The Hysteric's Guide to
the **Future Female**
Subject

The Hysteric's Guide to the **Future Female** Subject

Juliet Flower **MacCannell**

University of Minnesota Press
Minneapolis • London

The University of Minnesota Press gratefully acknowledges permission to reprint the following. Chapter 2 first appeared as "Perversion in Public Places," *New Formations* 35 (August 1998). An earlier version of chapter 3 was published as "The Postcolonial Unconscious; or, The White Man's Thing," *Journal for the Psychoanalysis of Culture and Society* 1, no. 1 (spring 1996): 27–42. An earlier version of chapter 4 was published as "Race/War: Freud, Adorno, and Jouissance," *Journal for the Psychoanalysis of Culture and Society* 2, no. 2 (fall 1997): 41–59. A version of chapter 5 was published as "Fascism and the Voice of Conscience," in *Radical Evil,* edited by Joan Copjec (London and New York: Verso Press, 1996), 46–72. A preliminary version of chapter 6 was published in *American Literary History* 3, no. 3 (1991): 623–47; reprinted by permission of Oxford University Press. Chapter 7 was originally published as "On Woman's Speech," *American Journal of Psychoanalysis* 58, no. 2 (June 1994): 143–58. Chapter 8 was first published as "Things to Come: A Hysteric's Guide to the Future Female Subject," in *Supposing the Subject,* edited by Joan Copjec (London and New York: Verso Press, 1994), 106–32. Chapter 9 was originally published as "Becoming and Unbecoming a Man: Mathematical Passion and the Other Jouissance in Stendhal's Autobiography, *La Vie de Henry Brulard,*" *Literature and Psychology* 18 (spring 1992): 1–22. Chapter 10 was first published as "Love outside the Limits of the Law," *New Formations* 23 (summer 1994): 25–42.

Copyright 2000 by the Regents of the University of Minnesota

Published by the University of Minnesota Press
111 Third Avenue South, Suite 290
Minneapolis, MN 55401-2520
http://www.upress.umn.edu

Library of Congress Cataloging-in-Publication Data

MacCannell, Juliet Flower, 1943–
    The hysteric's guide to the future female subject / Juliet Flower MacCannell.
        p.   cm.
    Includes index.
    ISBN 0-8166-3295-2 (hardcover). — ISBN 0-8166-3296-0 (pb.)
    1. Feminist theory.   2. Women and psychoanalysis.   3. Women in literature.   I. Title.
    HQ1190.M3   1999
    305.42'01—dc21   99–17021

Printed in the United States of America on acid-free paper
The University of Minnesota is an equal-opportunity educator and employer.
11 10 09 08 07 06 05 04 03 02 01 00   10 9 8 7 6 5 4 3 2 1

For Dean

Contents

Acknowledgments

A book that has developed from a lifetime of experience finds listing acknowledgments an impossible task. I can only say that what I have lived has lent as much to this book as what I have studied and learned. But I can remark some crucial milestones for my thought that have happily come to me in the form of friends and intimate acquaintances.

This book would not have taken shape as it has without the felicitous invitation to be Artist-In-Residence at the Marin Headlands Center for the Arts. The six months I spent there were crucial to much of the thinking I did and provided material support for the writing of three of the chapters. The collaboration with artists mentioned throughout my text shows how crucial this time was for me. I want especially to thank Ann Chamberlain, Bernie Lubell, Victor Mario Zaballa, Josefa Vaughan, Fritzie Brown, and Gabrielle Daniels for their interest, care, and support.

I would like to thank Charlene Engelhard, the Engelhard Foundation, and the Institute for Contemporary Art in Boston for granting me a residency that also furthered my work and provided insights into the question of the racial and the human as I experienced them at Moonhole in Bequia.

I want to thank my teachers in psychoanalysis, Willy Apollon, Danielle Bergeron, and Lucie Cantin. I know they will enjoy debating the issues in this book with me, and I am grateful for the firm understanding they and their colleagues at Groupe Interdisciplinaire Freudien de Recherches et d'Interventions Cliniques (GIFRIC) have given me of psychoanalytic matters and their ethics.

My warmest thanks to my friends Renata Salecl, Joan Copjec, and Slavoj Žižek, who seem to be sharing the adventure of following where insight can go in the world today.

I would like also to thank the University of California, Irvine, for its financial support for a great deal of the original research for this book, especially the award of an Irvine Faculty Fellowship. When I directed women's studies and the Organized Research Initiative in Women and the Image, I was not only able to pursue at length theoretical issues in the framing of women; I was also able to come into contact with some of the finest woman thinkers of our time, including Hélène Cixous, whose work first taught me about the creative range of hysteria.

My students at Irvine, Berkeley, and the Lacanian School have been exceptionally important to the way my work has developed. I would like to thank in particular Tracy McNulty, Armando Silva, Manya Steinkoler, Chris Meyer, Mark Calkins, and Sinkwan Cheng for their challenging questions. Thanks to my students at Berkeley in the seminar on perversion, and to those in the Lacanian School in the seminar on psychosis.

Without the encouragement and support of Will Murphy at the University of Minnesota Press, this book would never have seen the light of day. Thanks also to Robin Moir for her warm and lively correspondence, and to my copy editor, Louisa Castner, for her judicious, intelligent, and informed suggestions. I am also particularly grateful to Kenneth Reinhard and Richard Feldstein for their helpful insights.

Other colleagues have also been material to this work, including Julia R. Lupton, who team-taught a year-long graduate seminar on Lacan's ethics with me and Ermanno Bencivenga, which stimulated me to direct my thought in a certain direction. Thanks to my son Daniel, a screenwriter, who took this class and made me realize a side of maternity most people never experience. Thanks to my colleague Renée Riese Hubert, who always insisted on considering aesthetic questions with an eye to woman, and to Judd Hubert whose humor leavened our discussions.

Without my primary and secondary families this book would not have come into being; I am grateful to both, but especially so to my secondary one, to my *mari*, Dean, who helped me to sharpen and extend my ideas, to Daniel, and to my novelist son, Jason, who never failed to remind me what writing should be all about.

San Francisco, 1998

Introduction

Three threads may guide you through this book's sexual, ethical, and artistic passages. And possibly four.

One is *narrative*. Taking the literary scenes I have made use of here as your own signposts, scenes from Hitchcock, Sade, Kleist, Atwood, Duras, Angelou, Stendhal, you can trace a pathway for the *female subject* from the 1790s through the 1990s. My aim, however, has not been a historicist one. I have utilized these particular works because they have consistently sustained my own curiosity—and persistent anxiety—about the relation of *the girl* to ethics and to sexuality.

A second strand follows progressive (and at times, regressive) *political* lines. The paradoxes of the female subject's political position are nothing if not instructive. If you choose this way through *The Hysteric's Guide*, the path will not be straightforward, as the book moves along well-known political formations and some that are less understood: democracy and fascism, totalitarianism, atomic age politics, colonialisms, racisms, and utopian schemes. At all points, however, it keeps an eye on how political forms relate to the recognition (or misrecognition) of a *feminine ethic—* and a *perverse* one. I act here as if Sade's Dolmancé had returned to tell us (without preparing us for its difficulties), "Yet one more effort, women, if you would be free," and suddenly made us responsible for politics.

A third, more subtle, thread to be pulled out is an *ideological* one: the sexual and political contradictions of *woman* that are masked by, for, and to her. *Ideological* I take in its earliest definition, as the way in which power inexorably invades and sets up the sexual body. After Marx and Engels, ideology is considered a socioeconomic production, a set of distortions that effectively mask class conflicts and social inequalities and thus allow them to be experienced as if free of contradiction. But when Destutt de Tracy first coined the term *idéologie* (1796–1800)[1] around the same time as Sade's *Philosophy in the Bedroom* (1795),[2] he intended it to mean how different forms of government situated human behavior.

De Tracy's greatest disciple, Stendhal, extended his argument (1822) to read ideology as the purely political determinants of how people made love.[3] I prefer this Stendhalian version of ideology for woman, as it captures her libidinal investment in a distortion, as well as the effect the distortion has on her concrete amorous conduct. Given that she was not an acknowledged player in "society" and "the economy" until quite recent history, this lost French version of ideology seems more appropriate for the analysis of woman than the German one. *Idéologie* in this vein is a refined cultural instrument for analyzing feminine "masquerade" as something that can resonate politically, as it permits me to investigate *woman's desire* by making a place for the role the aesthetic plays in its construction.

Transcending without negating these three strands, there is a fourth that runs on the bias to the others, *freedom*. I have arranged my work to stage a series of confrontations among the feminine, patriarchal, and perverse versions of the *free subject*. I aim at a possible or potentially *free female subject*—her logic, her ethic, her unconscious. I find her potential in *the girl* who is not yet fully captured by patriarchal narratives of feminine submission and resistance, or by a symbolic politics of desire and loss, or by twisted capitalist, colonialist, or fascist ideologies of fulfillment.

With these lines in place—the female subject, "unmanly"/womanly ethics, woman's desire, and the free feminine subject—I address in this work two reigning and constraining ideologies that are, in my view, crucial turning points for the future female's history: sadism and psychoanalysis. *Constraining* and *ideology* are, I admit, an odd pair of terms to apply to this even odder couple, Sade and Freud. Discounting for the moment the manacles and cruelty that characterize sadism phenomenologically, Sade himself seems like a herald of vast new freedoms. He was the original voice calling for a full emancipation of the self. And without the Freudian revolution, who could have ever considered personal liberation today, despite its discovery of the guilt that holds our instincts in check?

Freud and Sade

In previous work I wrestled with some of the same issues I treat here by starting out from their political and ideological sides: the perplexities of post-Enlightenment democracies; the brutalities of fascism, colonialism, and racism; the impossibilities of various utopias.[4] Even in my earliest essays there is concern for the political always linked to a vexed relation to the feminine. Now, I have started from within to reach the heart of the matter with woman.

In that heart, I have seen the face of Sade. He is woman's internal alien today.[5] Not hers alone, to be sure: to attempt to comprehend woman's relation to culture and politics means facing squarely his unstated legacy with which, like her, we are all burdened.

Woman is no longer what she once seemed to be—not after Sade. She cannot be made to go back to some time before—the way that the Commanders try to make women behave in the Gilead of Margaret Atwood's satirical *Handmaid's Tale*—because even those modes have been deeply touched by Sade. Witness the way in which the few people in Gilead still able to reproduce (after toxic and nuclear pollutions) require a technically perverse posture for the "right to life" to take place. In Gilead's ironic utopia of sexual difference, Handmaidens (women with viable ovaries) must submit to sex with their Commanders, but strictly for reproductive purposes. Bound by traditional moral imperatives against adultery, however, the Commanders' (sterile) Wives must also be present at the monthly ceremonial sex act. Not just present, however: the Handmaiden must lie joyless and immobilized atop the Commander's sterile Wife during the act. The whole time the Handmaiden is terrified of showing she is in any way affected by the experience; she must be apathetic. Sade has already been here.

I have tried to approach political woman by counting her desire and modes of enjoyment as "political factors."[6] Looking in on that outside interiority that shapes moral life, however, I have come to appreciate the extent to which a perverse superego is what the girl any woman must grow out of chiefly contends with today. It tempts the girl away from assuming a social place, away from assuming a sexuality with attendant public and private responsibilities—away from becoming woman. This perception has guided my investigation of how and if the girl—after Sade—ever, indeed, accesses her "womanliness," her enjoyment, her culture, her sexuality, and her politics—in *her* way. Sade challenged singularly the right to existence of a feminine subject in the name of absolute sexual equality.

Today, following Michel Foucault and Judith Butler, we seem to have conceded that becoming woman is possible only in a parodic or surface form. Even Freud felt that a *woman's* development out of an originally bisexual creature had to do with a slight, aesthetic thing, a mask really, called femininity, and it was greatly flawed.

But Sade was there first, and he was most radical in refusing to credit the installation of the symbolic law in woman's unconscious, the point where psychoanalysis sees the subject anchored. Indeed, he discounted all claims of social coexistence, of law on the woman, except for a Natural law of unlimited total *jouissance*. For him woman was all lust and no *resistance*. Sade glossed his brand of lawlessness-for-woman as a *freedom* linked with progressive politics. We—she—still do not know if Sade's calculated impedance of her subjective process, the disruption of her desire, will have been a good or bad thing for woman—politically not least of all. Should she resist accepting Oedipal Law in the interests of realizing the liberty, fraternity, and equality Sade held out before her? Should she take her freedom on Sade's terms? Or should she insist that she not be confined to Sade's bedroom? His claims are undeniably attractive to her.

Perverse dreams of sexual equality as the basis of social equality are not "wrong." Those who reactively try to justify a worn-out patriarchy, its sexual nonegalitarianism, and the submission of any of its subjects to its barely credible Law and authority today sound shrill and out of step. And they are. Were the standard bearers of "traditional family values" really to face today's "perverse" ethics, politics, and ideological effects, they would have to notice, at long last, how an epoch-making change in the cornerstone of their cramped worldview—woman—has been in process for quite some time.

There is, however, something not right with a politics and an ideology rooted in a perverse call to absolute freedom. Something "of woman" was left out of Sade's rational calculus and transcendence of sex. This crucial missing element, if we discovered it, would reshape our political picture once again. At the very least, a *feminine* subject, with her desire, her resistances, her enjoyments, her questions, is missing from Sade. This subject is everything Sade's Dolmancé hates, especially the "anti-natural strength" that women employ "to resist the penchants with which they have been far more profusely endowed than [men]."[7] This feminine subject has been located properly only by Freudian analysis and its adherents. And by certain artists and thinkers.

I am hardly the first to treat woman and sadism.[8] Theodor Adorno and Max Horkheimer linked the sadistic woman to fascism, while Gilles

Deleuze conceived of a pseudosadism for woman to leaven her link to its radical evil. Slavoj Žižek regales us with the pure horror of a maternal superego that he, unlike Deleuze, considers inalterably sadistic.[9] I aim, however, less at the Mother (the traditional Evil, the bearer of the sadistic superego) and more at *the girl* who might choose (or not) to become one. My question is why and how the girl entertains the sadistic superego.

Am I claiming that Sade has somehow come into his own through the girl today? Yes and no. She is the "lesion," the weak spot in our cultural setup, and she needs to be frequented by analysis at least as often as she is by Sade. We know that Sade is long dead. Yet he persists in influencing a girl's feminine career and her cultural ambitions. We feel him in the subtle cultural imperatives that urge the girl toward a hysterical position of permanently deferring the assumption of her sex—as theorized in Foucault and Butler. We see Sade's shadowy contours in the expansive sadistic ethic of our public domain, from the workplace to the play space, an ethic that has yet to be adequately analyzed. It certainly remains to be understood as regards its effect on the girl.

Although few women will be entirely happy with my approach here, I have tried to look Freud and Sade directly in the face, to wonder where these two were and were not laboring on behalf of a *free female*. Do we who are *women* have any real sense of the concrete effect either has had on us, what the aftermath is for us of the knowledge that they put into the world? What effect are they having on the girl who now comes of age in that world?

In voicing these questions, which have long simmered for women's, gender, and queer studies—as for me—I am weighing out where psychoanalysis *critiques* and where it *participates in* the ideology of femininity and the way it has governed woman's body. And I am also weighing out whether Sade has been a blessing or a curse as well. I conclude that psychoanalysis has, can, and will have worked toward a *free* female subject, and in that work it will have distinguished itself from Sade's call for a total liberation of the self—but only just barely.[10] Moreover, we will be unlikely to estimate the proper contribution of psychoanalysis until it uses its powers to describe and then to credit a *feminine ethic,* a female subject, and a woman's way.

A Feminine Ethic?

Though they are the "silent ones," girls possess nevertheless an outstanding and crucial *savoir,* a *savoir faire* about how to deal with the ever expanding obscenity in our lives. I have wanted to pry it out of them, even though we, as a society, have never wanted to. In seeking what the girl knows about getting along with or resisting the sadistic superego, this Thing within her she has often hidden from herself, I have learned much. And I have learned more from those women who have started to speak.

I have learned from Hannah Arendt, as she scours the black hole where Adolf Eichmann's heart should have been. In that dark pit she heard an obscene voice and not the "voice of conscience" everyone else was probing and pushing Eichmann to break down and finally acknowledge. How was she confident enough in her truth to be able to *speak* it even when everyone else refused to believe her or refused to hear it? From where did she draw the courage to file a report on Eichmann's conscience when no one was ready to accept it?

For a long time I could only marvel at Arendt's discovery. But as I recently watched the film footage from Eichmann's trial, I began to understand. She clearly had started out from the fact of his sheer *apathy*, an apathy that had baffled all the moral reflexes and stifled even any animal pity in him. How different her ethical reflexes were, not so much from his but from those of the men and women who testified against him. In her difference from them, she betrayed her own moral *recognition* of Eichmann. The witnesses who stood before him denounced and yelled at him, and by doing so they showed that for them he remained within the realm of humanity. They implicitly framed their complaints as appeals to him to show *now* the humanity that he had so horribly lacked *then*, during the commission of his crimes.

Arendt knew he would never or, rather, could never do so. She recognized the inhuman Thing, the death drive, in him. Eichmann turns out never to have understood his work as a horrible crime against humanity, largely because *humanity* did not exist as a universal for him. He saw only a "rationally" sorted aggregate of groups and individuals, some of whom were expendable or had to be eliminated. With the unmoved face of an administrator, Eichmann stands tall, as if authorized in his every gesture by a metahuman force.

Arendt, alone among the commentators on this man, wanted to know where that authority really came from; she needed to locate its source within him. She did not name it what I do, the sadistic superego, but at least she *wanted* to try to find it, whereas others *wanted* to know nothing about it. Did being a woman have anything to do with Arendt's cold-blooded insistence on *knowing*?

What can we not learn also in this respect from Melanie Klein? I do not mean what Winnicott and object-relations theorists salvaged (the "good enough" mother) from the wreck of Oedipal civilization she witnessed in the child, as Oedipus and civilization alike crashed and burned all around them. Klein herself passed beyond good and evil in the actual mother: she went to the level of the Thing, finding it lodged, for the child, in the mother's breast. Yes, but its Thingness was more important than its breastness. It was a Thingness that even the infant, to become human, had to resist, even while it was being cruelly torn in two by the alternate tugs of cannibalism and reparation. With Klein, I think we did not witness just the arrival of yet another branch of psychoanalytic doctrine. We witnessed a *woman* trying to salvage the human from the Thing, the Thing whose power had come through loud and clear for the child in the wake of the absurd savagery of World War I, when Klein began her work.

It was almost impossible for me not to learn from Maya Angelou. As she found her way back from a devastating rape, without sentimentality, without bitterness, she also found her passion for the art that helped her recover from the worst. And I learned from men, too. Men like Stendhal, who wrote his book on love—please don't forget it—in order to combat the horrors of Sade's *Justine.*

We stand in need of these writers, artists, thinkers who, unlike Sade's fictional victims, managed to escape the libertine boudoirs and Silling prisons in which Sade sought to teach them their freedom—within, of course, the limits of reason. No innocents, these writers and artists have gone all the way with the obscene Thing. And they came back to teach us about the appeal of Sade.

The Sadean Future Female?

Am I trying to undo the damage Sade has done? No. Even if Adorno and Horkheimer despise her as the advent of a truly radical evil, Sadean woman seems to be one logical outcome of a truly egalitarian society. Should not woman, too, be granted the power to indulge, enjoy, to participate on an even footing in what was formerly the province of men? Female enthusiasts of Sade among writers, artists, literary and philosophical critics abound today, and I would guess that the appeal to "liberation" they find in his work is a major source of the attraction.[11] In my own experience, to teach Sade in the university classroom is to feel a corps of students galvanized, full of ambivalent attention.

And, yes, I am trying to undo Sade. I think Sade's fundamental skepticism concerning a difference between the sexes finally evinces a negative, if fascinated, reaction in women, men, and homosexuals alike. A desire to

critique Sade issues from the same student body that also finds him compelling. Something in the way Sade's pervert insists that he already *knows*
woman does not sit well with the young person of today. Many still want
to know who she is, where she comes from, what she wants.

In part I of this book I have shown the darker side of a sadistic ethic,
and woman's relation to it, playing itself out in what I earlier called "the
regime of the brother." Part II takes a lighter or brighter view of the same.
You may begin with either part.

The Hysteric as Guide

We will be guided in our quest for a feminine ethic by the one figure who
stands between Freud, who began to listen to her speech, and Sade, who
needed her for his partner: *the hysteric.*

We can learn from Freud and from artists, thinkers, and writers like
Kleist, Stendhal, Arendt, Lacan, Klein, who have been able to share with us
their knowledge of violence and sadism. We can also learn from those who
have avoided all knowledge of such Things in themselves—from foolish
pervert wannabes like Lori Davis, the girl in Martin Scorsese's remake of
Cape Fear.[12] She invites Max Cady up to her place for a one-night stand of
sadomasochistic fun and sex and ends up permanently scarred by the horror she experiences, literally bitten by the real she has wanted to avoid. We
can learn something about the death drive (in those who want to know
nothing about it) from the gaunt, somnolent femmes fatales who popu-
late Marguerite Duras's films and novels such as her Anne-Marie Stretter,
of whom it is said that nothing will ever happen to her but her death.[13] We
can learn from the hapless victims of a collapsed patriarchy like the bi-
racial Toni in Kleist's story, "The Betrothal in Santo Domingo."[14]

But most of all we can learn from the *hysterics,* those who have frozen
up during their halting progress toward a social and a sexual identity. We
can learn from those like Charlie, in Hitchcock's *Shadow of a Doubt,* that
the sadistic superego comes to the hysteric in a very attractive package.
The sadist fascinates her and tempts her. If she finally faces off against
him, she can begin to choose and to move beyond the domestic sphere.
Thus the *pervert,* too, has his uses in the construction of the female subject, however much he works for or against her.

I have tried to trace the outlines of an *ethics of femininity* to be read alongside of, and by the light of, an *ethics of perversion.* I have followed their
commonalities and antipathies, their political "outcomes" in this book.
Following the pervert's line, I have examined, at each point along it, its

effect on the girl. I have also tried to imagine her response to perversion's challenges, appeals, and imperatives.

Lacan writes: "Sublimation and perversion are both a certain relation of desire which draws our attention upon the possibility of formulating, in the form of a question, another principle of another . . . morality, opposed to the reality principle."[15] In this new formulation, only literature and art have been of real assistance. Art (Freud's "sublimation") often appears as perversion's close cousin: they both transgress the "reality principle" (the social morality we hold in common).

Yet art joins perversion only part of the way. Like perversion, it treats *pleasure* rather than *prohibition* as its starting point. When art approaches, and even oversteps, the bounds of the laws governing social coexistence, it is always granted public recognition (good or bad) for the news it brings back from that frontier. Until very recently, perversion has escaped this public acknowledgment.[16]

Let us now begin to consider our ethical situation as one also rooted or mired in Sadean desire. And let us also now begin to describe this "principle of another . . . morality, opposed to the reality principle" in art—and in perversion. For *the girl's* sake if for nothing else.

Part I

1. The Soul of Woman under Sadism

Femininity and Its Discontents

When I was a young graduate student at Cornell University, I went to hear a famous woman scholar from a leading Ivy League school speak on a subject that was not my specialization, though in a neighboring field. It would be better to say that I went to *see* her; I was drawn less by her topic than by her standing in the profession, and I was curious to learn, from her comportment and demeanor, how my generation of young women would be expected to "turn out," that is, to "turn into" professors. (There were only two women on the faculty of the Arts School at that time, and few women had ever become professors.) She delivered an excellent lecture in what I considered a normal, straightforward manner.

My admiration turned to dismay and disappointment, however, when this elegant sixtyish woman was challenged on some point by a tough question from a high-ranking male specialist in her field. Her immediate response was to take off her glasses, lower her eyes flirtatiously, bat her eyelids, and with a coy smile lapse into a hyperfeminine mode: "Now you wouldn't want to do that to me, would you?" Her sudden femininity had descended like a bolt from the blue. It was designed, I could see, to avert hostility on the part of the male corporation surrounding her, and to exhibit her as nonthreatening: what else is batting your eyelids but another form of the way eyelids work when you are afraid? Or the limp wrist—what better signal that you are not clenching your fist and readying a blow?

With great astuteness, Joan Riviere found out many secrets of womanliness by studying femininity as a masquerade.[1] In Riviere's case history, a woman who had made a stunning professional presentation to a company of men immediately afterward sought the men's approval—and their desire—with flirts and flutters. Riviere, of course, took her analysis of the mask of womanliness beyond my naive, ethological glimpse of its fight-or-flight response. She questioned the motivation of femininity's mask at a level deeper than pure defensiveness. Riviere asked about the woman's own aggressivity. What hostility and envy did she harbor within herself that needed to be masked by, or at least glossed by, her femininity? Did she not covet the phallic power the corporation of men around her wielded, individually and collectively? Did she not guiltily wish to usurp it? Was she afraid of their revenge should she do so?

For Riviere, classical feminine masquerade went only so far as to be a concealed weapon. But Freud saw it also as a shield—a shield a girl needed in order to enter and work in society, in however restricted a mode. Freud made his inquiry into femininity less because he wanted to know what a woman wants than why she seems unable to want after a certain point in her life. In the end, Freud decided that her femininity and the way it had been acquired were responsible for stunting woman's abilities and foreclosing her options. Her deepest sexual and libidinal choices were so masked to her and others by social constraints that she could almost never come to know her own desire.[2] But because she did realize how little desire she had been allotted by society, she grew embittered at the meanness of her patrimony and equally hostile to men, her mother, and any child she should have. If Freud may have wanted to find the path a woman had taken from girlhood toward becoming woman, his laying a girl's entry into society at the feet of femininity also marked his yielding on the question. The mask of femininity was its own double bind. For though it may have helped the girl to access her social place as woman under patriarchy, femininity, as Freud saw it, served ultimately to grant woman precious little leeway in that society.

Where Freud inflected femininity quite differently from Riviere, however, was in his belief that its hidden aggressiveness resulted from the girl's competition with and resistance to the Mother. Femininity was a shield because this rival female represented to the girl an obscene Thing, an obscene appeal that she had to ward off. In analyzing the mainspring of her femininity as marking a girl's bitter break with her mother—the sine qua non of her entrance into the patriarchal world—Freud thus stumbled onto something that may give us our own entrée into the way a girl becomes woman—or does not. As stinted, partisan, and partial as his analysis was, it still holds some important clues to the future female subject.

Why Become a Woman?

For Freud, femininity made a woman not out of a girl but out of an originally bisexed being: "Psycho-analysis does not try to describe what a woman is—that would be a task it could scarcely perform—but sets about enquiring how she comes into being, how a woman develops out of a child with a bisexual disposition."[3] Realizing that it was not society alone (which the Father represents as an ego ideal) that laid out a child's path to becoming-man and becoming-woman, he turned to the Mother. The Mother was, for her children, the first real source of prohibitions on enjoyment;[4] these predated the paternal "No" and were thus the original precondition for socializing the child.

Yet there was a paradox. A boy, who was a rival with his Father for the Mother, could psychically deflect the blame for restrictions on enjoyment onto the Father, and this boy could also expect to receive symbolic approval and appropriate rewards from him. In the end, he also got his mother back—figuratively—if he acquiesced. But as it was also the Mother who had herself been the source of such enjoyments, her impact on her daughter was more complex than that on her son. It is the Mother as the giver of life and therefore of death, the locus of pleasure without limit, that is the source of and the absolute repression of her daughter's pleasure—not the Father. Hygienic efforts on the daughter's behalf originally stimulated thrilling sensations in the girl child; but while the same held true for the boy child, the way each accepted being deprived of further excitements by the Mother was quite different. The Mother's "No" did not alienate the boy from her as it did the girl,[5] since a son figuratively regains all he loses by accepting "castration"; the daughter does not regain these losses. Castration represents the limits required by social coexistence; by accepting it (unconsciously and within), a boy is rewarded with a symbolic power, and proper object-choice, that is, a woman to replace his mother.

The girl's first love-object was also the Mother. But she could not follow the straightforward, publicly approved path of her brother—away from the Mother and toward a transferential second love. Nor could the girl, as powerfully attached to the mother as her brother was, make the compensating identification with her rival, since her love object (her Mother) and her rival (for the Father) were one and the same. As Freud notes in "Femininity," "the determinants of women's choice of object are often made unrecognizable by social conditions" (132). Her turn from her mother thus "ends in hate" (121). It is at this point that the girl adopts her femininity as the sign she has yielded her love for her mother and that she has also ceded the love-field to her mother: the Mother wins the Father. In short, a girl's acquired femininity marks her as having given in to the restrictions of society without much of value in return. Having been obliged, through the Mother's rather than the Father's agency alone, to give up even that small(er) portion of pleasure she had taken for her own, no adequate compensatory, satisfying, and socially approved transferential connection to her early thrills would ever lie in her future.

Femininity in her was thus very hard won—and very mystifying. However complex and heroic her struggles, this form of woman's castration was societally undervalued. The girl ended up without many clues to help her find her way back to the erotic. Her libido remained locked in a bitter hatred toward the mother, whose mere existence had landed her in this fix. The process of partition from the mother as seen by Freud, then, dwindled from the privilege and prestige of metaphor granted the son, to the daughter's assumption of a blighted *femininity*—a skimpy enough veil that all too thinly separated a girl from her equally disenfranchised Mother. The flip side of the femininity she assumed as a young girl was the frumpiness her mother also took on, especially in her daughter's eyes, in the process. "By thirty," Freud says, a woman's "libido" will have "taken up final positions . . . incapable of exchanging them for others" (135). Who else is this woman, freeze-dried at thirty, but the Mother?

If Joan Riviere's work had revealed femininity as woman's social and psychological oppression and her *ressentiment* all in one, Freud's work probed more deeply into the "why?" of its aggressive structure, finding in it a hostile response not only to male privilege, but also to the mother the girl had been forced to cast off, and to *the society* she was supposed, and not supposed, to enter.[6] A slender, fragile piece of aesthetic work—her mask of femininity—was to save her from the vile potential in the wider world outside the shelter of home and family, once she could no longer be at home in the primary family. She had to move swiftly and smoothly from primary family to her own role as mother, or something untoward could befall her.

Small wonder that femininity, as one of the very few recognized social requirements for becoming woman, was a prime target of early feminist attack.[7] My own generation regarded "femininity" with enormous suspicion, and I never considered my accomplishments, whatever they might be, as wrested from the opposite sex at their expense, as Riviere's womanly woman did. Personally, politically, and theoretically, I had always rejected Riviere's sort of femininity, and not only for its quivery, "uncool" features. Nevertheless, throughout my life, I was called the feminine one. It was a mystery to me, and Freud's explication of it left me even more puzzled. Moreover, there is a kind of excess residue of femininity that has settled on growing numbers of men and the very youngest of girls as it has been cast off by their elders: on the six-year-old JonBenét Ramsey, for example, whose sprayed hair, lipstick, rouge, and sexy attire shocked me one evening as she and others like her wafted across my television screen on the news.

For today, after the patriarchy, femininity and the narrative of the girl's social entry must be revisited by the psychoanalysis that first discovered their parallel structure. It is no longer as easy as it seemed to Freud to measure a girl's progress in achieving entry into society (and distance from her Thing) once we have given up the femininity index, the mask that indicates she has consented to certain rules, agreed to a certain set of social narratives and fictions, a certain symbolic seeming. His version of femininity looks only like a patriarchal ideology: the girl *must* yield to her Father in the competition for the Mother; she *must* accept her femininity as the castration she needs to endure in order to enter civil society (on however unequal a footing with her brother). What's more, she *must* do so with precious little reward: her libido is frozen at thirty, and she is transformed into a sexless crone after menopause—this is the end of her story. Or, rather, the end of her story at least as Freud read it, as it is determined by her unwinnable struggle against a "maternal" Other within. It is time, perhaps, to reevaluate the Mother and the girl she grew from.

The Task of the Girl: Social Requirements, Superego Commands

What is society supposed to mean to the girl, what are her obligations and duties to it, and what are the rewards it offers her? In Freud's time these were practically nil, and Freud countered feminist social demands with the claim that the moral superego is weak in woman. He was right.[8] The girl she developed from had been inadequately shielded from her drives (represented by the Mother) by the Father (society). Her stake in patriarchy was slight, its rewards to her largely negative in character. Because her portion of its official side was so meager, the paternal superego had little to offer the girl but the mask of femininity, the don'ts of moral conduct guides, and salvation through marriage. By the same measure, however, the girl remained uniquely attuned to the patriarchal superego's dark underside, represented by the Mother. Society and its ego ideals had a secret core or kernel of obscene enjoyment that they could never reveal. But the girl was always attuned to it.

The question of the girl's relation to society, of her becoming woman, remains unanswered today. It is especially troubling as no one has advanced much in describing an ethical pathway for her into the world beyond the primary family. She has assertiveness training and self-esteem propaganda, and she knows how to dress for success in any field of endeavor. That much is now possible. But we do not have a sense of how her way of relating to the public sphere differs, or does not, from that of those who have become men. She is no longer taught to be feminine, but there is the depressing possibility that the marked absence of femininity in today's woman indicates her continued capture by the "Thing," which has been variously characterized as a Sadistic superego (Klein), the invasive "*Jouissance* of the Other" (Lacan), and *"Das Ding"* (Freud)—a radical evil insofar as it cannot be exchanged for and leavened by law, metaphor, or other forms of the subject. I think I can pose some preliminary questions about the contemporary question of woman and ethics, by starting with the matter of what Freud called the superego, in particular, its relation to the girl, a question into which he never properly inquired.

Some fairly startling things emerge if we begin to frame the girl with a superego, especially now that official patriarchal dominion has lapsed, and a certain id character to the superego has been exposed (Freud recognized it relatively late in his *Ego and Id*). Whoever has had experience of the obscene side of the superego, of the unseemly underbelly of patriarchy, of the darker parts of the regime of the brother, will suddenly become a precious reserve of knowledge for us. That is why the girl can provide a wealth of material for us, even (or especially) because her knowing has remained largely unconscious. If only we can reach her.

To get to her, we must detour first through the Mother and the Hysteric.

The Obscene Superego and the Mother

The superego grows from the ego's twin, that other who always accompanies us and plays a running inner commentary on everything we do.[9] As our twin, it is also potentially our rival and antagonist. In no case is it only the providential though strict superego that early readers of a Kantian Freud imagined it to be. They mistook it, as Freud himself often seemed to, for the "voice of conscience" of a stable moral order. Today, we know that the superego's voice issues less from society's official morality than from its seamy underside. It harasses, hectors, and provokes you to do just what the moral code has repressed or prohibited: "Just do it!" an anonymous undertone insists, even from T-shirts and bumper stickers.[10] Official morality counters with, "Just say no!" But even this vocal counter-imperative, read in that obscene accent, becomes the very same superego pressure to let go. Simply inflect it this way: "Just *say* no (but go ahead and actually do it)." That undertone, that muttering you hear is where the obscene superego speaks to you. It tells you that the enjoyments you lack are nonetheless owed to you. It then challenges you to go ahead and take your portion—"Enjoy!" But (this is the sadistic part) you can do so only under conditions that would humiliate you in front of others. The obscene superego is what induces your enjoyment and punishes you for it at the same time. If its voice touches you in your heart, it also stains you on your surface. It is the postmodern form of guilt.

This urging and punishing superego is tied, psychoanalytically, to the mother's voice. She is the first to prohibit certain natural pleasures, and yet she is their first cause as well. Her prohibition seems to carry the fullness of forbidden enjoyments along with their privation. Because she is the site of all provisioning, her denial, her "No!," seems as unreal as it is arbitrary. Contrast her "No!" with a father's "No!": his is properly negative, since he has literally given the child nothing to begin with. The Mother's "No!" will seem capricious, dictatorial; the Father's "No!" will seem to have a formative effect, the way a sculptor's removal of stone makes a figure. Hence the Mother will appear to be selfishly withholding what she has; the Father will not even have to deal with "having"; he makes a virtue of lack. Of the two figures of authority it is the Mother who comes to denote an irrational pressure to do and not do; she represents an arbitrary injunction to enjoy and not to enjoy at once. It is from this structure that the obscene superego has been dubbed a "maternal" one.

I question the psychoanalytic attribution of maternity to what can only be called an *obscene* superego today. To blame the mother is no longer valid or very meaningful. The obscene superego represents to our psyches a figure whose very lack puts us under pressure to fulfill it, fill it out. This pressure is a simultaneous incitement and unbearable humiliation: someone, something has inflicted on us a fundamental injury, an intolerable insult to our dignity. But the exclusive administration of this abuse has long since passed out of maternal hands.

It now escapes any primary articulation through the family, having run the gamut of the family's principal members: in the 1950s, the Mothers took the rap; in the 1990s, the Fathers have quickly become prime suspects, accused everywhere of spousal and child abuse. But in the historical long view, as I pointed out in *The Regime of the Brother,* the "elder brother" came to carry this onus in the eighteenth century and beyond. We have reached a saturation point in our blame mania when we now attempt to attribute the sadism roaming at large in the land today to "peer pressure." The search itself for someone, anyone, to pin our humiliations and privations on is itself a symptom, not a solution. We look everywhere, except within, to the way we cope or fail to cope with an inner violence that appears to come from without.

Freud called this inner violence the "death drive" and Lacan called it the "lethal *Jouissance* of the Other."[11] But the name does not matter. What matters is that we face the fact and logic of its existence. It is even more important for us to figure out a way around it. So while it is absolutely necessary to uncover and pinpoint empirical abuses, however blinded to them we are ideologically—to nab brutes and bullies in all their hiding places, from families and gangs to corporate boardrooms—it is equally important for us to learn how to free ourselves of their mental effects. If we cannot shake these off entirely, we should learn at least to shrug them off—with humor if all else fails.[12]

There are also social and economic reasons why it is no longer appropriate for psychoanalysis to focus on the mother as the singular figure where the abusive Other shows up in the mental picture of most individuals. Mothers are no longer the site of such absolute social lack as they once were. Women now enjoy a less restrictive field of play for their cultural ambitions than they did under classical patriarchy,[13] and even *mothers* have dramatically increased their participation in social and economic life. As a result the unconscious figure of the mother cannot fail to have altered; she could hardly continue to represent to the child's psyche a wealth of enjoyments that she has arbitrarily and despotically deprived him of. Nor does she alone stand for and unconsciously represent some pure existence beyond the system of social credits. That role may have fallen to perverts.[14]

More important, society itself seems less and less a stable moral order, with appropriate rewards and punishments to contrast it sharply with maternal tyranny and caprice. From the beginning of a child's life today, society is painted as the site itself of lopsided divisions of wealth, aggression, violence, and interpersonal antipathy.[15] As the original contrast Mother/Nature/Antisocial versus Father/Culture/Social breaks down, we stand in need of a better figure to reference the despotic, obscene superego: but if its proper name can no longer simply be the Mother, then who, if not Sade? And who is his victim of choice but the girl?

The Hysteric and the Sadistic Superego

Though I am not a clinician, I am exceptionally interested in how the theories I have constructed actually work. I am likewise attuned to what is ideological in the imperatives a girl is supposed to hear. In the absence of a clinic and of a good ideological critique for women, I have had to look to narratives, not only analytic case histories. So when I sought confirmation of Freud's picture of the mother-daughter break in "Femininity," I turned to art rather than to psychoanalytic case histories for examples. Narrative is traditionally valued as equipment for living, though underappreciated in contemporary life. Artists and writers provide an experiential dimension in a universalizing context that I find exceptionally meaningful. But I see in contemporary art something even more precious than "wisdom." Art in our time has had to go beyond certain limits in order to re-mark again the limits of the human, to refind what of the human remains after a certain human limit has been surpassed. Art highlights the line between the human and the Thing. If the Mother *is* the Thing (Freud's *Das Ding*), then this mother-daughter relation should have been a central figure for an art focused precisely on that line.

When I looked into narratives of the mother-daughter break, though, I was in for a real surprise. Authors and filmmakers of all sorts have been drawn to the mother-daughter relation. But in what the artists had to say about it, I found enormous suspicion of the demand made on women to break with their mothers on patriarchal terms. Many implicitly questioned the motives, aims, and sources of this demand. They saw patriarchy as itself in shambles and perceived specious political, racial, and even colonialist designs behind the supposed ethical requirement of a rupture between the girl and her mother. But the big news they brought me was that the girl's relation to the mother had never been exclusively mediated by the father. Instead, a perverse, sadistic figure that is both conflated with and distinct from the Mother stands between her and the girl. The obscene figure with which the girl contends is not maternal but sadistic. With the sadistic, the girl comes to an original crossroads. The obscene superego commands her as her mother was supposed to, but where the mother's dominant tone was that of a privation, the obscene superego promises fulfillment.

The most privileged access we have to this confrontation, however, is not yet directly with the girl. We don't yet know very much about her personal relation to her id. But we do have quite a bit of material from one way in which the girl can go or, rather, refuse to go: the hysterical direction. In the girl who is a hysteric, faced with the obscene, sadistic superego, and not yet having secured a sure sexual orientation, we find the perfect foil. For the hysteric remains something like the bisexed child out of which the woman was supposed to grow: the *hysteric unconscious* is defined as one that has no sure sexual guide; its question to itself is, "Am I a man or a woman?" It is therefore the perfect target for a sadistic superego, and prey to a perverse ideology that discredits all sexual differentiation,[16] for she credits neither the phallus nor its puny counterpart, femininity.

What happens to both mother and daughter when the hysteric meets the pervert? An artist will tell us. Hitchcock's *Shadow of a Doubt* draws together the main elements in the girl's sadistic superego link, and the lure and thrill the pervert holds for her. It also adds a dash of the hysteric's confusion about sex and her quiescent rivalry with the mother.

Hitchcock's Shadow of a Doubt: The Pervert's Guide to the Hysteric

I was searching for films I had loved as a child to watch with my young sons, much as I had dug back and shared favorite, half-recalled old books, when I accidentally refound Alfred Hitchcock's *Shadow of a Doubt,* a film I had seen as a girl younger than six years old.[17] I was surprised when I ran across the paired faces of Joseph Cotten and Teresa Wright on the cover of a rental box in the Hitchcock section of the video shop. I had always remembered the story of Charlie and her Uncle Charlie, the characters these two played, but I did not realize Hitchcock had directed the film. I did not even recall its title, and still less was I aware that Thornton Wilder, author of *Our Town,* had written most of the script while consulting closely with Hitchcock. The movie had simply been a sort of mental backdrop for me throughout my youth. Its central focus is a girl, a very special case who will instruct us about the sadistic superego. For she is a girl who has yet to assume her sexuality, who has not taken responsibility for her feminine subject position: psychoanalytically, she is a hysteric.

The film depicts an adolescent girl from the most normal-seeming of families hailing from the most normal-seeming of towns. Charlotte "Charlie" Stewart (Teresa Wright) lives with her parents and her two younger siblings in a big frame house in Santa Rosa, a town in northern California. She seems very feminine, but there is some gender ambiguity about her: her name or, rather, nickname, is after all Charlie, and she somehow considers herself head of the family, despite the presence of her father and mother. When we first see her, she is listlessly sprawled across the bed in her room, thinking about how dull and fragmented her family is, even though they lead a stable, comfortable, perfectly normal life. She is particularly concerned that her mother works far too hard; she tells her father that their family is all talk and that she needs to do something to "shake up the family." She decides she will call on her Uncle Charlie on the East Coast, discounting her father's weak assertion in the scene that all is well.

Her complaint is somewhat mysterious; her life is well run. Her parents are typically middle class; the mother, Emma (Patricia Collinge), takes care of her family, shopping, cooking, working with a ladies' club, and generally flutters about; the father, Joseph (Henry Travers), is the stereo-typically token presence in his three children's lives, his appearance among them largely confined to being background noise at the dinner table.

But there are some quirks in these parents. The mother, who is very matronly, shows a rather unseemly libidinal attachment to her brother Charlie (Joseph Cotten), who lives in Philadelphia; the girl is nicknamed after this uncle. Despite the physical distance between them, the mother's tie to her brother is quite a bit more visible than any to her husband. So is Charlie's: just as she runs out to send him a wire to come "shake up the family," she finds that her uncle has already sent them one. She has no relation other than a civil one to her father; she dismisses him as largely irrelevant, but she is neither cold nor particularly emotionally linked to him.

The father, too, is peculiar. His chief leisure activity is to plan the perfect murder with his next-door neighbor Herbie Hawkins (Hume Cronyn) each night after dinner.[18] Finally, the girl, young Charlie, is just slightly too old to be still living at home, without any social life or ties to the world that would supersede her attachment to the family. She has graduated from school, with apparently no prospects for marriage, no plans for college or work (even though her father says she has "brains"), and no emotional focus but her immediate family, especially her mother.

Their quiet, if lightly quirky, lives are interrupted by a telephone call: Uncle Charlie's telegram announces his imminent arrival. The mother is thrown into a state of agitation; the girl can hardly contain her joy. These two are entirely captivated by the thought of the visit, while the father, younger sister, and brother are largely indifferent, if not slightly hostile, to the prospect. In any event, the call has certainly animated the mother and the daughter.

Uncle Charlie arrives by train; he is a handsome, almost rakish, magnetic man. His niece, like her mother, clearly adores him. And he is rich.

He tells them he is world-weary and wants to retire to this simple town. But we have already seen him in some kind of trouble with police back on the East Coast, though precisely what remains unclear. He, too, has quirks. One night at dinner, as the father merrily plans another perfect murder, the subject of widows arises, and with obvious intensity, but no recognizable emotion, Uncle Charlie denounces widows as useless, fat, wheezing animals, feeding off the dead bodies of their husbands, drinking, eating, and smelling of their money. In town, he deliberately baits the good burghers with his contemptuous, highly cynical remarks, a provocativeness that nevertheless charms all the ladies he meets. When young Charlie objects, he gaily replies, "The whole world's a joke to me."

Uncle Charlie enchants the town with his money and looks. He becomes very popular with its citizens, and the ladies' club invites him to give a speech, which is loudly applauded by men and women alike. But his niece puts an end to his aspirations to beguile the town in a rather dramatic fashion.

Even now, as I write, I can plainly see that in addition to the argument I am making about hysteria and perversion here, this great film also contained the thesis of my earlier work, *The Regime of the Brother,* in miniature. One of the film's monologues (usually cut from rental video versions) focuses on the intensification of the brother-sister relation that appears when the patriarchal organization of society is weak or absent. The monologue is delivered by Patricia Collinge (Emma) during a scene in which Uncle Charlie attends a gathering in his honor at his sister's house. He has been expected to announce his plans to settle down in the town. Quite abruptly, he announces instead his imminent departure. Upon hearing that he will not be coming to live near her in her town, his sister, this very motherly mother of three, breaks down and weeps in a startlingly indecorous manner. She moans that a brother is the only irreplaceable relation a woman ever has, and the most important one to her. With her husband and children, a woman loses who she is; she only recovers herself through her brother.

Emma's overwrought speech, which violently disrupts the party's decorum, is a modernized reprise of Antigone's speech to Creon and is marked by something of the same oblivion toward the normal social world around her. Antigone laments that once her parents are buried, a dead husband or a dead child can be replaced, but a dead brother cannot.

Antigone's speech was, of course, an ethical one: she was trying to get Creon to follow proper ritual and bury her brother's bones, respecting a law of humanity beyond the petty interests of the state. Collinge's speech in *Shadow of a Doubt* inflects the brother-sister nexus completely differently, giving it incestuous or at least excessively libidinal overtones. It confirms the pettiness of the rules and laws of bourgeois society, the insignificance, for a woman, of marriage and children.

What Hitchcock's mother/sister does not know, of course, is that her daughter has discovered her beloved Uncle Charlie is the Merry Widow Killer, a serial strangler whose wealth is steeped in crime, and his personality even more so. And the part of the film that follows is, I think, what must have inspired my lifelong concern for the girl's sexual journey. It makes the movie a paradigm of the hysteric's confrontation with the sadist. This confrontation is no simple triumph over a cruel, perverse murderer, however, and this is the crucial element in the way the plot of the *Hysteric's Guide* also unfolds—for Hitchcock's Charlie is also compellingly drawn to this sadistic strangler, growing ever more spellbound by him as she comes closer and closer to discovering his secret. Whereas she feels she has found out her father's secret (his insignificance, even impotence), Uncle Charlie's secret makes him the real man she had wanted her father to be. If he is a killer, after all, he has done the deed her father can only talk about.

Even after Charlie is certain about her uncle's guilt, she does nothing to protect herself from him, even though she knows he knows she knows. He tells her they are the same person, same name, same identity, that she must therefore protect and save him. She thus never reveals his guilt to her parents, or to the world at large. Only the detective Jack Graham (the dick, I guess) eventually gets let in on her knowledge, when it no longer really matters, and he defers to her demand that her family must never know. He allows her to try to get her uncle away from her family before he attempts to arrest him.

Her permanent deferral of disclosure puts her at risk of her own life (Uncle Charlie tries to gas her in the family garage; he booby-traps the stairs she uses, and so on). This failure of speech on her part does not prevent her, ultimately, from acting against him. Whether hers is an ethical act or not remains, however, to be seen.

At each step in *Shadow of a Doubt* we find Charlie caught up in and paralyzed by a fascination with something that consciously repulses her. Charlie ties her inability to speak out directly to her mother ("It would kill her if she found out" is the constant refrain). The reason she cannot denounce her uncle outright, she tells the detective (McDonald Carey), is that she needs to protect her mother from the truth. Her ambivalence toward the sadist is thus paralleled by a certain ambivalence toward her mother.

For Charlie has refused in every way to compete openly with her mother (for her Uncle's if not her Father's affections). But Uncle Charlie is her dream man here, too: he obviates the need to compete, as he treats both her and her mother equally—a mink stole for Emma, an emerald ring for Charlie. Her giving up the field of competition for the male object should denote, according to Freud's feminine agenda, that she has yielded ambition to her mother and must seek outside the family for an object-choice other than her two parents. However, she has done everything, including finding out his secret, to draw her uncle's attention, no matter how destructive it proves. The dual pull in Charlie reveals a hysteric's arrested feminine itinerary, a hesitation before the full entry into assuming a sexual identity (and its attendant social responsibility) that marks her as a hysteric.

As a feminine/masculine figure, she carries within her the hysteric's vulnerability to the pervert. The hysteric is the perfect prey to the pervert because she refuses to name her mother as the culprit: she will not accuse her mother of being the agent of some original abuse, she will never break with or "kill" her mother mentally. (In contrast, her bookish, science-oriented, cool younger sister, Ann (Edna May Wonacott), is happy to break completely with her mother; she skips down the sidewalk deliberately stepping on the cracks so she can proudly announce, "I broke my mother's back three times.")

Charlie has not, in other words, accepted castration as relevant to her. But this puts her in a precarious and vulnerable position: she is left without the means castration offers the subject—speech—to relieve her of the pressure and burden of her Thing. Because she cannot denounce her mother, she must become her *and* her evil twin, the brother.

Even as she realizes who and what her uncle is (she has the rock-hard proof she knows can incriminate him, even though another man is thought to have been the murderer), Charlie will not denounce him. But she does want to be rid of him. And here the story becomes most interesting for us. While the ring with a rather large stone in it that she recovers from her uncle's bedroom is not exactly the "bedrock of castration" that Freud ran to to determine sexual difference with certainty, it serves as an adequate simulacrum. Since the inscription on the ring is the sole evidence left confirming her uncle's guilt, Charlie uses it to accomplish his riddance. Her majestic, silent sweep down a grand staircase wearing that rock prominently on her finger and aiming it directly at Uncle Charlie (who recognizes it immediately) prompts his sudden decision to head out of town. So, even if she does not bear her castration within, Charlie can wear this rock to good effect.

Hitchcock's parody of an engagement party here is, in a way, just that: it marks the hysteric's new stage of engagement with the sadist in which she is no longer completely under his spell psychically, while their fates actually become even more inextricably entwined with each other.

The Hysteric, the Mother, and the Pervert

Even as a very young girl I think I saw, or felt, the hysteric's ambivalence toward the Mother and her parallel ambivalence toward the sadist in this film. Charlie loves her mother and reflexively moves to protect her from all sinister knowledge. However, she must still get herself free of the sadistic superego the Mother represents (or used to). The mother still constitutes a rival, but the object of competition is a neutered man's love: not a father, but an uncle, too close to be a sexual love, far enough not to be properly or primarily incestuous. Uncle Charlie allows her to compromise, to keep her mother's obscene, thrilling part, and kill it at the same time. For if her father were ever really murdered by Herbie, Emma would become a widow, her uncle's victim of choice.

The hysteric also loves the sadist. He brings a *jouissance* to her, a secret knowledge about the nihilism of human life, its petty morality, its fenced-in restrictions—her "normal" life—so flat in comparison with her secret *jouissance* within. There is no other explanation for Charlie's barely contained excitement at the mere thought of his arrival into her dull life. She ultimately knows she must oppose the sadist's promises if she would "become woman." From that vantage point she would have to hate in him what he bears of lethal *jouissance*, death drive—those Things Charlie has never seen, or refuses to see, in her mother. But they still persist somewhere, troubling the boundaries of the reality and pleasure principles our societies have lived by. And she wants them to persist. Uncle Charlie tells her what she already unconsciously knows, that they exist in the midst of a foul sty of a world and that she must, at all costs, protect herself and her family from it. Yet as he represents this evil at large in the world, and as it is she who has invited him to share her bedroom and to take his place in the family circle, the allegory of evil warded off grows murky.

Psychoanalytically, what has happened is that a pervert, her uncle, has materialized to embody the sadistic superego that has already urged her, languishing across her bed, to "shake up the family," to get it to break out while keeping it within the safety zone, the boundaries of the home. The pervert, who has a very specific skepticism regarding sexual division (Uncle Charlie tells Charlie she is he; his sister also identifies with him), is the cardinal and unremarked element in the way the girl today encounters what stirs her. Her pleasures, her thrills that her superego urged within her, are brought out in her by the person of the pervert, who acts out what the mother no longer has to: the power to enjoy, and to foreclose her need to join society, the world of others, of other subjects in which her joys would be restricted.

The Pervert Displaces the Parents

What Charlie helps us to see is that now, as a part of the girl's logical structure, the most important relation for her sexual life today is to the pervert, and not to her Mother or her Father.[19] We must recognize this if we ever hope to see her take a next step. Let me be clear about what I mean by *perversion*. Perversion does not have much to do with the crazed, out-of-control violence the popular and movie imagination conceived it to be, around the 1950s and '60s, in an America newly conscious of "sex crimes."[20] It has to do with a certain skepticism regarding the law, including the law of sexual difference.

Charlie, sprawled listlessly across her bed, is clearly at home in her mother's house, but she is also trapped there. Her posture mirrors that of her uncle in the opening scene in which he apathetically awaits his fate, lying slack faced and limp abed in his rooming house as detectives encircle the area outside. She is excited only by this murderer who literally takes over and occupies her bedroom. Like him, she waits for her death. In the end she remains entombed within the circle of the family. The coziness of her small town, supposedly untouched by the vile elements she has invited in, is where she will figuratively bury herself. She has had to take her uncle's life; he ends his death drive ensconced and buried in a coffin in that same town, eulogized by that same family. With the exception of her lame courting by the detective, Charlie's focus as the film closes remains entirely on her uncle's vision of the world as pure evil, and she remains locked in her primary family; she is still not a woman, she has still not left her home or her mother.

This parable of the hysteric's failed confrontation with her own sadistic drives did not go unnoticed by Hitchcock, and we must not overlook it either.

Perversion's Promise of Jouissance

What the girl in the film cannot really give up is the odd and frightening promise of fulfillment that Uncle Charlie represents: the world as vile and foul. Her sadistic superego has already whispered about this *jouissance* to her, and her sadistic uncle seems to embody it for her. "Why?" requires a psychoanalytic explication. The pervert (who denies the Father and dreams that the Mother bears absolute *jouissance*) represents or wears the super-ego mantle today, lending the girl her ideological contours. He represents a "total man" to the hysteric who finds the Oedipal man ridiculous: he shapes her dreams. I think this is true on not only a literary and theoretical level but an empirical one as well: a young woman reports that no girl fantasizes about having sex with a "sensitive man." A much larger role than we have previously imagined for the sadist, who is according to Lacan, the *self-appointed* administrator of a maternal will-to-enjoyment,[21] looms in the formation of the girl and her ethic (her relation to her sex). (Lacan even noticed that a man can make love to a woman only by becoming a bit of a pervert, too, fetishizing his partner's body just enough to make up in a small way for the nonrelation between the sexes.)

The pervert is interested in a fulfillment, a specific *jouissance* beyond gender, beyond even the pleasure principle, beyond the difference of sex that makes "relation" impossible. He thus carries a particular appeal for the hysteric, who does not know if her sex is hers or not. Perversion can be formally decoupled from homosexuality: any given homosexual might very well have unconsciously adopted Oedipus (castration, the "Law" of sexual difference), if perhaps in inverted form.[22]

In the film by Hitchcock, the promise of fulfillment does not issue directly from the mother as in Freud's analysis, but it comes to the daughter through the agency of the sadist, her Uncle Charlie. The girl and her mother are, in fact, equally magnetized by his hidden promise of *jouissance*. Even though she does not break with her mother à la Freud and does end up shoving her Uncle Charlie off a fast-moving train to escape his murderous designs on her, Charlie does not herself escape. She gets off the train, she doesn't leave town, and she will not tell her family the truth about him—the truth that is, of course, really about them and about herself. If she has managed to detach herself somewhat from his compelling allure, she becomes focused exclusively on her uncle's view of the world as a place of horror. Uncle Charlie always seems to be out in the street whenever Charlie or her mother happens to look out the window in the film. This fascination is what really keeps her riveted to her family, and to maintaining its appearance of normality at all costs.

How does the pervert communicate so directly with the hysteric? The founders of psychoanalytic doctrine did not think to bring the pervert into the heart of any question concerning how the girl becomes woman. Quite the reverse: rather than accomplishing the sexual merging we find in the pervert, the girl was supposed to achieve her womanliness by growing *out* of an original bisexual disposition. The perverse unconscious, in contrast to an Oedipally sexualized one (hetero- or homo-) is consistently indifferent to sexual difference. When the pervert arrives to place himself (or itself) between the girl and her mother, and to make a breach between them, we can be certain that he is in no way assisting her to break with her obscene Thing, the sadistic superego inside her. That Thing holds him, too, in its grip—that Thing that is death drive or obscene will-to-*jouissance* that we have all too casually identified with the mother.

The pervert sometimes wins and more than once has a fiercely incisive message to relay to a girl, who in general refuses to hear or understand it. Without their mutual engagement, the hysteric will be forever blind to what is moving her, moving through her. She will never come to "know" the structure of her own relation to *jouissance,* or her unacknowledged competition with her mother: she will, most crucially, miss her chance for her own subjective freedom—freedom to leave Sade's bedroom. Failing that, her unconscious choice *not* to know her Thing will keep her confined there, fearful of, yet waiting for, the news he brings her about her *jouissance,* and kept under its constant threat.

That third figure with whom the girl must contend in her route toward social coexistence—Sade—has left his legacy, a sadistic superego, that has perhaps permanently altered the patriarchal parameters of the "society," the "symbolic seeming," whose shelter the girl once sought. It has certainly altered her relation to her mother. A break with her mother is no sure sign that a girl has mentally staved off an internally stifling, oppressive force, the Thing her mother represented to her. She may instead have become, like the pervert, its instrument. Or she may, like the hysteric, have found a way never to leave her mother, believing the pervert's contention that a negative side, the death drive in Things does not exist.

Freud, at least, had reserved a crucial psychic functionality to the sexual division of the parents, so that the child, even the girl, could attain some sort of dialectic or balance between their opposing choices, their different versions of "No!"

Indeed, it appears that rather than the "pure" motives of patriarchy, the only imperative that happily slices mother from daughter as preliminary to her passage into her sexuality, her society, and her womanness comes from a fairly creepy set of figures who insinuate themselves into the family link between the Mother and the Girl. It is they the girl must break with to win her womanhood. With the sadistic dimension now front and center, I can move to quite a spectacular example. Chief among those who split mother from the daughter, femininity from maternity, and fired the first modern salvo in the mother-daughter war was the Marquis de Sade, in his *Philosophy in the Bedroom*. In this text, a mother-daughter relation is not only destroyed, it is questioned down to its root: in it we can no longer even tell whether or how to distinguish mother from father. Sade blended the two parental figures and had both participate equally in the girl's liberation—or is it capture?—a fusion that leaves the girl in the grip of a single, totalizing sadistic superego.

Sade's *Philosophy in the Bedroom*:
A Treatise on the Education of Young Girls

Sade paints the picture of absolute liberty within the walls of a private boudoir that figures as a fantasy place where everything is permitted, yet kept under purely rational control. His libertines come to "educate" a girl to *her* own reason for existence, a reason that, carried to its logical extreme, should free her completely from any irrational domination, including that which comes from her mother.

Philosophy in the Bedroom opens with the induction of a young virgin, Eugénie, into the demimonde of libertinage. She has been invited by Madame de Saint-Ange to spend time in the older woman's home, over Eugénie's mother's suspicious objections. She does, however, have the blessing of her apparently naive father. Full of caresses and kisses for each other, the two women repair to Saint-Ange's private bedroom. Once they are there, however, Madame de Saint-Ange reveals that she has arranged for her brother, the Chevalier de Mirvel, to be present, and, moreover, he is to initiate the girl sexually (or, rather, to supplement the initiation Madame de Saint-Ange herself has commenced with Eugénie).

This bedroom scene, it turns out, has itself actually been orchestrated by an archlibertine, Dolmancé, who assigns everyone a sexual act and role to play. In this boudoir, everyone is made accessible to everyone else: attendants are called in to witness and to service, sex takes place among the four principal characters in every available combination (except for one or two: there is no male fellatio, and Dolmancé himself will never touch a female organ; this is Sade's way of detaching *jouissance* from the Oedipalized erogenous zones and allowing it the freedom to flow throughout the body). Dolmancé stage-manages Eugénie's defloration so flawlessly that in the space of a few hours he incites her to the most absolute sexual excess. Along the way, he expounds the logic of his procedures and demonstrates the irrefutable political correctness of inducting Eugénie into the corps of libertines. His is a logic neither she nor anyone else in the scene can adequately refute, or even care to. Although the

Chevalier makes a few weak stabs at it, his mincing moral objections to Dolmancé are only rhetorical gestures adopted for the pleasure of the debate, and to demonstrate further the implacable reason in Dolmancé's stance.

Eugénie's virginal resistance requires only a brief surmounting: she not only submits, she enjoys. She enjoys so well, indeed, that she ends by rejecting her mother, and more. She participates in her mother's murder. When her mother, suspicious of Madame de Saint-Ange, storms in to "save" her daughter from debauchery, she is immediately subdued by the group and forcibly infected with a deadly pox. Eugénie emphatically urges the others on and punctuates her own newly liberated position by taking a curved needle and thread to stitch her mother's vagina together to ensure that the pox will not escape—and that she will never have a sibling. To top things off, it is finally revealed that the entire course of events, from the girl's sexual initiation to the infecting of her mother, has been accomplished at the behest of Eugénie's off-stage father.

Philosophy in the Bedroom cannot be dismissed from my discussion of the girl just because it is old and therefore irrelevant. It cannot be left out because it is a writing that *makes history*: it marks out a particular space for a hitherto unheard-of freedom, an absolute freedom for the girl, within the limits of reason alone (to paraphrase Kant in a way that would most likely horrify him)—freedom for her as for everyone else. Once Sade undertakes to teach woman her freedom in the form of an absolute relation to enjoyment, it cannot be undone. Even though all Sade's work was banned from 1814 on, it was considered precious enough to have been passed lovingly from (male) hand to (male) hand until it finally saw the light.[23] So, even though few if any girls, before Guillaume Apollinaire first published pieces by Sade in 1909, probably ever had direct access to Sade's general thesis on girls, it was clandestinely put into circulation a long time ago. His liberation of the girl, then, will have already taken place, even before she was born, and even if her parents had never literally heard of Sade. Once Sade put his ideas in play, however quietly whispered, they became part of a new patrimony of the girl-child. She can still hear its undertone in every rule regarding her.

In Sade's fictional bedroom, in his private fantasy chamber that lies beyond the jurisdiction of every authority, something singular takes place: a general will to enjoyment, regulated only by unfeeling reason. Like capitalism, this will stops at nothing. Absolute enjoyment is promised freely to any and all who agree to the boudoir's *rational* terms: nothing occurs in there that cannot be assigned its logic. Recoil we must at the infection of the Mother, yet Sade's Dolmancé has already provided us with its impeccable rationale: to "kill" the Mother in the woman is to end the only real or native limitation on her potentially absolute sexual freedom—procreation (with its fundamental admission of mortality)—and deny any special quality or distinctiveness to her sexual parts.

The "Father" under Sadism

Eugénie's off-stage father plays a bizarre role, that of the "good" bad guy, inasmuch as it is he who secretly orchestrates his daughter's liberation. Eugénie's mother is made into the agent of a moral authority that normally resides in the paternal. As the sole moral authority, the mother must be humbled and ridiculed.[24] Yet from the very beginning, her authority is razor thin; she has nothing but an apoplectic outrage on her side. She does not scold her daughter from some sense of deep commitment to the laws of social coexistence. Moreover, the father's obscenity is nothing more than the mother's rules in reverse, just as thin and arbitrary as his wife's morality. We are given no motivation for his espousal of evil and transgression.

Neither a mother nor a father, then, really functions in Sade's fantasy production, at least not in regard to their roles as Freud laid them out. The psychoanalytically perverse structure of Sade's fantasy scene is completed by overcoming all parental authority. The pervert considers authority nil; he acts less to break down the law than to show how a will-to-enjoyment defeats or supersedes it. The so-called father in Sade's *Philosophy* has nothing left of paternal function but pure command; he bears no partitioning metaphor. He is reduced to the dimensions of Lacan's "unbarred Other," or Freud's mythic *Ur-Father* of *Totem and Taboo*; he takes over for and holds the place of the creature whose full enjoyment is supposed to be located for the child in the Mother.[25] Eugénie's two-dimensional, caricatured mother and her providential father, then, simply represent two sides of the same sadistic superego coin: they do not represent the dialectic of Law and desire that the Mother and Father do in psychoanalysis.

Sexuality Lost under Sadism

Sade's fantasy was of a sexuality so equal it ceases to have any meaning, especially for the girl. We're getting near that point with the girl today: recently, my son overheard two girls replying to the question, "So, what are you doing this afternoon?" Their response was, "Oh, we're going thrift-store shopping and then we're going to watch some porns." A thirteen-year-old girl queries the family newspaper columnist about why she gets a thrill when she reads *Playboy*. A young woman complains that twentysomething girls are exceptionally "hard" when they discuss sex, much rougher and cruder than young men at that age used to be. This past year girls have pulled even with boys in the commission of violent crimes.

This form of equality may not have been what either Sadism or feminism set out to demand, but it is at least a portion of what they have received. Women have lost the only job—mothering—for which their culture ever prepared their psyches. Their mental preparation for other tasks has been given relatively little attention, despite courses on assertiveness training, consciousness raising, self-esteem, and the like. No one knows just how to direct the girl, nor has woman been challenged to find out something more about herself—and tell about it analytically—than what she reads in propaganda magazines and popular news columns. The only treatise we still have on the education of young girls remains Sade's little pamphlet.

Yet it is my guess that she remains hungry for knowledge about herself, even if she doesn't know it. This hunger forms part of the girl's attraction to the pervert—his promise of knowledge about her.

A girl's "innocence" and her sexual ignorance are not the issue. It is how she deals with that knowledge for herself that counts. Rousseau once said (in *La Nouvelle Héloïse*) to those who complained about his fiction's moral unsuitability for young girls, "No chaste girl has ever read a novel. If she has thought even to open its pages, she is already lost."[26] His irony would be most apt today; no pretense of feminine innocence should deter us from questioning in some detail how well the girl handles the bundle of obscenity that has landed, so to speak, in her lap.

When I say *obscene*, I do not mean only what the televangelists and telemedicos today insist on putting out over the airwaves: presidential anuses (Reagan's operation) and penises. (Clinton's supposed "distinguishing characteristic," semen-streaked dresses, foot fetishes, and phone sex—those items that would give Sade, and the sadistic in us, merry proof that the moral order is nothing more than its grossest underside. One can only wonder why Clinton's prosecutors have not been the least concerned about their impact on the girl, daughter Chelsea, for whose sensibilities Kenneth Starr has been sadistically unconcerned, in the technical sense.)[27]

But by *obscene* I also mean the real events, the genocides, the carnival of carnage, the unthinkable and unspeakable horrors to which we are daily exposed, and to which we are growing increasingly numb.

Becoming Woman under Sadism

The classic question the hysteric asks mirrors the pervert's antipathy to sexual difference. She wonders, "Am I a man or a woman?" The hysteric wants and does not want the measure of protection from her inner Thing that social coexistence offers her. Or maybe she knows a secret truth: that at some fundamental level, social coexistence, the Law of society, is at best a fiction, one that may not indeed ever be fully believable. At worst, society, too, may have its own hidden Thing. Following Sade, the girl has nowhere to go but toward hysteria. The inevitable question that follows from Sade's challenge to the logic and the laws of sexuality comes down to this: how does one know, after Sade, *if* one is a man or a woman? Even for Freud, who masterfully delineated how to become a man, the process of "becoming-woman" was completely mysterious and perhaps impossible.[28]

With recent theory, Foucault and Butler in particular, we have begun to believe that becoming woman and the reverse, becoming and unbecoming a man, are essentially arbitrary decisions.

Is this where we must stand regarding the ethics of woman's sexuality today? Must we weigh the sadist's antipathy to sexual difference, an antipathy now widely shared by feminists and politically correct others of the past decades, against the proposition that sexuation is an *ethical* matter? To speak of sexuation as ethical means that it is neither natural nor essentialized, but it does not therefore mean that assuming one's sex is only an arbitrary or a conscious decision.

Sex and the Girl after Sade: Ethical Questions

The illusion of symbolic seeming, which sustains the moral order as we once construed it, has been pretty well taken down for the girl. Sade has her right where he would have wished. How can she get out of his grasp? Does she even need or want to? Sade's perverse scenario is more than just a startling fiction, an alternately stirring and horrifying tale. It is being reenacted in one variation or another all over the world. Sade's readers uniformly agree that no matter how cruel, his very distillation and surmounting of sexuality render his fantasy more than a mere *histoire*. The thrill of Sade is more than what comes with mere sex.

Sade may have left the girl in the dark and on the dark side of her relation to her mother, and he was probably pretty off-base in his conclusions about what she liked, but he was the first to have taken a step, in modern times, toward defining the girl's enjoyment. But he will never get past the hysteric to get to the girl, really. The pervert's controlled fantasy becomes, for the hysteric at least, a site where *jouissance* itself will both come alive and be at last fully controlled. The hysteric is wrong, of course, to imagine it will not touch her at the core. Like all pornography it will, but his even more so: its construction aims at a logic that would define for all time the girl's capacity to *relate to her sexual enjoyment*. We have, within our ethics, our politics, our psychologies, no means of contesting Sade's epoch-making, inaugural rules in this respect.

Perversion's implacable recourse to reason and logic makes it impossible for us to dismiss as deviant, insane, and marginal its assault on Oedipus. Nor in some of the deepest parts of ourselves do we want to: "The right to jouissance, were it recognized, would relegate the domination of the pleasure principle to a forevermore outdated era. In enunciating it, Sade causes the ancient axis of ethics to slip, by an imperceptible fracture, for everyone."[29] Freedom in the bedroom is intimately linked to at least one aspect of our necessary sense of subjective freedom and liberation from the Master. Freedom in the bedroom, fully bound by the rules of reason, and guaranteeing sexual liberty for all, is the heart of bourgeois life. Our demand to keep the bedroom out from under the noses of authority is something that nobody I know is prepared to give up, to special prosecutors or to anyone else.

And yet, and yet. It is a fragile, precarious freedom—this freedom claimed and partially won by Sade's work (if not by his life). It has its limits, and they are not those imposed by his own reason, though he desperately wanted things to work that way. Although it is not that of a slave, Sade's is after all a *prisoner's* dream. Sade is finally in no position to think the girl's freedom, really. Still, he has done his part. True, he does not give the girl what she really needs, the "free-*thinking*" part of libertinage, and he offers her only a walk-on role: she gets to show in her body the working of unlimited *jouissance* and to prove, by remaining unscathed by it, that it is not a death drive, that it is neither lethal nor dangerous. Sade was perhaps the first to give us the idea that girls can have their fun without the patriarchal cautionary tales that leave them seduced and abandoned, indelibly scarred and made dead by their enjoyment. He writes his stories in fact to demonstrate the opposite.

Nevertheless, although he might have given us this idea, Sade never delivered the goods. To create a proof that fulfillment, and enjoyment, really exist, Sade had to override the *truth* of the girl's experience. If Eugénie really had begun to exist as "woman," once she joined forces with the libertines and symbolically killed off her mother, that would be one thing; it would justify even to patriarchy the education Sade puts her through.

Does Eugénie become a woman so easily by doing away with her mother? Or does she merely become part of a larger, unisexed body, a natural, or better, a corporate body vastly greater and more engulfing than her mother's ever could have been? She does not enter the body politic, because Sade has told her she does not need to. She need never contribute to the public sphere as long as she achieves freedom, equality, and fraternity within his bedroom walls.

Will Eugénie have actually comprehended enjoyment to its depths, or will she have used its overwhelming her as a way to refuse to know anything about it? Will she really have been "educated" by Sade, or will she have learned from him only how to deny that woman has a problematic relation to enjoyment? Will Eugénie have been enlightened, or will she have simply adopted, as victims often do, the slant of her abusers and abductors?

Dolmancé, making woman out to be the object of "an equal right of enjoyment" by "all men" (319), declares:

> If we admit as we have just done, that all women ought to be subjugated to our desires, we may certainly allow them ample satisfaction of theirs. Our laws must be favorable to their fiery temperament. It is absurd to locate both their honor and their virtue in the anti-natural strength they employ to resist the penchants with which they have been far more profusely endowed than we. . . . I want laws permitting them to give themselves to as many men as they see fit; I would have them accorded the enjoyment of all sexes and . . . of all parts of the body. (320–21)

Sade's "total *Jouissance*" here ironically re-places woman squarely in the arms of a Mother other than the one he tore her from: Nature. His logic has required it. But if he has evaded the question of the specifically *feminine* subject, the subject that cannot be found "in nature" or without resisting the mother, then he has mapped only part of the terrain we need to traverse. He has not offered the girl any entry into society, not given her any guidelines for coexisting with others under conditions where *jouissance* cannot reign supreme. His world, however utopian, is still restricted to the bedroom, not generalized to the level even of a collective ego. The drive he set in motion is still among us. Today, as Oedipus wanes, we are experiencing an urge toward expanding his bedroom walls and toward bringing Sade's vision to public fruition. I analyze that populist impulse in chapter 2, "Perversion in Public Places." But here I am focusing on Sade and the girl.

Judith Butler: Between Patriarchy and Sade

The current alternative of choice to Sade as well as to Patriarchy is Judith Butler's work, which challenges the way sexuality is psychologically *formed* under Oedipus with the way it can be *performed* in postpatriarchal culture. She stops well short of the complete Sadean dismantling of the Law and suggests instead a compromise between patriarchy and Sade.[30] It would bypass patriarchy by removing *agency* from the *subject,* which is sexed and therefore subject to the law of Oedipus, to a *self* that would actively perform gender.[31] In *Gender Trouble: Feminism and the Subversion of Identity,* she suggests fiction, simulation, and parody as a set of "subversive" strategies that go beyond the "camping" of femininity created by the gay community, to overcode gender and disrupt sex role expectations. Not just women, but everyone, Butler's work implies, can now take on gender the way only women were once supposed to, through masquerade. But it is a masquerade pushed to the point where the mask self-destructs: "The task," she writes, "is not whether to repeat, but how to repeat or, indeed, to repeat and, through a radical proliferation of gender, *to displace* the very gender norms that enable the repetition itself."[32]

Butler's aim is to free us from our sexed subject, whose dull duties, tired narratives, and singular fate we all already know, in favor of an openness and flexibility appropriate for the postmodern world of surfaces. The outcome is a performed gender whose social and cultural meaning is radically unreadable. She has thus attracted many followers eager to undo the ideologies of feminine masquerade, the shopworn codes of Oedipal sexuation, and the stereotyped assignment by gender of social roles and duties.[33] At the juridical, social, and political level, such a reconfiguration is long overdue, and it surely plays a large part in the appeal of her theory. But at the mental level, Butler's popularity may also stem from a darker source. For looked at closely, we can see that Butler's thesis is essentially adapted to the mental set of the hysteric, who asks, "Am I a man or a woman?" and who finds no adequate response in the symbolic to support her either way. As Butler has chosen to deal with the juridical rather than the psychoanalytic subject, a brief detour through both is in order.

The Juridical and Psychoanalytic Subjects of Sex

What renders the subject a *juridical* subject is its appointment within a social context—its placement within a family, group, tribe, nation, and a "sex." There is a secondary effect to this placement: it also provides the subject with an unconscious *sexual* location as well. The subject is not only granted citizenship by the laws under which it is born; it also concurrently receives its unconscious "anchoring," its inmost bearings, from them. How so? This orientation, sexual orientation, comes from the way the subject originally responds to what it feels the social has said about it, to what it has "heard" in the tone of voice that secondarily denotes an attitude, and an evaluation of it.

To psychoanalysis, therefore, the *subject of the unconscious* exists only as a by-product of a specific questioning: "Who am I for you, the other?" This question has two answers: a *symbolic* one that mentally locates the questioner in a legal, moral, and social network; and an *unconscious* one. The symbolic answer—the more or less legal placement of the subject within a specific social system (e.g., as someone's son or daughter)—has an unconscious correlate or precipitate: the subject's placement of itself with respect to a sexual divide.

What the subject of the unconscious "hears" in the undertone or underside of the response of the symbolic furnishes its unconscious sexual position. Society says, "You are a woman" as it situates you as daughter, sister, wife, mother. Your unconscious, responding to the tone in which this assignment is made, says: "I am not!" Or, "Yes, indeed!" Or, "Am I?"

There is even more to its sexuality than finding a proper place, however. The subject "takes" the social answer to its "question" ("Who am I for you?") in a broader frame, answering itself with a longer term rationale for its life (and eventual death). The subject can tell itself several different stories as to why it finds itself constrained, fulfilled, or confused by the divisions that Freud called "the reality principle" of social coexistence:

• *Sexual (Oedipal) reason* hears in itself the requirements of civilized social coexistence and the imperatives of a Law of reproduction for continuing the life of the group. This unconscious reason rules the Oedipal subject, whatever the consequences, negative (castration, individual death) or positive (care for children, ethical behavior, etc.). It demands that the subject take up sex, in the interests of this reason. Sexuality—that is, Oedipus—therefore may be internally accepted by heterosexuals and homosexuals alike in all its serious, even tragic dimensions, as long as a sexual position is taken by the subject: "I am really a woman." Or, "I am really a man."

• *Hysteric reason,* in contrast, cannot "hear" any definitive judgment on the question of its "sexual" placement in the symbolic's muttering. The hysteric subject unconsciously demands, "Am I a man or a woman?" and never hears a clear or final answer. It can give itself no real reason to choose.

There is a hesitation, and even a fear, before the possibilities in its two alternatives, Oedipus and perversion.

• *Perverse reason,* in contrast to either of these two, turns a deaf ear to the Law. It hears only one tone, one superego voice, that of its rival twin. It can oppose or embrace it freely, since in the long run this other is only itself and has no ultimate authority. The subject, society, the law, and thus sexual difference do not exist for the pervert. He denounces all symbolic seeming in favor of the Real: *jouissance,* death drive, the beyond of sex (although, of course, unconsciously, the pervert mentally aligns him or herself with a more powerful and implacable Law than that of sexuation, the Law of Nature).[34]

The Ethics of a Subject of Sex: The Peter Pan Option

Psychoanalytically, the social encoding of one's gender and one's unconscious sexual position, then, do not always line up. However, Butler's position, following Foucault's lead, is to do away finally with the distinction between social role and unconscious sex. She brings the id to the surface, so to speak, but she *neutralizes* this uncontrolled substance through play and parody. Her innovative strategy is to offer a permanent deferral of sexual identification, a reduction of sexuality to a mere discursive form, and a taming of the drives in the unconscious. This strategy cannot fail to attract the hysteric. In Butler's most recent work, indeed, she has begun theorizing why the girl and boy never need break, psychically, with their mother—like the hysteric.

Still, Butler's work seems to me less a theory about than a reflection of the education of young people *to* hysteria today. And here is where we need more analysis, not just a supportive or confirming philosophy. What are the goals and ideals of educating middle-class youth in our time, and why does a hysteric-like structure predominate among them? Hitchcock's hypernormal Charlie has, after all, been instructed only in how to inhabit a room in her family home, not how to live in what we used to call "society."

Of course, after Thatcher and Reagan, "society doesn't exist"; could we, in all honesty, say that this does not hold for our children (as it did for Uncle Charlie, who admonishes his niece that society at large is a foul sty)? Schooling our young now ideally consists of their being scheduled every minute *after* school, ostensibly to meet the work needs of the parents.[35] But is there not fear of what is lurking outside their homes and inside their heads, as well, behind this frenzy? If, by contrast, children simply play outdoors in their suburban neighborhoods, they are watched more visibly by the eyes on the decals of Neighborhood Watch crime alert signs than by actual parents. No particularly responsible adult monitors their play together, what little there is, to ensure that each learns how to be a proper citizen of the world of childhood, playing fair, including everyone, practicing how to be grown up, and so forth. Adolescents may volunteer for good causes or have huge loud parties, but rarely do they have a chance just to hang out with a mixed sex batch of pals, idly, thinking up things—even subversive things—together. They might be thought of as a gang.

The girl today is being taught to be her own man, or, rather, her own quasi man: she will not be the emotional, flighty girl of yesteryear, she will not be feminine, but she will also never quite have to become a woman. Nor does the boy ever have to become a man the way it used to go. We see the girl today with a perpetual, but oddly unwelcoming, smile, her statements framed with the intonation of a question. The boy has learned to groom himself for being on display, and knowing that young girls often feel more at ease with gay boys than sexually threatening males, he learns to fold an ingredient of mystery about his sexual orientation into that grooming. This is the hysteric setup, the uncertainty about sex, in action.

Butler is thus very appropriate for today's society; she is providing our young people with a way of relating to their absence of sexuality, their post-Oedipal situation. Her work confirms to the young that, in fact, they may never have to grow up, like Peter Pan;[36] they can remain forever, mentally, in their bedroom of the parental house. And she might be right. The world is different now from the way it was a few decades ago. Society is different. It has much more of a sadistic, id character than we ever admitted in the past. No parent can want the child to step out of the charmed family circle into that "foul sty." What's a girl to do? If it was the existence of a so-called maternal obscenity that propelled the girl out of the house and into the arms of a waiting man, Sade certainly did his part to make us skeptical of that man as a resolution. The excuse of a generalized obscenity in society keeps the girl trapped in her family, where it may be even worse. Recently, a mother and the male stripper she permitted to perform at her fifteen-year-old daughter's birthday party were both indicted for corrupting a minor. One girl who attended paid the stripper twenty dollars to let her perform oral sex on him; others said such parties are held all the time. What's a girl to do?

Lest we forget, however, the vaguely Sadean threat the negation of sexual difference always carries with it, that of erupting within the family circle, we might do well to remind ourselves of what the converse, an ethic of sexuality, is.

An Ethics of Sexuality

To assume, ethically, a sex means to have some relation to "the public sphere," some responsibility toward a society that requires certain things of certain sexes. Responsibility toward and for society is something women, classically, have never been asked to have beyond motherhood and its attendant duties. Today, maternal duties are no longer demanded of women: just as Sade envisioned, women are free of maternity as our absolute and sole obligation to society. Women are everywhere out in "the world," certainly. Still, the "work world" of our corporate economy is not exactly what we once understood society to be: the place where each must recognize the other as a subject and must therefore grant that other dignity. This is the minimum necessary for social coexistence, but a commitment to the other's dignity could hardly be said to characterize either version of the *eikos* today: the household or the economy. That is why Butler finally cannot help the girl out of the room and the bed that her mother and Sade, respectively, have made for her. There is no alternative version of the public sphere, or society, for which she need leave them. At bottom, their structure is the same, and neither mother nor Sade really credits the existence of a society of subjects.

To be ethical means finding your own bearings; it means relating knowledgeably and courageously to your own drives. It does not mean disavowing their existence. The ethical aspect to sexuation is not a matter of will: it cannot be understood as an act on the part of the ego and its twin, the superego. A subject is what assumes responsibility for itself; it produces a specific work, a mental labor, in order to deal with its drives. This should be true even for a female subject, especially after the one piece of work—femininity—patriarchy used to hand her to accomplish no longer serves her very well.

Only if we can get to the point where we can begin to attribute a subject to the woman, an ethical subject, will we have a guide not only to hysteria, but through hysteria to *the future female subject*. Our world has negligently charted the girl's course right through the Sadean minefield. I am trying to sketch her "way through" it. If we cannot get through to that female subject, then our only alternative is to face squarely what the fulfillment of Sade's fantasy means for the girl. She will have to go with Butler without thinking through how vulnerable she may therefore be to the perverse. She will never exist *as* woman.

An Ethics for the Feminine

Perhaps it is only a matter of people needing a little mystery in their lives; as Bakhtin once put it, if you carnivalize the body too much, it becomes a meaningless, lifeless corpse.[37] Yet I am seeing a resistance to Sade today among young women. In my courses, the critique of Sade has come particularly from women, even those who are self-identified lesbians. (Their resistance may have something to do with Dolmancé's belief that using bigger and bigger "engines" to penetrate Eugénie and Madame de Saint-Ange with *jouissance* will render the women equal or superior to men in their capacity for enjoyment.) Still, my female students seem bereft of any incisive terms, any technical vocabulary to articulate the ways they demur from his stance, however much they would like to criticize Sade, even as they appreciate at some level his recognition of their enjoyment. At their disposal they have only a conservative, fearful, patriarchal-ish rhetoric. They fall silent, then, because the patriarchy doesn't exist for them any longer, and because they are neither conservative nor fearful enough to use its worn ideology as a guide. Any analysis of what may be going wrong (as well as, in some ways, right) for woman after Sade escapes their powers of ideological critique. They lack the words to say it.

That is because we lack a good record of the girl's relation and response to the sadistic superego, a record that might serve to guide us. We mainly have the testimony of the hysteric. But we can begin to make our inquiries. We can ask and ask, until someone answers, about how the girl hears the superego's imperative voice, that voice cultural patriarchalism was never quite sufficient to counter for her.

The importance of this inquiry goes beyond the girl herself. Because the appeal of that sadistic superego voice now threatens to drown out all others in *everyone's* mental airwaves. Patriarchy's shield against the obscene superego, *the word* (which Freud, Lacan, and Apollon all call "paternal"), grows ever weaker the more our social laws appear to be arbitrary, despotic, and unreliable. The word, as metaphoric release from Thingness, is blocked when the ego's evil twin, the superego, is our only interlocutor. And even where the word retains the power to displace the obscene call of the superego, we can no longer confidently expect it to come from the lips of poetic fathers. I have had to search for it especially from those women who have withstood the inducements of Sade (used here generically to indicate the sadistic superego). But our best resource, if we could only access her, would ultimately be the girl. Duras called her word a "hole-word" in *The Ravishing of Lol V. Stein*:

> It would always have meant, for her mind as well as her body, both their greatest pain and their greatest joy, so commingled as to be undefinable, a single entity but unnamable for each, of a word. I like to believe—since I

love her—that if Lol is silent in her daily life it is because, for a split second, she believed this word might exist. Since it does not, she remains silent. It would have been an absence-word, a hole-word, whose center would have been hollowed out into the kind of hole in which all other words would have been buried. . . . in one fell swoop it would have defined the future.[38]

To hear it, we may need something like this odd, negative force, this hole-word, which Walter Benjamin also named "the destructive character."[39] This is the impossible character who can find a way through the limits and impasses of an established situation. Only such a character could discover an exit from Sade's bedroom, at least for the girl, without giving up whatever portion of freedom he had secured for her, and without attempting, however futilely, to put her back into her "father's house." Futile because the limits the paternal metaphor once placed on *jouissance,* too phallic in character, no longer permit the "return" of the girl who has been touched, in her core, by Sade. How can she, or anyone else, attempt to resist on patriarchal grounds a *jouissance* that everywhere exceeds the Father's symbolic grasp? The answer for the girl is not traditional patriarchal society's answer. It is not exactly Freud's femininity, either. Answers will come only if we can invent new ways for coping with a dramatically expanded excess—Sade's excess—at large in the world.[40]

It is unclear whether the girl will ever be able to leave the confines of Sade's bedroom, and take a step, as woman, toward another sort of freedom, another sort of *jouissance* than what perversion has mobilized. Will she find her invisible incarceration in Sade's bedroom perfectly bearable? Will she or won't she find a "way through"? Still, attempts have been made—by artists and a few psychoanalysts.[41] I consider Marguerite Duras chief among them. Her *Destroy, She Said* is a "last" text because it is, in some sense, the "first" of a new series.[42] While it does not show where the sadist wins or loses, it does show sadism's bedroom, the pervert's scene, as reinhabited, retrofitted, and adapted for entirely fresh interests and uses— those of the female subject. A new scene opens before us. A field, feminine, creative . . . But I anticipate.

Conclusion

Sade attacked both maternity and femininity and with them the specialness of the female subject. Likewise, Freud never really viewed the feminine option as anything but a loss, a constraint on the girl's bisexual possibilities cut short by a harshly patriarchal society. His unavowed "myth" of the girl is a little like Rousseau's savage: her fall into the ills of femininity parallels her abject submission to an arbitrary social order. But it was Freud's romance with the hysteric that blinded him to woman: one glance at the index to his *Collected Works* shows Freud progressively giving up, and contenting himself with, the masculine yet womanly hysteric at the expense of whatever woman he might have conceptualized in her place. Freud remained as firmly attached to the hysteric as to his daughter Anna, taking only brief—and chilling—detours through hysteria's counterpoints, "femininity" and "female sexuality," and whenever he did so, he beat a hasty retreat back to his first hysteric loves.

Freud's preference for the hysteric, I suspect, had something to do with her fidelity to "true" nature, her closeness to the bisexed origin. But it also had to do with the hysteric's fantasy of the total man and Freud's unwillingness to analyze where he stood in that respect. He unconsciously sustained and protected the hysteric's fantasy of man as he who brings out the *jouissance* she cannot acknowledge in herself. Was Freud perhaps afraid to scrutinize the perverse underlining to the masculine ideals he upheld?

When Jacques Lacan elected woman for his study in *Encore*, he regarded it as a not entirely fresh undertaking but as a return to a meditation interrupted a decade and a half earlier in his seminar on ethics—on Sadean ethics in particular.[43] If indeed, as I have argued, the girl must contend with a *third figure* beyond Mommy and Daddy en route toward social coexistence, then it is Lacan, not Freud, who hits the mark with the girl Freud missed.

The value of femininity is, finally, in Lacan completely different from that in Freud. Lacan expressed the moment of acquired femininity as a gain—for better or for worse—rather than as the loss and constriction Freud's picture laments. In everything that Lacan invokes regarding feminine logic, we see it as more demanding, more complicated, more hazardous, and more hard work than either the masculine or hysteric positions require. For Lacan, the feminine was what has to deal with "more"—supplementary *jouissance*, a double focus toward the other/Other. More than the hysteric. More than the masculine. Encore.

When Lacan concedes to the feminine a supplemental *jouissance*, he takes the same biological model as Freud's—the dual siting of sexuality on the feminine body, vagina and clitoris—not as proof of an essential bisexuality (organ of generation, organ of phallic *jouissance*) but as proof that not all of woman is under the phallic signifier. She therefore has a wider experience of the fundamental problematic of our time—how to deal with *jouissance*—than does man. This is not to paint a picture of Lacan as exalting female sexuality. Not at all. Because she must face an unwieldy *jouissance* on two fronts, so to speak, without the sure support of the phallic signifier, her battle is more complex and more fraught with danger than the man's—or the hysteric's. In any event, where Freud saw "less" in the feminine, Lacan saw "more," and as such it is Lacan's theory that permits us greater access to that feminine experience, that *savoir*, that knowledge of *jouissance*, than was really possible under Freud's oddly more romanticized view.

2. Perversion in Public Places

A mere fifteen years ago when the media reported on a respectable grammar-school teacher in a midsized northern California city who, after school, was a highly paid dominatrix ("Ms. Brandy"), the tone was that of shock, though a titillated shock. As the police relayed descriptions of the fully outfitted dungeon beneath the teacher/dominatrix's suburban tract house and revealed her clientele to be members of the local chamber of commerce, they also expressed a certain befuddlement: could they charge her with any crime? She was, after all, not selling *sex* but *punishment* to her johns. And her johns were equally difficult to imagine prosecuting: for how could a masochist be punished by the forces of law and order, since any punishment would have to take the form of the very punishment he would be being punished for? More recently, episodes of the popular television series *NYPD Blue* and *Nash Bridges* have featured police detectives unable to decide whether the people they find tied up and handcuffed are robbery and murder victims or simply masochists who succumbed to their own demands.

Somewhat greater uneasiness attended the underground rumors of perverse behaviors involving the highest officials in the United States (or their closest friends). The mistress (now deceased) of a well-known business magnate alleged that she had documented sadomasochistic acts with public figures (including some in the White House) on videotapes. Certain people, purporting to have viewed them, released salacious details. With these allegations by Vicki Morgan sadomasochism came out of the dungeon for all of America: perversion threatened to go public on a national scale. (Even the youngest children at the time could hardly fail to escape awareness of, and curiosity about, the sensationally half-revealed images; one very small boy of my acquaintance took to calling Vicki Morgan "Puss in Boots.")

Hypothetically, at least, perversion as an official way of life had become conceivable to middle America. The Reagan administration's swift reaction—a vigorous and successful effort to countervail (or to veil) the soupçon of perversion—was comforting, to be sure. Still, something had changed forever for the American psyche.

Any tone of puzzled shock has long since disappeared from our media accounts of perverse behavioral styles. Today, it is not perversion, but the hint of a once-standard adulterous or heterosexual liaison that is deemed "scandalous." Several top U.S. military officers have resigned while others have been forced to step aside upon being confronted with evidence they have had adulterous or extramarital affairs. The presidency itself is currently considered "threatened" by just such an allegation.[1]

Meanwhile, a sadism cafe, La Nouvelle Justine, has opened in Manhattan, where light spankings are served up by waitresses along with meals. "S&M is a big hit South of Market" in San Francisco, where "couple after couple, clad in black leather, silver chains, or barely anything, are taking turns whipping, slapping, and pinching each other all for the benefit of the crowd of drooling tourists, articulated voyeurs and S&M practitioners." Clubs like Bondage a Go Go and sex toy stores like Stormy Leather report that "a good chunk of our business is heterosexual, middle-aged couples."[2] A birthday party thrown in May 1997 for a political consultant who successfully managed the vote for a new city stadium entertained guests (including leading San Francisco politicians) with a sadomasochistic act featuring a dominatrix who "carved a pentagram on a man's back, urinated on him, and sodomized him with a Jack Daniels [whiskey] bottle."[3] "Gothic" societies have formed around adopting sadomasochistic paraphernalia.[4]

Lest we too quickly conclude New York and San Francisco are simply the new Sodom and Gomorrah, however, let us note that academic lesbian sadomasochism is now considered a fully legitimate form of feminism with high ethical standards inspired, in part, by Gilles Deleuze's influential 1967 book, *Coldness and Cruelty*.[5] Deleuze called for a new ethics in which women would conscientiously give up their traditional "masochism" and "play at sadism" to afford men an opportunity to change their ways, get out of their traditional sadism, and adopt a new masochism.

Such suggestions as Deleuze's have been amply implemented in the lesbian sadomasochist world, where "sadism is a pleasure in mastery and not a perversion . . . an active life-preserving aggressivity [that aims] to assert control over power and violence in sexuality by using it. [It is] potentially liberatory, harnessed and theatricalized for greater sexual pleasure and greater understanding of that pleasure."[6] Self-limited by mutual consent, without having to pass through the unascertainable desire of the Other (Lacan's "castration"), full enjoyment unhampered by arbitrary power: how, indeed, could anyone demur from this utopian picture of pleasure-filled existence?

The current publicity surrounding perverse behavioral styles may index the extension of this new ethic. Or it may merely be a fad. To determine its nature requires investigating the degree to which perversion is the new ethic in our contemporary politics, economies, and psyches. This has further implications for the girl who must choose, unconsciously or not, her pathway into our society. Whether an increasingly familiar phenomenological "sadism" and "masochist violence," glamorized in the media, have any real (if only lingering) connections to a perverse *unconscious* not under rational control remains, however, to be seen.

The interplay between public life and the structures of perversion—the disavowal of the law and its violation, the staging of violence with alternately submissive and dominant partners—clearly merits exploration because it seems to mirror a process that can no longer easily be termed either conscious or unconscious. Perverse sadistic violence practiced on a willing "victim"—is it violent or not? Can we distinguish "playing at" sadomasochistic violence from an allegedly true sadomasochistic pervert's acts, whose cool and reasoned cruelty poses so important a challenge to the Law?

Since the pervert always requires a theater, we might take a scenic route into perversion and its connection to the form of social relations today. Two different scenes of instruction follow.

Scene I. In the Lacanian Classroom

Recently, I began teaching a course on treating psychosis at a Lacanian school. I started out by emphasizing that unconscious psychic structures may exist without being manifested. As I began telling my students (many of whom worked with psychotics and the mentally ill homeless) that someone might have a psychotic unconscious and yet function perfectly and even very effectively within society for quite some time,[7] the class became visibly disturbed, though they remained quite obviously incredulous.

I persisted in my theoretical exposition, pointing out that, after all, just before he became ill Judge Daniel Paul Schreber (a psychotic man whose autobiography was analyzed extensively by Freud) had been functioning so well that he was about to assume a role equivalent to Chief Justice of the Supreme Court. The manifestation of his delusion showed he had fundamentally and unconsciously foreclosed believing in Law. Yet here he was, about to become one of its most prominent public representatives. For Schreber, for the paranoiac, the Law—the beliefs we hold in common, the fictions we collaboratively produce, the stories we tell each other to support and sustain our mutual coexistence against the unpredictable Other—was null. His own inner constructions, built on a void where symbolic Law should have been, inevitably collided with the positive existence of law and induced Schreber's breakdown.

What is this symbolic Law ("castration") Schreber foreclosed? Symbolic Law is what enables mutual coexistence: it is a *partition* that intervenes between the pair ego and other. To the paranoid unconscious, the ego-other couple is constructed out of a dialectic of self and other as mutual objects of envy and competition—mutually *destructive* objects:

> This dialectic always carries the possibility that I may be called upon to annul the other, for one simple reason. The beginning of this dialectic being my alienation in the other, there is a moment at which I can be put into the position of being annulled myself because the other doesn't agree. The dialectic of the unconscious always implies struggle, the impossibility of coexistence with the other, as one of its possibilities.[8]

The paranoiac cannot even be said to have a subject, so pronounced is his avoidance of the Other. (Lacan puns that the *S* of his diagram is replaced by *Es*—the German "It" in the paranoid unconscious.) By contrast, "normal neurotics," who unconsciously believe that the Law protects them, by means of a painful but bearable separation of subject from object, have a modicum of unfounded faith that peaceful coexistence is possible within the Law. They can suffer the presence of an other, however unknowable. Lacan put it this way: The distinction between the Other with a big *O*, that is, the Other insofar as it's not known, and the other with a small *o*, that is, the other who is me, the source of all knowledge, is fundamental. It's in the gap, it's in the angle opened up between these two relations, that the entire dialectic of delusion has to be situated."[9] In the neurotic unconscious, subject and other are mutual question marks: what does s/he want? In the psychotic unconscious, voided where the Law should be, the infinitely unknowable Other who "causes" us as subjects is unendurable. Only the other, me-as-other, who contains and/or envies the object (of enjoyment), exists.

The paranoiac, because he *knows* exactly what the other is, has, or wants—himself-as-object—finds the concept of the Other intolerable. He *knows* that in the Real there is no Law, no shelter, no shield against the lethal other, small *o*.

Schreber saw, therefore, in the mirror both a Supreme Court Judge, a representative of the Law, and his murderous rival. He disguised himself to himself by wearing women's jewels and finery whenever he looked in the mirror: was he trying to deceive the persecutory other? His breakdown was inevitable, yet up to the crisis he had been able to work, and work well, sustained by means of an inner construction of his own devising. Then it gave way. After the crisis, he repaired his system, the original elaborate delusion that had held him together, his self-made system. He then felt the urgent need to publish it in order to save not only himself but the whole world from the defect in the Other: its unchecked violence that he alone *knew* to be its essence.

As I went over these points to the psychoanalysts-in-training, I noticed their becoming uniformly anxious, as each turned increasingly inward to wonder about their own unconscious structure.

Scene II. In the University Classroom

By contrast, my literature graduate students at the University of California responded completely differently from the psychoanalysts-in-training when I began presenting my proposals on perversion. Where the latter had become unnerved at the suggestion that psychosis was a structure that can exist without overt manifestation in those whose behavior appears "normal," the literature students in my seminar "On Perversion" started out by eagerly identifying themselves with and as perverts: "Perverts are good, right?" one student declared early in the class. As they expressed their earnest feeling that perversion was about an *agency* that "straight" life denied them, I could see the challenge before me. Not only did they initially discount the unconscious: the thought of its independent agency was foreign to them.

I gently began examining perversion as an unconscious structure that was neither good nor bad, nor fundamentally tied to homosexuality. (Homosexuality is a question of object-choice by the ego, and a matter of ultimate indifference to the unconscious structure: homosexuals come in the same varieties as heterosexuals—neurotic, psychotic, and perverse). In time, the students' responses to my lectures on hysteria, sexual difference, and the work of Lacan, Deleuze, and André on perversion suggested to me that my listeners were not nearly as perverse as they might have liked.

In this second classroom scene, the complications of analyzing the perverse came to the fore. Apart from some clinical books (which often insufficiently distinguish perversion from homosexuality), we have little to go on to determine the relation of sadism to the Law—little, that is, besides the fictional writings of Sade.

Lacan on Sade

Lacan did his foundational work on perversion by setting out from Sade's work, and his insights have been convincingly updated by Serge André.[10] From them we learn that the sadist, like the psychotic, does not accept the Law. But, unlike the psychotic, the basis for the pervert's rejection is less unbelief than it is a *reasoned* conclusion. And he does not fear the violence of the Other, because this violence can, he believes, be controlled by reason. The pervert's skepticism stems from "knowing" that "the form of the Law is its only substance."[11] The sadist wants to demonstrate the insubstantiality of the Law—to discount, preempt, humiliate, and expose the Law as merely formal. Sadism acknowledges the Law and dispenses with the need for it in one stroke.[12]

The pervert Dolmancé appears in Sade's stage-lit *Philosophy in the Bedroom* as the paragon of rationality. Controlled to the point of apathy, he demonstrates why taking the Law (Oedipus) as merely formal is most consequential: it allows a sheer mutuality, among a set of equals, to take the place of, and to take over for, any centralized authority over enjoyment. As the impresario at the advent and enactment of this purely formal law, Dolmancé's role is to demystify that Other who traditionally brings a partitioning Law in its wake—God and the Woman. The atheist Dolmancé ably demonstrates that woman, like the God he provokes, is reducible to a quantifiable dimension: her capacity to enjoy the other. She holds no mystery: her desire is fully plumbed. The girlish "victim" Eugénie instantly drops her modesty and abandons her virginity in favor of equal participation with her fellow bedroom occupants in the *Philosophy,* and plunges with zest into the general *will-to-jouissance,* "the V" (*Volonté*) "that dominates the whole affair," Lacan calls it.[13] Dolmancé proposes will-to-*jouissance* as a new "social" contract (Deleuze would say "institution") to replace all prior forms of social relation. He induces rather than seduces the participants with this proposition. (Seduction means giving your word, even when, or especially when, you are lying. Words for the pervert are strictly logical demonstrations correlated with acts.)[14]

Will-to-Jouissance

What does will-to-*jouissance* mean for the Sadean character? Whereas an unfathomable, unknowable *desire* of the Other founds social reciprocity, will-to-*jouissance* solves the mystery of desire. It is so radically nuanced toward *knowledge* as to revolutionize the social relation itself. Since the other's desire is a known quantity, will-to-*jouissance* can become a cooperative collective construction, in which everyone present knowingly participates. Its "natural law" is that of a *jouissance* that is posed no limits. Indeed, immersed in the will-to-enjoyment immanent in the acts ordered up by Dolmancé, not a single one of the participants in the bedroom scene gainsays their collective power to achieve unlimited enjoyment for all. It is self-evident. Nor, since their pain is always ultimately converted to pleasure, can anyone in the bedroom grouping believe in ultimate violence—death at the hand of the other. (Nor do they believe in castration: for Freud, fear of death and fear of castration amount to the same thing.)

The subject-object dialectic, so overwhelming to the paranoiac, is effectively declared null and void by Sade's mouthpiece. The partner of the pervert will consecutively be the fully enjoying subject and the fully enjoyable object: "I have the right to enjoy your body and you have the right to enjoy mine." All can enjoy all at no cost to one or the other. The object, for the pervert, will replace the rivalrous other entirely by the object of enjoyment he stands for. This object will become a fetish penetrated with enjoyment, its place held alternately by both self and other.

The sadist looks to the other, then, not as a *semblable* but as an unequal, destined to be more himself than himself. This "dominant" other will be, however, someone with whom the "submitted" partner will exchange places. No matter how monstrous the dominant, the submissive sadist-as-object has the ultimate right to trade places with him and to become the dominant himself—and thereby, the full subject of enjoyment.

But can he? By analyzing the fantasy and the placement of the object in its scene, Lacan gave us access to the pervert's unconscious. There, the story is different. In the *fantasy* underlying Dolmancé's sadistic script, the full, "raw" subject of enjoyment inflates to the dimensions of that *surhomme* designated by André's perverse Violette—the One beyond gender who can enjoy so much more than mere men and women can.[15] The other (small *o*), proportionally diminished, is cut down to the dimensions of the (small) object *(a)*.[16] The fantasy's secret wish, which *precludes* the "even trade" Dolmancé promises, is the wish to *remain forever a mere object.* "Sade rejects the pain of existing into the Other, but without seeing that by this slant he himself changes into an 'eternal object.'"[17] Why? Because only as a fully petrified, apathic *object* can he hope to escape the fate of all *subjects*—to be subject to death, to pain, to the invasive violence of the other. Sade's fantasy denies his own torture and imprisonment at the hands of Madame de Montreuil as much or more than it claims his unrestricted enjoyment.

The pervert, trumpeting an entirely new basis on which ego and other, subject and object, can be bonded, unconsciously reveals that his dream is only an unconscious desire, a way of making up for the fact that he is already the object of an Other's invasive *jouissance.* Sade's attempt to convert himself from object of the other's abuse to the dual object and subject of enjoyment indeed appears so desperate that it has created great sympathy for him as a sad victim of persecution, not as the dominating sadist.

Politics in the Bedroom

To bring out the unconscious of the pervert even more, we should note that in addition to the structural terms (subject/object) that Lacan employed, he also used conspicuously political imagery to describe the perverse unconscious. These terms help distinguish between two unconsciouses—paranoid and perverse. They, in turn, sharpen the contrast with the hysteric's unconscious. For the hysteric, *jouissance,* the object of unconscious desire, is always (happily) "lost" to the veiling symptom. But in the paranoiac unconscious, the object remains a principal player. The paranoiac looks in the mirror and sees the object that torments him— himself. He *is* the other, his reflected rival who is also the object of his envy. Likewise for the pervert, the object remains crucial, but here the object fully replaces the subject. This is to be followed by the reverse, in its turn.

Lacan's political fables regarding psychosis and perversion illustrate their distinction another way. For Lacan, the paranoid unconscious is a parable of a master and a slave, whose dialectic's final stakes are the death of the subject or its object.[18] Taking his cue from Sade's formally "Republican" pamphlet in *Philosophie dans le boudoir,* Lacan pulls the object out of the master-slave dialectic and puts it into a scenario of the "Rights of Man." These Rights are supposed to supplant the master-slave dialectic by a simple declaration: no one may henceforth be the property of another; as a result, the power of life and death over another is eliminated. (Note that

Lacan skeptically remarks that despite the pervert's rhetoric of liberation from the Master—death or castration—Sade remains "a serf of pleasure.")

No one could blame an enlightened and liberated bourgeoisie for concluding that suspending the master's right to life or death over his slave put an end to arbitrary actual violence and inaugurated the reign of "perpetual peace." And no one can blame Sade for his personal and political dreams, either. Such an inmixing of the political does not, however, necessarily follow from the philosophical dreams of Kant and Sade.

In the quadripartite structure of the unconscious, an ego-object (or ego-other) dialectic is crossed by a subject-Other relation. What the pervert unconsciously denies is less the purchase of formal Law than the power of the entire field of play of Other to touch him. That field of the Other is the site of death, and pain: the field of castration, the real threat that flesh might be cut, blood might really flow. The pervert instinctively refuses all but stage blood.

Sadism's essential hallmark is that violence is only a dramatic device. It does not consciously credit the existence of the Real Thing. But unconsciously it remains fully in the grip of that Thing lurking just behind the object.

Sacrifice, Sadism, and the Real Violence of the Other: The Law

The violence of and by the big O Other is called "castration" by Lacan and "law-creating violence" by Walter Benjamin. It is the law of society, the dimension linking Subject to Other, as distinct from the twisted tie bonding ego to object.

This Law the pervert fundamentally disavows. Sade's writing, to be sure, touts the "Law," but it is a Law of Nature, not *the Law* in the way we understand it from Rousseau, Hegel, and Marx on down to Benjamin and Lacan. Pierre Klossowski showed Sade's as a Law of pleasure, a Natural Law of creation and destruction rendered so extreme as to vitiate the very category of the subject. *The Law* breaks with this Natural Law and founds itself as a *pure* violence. *The Law* is the province of the wholly Other. It alone makes the subject.

For Lacan, who interpreted the origins of Judeo-Christianity this way,[19] Law-creating violence is the *law of language* that accompanies and founds all human society (speech). Origin and by-product of speech, the Deity— God's Law—is the most common way of representing the alterity and founding violence of what institutes society.[20] But even the atheistic Enlightenment found Rousseau offering the Law of the stranger in the *Social Contract* as a substitute: the Lawgiver, Rousseau tells us, can never come from within a group; he or she must always be a foreigner to the society they institute.[21]

Figured as a transcendent alterity—God, Society, the State—and apprehended as a violent force intervening between you and your fellows, Law-creating violence is one way of characterizing the violence language has *already* done to one's nature. Castration is the violence Lacan portrays in *Television* as "carving out" a body from a mass of animal substance.[22] That this separating, shattering violence is also the very same as that Law we discussed earlier, with paranoia, the Law of Partition (the paternal metaphor) that shelters us from the other's murderous intentions, cannot be iterated often enough. Like partition, the violence of the Law is no mere dramatic effect, no deus ex machina. It never shows itself. God's justice, in Benjamin's "Critique of Violence," has no phenomenality.[23]

Blood Rituals

How, then, can psychoanalysis respond to contemporary stagings of violence?

One of the most publicized aspects of "modern primitives" today is the flagrant and extreme piercings, scarifications, brandings, and corsettings now commonplace among working- and middle-class youths in every major urban environment, with countless imitators in small towns and peasant settings everywhere. Even the Rich and Famous are caught up in it. Some rituals are legible as secondary effects of *The Law*; others are not.

It seems that blood must be spilled. But spilled within in a perverse scenario or in a scene of imaginary castration?

Serge André studied certain men's groups that, in private ceremonies, require the shedding of blood. Initiation rituals (even secret handshakes) are imaginary representations and public demonstrations of a reparation applied to a failed symbolic castration. They resolve the castration complex when there has been a failure of the paternal. For example, André interpreted institutionalized coitus between an adult male and a noninitiated youth, common in warrior peoples, as the ritual exorcism of a youth's femininity that dies as he is "reborn" to himself as strictly virile.[24] His violation effectively "completes" his castration process, albeit in the form of an imaginary (not symbolic) simulacrum. Still, even as a simulacrum, Real blood must flow, as a sign of the mortal danger the Other brings:

WEST POINT, N.Y.—About 50 West Point seniors were punished for taking part in a "blood branching," in which pins designating their branches in the Army were pushed through their uniforms into their chests. Calling it a "stupid rite of passage," Lieutenant Colonel Rick Machamer, director of public affairs for the military academy, said yesterday that the cadets face demerits, extra duty or restrictions for the ritual.[25]

This is "sacrifice": compensation for a missing paternal metaphor. It demands that a real violence mime, but attenuate, the horror of the "carving out of the body" by language's original law-creating violence. The tone of the sacrificial mise-en-scène is less to deny the reality of violence than to remind us of it. Blood must flow. Just not too much blood.

In true sadism the purpose of staged violence is different. It is to show that the Other's violence can be limited contractually. The sadist displays violence and even puts "castration" on stage, but as never more than a scene, never more than a perverse imposture. He mocks castration, like death, by denying it. He refuses it altogether precisely by admitting it as a mere *fiction*.

Masochism and Real Blood

Self-mutilations naturally fall toward the masochistic side and further complicate the analysis of today's "sadomasochism"—that conflation of sadism and masochism that Deleuze denounced roundly as a "misbegotten name, a semiological howler."[26] A recent newspaper article by Joan Ryan treated a case of masochism with surprising equanimity:

> Amy's parents wouldn't recognize the bookish daughter who once earned straight A's and sang in the choir at a Texas boarding school. The smiling 20-year-old is in a South of Market club surrounded by other pierced, tattooed, branded and scarred patrons. She's wearing a red corset with the waist cinched to an uncomfortable 20 inches. She has a ring through the septum of her nose and two more in each nipple. She recently got a second tattoo on a shaved patch of skull. . . . Amy is part of a growing subculture that is exploring the line between fashion and mutilation, design and destruction, choice and compulsion. . . . Pain is part of the attraction. . . . "I like pain," she says, as if telling you she likes ice cream. Her 21-year-old friend Ivy is . . . branded . . . she has faint lines like railroad ties on her legs and wrists from more than six years of cutting herself. "I like pain. I like blood," she says. "I like testing my limits."[27]

The girls' high-profile, public, "fashionable" female masochism is hardly the masochism Deleuze hoped would escort male sadism back to a place within the Law. Their blood flows to re-mark the sacrificial way castration has been written on their bodies, but the ritual scarification of Amy and

Ivy, whose "initiation" ceremonies could never parallel those of males, may also be a masochistic twist to sadistic perversion. There is, after all, a dash of perversion as the girls scoff at the Law as mere form: "I like testing *my* limits."

In genuine masochism, which must be male, Deleuze says there is an "aestheticism" whose hallmark is "coldness" rather than Sadean apathy.[28] This couldn't apply more than in the case of the late Bob Flanagan, who purposely made an aesthetic-masochistic example of himself. Flanagan suffered from cystic fibrosis, a degenerative disease whose victims rarely live to, let alone past, adolescence. Flanagan died in his midforties, one of the disease's oldest-known survivors, "a distinction largely credited to his masochistic lifestyle and the strength he derived from learning to live with, and tolerate, pain."[29] Flanagan became a performance artist who movingly described (and videotaped) the ways his longtime dominant partner and collaborator, Sheree Rose, enabled him to feel alive by subjecting him to whippings, pain, and so on.

Something more of the real is involved with Flanagan's masochism than we easily feel comfortable with. When news reporter Craig Marine tries to describe Flanagan's theater of pain, he has quite a bit more difficulty than Joan Ryan had discussing Amy's and Ivy's scars. Depicting one scene of a penile subincision (an alternate form of ritual circumcision that involves splitting the penis end to end), Marine's text demonstrates amply how the Law of language, metaphor, and figure shelters us from direct experience of the violence a masochist goes to extreme pains, so to speak, to acknowledge:

> Let's see if we can describe this one scene for publication. You've got Mr. Two By Four, Mr. Hammer, Mr. Nail and Mr. Distinctly Male Appendage. There is a meeting of the aforementioned—a rather violent one at that. There is an extraction, and plenty of resulting blood on the camera lens.[30]

Flanagan does not deny death. He resists it. He stages its horror not only to remind himself of its power, as in male initiation, but to mobilize his body to fight against it. Kirby Dick, the documentary's maker, says: "I view it as a form of cross-training. Bob came to know the limits of pain and methods of tolerating pain. A large part of masochism is mental training." Flanagan's idiom of masochism permitted him, overwhelmingly threatened by the Real, to formulate a defense, there where the Other's *jouissance* had him in its grip. Flanagan's self-"violence" fought the death drive with its own weapons. The Sadist scoffs at death yet unconsciously submits to it.

So Flanagan's is the inverse of the pervert's scene.

Scene III. Perversion in Public Places

Still, we can and will return every effort to violate the norm to the catalog of cultural stuff we hold in common. Thus the recent vogue for publicly perverse behavioral styles is being taken as an opportunity to retrieve normality from sadism's formal dismantling of the Law. Pundits now say, "S&M is still at the far limits of the sexual envelope [but it is] filtering down into the mainstream. . . . We're a large populist culture. We'll take anything and normalize it."[31] An unmistakable ethical propriety and a faith in personal agency appear in comments like these, tolerant, urbane, witty. They show a general public comfortable with sadomasochism and perversity as mere styles. So little anxiety attaches to these remarks, though, that we must wonder whether indeed the radical nature of the perverse unconscious has been rendered obsolete, or is being naively misrecognized.

A look at the rhetoric accompanying the S&M and BDSM[32] practices (private and commercial) the Berkeley students brought to my attention shows a discourse of progressive social ideals: brotherly love, mutual respect, interpersonal trust, restraint, and self-control—the same things we generally (though not psychoanalytically) think of as requirements for communal coexistence. Indeed, my California students were quite certain that S&M culture offered them an agency, a sense of community and of decency that the worn-out forms of neurotic sexuality could not. This explains, for example, such odd crossovers as the Christian singer Pat Boone's showing up in full leathers, tattoos, and a dog collar for the American Music Awards in January 1997.

BDSM practices have come to stand as codified models for a trust that long ago fled a society awash in tales of out-of-control crimes and punishments. Sadomasochism offers a welcome relief—"guarantees," signed contracts—to young moderns bereft of the once taken-for-granted coordinates of civil society. Couples today, entering their second or third serial marriage, and wanting to "do it right this time," can now purchase by mail order from Colorado a ready-made prenuptial contract for remarriages. It promises the partners they will be able to live together tension-free by specifying in advance everything that usually causes friction in recombined households: whose cats are kept, whose given away; which partner is responsible for seeing that the automobile's tank is filled; how often the laundry gets done and by whom. In a similar spirit, so-called perverts can pick up their preprinted sadomasochistic contracts at Good Vibrations, a female-owned, family-style sex emporium in San Francisco.

The hallmark of these S&M contracts is that the threat of violence is contained or controlled within them by agreement. The rules governing what can be done are explicit, the limits clearly drawn. These documents establish and regulate "trust"—the very thing that we, at the mercy of ordinary human verbal (and sexual) intercourse, will never find guaranteed.

A laundry list of rules and regulations is, we also know, the sign of the sadistic superego—not of the Law, and as far as I know, no human society has ever come with money-back guarantees. Still, I wonder. The immensely popular adoption of perverse sexual forms and styles associated with "neotribal" or "modern primitive" subgroups certainly leads us to conclude that the world has indeed rolled joyously over a sadistic edge. As BDSM has gone public, coming out of private clubs and made into tourist attractions, the utopian side of Sade's vision does seem on the point of being fully realized. In today's scene, gay men and lesbians play BDSM games together without being segregated by "gender": "femmes" can experiment with being "tops," "butches" can date "daddies," and anyone can pick any role—"Daddy," "Mommy," "Boy," "Girl"—to play with anyone else.[33] Sade's theater appears not only to have triumphed: Dolmancé's dream of a new form of social relation that neutralizes all real violence is being institutionalized.[34]

Perhaps Sade's "utopian" vision has been implemented through that new social contract his Dolmancé anticipated. Perhaps his dream is being realized. Has the human creature begun at last to shed its "subjectivity" not for the *Es* of the psychotic, but for an enjoyment without limits.[35] This may be too fast. More traditional interpretations are possible.

Our collective fascination with "perverse" behavior and style may index a collective hysterical fantasy more than an actual rise in the pervert ratio in the population. The public staging of perversion-as-entertainment recalls a long-standing dream of blissful existence outside the pale of civilization and the confines of the law. Thinkers of the eighteenth century dreamed of savage life just as an industrial age that would forever eliminate that getaway plan was dawning. Neurotic perversions are scenes of a *jouissance* lost to civilization (or industry) and its discontents—to some Thing—and available only in fantasy. If we take the pervert as one who acts out his or her own fantasy, but who must confirm its logic by inducing the hysterical other to go along, we can begin to assess the commodification of perversion and its proliferation of prestaged fantasies for sale in socioeconomic terms. Why is it selling so well? For despite its denial of the Other's violence, perversion can ultimately do nothing, really, to prevent it from breaking out, no matter how carefully it is fenced in, contracted with, regulated. Just why does the hysteric get involved in the pervert's scenario?

Apollon and André distinguish pervert from neurotic this way: the neurotic fantasizes about perversion; the pervert acts. Yet as the "heterosexual, middle-aged couples" who consume sadomasochism's commodities purchase their paraphernalia and their tickets to Bondage a Go Go, the line separating fantasy and act becomes uncertain: Is a fantasy your own when you've bought it off the shelf? Is then acting it out the same as the pervert's passage to act? If we set up the question of violence and perversion on the model of this neurotic structure, we end up dealing only with outcomes, or comings out, or comings apart, and not with *causes*, the Thing psychoanalysis must discover. If we only count the pervert wannabe as a hysteric induced to having their enjoyment stage-managed by a pervert, we would still not have located where the real pervert is, nor his or her partner.

Does the hysteric become the pervert's partner to avoid knowledge of the abusive Thing? Are we as hysterical wannabe perverts in complicity with a deeper perverseness, a greater loss of agency than our thematization of "ready-to-wear" perversion, "made-for-TV" and "for-sale-to-tourists" indexes? Taking on the perverse stand without meaning it is a political danger not only in the old-fashioned Adorno/Marcuse/Horkheimer sense of a "repressive desublimation." It lies with the fundamental problem that by averting knowledge of the *Cause* (the violence of the Other; *la Chose*) the real violence potential even in the Law, the permanent threat of violence of the unbarred Other, goes unchallenged.

Sade's Dream or Nightmare?

The next question is whether perversion in public places today marks the triumph of Sade's *conscious fiction*, installing a new, workable social contract without need for the Subject-Other relation marked by the institution of the Law. Or is it the ironic realization of Sade's *unconscious fantasy*—the desire to become the "eternal" object and thereby cease suffering from intolerable abuse? Are hysterics, too, like the miserable Sade, unconscious witnesses to our own abuse, to our subjection and torment by an uncontrolled and unacknowledged other? Who is the abusive Other today? And what ethic could contest It? The perverse (im)posture and its consumers may end not with freedom but with complicity in blinding ourselves to serious abuse. If so, we will see the Sadean comedy (in French, English, and Freudian meanings) finally turn tragic.

A return to some well-worn political, economic, and sociological concepts may permit some purchase here. Alongside the spread of sadism, masochism, and the ideals of violence-lite, we are also undergoing an unprecedented and revolutionary extension of the means of aesthetic production. Computer-driven technologies are setting the work of art into an age of electronic production that may exceed the domain Benjamin carved out—the work of art in the age of mechanical reproduction. If the master-slave issue is not yet overcome by the sadist's formal skepticism, part of the reason may lie with the unlimited free play of the imagination now available technically. This free play appears, however, in a domain where the apparent conquest of the master-slave field is being rapidly reversed. Only an ethics can face the situation. At our disposal, we have Lévinas's religious ethic of the Other; Deleuze's neomasochist ethics; Žižek's ethics of Lost Cause, which gets close to my concerns; Lyotard's passion; and Badiou's general reflection. But Lacan still serves as the best guide, if we want to follow the detour he needed to take through aesthetics to get to ethics in the time of Sade.

The Object in the Aesthetic Relation

To fathom the new, wily ways of the Other unwittingly freed from constraint by the sadistic unconscious, we must pay stricter attention to the pathway Lacan took from "Kant avec Sade" toward ethics: aesthetics. Lacan's confrontation with the ethics of art and those of sadism is still the best account of the "aestheticization of violence" and the investment in violence-lite and phony wars now around us. And it alone seems powerful enough to comprehend the new means of exploitation we face today.

When Lacan embarks on an ethics of psychoanalysis in *Seminar VII*, he encounters two versions of relation to the object that similarly discount or formalize the relation to Law. The perverse we have already discussed. The *aesthetic* partakes of the general problematic of sublimation. Lacan discovers that the two oppose each other structurally, if not phenomenologically. But they also each engage in a unique mode of confronting contemporary life, or life after Kant, we might call it:

> I have thus brought together for you two cases which Kant does not envisage, two forms of transgression beyond the limits normally assigned to the pleasure principle opposed to the reality principle considered as a criterion, namely, the excessive sublimation of the object, and what is commonly called perversion. Sublimation and perversion are both a certain relation of desire which draws our attention upon the possibility of formulating, in the form of a question, another principle of another . . . morality, opposed to the reality principle. For there is a register of morality which is directed from the side of what there is at the level of *Das Ding*, namely, the register

which makes the subject hesitate at the moment of bearing false witness against *das Ding,* that is, the site of his desire, be it perverse or sublimated.[36]

Lacan gently mocks us with an image of our failed creativity: "We haven't even been able to invent a single new perversion."[37] Yet Lacan had set out to reach the aesthetic, as a form of "creative destruction," by way of Sade. He first looked to courtly love poetry for the apparent sadism of the Lady, and perhaps also because Laure de Sade—Petrarch's Laura—was Sade's supposed ancestress. While an aesthetic superego is presumed to share some features superficially with the sadistic one,[38] a major distinction must be made between Sade's notion of creative destruction (the material principle of Nature's cycles) and the aesthetic "destruction" Lacan happens upon.

Let us see how Lacan laid out the structural relation of subject and object in the aesthetic before setting it into the new context of electronic production. In contrast to the realm of the unconscious—neurotic, psychotic, or pervert—the aesthetic marks out a unique relation to the object that does not have to do, strictly speaking, with the unconscious or the superego.[39] That the object not remain for the artist what it is for the neurotic, forever unreachable, or become the persecuting object of the psychotic, is already the risk the artist takes each time. But what does the artist risk vis-à-vis the sadistic object? Does art entertain an intimate relation with sadism? After all, art too designates the object as fully enjoyable. It brings "delight."

The aesthetic demands a fundamental clearing of the field of the Other in order to establish a fresh relation to the object. This entails a risk. Wiping away the Other and the Law that have stood between and partitioned subject from object—sweeping out the whole of tradition, metaphor, and unstated social agreements—leaves the object again a freestanding entity, renewing its threat to the subject. The subject's sense of awe (wonderment and fear) before the object is restored. The crucial difference between the artist and the sadist, then, is that in brushing aside the Law the artist risks encountering the Thing, the Real in all its violence and brutality. Where the sadist consciously imagines he can control the Thing but unconsciously plots his own subjective destitution to escape It, the artist risks everything in order to raise anew and quite differently the Law of partition that shields us from It. The work of art reconstructs, on the basis of a void in the Law, a new form of shelter, a beauty that forms a "barrier so extreme as to forbid access to a fundamental horror."[40]

This miracle is operated, Lacan tells us, by granting the object dignity, raising it to an untouchable Thing. Again, the sadist seems close: both sadist and artist value the object; for each, the object is penetrated with *jouissance*. But the sadistic unconscious falls short. It cannot divide subject from Thing. Having formally discredited the laws of language and speech, the sadist is impotent to reestablish a sanctuary from the Other.

The aesthetic, too, contests the law of the signifier, but unlike perversion it also partakes of its function. Art retains its direct relation to *jouissance* yet still manages to put its experience of enjoyment into circulation. Like the signifier's, this circulation cannot be controlled in advance, nor can its itinerary through time and space be predetermined by contract, rule, or regulation. Lacan devised the term *sinthome* to coincide with this aspect of the artistic sign, designating the artwork as a *signifier* and not as an *object*. But it is a signifier penetrated with *jouissance* and not only, as the signifier of language is, the mark of a loss of *jouissance*.

Art—Freud's *sublimation*—functions to re-place, put back in place, a kind of Law of the Other. Its fiction differs from the Law-lite and violence-lite of the sadist, however, because it includes knowledge of the violence of the Other. Without hiding the shock of the Real that inspires it, without giving that violence an alibi, as sadism does, art goes about constructing new barriers, new and necessary partitions, new forms of relation to the past and to tradition. It constructs a new difference between subject and object and, more important, a new distance from the violent potential in their relation. It does so especially where the paternal law, God and society, are in default or lie discredited. Hence, perhaps, the misguided accusation that artists are perverts (e.g., Robert Mapplethorpe or Karen Finley) in the United States today.

The Vel

> "Who's the boss—you or the pain? Come on, show me who's the boss?"
>
> —Jay Wiseman, *SM 101*

When Lacan speaks of the aesthetic clearing necessary to refabricate a barrier between subject and Thing, for him it's only a metaphor. Let's take it literally—as a *playground* where the crucial new relation to the object takes place. A preemptive strike against the arts and their playgrounds is under way. Its pressure announces more than simple "natural" market forces, rising real estate prices, and popular targets for professional moralists in government, religion, and art criticism. Rhetorical attacks, arts administrative protocols, and sheer economic demands are combining to preempt a mental free space, a space where no one, unlike the sadist, need ever work for the *jouissance* of the Other.

The shutdown of "creative play spaces" arrives at the same time as an acceleration in the conversion of "creative production" to the electronic.[41] If the artistic relation is ever completely commandeered for what Disney has generously given us a name—"imagineering"—we may find ourselves more open to the revenge of the Thing than ever. If the energies of art making are taken up for someone else's profit (the *jouissance* of the Other captured in a financial image), the cardinal aesthetic itinerary I describe above risks being fundamentally hijacked.

I do not mean that artists should not make money, but that the exhaustive conditions under which artists work to secure a new and crucial relation to the object are being mimicked industrially for quite other than the aesthetic aim of refounding the subject's relation to the object. For why else should tampering with the conditions of production of the work of art correlate with a high profile for sadomasochism (or its hysterical converts) in the age of electronic production? Is the essential work that art does for us with respect to the Law being blocked here?

Of course, the computer/graphics/software business has taken extraordinary pains to configure itself as the opposite of heavy industry. It classically exhibits the Marxist problems of any industry taking off (intense exploitation of capital and labor), and its spectacular growth has often found governments willing to cut this enormous wealth-generating machine some slack, relaxing labor, overtime, and financial laws, and lifting certain traditional safeguards protecting workers and investors.[42] But the industry has innovated in a direction that is by all accounts reasonably enlightened. Because everyone is working in a "creative" industry, everyone understands that they should give more than the usual to the "project." In return, however, the workers are offered sabbaticals or given stock options and time off for working in think tanks in research parks, and so on. The factories they go to work in are sometimes called "campuses."

Notwithstanding, the conditions of production of the aesthetic means of reproduction are viewed by those employed in them as harsh—from Burbank to the Silicon Valley, throughout the global economy. There is an undeniable demand for excess from workers; it is even written into their contracts, justified by the point that projects in these settings are creative and thus consume the same kind of energies as the work of sublimation— enormous creative energies. Yet situating the creative process within what is essentially a field of economic warfare (competition) is still to model it on the demand for *jouissance* by the Other, not on resistance to it. With this twist, we may collaboratively be producing the model for a unique new exploitation of the human soul, possibly deeper than ever before devised. Freely decided on, this model nevertheless forces open the royal road between the *jouissance* of the Other and the subject, and closes the "angle between Other and other" that Lacan saw as essential to our *humanity*. We will have given up on sadism's egalitarian dream by giving in to its unconscious desire.

Such exploitation anyone subject to it might understandably flee, if only in their unconscious.

South of Market, where the BDSM clubs are located in San Francisco, is also the site of Multimedia Gulch, the "creative" end of the software business. One of the most telling comments from the young people flocking there for S&M these days unknowingly reproduces Lacan's *vel* of "Kant avec Sade." It is a "people's critique" of the extreme working conditions encountered in this alluring, new, high-paying industry: "It's a choice. You can have money—or a life."

If it does not contest but instead allies itself with the abusive Other, the postmodern pervert becomes its permanent plaything, its fetish and its victim all in one.

3. The Postcolonial Unconscious;
or, The White Man's Thing

The good is what keeps us a long way from jouissance.
—Jacques Lacan, *Seminar VII*

Here I was, invited to speak about Lacan and postcoloniality, and only a single mental and visceral response flashed through me, which I can best sum up with a slightly incredulous inflection: "Post?colonial?" How hopeful, yet how unsecured that term sounds. Globalized economic systems, run-down information superhighways, and the "glamorous tentacles of media colonization"[1] are taking to a higher perversity Lacan's early image for our latter-day patriarchy: "La grand route—être père." While it is more intent on acquiring sales than national territories, and on conquering corporate and not mere human bodies, colonialism seems only to have shifted ground where the subject's alienation is concerned. Something in the new transparencies of cultures to each other has unmade our local lives in the West and has left us less cosmopolitan, less confident, and less knowledgeable than anyone with a *local* life ought to be. The Disneyized version of everything seems to touch us everywhere we turn, perhaps even more in the metropolis than in its former colonies.

Still, we in the center have been cheered by the news from the periphery, by the word, coming to us from former colonies, that we are about to enter a truly postcolonial era. Brilliant ex-colonized writers like Homi Bhabha have secured important new models of sublime social bodies that will escape the predations of colonialism, capitalism, tokenism, and the general runaway rationalism (in Max Weber's sense) that has overtaken world cultures. His new "locality of culture" would be "a form of living" that is

> more complex than "society"; more connotative than "country"; less patriotic than *patrie*; more rhetorical than reason of state; more mythological than ideology; less homogeneous than hegemony; less centered than the citizen; more collective than "the subject"; more psychic than civility; more hybrid in the articulation of cultural differences and identifications—gender, race, or class—than can be represented in any hierarchical or binary structures of social antagonism.[2]

Bhabha's utopia is compelling. But it is rather far from what I had been seeing recently in "first world" cities as, for example, on Paris subway walls.

In the spring of 1997 I traveled to Paris to participate in an international art exhibition.[3] I was looking forward to seeing once more this capital of quality in everyday enjoyments—exceptional food, artful design, well-made goods. Joie de vivre seems to look back at you from the extraordinariness of the ordinary objects that surround you the moment you arrive in Paris. I was even looking forward to its crowded Métro stops, with their wall posters filled with goods that gladden your eye and make your pocketbook despair. These commercial posters have always given me a sense of contact with the experience the French themselves are having, for better or for worse, of their own lives. Even the Métro graffiti, that visible free speech that graces the subway's corridors, usually has the perfect mix of image, word, and risqué innuendo the commercial advertisements aspire to.

That spring, some examples of each were still around. The majority of the advertising area, though, had gone to a higher power or a higher bidder. Bland global corporate ads now occupied much of the wall space. Floor space, too, as the once trash-free Métro platforms were loaded with fast-food wrappers and their blaring, colored logos: fear of terrorist bombs had sealed the platform garbage cans. "Signs of a particular historical moment," I thought to myself. "Funny how the movements of peoples across borders in the global economy seem to need some threat or menace, real or imagined, to accompany it."

One advertisement among these largely drab examples of the genre nevertheless caught my attention: it was a triptych for a foreign (i.e., not French) manufacturer of 35 mm film. Using nude models, it advertised the permanence of the images its product could capture. Now, nudity is hardly unusual in French Métro ads, but the tone of this one was distinctive and rather more frontal than the image itself. The caption that glossed the young woman whose bosom was being caught by a camera lens was asking: "Do you like my breasts?" Another panel showed her round, adolescent buttocks, captioned, "Do you like my ass?" A French woman I mentioned it to later in the day said she had seen the ads and that they had "shocked" her.

It is pretty hard to shock a Parisian on any matter; they are a mostly cool-headed lot. But that ad had gotten to my friend. The poster had disturbed something more fundamental than Parisian cultivation and good taste. Its directness, its absence of nuance in wording, its appeal through those parts of the body Lacan called "objects a," that *breast*—they all got me thinking, too.[4] The poster could not have been more direct in proffering these objects, but it did so in a cynical, mocking tone. It put you near the Thing and held it completely out of reach at the same time. There was a sadistic, superegoic air about it. "Enjoy! (if you can)!" If colonialism has a superego dimension, I thought, perhaps after all my invitation was justifiable, and psychoanalysis might really have something to say about postcolonialism today.

Bhabha's effervescent reuse of social excess is the precise opposite of the reductiveness reflected in that poster. Where his new formations have an additive "more" based on by-passing cramped and outworn social forms, the Métro poster lacked such lack, such freedom. It was unnerving to think that two rich cultures had been brought into contact in that poster frame and had produced something much less than either, something suffocating and scary, something neither culture alone would have been at all happy with. Or held responsible for.

That absence of specific responsibility—one leading world culture had been invaded not simply by another world culture, but by a third thing that neither of them would have produced, desired, or admired—also seemed to have superego overtones. I was reminded of Albert Memmi, who wrote eloquently and very early about how the perniciousness of colonialism insistently inserted irresponsibility into the colonized:

> The most serious blow suffered by the colonized is being removed from history and the community. Colonization usurps one's free role in either war or peace, every decision contributing to his destiny and that of the world, and all cultural and social responsibility. . . . The colonized man feels neither responsible nor guilty nor skeptical, for he is out of the game. . . . He

has forgotten how to participate actively in history and no longer even asks to do so.... All memory of freedom seems distant.[5]

Yet no single class, race, nation was in any way the cause of my feeling of being colonized: who was colonizing whom? Why, after all, did the crude subway ad shock a sophisticated French woman used to nudity for selling goods? Would the foreign manufacturer have approved the same ad at home? There is a free play in the system that does not have the look and feel of freedom.

The discomfort I was experiencing is new to the peoples of the "first world," although similar effects are being felt by everyone dwelling in the world cities today. It is perhaps time for the West to reassess its own understanding of the damage it produced in its classic colonial period, because that damage seems to be coming back to haunt it. The power to move you without any concomitant responsibility for the effects of that power repeats the essence of colonialism. But *then* it was experienced as a political and economic power with damaging psychological side-effects; *now* it is a psychoeconomic power whose political after-effects are as yet unknown.[6] Has the psychic damage the first world inflicted on its colonized now come back to bedevil it as well? The classical Western subject was either distorted fundamentally by classical colonialism, or colonialism exposed its unconscious truth. But well before colonialism, this classical subject had, we know, suffered traumatic blows—it just didn't know it. Some of these blows were delivered by what Adorno calls simple "bourgeois sadism." Others came as a reflex of the colonial adventure. The classical subject's failure of knowledge (of its own sadism) was undoubtedly a component of its colonizing force.

Between our experience now and the compelling, uncannily familiar narratives of colonialism's psychic damage then, there may be analogies, parallels, cautionary tales. What happens to the subject when the laws of social coexistence it is submitted to are fundamentally disturbed? I will provisionally call it a "colonial complex," a personal, political, but most of all, an ethical disorder. But if the subject is again the issue, it is not the dispersed, proliferated, postmodern subject, because its proliferation may be as much a part of the problem as of the solution. The issue is our very own Western classical subject in its three dimensions—as *sovereign individual, citizen under law,* and *person before God*—that must be analyzed and in its fourth: the unconscious.[7] The unconscious is where your humanity and your inhumanity touch and clash for dominance over your body, your mind. And colonialism is the exemplary site of man's inhumanity to man—and woman.

It is not easy to find our way into a psychoanalysis of colonialism that would provide a guide to the future ex-colonial Western subject.

The body—those breasts, again—rather than the mind may be the psychoanalytic place to begin.

The Classical Colonial Complex: Race and Rights

The colonized body was a racialized body. But race is hardly the overt principle of organization in global culture today. The chief colonial offense, racial policy, is no longer official in world capitalism; indeed, quite the reverse—capitalism freely moves and mixes peoples. While new fascisms, racisms, and right-wing nationalisms still flourish in "first world" and now in some "third world" countries, they have a retro feel and are marginal to the central political discourse in Europe and America, unlike the sustained, mainstream policies they constituted in the 1930s. So if we are to learn where the lesion, the bodily affront we bear today is located, we will have to understand the underlying *mechanism*, how colonialism connected body to mind in a way that short-circuited cultural defenses and permitted race to become a psychic trauma under its regime.

Race

Race was central to the way colonies were administered after eighteenth-century revolutions and rebellions freed slaves and deprived European nations of their "white" colonies (the ones where their settlers had largely vanquished indigenous populations). Racial separation and racial purity were the cardinal principles and ideologies of official colonialism, but they had sailed from Europe under a false name. The real name of race was politics: race was one of Europe's most destructive inventions (Linnaeus) as was racial purity (of French origin). I discuss the history of race in the following chapter, but the history of racial purity was purely political, originally devised to explain a class rout: why the nobility lost France to "the rabble." In the wake of the French Revolution, the defeated aristocracy (de Gobineau) looked into itself and wondered how the descendants of the Frankish warriors, who had conquered and continuously controlled inferior celto-Latin peoples, could now have lost their power to rule. The only answer for Gobineau was that the purity of the noble stock, the aristocrat's original race had degenerated, through intermarriage, effeminacy of manners, or both.[8] A political problem (class versus class) thus sailed out to the colonies in a racialized viral form. It returned with even greater virulence to Europe, undoing its own civilization in the twentieth century, having married Enlightenment ideals of national liberation and self-determination of peoples to a purified, armed, and dangerous Master Race.[9]

The virus was cultured in the colonies. Aimé Césaire, in his *Discours sur le colonialisme,* said that Europe had actually practiced Nazism in training in its colonies, "employed only against non-European peoples. . . . That Nazism they encouraged, they were responsible for it, and it drips, it seeps, it wells from every crack in western Christian civilization until it engulfs that civilization in a bloody sea."[10]

Today, of course, we have learned the horrible lesson of racial thinking; the apartheids it required have now lost their last adherents. And we have been given renewed hope from the ex-colonized, hybrid,[11] bicultural, or composite subjects[12] who have carried out the most complex maneuvers and managed to balance all the competing claims to their alienation in exemplary ways. We can learn much from artists and writers like Coco Fusco, Guillermo Gómez-Peña, Teshome Gabriel, and Greg Sarris, who have taught us that the juggling act, the finding yourself in the mix, is a *human* operation that anyone is capable of executing.

In the complaint of the postcolonial writers of the first generation against the abusive use of race by colonialism, though, there is more than biculturalism at issue. In the voice of Fanon, there is a second tone, a second note of fear and of bitterness that makes even race itself seem epiphenomenal. There is something of the *body* that race is written on that remains unresolved in Fanon's writing and still constitutes an opacity for us today.

The challenge Fanon threw down was that race, which was an administrative category for running the social organization of colonies, unpredictably turned out to have an enormous traumatic psychic consequence: dehumanizing the colonial subject. "Fanon's only white is *human*" (98) does not say the same thing as "only white is *superior* or inferior." How did race enter the colonized psyche in so traumatic a fashion that for the colonized it had the power to displace and efface their humanity? What is the aggravated assault that is so pernicious that Fanon writes of it, "If Martians undertook to colonize the earth men—not to initiate them into Martian culture, but to *colonize* them, we should be doubtful of the persistence of any earth personality"(95)? What parallel point of bodily weakness do we show today?

Perhaps global capitalism unthinkingly uses the body in a way that repeats the dehumanizing effects Fanon decried. Despite of or because of our efforts to rationalize, digitize, and market-niche it out of any but its consuming mode—binge and purge—the body provides fertile soil for abuse, even if race is no longer the recognizable sign of that abuse. Something irrational attaches to the body, something that my Paris subway poster's promise of *jouissance*, stripped of the customary cultural, social, and fantasy framing around it, reveals.

Psychoanalytically, the question of race can be simply put. How can the identifying trait of one person, the white man, have become meaningful as an internal, unconscious identifying trait to someone of color? All primary social and cultural identifications are alienating; they always produce a subject with an unconscious full of unthinkable things. While the constitution of that subject means an initial severance from nature, something of that nature remains to appeal, haunt, and trouble it. Lacan called the first break with nature an identification with a singular or "unary" signifier, some mark or trace that remains indelible for you psychically. You can't repeat that first marking. And you are never conscious of it either. Nor are you conscious of that first "Thing" that is its necessary correlate, the Thing the signifier separated from you. The line between you as a human ("social") being and your Thing is not straight but crooked. A little bit of the Thing is carried along with you—in your fantasies, your dreams, your superego—and in your body's erogenous zones, its symptoms. Žižek calls this a kernel of the Real, and it is traumatic because it is where your nature and its sacrifice meet. You should not like to be present at the encounter.

There is, then, always a traumatic center to social identification, a "specific way people relate to . . . traumatic determinations (nation, race, sex) around which they form their identity."[13] To assume your identity (as sexual, racial, etc.) means that some mark, some sign indelibly stamped in your unconscious, has made you a *place* in an interhuman network. This social place is inscribed negatively, in the hollowed-out way a letter is stamped into metal. It marks a loss, that of your place *in nature*. This loss is so fundamental that your culture can only partly make up for it. Fantasy alone can attempt to fill out that lack, to provide again the nature your society disallows. But it usually redoubles your allegiance to social Law. Why? Because your nature is not always a pretty sight: its return is thrilling, terrifying, horrifying all at once—forbidden sex, forbidden enjoyments, aggressions, and death drive.

In every official, conscious, social identification, then, a bit of the Thing lurks, a kernel that represents what your official identity has had to rule out for you to be human. It lurks in your unconscious, but it breaks out, like a rash, in your body—in its symptoms, and in those zones that carry a heightened libidinal charge.

We begin here to approach the heart of the matter. Everything in Fanon's description makes it seem that something much more injurious, much more grievous was involved in colonialism than any hitherto known form of interhuman exploitation. Yet if the white man pretended simply to displace the colonized's primary signifier with a modernized, new, and improved one, "white," the colonized person ought to have been able to laugh it off, shrug it off, or revolt directly against it, as any bicultural person can. That the colonized were unable to do so indicates a more ominous process at work. To Fanon it was dehumanizing; to Albert Memmi, it blocked the very life's course of any individual and his society. Memmi knew the need for Oedipus in any human being, a need the colonizer blocks:

> As an adolescent, it is with difficulty that [the child] conceives vaguely, if at all, of the only way out of a disastrous family situation . . . revolt. . . . Revolt against his father and family is a wholesome act and an indispensable one for self-achievement. It permits him to start his adult life—a new unhappy and happy battle—among other men. . . . Now, into what kind of life and social dynamic do we emerge? The colony's life is frozen; its structure is both corseted and hardened. No new role is open to the young man, no invention is possible. The colonizer admits this with a now classical euphemism: He respects, he proclaims, the ways and customs of the colonized.[14]

Memmi's early theorization implicates colonialism in a manipulation of the unconscious. His "mythical portrait of the colonized" depicts a "social and historical mutilation" in the lure of identification with the colonizer, an acquiescence to the colonizer's judgment concerning the "best" in the colonized's own culture.[15] That Paris poster, too, "respected" French desire for and tolerance of nudity to sell things . . .

But as crucial as Fanon's and Memmi's statements are, and as psychoanalytic, they leave a certain core untouched. They represent the overthrow of a local civilization vividly, but they do not show how its Oedipal structure is overthrown by the colonizer, how its own humanity is lost. If we do not understand how colonialism gained this supreme power over the deep structure of the psyche, we will reinforce it. We will assume it is due to the colonizer's technological, cultural, or ethical superiority. Memmi depicts the problem very well, but he has not gone absolutely to the root.

That is because the colonizer seems driven to appeal to that hidden kernel, the hidden aggressivity, the unavowed Thing in you that will push you toward the inhuman that Fanon sees. I do not mean that the colonizer will look down on you as an inferior being or see you as an animal, for that is a different notion altogether from what I am looking at here. The solicitation of your traumatic kernel cannot come through consciousness, yours or his. Officially, the colonizer has only offered you a new brand name, and it should not have to touch the core of your humanity. But it does.

I would suggest that rather than the official policies, ideologies, and technologies the colonizers brought to the colonies, it was a Thing that inflicted a secondary, traumatic, psychic damage to the colonized: the colonizer's own Thing. Their death drive enters the colonized subject, a subject to whom it does not belong. It enters at its point of least resistance, his body.

The body is where drive returns the Thing to us. We learn to deal with our drives, and the cumulative result of this learning is called, by Freud, culture. The colonized body is one that has been exposed or invaded by drives other than its own. The colonization of the subject arrives through the White Man's Thing. The signifier that had granted one person his humanity is displaced by a dehumanizing Thing not his own. The signifier *white* carried its own traumatic Thing in its wake and invaded the colonized with it.

Colonialism and the Sadistic Superego

The colonized subject is thus doubly inscribed, not simply because he is bicultural and playing a new role. His or her primary break with nature has been broken into—by some Thing of the inhuman in the other, some drive he encounters in the colonizer. Death drive, the *Jouissance of the Other.*

The charge against classic colonialism is that the colonizer blighted the human distinctiveness of entire human communities. My thesis is that this particular damage would have occurred even without its originally being a conscious policy, though in time that, too, became possible.

One of the best descriptions of the distinction between an unconsciously perverse colonizer and his conscious counterpart can be found in J. M. Coetzee's *Waiting for the Barbarians*.[16] The unnamed narrator, the Magistrate, is a man of good will whose outpost is in some unnamed land, and whose job is to keep the barbarians out of his territory. Eventually, he suffers and shares the fate of the barbarians, but to start with he does his job properly, though in a desultory way and without fanaticism. One day, he is horrified and galvanized by a sadistic torturer, Joll, sent by the central administration who comes to produce better and more efficient results in rooting out the barbarians. After the Magistrate's horrifying encounter with the torturer, he moves beyond his town's limits into barbarian territory. When he asks Joll how he knows when to stop once a prisoner has told the truth, Joll replies, "There is a certain tone. . . . A certain tone enters the voice of a man who is telling the truth. . . . Training and experience teach us to recognize that tone. . . . First I get lies, . . . then pressure, then more lies, then more pressure, then the break, then more pressure, then the truth." "Pain is truth," the magistrates sees.

What Coetzee lets you know, however, is that even the good Magistrate has had his perverse side, too. He has taken his tortured, semiblinded, barbarian servant as his mistress, and his sexual treatment of her is not "missionary." He treats her body as a suite of zones or objects to be traversed; there is no conversation, nothing of the properly human in their intercourse. By the time you finish this allegory, you see that the administrator from the central office is the Magistrate's own sadistic superego, embodied in its conscious rather than unconscious form.

Coetzee's tale makes you feel that the injury inflicted by the colonizer is perhaps all the more grievous if it seems to emanate directly from his id, discharged directly from the unconscious of the colonizer. It accounts for the colonized's experience of it as a greater evil than any other form of conquest and territorial occupation.[17] The colonized is invaded by the *jouissance* of the Other.

Uncontained *jouissance* is not without its effect on the colonizer, too. The case histories Fanon details in *Wretched of the Earth* leave little doubt that there was a two-way psychic street between torturer and tortured, colonizer and colonized in the Algerian war. *Jouissance* was a road or inroad whose existence early psychoanalytic attempts to analyze colonialism did not suspect; witness Octave Mannoni's *Prospero and Caliban*, with its thesis of colonial dependency.

That is because the abusive *jouissance* of colonialism arrives packaged in the form of the Good. The proper name of the White Man's Thing is "the Good." Now, the Good should be part of any ethical discourse and have nothing at all to do with the inhuman emissary from the id I have been invoking in colonialism. Still, ethical discourse after Kant no longer centers on the Good, and interhuman discourse, after Freud, brings in the superego and thus sends the relation of self and other in the direction of the inhuman.

If what I have just outlined is the case, we should be able to develop an *analytic process* adequate to colonialism's extreme pressure, a process involving the sadistic superego. It was able to draw not only sex, but race and nation into the nexus between the signifier of identity and the obscene Thing.

In colonialism's dark heart it appears that we are seeing the outlines of a sadistic superego, implanted in the colonized subject from the unconscious of the colonizer. The damage Fanon fixates on certainly smells of it. This would account for Fanon's frustration, in *Black Skin, White Masks*, with an anodyne European psychoanalysis that refused to recognize the psychic damage colonialism wrought, for the colonizer as for the colonized: "What we wanted from M. Mannoni was an explanation of the colonial situation. He notably overlooked providing it" (94). Mannoni's analogy between the colonial and the "child" failed to consider the effects of an abusive "parental" superego on such a "child."

My proposition is that in colonialism not only the white man's official culture (his "civilization") but also his fundamental fantasy, his Thing, collide with that of the colonized and displace it. This sounds extreme, but let us read Partha Chatterjee. We all cheer and are cheered by his desire "to claim for us, the once-colonized, our freedom of imagination"; "if nationalisms in the rest of the world have to choose their imagined community from certain 'modular' forms already made available to them by Europe and the Americas, what do they have left to imagine?"[18]

I am drawn up short with horror at a colonization abrogating not only a private but a whole people's imagination. Albert Memmi had criticized early and trenchantly colonialism's blockage of a colonized's *society* in addition to the colonized *individual*: neither could go on and take their own next step.[19] But as if in revenge, the immense infatuation for Commander Marcos and the Zapatista rebels of "first world" Westerners (whom Dean MacCannell calls "Zapaturistas") indexes our own alienation, our barely disguised desire for the "third world" to do our dirty work, throw off the oppression we feel, and return our imagination to us.

The Good

In the eighteenth century there was a period of great transition, revolution, and reaction, in colonization. The idea of the Good as the ethical foundation of human society was overturned by two thinkers: Rousseau and Kant. (Sade, their menacing shadow, played his role, too.) Aristotle's Supreme Good, the Good that organizes our pleasure principle—these Kant swept away by ruling out the Good as determining Reason for the individual.[20] His favored author, Jean-Jacques Rousseau, did the same for the social level, in his *Social Contract* and his *Second Discourse*.[21] Each in his own way saw the Good as the site of narrow self-interests. Individuals and factions promoted their own Good as if it were identical with the Good of everyone. After Kant and Rousseau, no one was permitted to count their own good in any ethical process. Nor their own "goodness" either, as the very quality of goodness was contaminated by the aggressive drive from which it originally stemmed.

The European colonizer, sailing forth under the flag of Christendom, wrapped himself and his exploits in the mantle of God. Yes, but psychically this mantle took the form of the Good. "Being good" oneself legitimates placing others into the service of the Good, your Good. The distinctive character of colonialism was that rather than simply seeing itself as a form of conquest it saw itself as a purveyor of goods, in both the material/ commercial and the spiritual senses. Colonial power was thus marked by more than military superiority or more elaborately lethal technologies than its enemies. It was supposed to love thine enemies, to work on their behalf, for everyone's mutual good. (Ideologically put.) This purveyance of goods accelerated (and became perhaps more destructive in Fanon's sense) after the Enlightenment had, by its account, "unmasked" a self-interest and greed hidden under the religious "covers" of the earliest colonizers. The colonizer's role as purveyor of goods became less well understood by the purveyor himself from that point on.

The result in Kant was his categorical imperative that demands the individual remove all "pathological" interests (anything based on irrational, emotional factors) from his will, ensuring that its course could be set throughout all of mankind. The result in Rousseau (who probably inspired Kant) was not an ethical imperative to a will devoid of pathologized "interest," but a social imperative to a general will, in which the Good (the self-interests of individuals and parties) could no longer claim it coincided with the best interests of everyone. Thus, with these two crucial thinkers, the Good was disqualified as the determinant of individual and the social reason, respectively.

Let us look briefly at an artist's rendering of the colonial wake of Kant's and Rousseau's ethical revolutions. Heinrich von Kleist's story "The Betrothal in Santo Domingo" provides a most succinct meditation on the Enlightenment's self-conception as "good," its theoretical overthrow, and the unconscious and hideous way it returns to be played out experientially. That he chose a colonial setting is prescient. Kleist grasped immediately what Lacan would come to know theoretically only a century and a half later: that the Good and the Thing are the same. Kleist also understood that the body, through the signifier of race, nation, and sex, is its point of attack, the lesion where the *jouissance* of the Other invades. His stories are always startling, and this one is no exception.

Kleist's "The Betrothal in Santo Domingo": The "Good" Colonial Master

Like *Das Ding* for Kant, relegated to unknowability, your own Good, too, had to be rendered entirely opaque to you. Its ethical bankruptcy was relentlessly exposed by Rousseau. Yet, as Freud put it, no one ever gives up an enjoyment; no one can really sacrifice their own good no matter how rational the sacrifice is. As Lacan states it bluntly, at the "level of the unconscious," the Good and the Thing *(Das Gut, Das Ding)* are interchangeable: "The subject makes no approach at all to the bad object, since he is already maintaining his distance in relation to the good object. He cannot stand the extreme good that *Das Ding* may bring him, which is all the more reason why he cannot locate himself in relation to the bad. . . . At the level of the unconscious, the subject lies [about evil]."[22] Heinrich von Kleist was a follower of Kant (himself a follower of Rousseau), who had suffered in his early youth a "Kant crisis." Originally an adherent of Christian Wolff and the Leibnizians, Kleist had given up his Leibnizian ideals and his commitment to the goal of *Das Gut* upon reading Kant. The destruction of his ethical foundation threw him into despair. He wrote to his sister Ulrike that after reading Kant, "My goal has sunk!"

His story of "The Betrothal" demonstrates his Kant crisis in a colonial context. It begins with an ex-slave who kills his master after being freed by him. The setting is the island now called Haiti, during the successful slave revolt of the late eighteenth century. You will hear more about a young couple, Toni and Gustav, but the background story of Congo Hoango, Toni's mother's mate, comes first. His trajectory demonstrates the fall of the Good:

> On Monsieur Guillaume de Villeneuve's plantation at Port-au-Prince in the French sector of the island of Santo Domingo there lived at the beginning of this century, at the time when the blacks were murdering the whites, a terrible old negro called Congo Hoango. This man, who came originally from the Gold Coast of Africa, had seemed in his youth to be of a loyal and honest disposition, and having once saved his master's life when they were sailing across to Cuba, he had been rewarded by the latter with innumerable favours and kindnesses. Not only did Monsieur de Villeneuve at once grant him his freedom, and on returning to Santo Domingo make him the gift of a house and home; a few years later, although this was contrary to

local custom, he even appointed him as manager of his considerable estate, and since he did not want to re-marry provided him, in lieu of a wife, with an old mulatto woman called Babekan, who lived on the plantation and to whom through his first wife Congo Hoango was distantly related. Moreover, when the negro had reached the age of sixty he retired him on handsome pay and as a crowning act of generosity even made him a legatee under his will.

No colonial Master has ever been pictured as more enlightened, more "good."

And yet all these proofs of gratitude failed to protect Monsieur de Villeneuve from the fury of this ferocious man. In the general frenzy of vindictive rage that flared up in all those plantations as a result of the reckless actions of the National Convention, Congo Hoango had been one of the first to seize his gun and, remembering only the tyranny that had snatched him from his native land, blew his master's brains out.[23]

The literal explosion of de Villeneuve and his purveyance of the Good has been authorized, legitimized, by the Declaration of the Rights of Man— "as a result of the reckless actions of the National Convention." Kleist's insight is impressive: it was the power *to declare* these rights, to demonstrate that they were neither inherited nor inherent (natural), that abolished the old discourse of the Good. In the course of the story, de Villeneuve's personal "goodness" comes under a Kantian skepticism as well.

Whenever I teach this story, my students universally side with M. de Villeneuve, an enlightened man of obvious good will. Once I explain to them that the National Convention was what instituted the Universal Rights of Man and remark further on the difference between natural and conventional rights, the students grow quiet. Should they side with Master or Slave? Natural and inherited rights, as Rousseau and later Kleist's contemporary, Hegel, had shown, were artificial fictions, made up by the noble, landowning, warrior castes to institute and maintain their rule. With the Rousseau-inspired declaration of the universal rights of man as *conventional,* as the product of a social contract, a fundamental new Law granting equal rights to all superseded these old claims.

Something new had entered the world, something concerning the freedom of the subject, the person, with the new form of the Law. It was chiefly a freedom from an original falsified set of values concerning what was Good or Great or Best. It constituted a large step forward in the progress of sharing power among all of humanity. But because certain features of the old order were not confronted enough, perhaps, this new Law unwittingly empowered not only the People but their Thing.

Let me be clear about what this new social contract meant. It abolished slavery instantly, as a legitimate concept even though positive law would take some time to catch up with it. Congo could not wait. Indeed, Congo's is not the act of a man anxious to be "freed"—he already is—but to *mark* his as an original, legal freedom that voided in advance all the power to enslave—or to free—him. De Villeneuve had never had the right to enslave him to begin with.

Congo Hoango could, with reason, rise up against an arbitrary man-made law that had instituted a hierarchy of unequal rights as a natural-seeming hierarchy. Hoango could not have revolted against a truly *natural* law: you cannot shoot Nature in the head. Congo's pistol shot, then, puts a formal punctuation mark to the idea that a man—*any* man, no matter how superior, in terms of wealth, class, or morality—could *enslave* another. Or, by the same token, *free* him. De Villeneuve did not own the freedom he "gave" to Congo Hoango; the Negro had that freedom by right, a right once hidden but now made manifest by the universal Rights of Man.

Colonization, Superego, and the Law of the Good

How much radical alienation of freedom there is in the master himself.

—Jacques Lacan, *Seminar XI*

Das Ding presents itself . . . as that which already makes the law. . . . It is a capricious and arbitrary law, the law of the oracle, the law of signs. . . . That is also at bottom the bad object that Kleinian theory is concerned with. . . . The subject makes no approach at all to the bad object, since he is already maintaining his distance in relation to the good object.

—Lacan, *Seminar VII*

The waning of Oedipus, Freud tells us, is marked as the acquisition of an *internal* sense of the good in the form of the superego. Freud sees it as the way we overcome our mythified relation to our parents. But as Lacan noted, this "internalization of the Law" as the superego's good has "nothing to do with *the* Law": Oedipus.[24] The sadistic superego makes its entrance as an interior yet alien entity, which, Lacan tells us, issues "strange, paradoxical, and cruel commands" that echo that undertone of the Law, but for other aims.[25] Its appearance in us is a modality of our *Thing*: that bad object that is also our good object: a good so supreme, a *jouissance* so absolute we never allow ourselves to come near it.

What's more, we lie to ourselves about the nature of that Thing in us.

The superego is not only, we know, a moral voice, the voice of conscience, the call to duty, as Freud once thought; it is also that voice's obscene incitement to take that Good for yourself, even as you know it must not be touched. Freud's chief example is masturbation, once the child has realized that threats of real castration are idle and that his parents will not, as they claimed, cut it off. So the superego appears as an authority superior to that of the parents: it says, "Go ahead." At the same time, it mires you in the deepest guilt, potential shame, and embarrassment.

Now, just as post-Kantian Law is telling you officially that for the common good your own particular Good must go, its obscene underside, its superego, tells you the reverse: "Go and take that Good for yourself; you are entitled to it. Only the competition from your fellows for it prevents you from enjoying it fully." Thus the superego situates you at the site of the lesion where your good and its sacrifice meet, right where Renata Salecl calls the "place of traumatic enjoyment": it is precisely where "some act, some sentence . . . can unmake [your] world."[26]

After the eighteenth century, we encounter on the one side unbearable superego pressure to enjoy, and on the other society's counterpressure to give up your private good for the common one. Colonialism provided the perfect outlet for both the guilt of enjoyment and the imperative to enjoy the colonizer's own superego imposed. The colonial act alleviated internal suffering from the Thing, by imposing the colonizer's Good on another and claiming he was acting on the other's behalf. The unresolved part of the complex he handed off or loaded on to the colonial subject, however, is the work not only of the Good but of the Evil in him, the bad object. His move thus constitutes, so to speak, the black man's burden. "We" will have rid ourselves of that pressure to enjoy; "they"—the colonized, racialized other—will be the only ones still focused on the stuff of enjoyment, the good, including the good of their people. Only "they" will be caught laughing and singing and dancing. Only "they" are violent, aggressive, uncivilized. "Their" good makes them less than universal, less than human. We seem to have successfully infected them with the Thing in us we cannot acknowledge.

The White Man's Thing: The Racial Body in Colonial Fantasy

Now we come back to the concrete question of the colonized: what makes the colonized susceptible to its invasion by the White Man's Thing? I have not yet made entirely clear the circumstances where race and nation can claim equal status with sex as source of trauma at the psychoanalytic and not simply social, political, and economic levels. If it is true that *"Das Gut,*

Das Ding"—the White Man's Thing—increases the power of exploitation in the colonial situation, I have argued that is because it insistently replaces the kernel of the colonized's identification with that of the colonizer.

Today its field lies in the commodity and the competition for and the service of *goods* that structure the colonial experience the way they structured that Métro poster. But under classic colonialism, where commodities were just in their infancy, the Thing operated directly through the body. The body as racialized.

Race was the weak point or lesion where the alien's Good was inserted. Lacan says that something in the body is structured in the same way as a subject's relation to the signifier.[27] The body bespeaks *the letter.*[28] The return of *your* Good enters your body—in a way that escapes the sway of the Law. It stamps a new letter on your body over the one stamped by your original encounter with the unary signifier. This letter has its own agency over the body and contests the rule not only of your signifiers but of any balance you have achieved toward your Thing. But that letter, for the colonized, is the white man's color chart of his skin.

Racialization was historically an effect of the *class* struggle involved in democratic revolutions (Le Conte de Gobineau, Boulainvilliers, etc.).[29] But in colonization, not only was its European class base obscured, it blended directly with the problematic of the good to compound and devastate the subject on the basis of the racialized body. This is what happens to Toni as we return to Kleist's "The Betrothal in Santo Domingo." Its sequence is chilling.

The first trauma of enslavement is followed by a second and graver stage of pathology. In Toni's case it is not a sexually ambivalent hysteric, but a racially ambivalent, bicultural girl who is forced to choose psychological enslavement over her own subjective freedom.

Kleist again: The Relay of Radical Evil from the Mother to the Good

Toni is a *mestiza* (one-fourth Negro), the daughter of Babekan (common-law wife of Congo Hoango). Babekan is a mulatto with a Spanish father: Toni is not Congo's daughter but was fathered by a French nobleman who refused to acknowledge his daughter. The illegitimate birth caused Babekan to suffer sixty lashes from the good M. de Villeneuve, her master, injuries that left her permanently disabled.

Toni is fifteen years old when her story begins, set in a tumultuous revolutionary era, the late eighteenth century, in a remote place against the background of the only successful slave revolt in the world, led by Generals Dessalines, Christophe, Toussaint-Louverture, and other French-trained black military men. Toni and her mother live on the former estate of the deceased French settler, Guillaume de Villeneuve, the one who had emancipated Babekan's mate, Congo, after the slave had endured severe hardships and saved his master's life. In Congo's absence (he has gone off to fight with the generals) Toni and her mother are instructed to slay all whites who might come to the estate by any means necessary: trickery, seduction, and so on. Congo has warned the girl not to lose her virginity in the process.

The women's paths cross with Gustav van der Ried, a young Swiss settler who is trying to escape the advancing black armies. Leaving his family to hide in the woods, Gustav has made his way to the estate hoping its occupants are still white. Babekan and Toni greet him and, stressing the "white" part of themselves, invite him in—but only after he has laid down all his weapons.

Their move is both defensive and offensive: they know perfectly well, just as he does, that it is kill or be killed. He has also, in truth, kept one weapon concealed on his person. When Toni hospitably prepares his sleeping chamber for him, he calculatingly reveals his weapon to her. At the same time, he draws her to him, putting her on his lap and folding his arms around her. He not only holds her physically, he holds her with his speeches: he flatters her resemblance to the fiancée who gave her life for him; he highlights and praises the white elements in her beauty; and he promises to shelter her in the most exquisite patriarchal home back in Switzerland if she will only agree to marry him. The sexual culmination of this seduction (or is it rape?) takes place off-stage. It has a profound effect on Toni, who can no longer move, respond, or act, except to lie rigidly with tears streaming from her eyes. She alarms Gustav, who manages to get her almost catatonic body back to her bed just in time before the household stirs. When she awakens, she is completely recovered—and she is completely on Gustav's side.

But even before Gustav had taken Toni with his own horrible form of seduction, he had prepared the ground with a set of morality tales in which good faces evil. Gustav first tells the mother and daughter the terrible story of a Negro slave girl who took revenge on her wicked former master, a "Judith and Holofernes" kind of tale of retribution: she sleeps with the man, who thinks she now loves him and has forgiven him for having enslaved her. Instead, knowing she is infected with the plague, she has brought him death with her "love." Next, alone with Toni, Gustav tells her she "resembles" someone from his past, Marianne Congreve, a white French woman who was once Gustav's fiancée. Not only does this serve to distance her from her mother and link her with her French father (who denied his paternity); it also works as a parable. Gustav tells how he had recklessly criticized the Revolutionary Tribunal (the Terror), was denounced, and his arrest was sought. He escaped to the outskirts of the city, but

> the bloodthirsty band of my pursuers, failing to find me but insisting on some victim or other, even rushed to my fiancee's house; and so infuriated were they by her truthful declaration that she did not know where I was, that with outrageous cynicism, on the pretext that she was my accomplice, they dragged her instead of me to the scaffold. No sooner had this appalling news been conveyed to me than I emerged from the hiding-place into which I had fled, and hastened, pushing my way through the crowd, to the place of execution, where I shouted at the top of my voice: "Here I am, you inhuman monsters!" But she, already standing on the platform beside the guillotine, on being questioned by some of the judges who as ill-fortune would have it did not know me by sight, gave me one look which is indelibly imprinted on my soul, and then turned away, saying: "I have no idea who that man is!" And a few moments later, amid a roll of drums and a roar of voices, at the behest of those impatient butchers, the iron blade dropped and severed her head from her body. (246)

His presence at the event of a cutting off that is not merely threatened but carried through indicates we are in superego territory. It is an object-lesson to Toni. Indeed, Gustav tells Toni that it was Marianne's "death alone that taught me the very essence of all goodness and nobility." To be good, Toni must die for him.

This point in the story causes Toni to throw "her arms round his neck . . . mingling her tears with his" (247). Calculating the effect of his morality tales, Gustav, knowing

> that there was only one way of finding out whether the girl had sincere feelings or not he drew her down on to his knees and asked her whether she was already engaged to be married. "No!" she murmured, lowering her great black eyes with a sweet air of modesty. . . . when the stranger, whispering playfully into her ear, asked whether it was necessary to be a white man in order to gain her favour, she suddenly, after a fleeting pensive pause, and with a most charming blush spreading suddenly over her sunburnt face, sank against his breast. The stranger, moved by her sweetness and grace, called her his darling girl and clasped her in his arms, feeling that the hand of God had swept away all his anxieties. He could not possibly believe that

all these signs of emotion she showed him were merely the wretched antics of cold-hearted, hideous treachery. (244)

It is completely undecidable at this point which of the two is tricking the other, or if neither is and Kleist is depicting a genuine spontaneous mutual "love": Toni may be doing her job of seduction courageously, given the context of Gustav's physical power over her (the sword on the table); Gustav may be genuinely attracted to her, in his limited, racialized way: "But for her complexion which repelled him, he could have sworn that he had never seen anything more beautiful" (243). Decision will come through sex:

> There is no need to report what happened next, for it will be clear to anyone who has followed the narrative thus far. When the stranger regained possession of himself and realized what he had done, he had no idea what its consequences might be; but for the time being at least he understood that he was saved, and that in this house he had entered there was nothing for him to fear from the girl. (247)

Gustav is "saved" by his taking of Toni. But Toni has, in one of Kleist's famously elided scenes of sexuality, experienced a traumatic blow, which for her is irreversible:

> Seeing her sitting on the bed, with her arms folded across her and weeping, he did everything he could to console her. He took from his breast the little golden cross which was a present from his dead fiancee, the faithful Marianne, and leaning over Toni and caressing her with the utmost tenderness he hung it round her neck, saying that it was his bridal gift to her. As she went on weeping and did not listen to him, he sat down on the edge of the bed, and told her, stroking and kissing her hand, that he would tomorrow morning seek her mother's permission to marry her. He described to her the little estate he possessed on the banks of the Aar; a house sufficiently comfortable and spacious to accommodate her and her mother as well, if the latter's age would permit her to make the journey; he described his fields, gardens, meadows and vineyards, and his venerable aged father who would welcome her there with gratitude and love for having saved his son's life. As her tears continued and poured down over the pillow he embraced her passionately, almost weeping himself, and begged her to tell him how he had wronged her and whether she could not forgive him. He swore that the love he felt for her would never fade from his heart and that it had only been the turmoil and confusion of his senses, the strange mixture of desire and fear she had aroused in him, that had led him to do such a

deed. . . . she made no answer to anything he said and simply lay there motionless among the scattered pillows, cradling her head in her arms and sobbing quietly. (247)

When morning comes, Toni awakens pure white. Not literally, of course. But her entire identity has now become sensitized, as it were, to Gustav's "good." She tells her mother it is "shameful and contemptible" to violate the laws of hospitality as they had done, that her home is a "den of murderers" (249). She defends the young Swiss because "he is not even a Frenchman by birth" and therefore not an enemy, claiming that he is "entirely noble-minded." Moreover, she now proclaims she has a "soul," which is sickened by the killings. Toni, in short, has been converted to the "good." Gustav's good. Psychically, her good has been displaced by Gustav's. He has forced her, through her sex, to choose between two equally self-destructive alternative identities. Each is morally focused on his good, not hers, not her family, her home, her people, her mother. She can choose to be considered a plague-infected ex-slave, duplicitous and evil; or she can choose to be considered a self-sacrificing, good, and noble lover à la Marianne. Between pure evil and pure good, Toni loses either way.

It is within a restricted moral—superego—frame that Toni becomes a *psychological* slave despite her *political* freedom. She now repeats Congo Hoango's original gesture, that of rescuing the Master. Because she is a girl, Gustav's sadistic superego will have urged her along a different pathway from Congo's response to the "good," bull-whipping Guillaume: it is she who will be shot by Gustav, not she who will shoot him. In contrast to Hoango, that is, Toni is much more dominated by the love-masked sadism in Gustav than Congo is by Guillaume's moralistic one, which he answers with his own empowerment, his *rights*, his *jouissance* in a way that the girl obviously can neither know nor bear. Her submission to the sadistic and invasive *jouissance* of Gustav imprisons her mentally and enslaves her as no other physical form of entrapment and torture could.

Toni manages to find Gustav's family, arm them, and have them arrive to liberate him. She has tied Gustav to his bed while he sleeps, to ensure that no one in her own household suspects her of disloyalty to Congo Hoango. But Gustav is unaware of her plan. Once he is freed by his relations and armed, he shoots Toni "right through the breast" (265) in front of his appalled family. They know the real story, and they blame him severely. Facing their disgust, Gustav places the pistol in his mouth, blowing out his brains and scattering pieces of his skull, which stick to the walls of the room. No longer unequivocally good in the eyes of his fellows, or no longer its exclusive possessor, Gustav cannot continue to live.

Most students react to a first reading of the story as though it were a romantic love-death, a Romeo and Juliet story. But the only real stake in the tale is a struggle for the good, that "good" associated with the forbidden Mother. As we all know the importance of separation from the Mother under Oedipus, we at first imagine that, with her choice of Gustav over her mother, Toni has chosen the good. She has symbolically "killed off" her mother for the better, more ethical part of herself: after all, she decides she will murder no more whites. But it is no ethical commandment, no true *civilization* that has demanded this decision of her: it is actually only an enemy from an opposed group. Gustav's evocation of a paternalistic civilization is pure sham: could anyone really believe his promises to Toni—marriage, children, a blissful Swiss home—when we are told that her skin color "repulses him"? It is he, ultimately, who has acted most unethically toward her.

But why is this girl so susceptible, so vulnerable to him? We cannot know if it is due to his seductive powers, to that sword of his lying on the table, or to her own psychology. She is not painted, like Hitchcock's Charlie, as a *hysteric,* but she is painted as troubled by a failed identification. Her ambiguous racial identification resembles that of the hysteric's undecidable sexual one. She is missing a symbolic father, and Gustav deprives her, mentally, of her mother's support. So when Gustav calls on Toni to give up her life for his, she has already been stripped of all parental defenses. By the time we see Toni fully complying with his aims, she is also fully destitute. She has been internally invaded, colonized, and occupied by Gustav.

Gustav is entirely specious as well as selfish in his appeal to Toni's "better" self: he is asking that Toni reject her commitment to her people for the role of an inferior, a slave to his interests. In breaking with her mother, Toni has, moreover, unwittingly prepared her own murder: having killed in herself what her lover demands she reject (her race, her mother, her sexuality), she is already gone. Her subjective essence cannot be extirpated by choice and fiat, Gustav's pleading notwithstanding. To reject them entirely, as Toni does, is to die already a symbolic death. Gustav's final shot through Toni's breast is only a second death for her. She has already killed in herself the knowledge of the Things her mother had passed on to her: her dark skin, her life, and her hatreds, too. Submerged by an ideologized "brotherhood" to which she has sacrificed everything she received from her black mother, Toni erroneously accepts the fake patriarchy's rules of the game: cut off your mother if you want to access your "patrimony," your great white father's world.

Kleist's vision is of the feminine at its most vulnerable to this perversion of patriarchy's promise to the girl. The reason I have retold this story here is not to accuse yet again "the patriarchy," but to show another aspect of an obscene superego in its destructive relation to the girl. While it is not technically a sadistic superego we find working through Gustav, it participates in the superego structure: "the patrimony" promised to Toni by Gustav is precisely what is off-limits for an ethical function of the "Father." Gustav is dangling the same kind of promise of fulfillment, one that he can arbitrarily withhold, that the "Maternal" superego does.

What makes colonization so traumatic an encounter for the racialized subject is always something like the story of Toni. We can even go one step more, to reinterpret the problematical *ethical* position of colonizer and colonized here as parallel to that struggle with the peculiar, yet compelling power that an Ideal ego and its Good has over any subject of the Superego, as aggravated in the case of the colonial subject.

The Sadistic Superego and Neocolonialism: The Bad Breast

The superego must be dealt with if the subject of a new ethics, demanded by the birth of modern democracy and real postcoloniality, is ever to replace the older ethics of the good. Democracy needs not a greater, clearer, better, more expansive version of the good—a superpower—but, rather, an accounting for the idealization of the very one who has the power to deprive us of our good, our *jouissance.* This good is nothing other than *Das Ding,* the unapproachable and unfathomable and unmovable entity around which our unconscious moves and against which it defends itself.[30] Under the superego, replacing the ego ideal of the Oedipal father ("the power to do good") with an ideal ego does not remove the power of the good inherited from Aristotelian ethics (and the pleasure principle) but, rather, restores and further distorts it. It is to idealize and render yet more powerful precisely that imaginary other who, in Lacan's beautifully succinct definition, "has the power to deprive us of the good" (1992, 234), much as Toni idealizes Gustav's definitive replacement of her good with his.

"Second-stage" colonialism is, therefore, most damaging to the colonized psyche precisely when the colonial subject incorporates a bad object—the colonizer's good, the white man's Thing—in the form of a good that "determines their reason." Far more damaging than simple enslavement,[31] or pitched battle with an alien adversary, it blocks the colonized subject from finding their own desire. It insists that the Other's *jouissance* is the only good.

The Political Subject and Its Unconscious

The classical political subject was first fully transformed in early modern Europe by bloody religious (and therefore economic) warfare—the Protestant Reformation, the Counter-Reformation, the several inquisitions, the institution of capitalism, and so forth. Second, the painful birth, through literary and philosophical labor, of the political subject as *individual* (Descartes) and, simultaneously, as *member* of a collective body called "The People" (Rousseau) worked its own transformations. Finally, the death agony of God helped transform the legal category of *person* into its shadow-form, the *personality*. These mark the advent of a new subject suited for modern democracy, that form of governance that fundamentally altered the European social order—the political subject. It is not accidental that a fundamental reaction against this new subject also opened the door to colonial forms of governance, the very antithesis of democracy.

A key component of this new formation of the subject in the seventeenth and eighteenth centuries was the emergence of an idea that "a people" was not determined by divisions into natural (economic) classes. It ironically parallels the emergence of an entrenched division or, better, opposition of human beings—the colonizer and the colonized. I would not say, à la New Historicism, that the birth of modern democracy depended structurally on colonialism, that the acquisition of the "rights of man" was a function of, or a cover for, the elaboration of a capitalist-exploitative-racist logic. Rather, I would approach the matter from the other side, examining how the earliest formulations of the terms of democracy were *blocked* precisely as a *result* of the colonial adventure, which itself was, in no small measure, a negative response to democracy.

Hannah Arendt has already shown how Europe exported to its colonies a decidedly pre-Rousseauian form of social and political thought well after the modern democratic model had been decisively formulated. Though it sloganized democracy, what Europe brought to its colonies after the democratic revolutions of the eighteenth century, she tells us, was still rooted in predemocratic forms, rather than in a working program derived from the revolutionary principles of modern democratic thought: liberty, equality, fraternity.[32] The most pernicious effect of this export (which was no longer fit for consumption at home), according to Arendt, was that it ultimately hindered the development of political democracy in Europe itself. Arendt is no ardent fan of democracy per se, which she finds inherently susceptible to totalitarianism. Yet even she sees that the distorted version of itself that it exported to the colonies exacerbated the weaknesses in the fledgling modern democratic form.

Arendt's own stress is also unwittingly telling as far as Eurocentrism, like egocentrism, blinds one ethically. As a woman and a Jew, Arendt—unlike many political theorists—makes common cause with the colonized. Yet she seems unable or unwilling to assess the harm done to the colonized—psychically or politically by this inferior product. She is everywhere centered on the European and the effect of his external colonial adventures on him, on his own internal political development. The fact that so astute a political analyst as Arendt is blind in this instance to the most salient feature of the system she denounces—its dehumanization of the colonized—shows the extensiveness of my earlier claim that the colonial complex is an *ethical* disorder. Does it have something to do with a willingness to accept the excision of the Good as a criterion in European affairs, while not expecting the same from the colonies? It seems that the unconscious side of the political subject must now be considered more closely. And that means turning to Rousseau.

Rousseau and the Political Unconscious

Most people read Rousseau backward, from the revolutions and reactions that followed him. I do things a little differently, starting with the real radical in European thought, Descartes, and I watch where Rousseau attempted, in my opinion, to stand Descartes on his feet. Rousseau, I believe, aimed to do for "society" what Descartes did for the "subject": to found it, and its conditions, free of all inherent and predetermined characteristics or properties. To do so, Rousseau turned Descartes around: if Descartes founded the subject as thinking substance, free of all a priori attributes, Rousseau founded a political substance, "the social body," free of all acquired and inherited properties. Where Descartes took the individual mind for his theme, Rousseau took the collective social body for his. The consequence in Descartes, according to Lacan (1978), was the simultaneous opening of the subject of the unconscious. Rousseau's efforts likewise opened, I would argue, the political unconscious.

Rousseau had insisted—and Kant tried to follow him here—that in his time a new subject was in the process of being born.[33] It was to be subject to no natural or divine law, but only to a law of its own. It was the *product* of and the *origin* of a social contract whose contracting "second party," as Althusser pointed out,[34] had absolutely no existence before the contract was signed. In contrast to positive law as it had previously existed, this law was negative.

What does this "negative law" mean? Rousseau identified historical society, which he called "civil society," society as we know it (and, as historical beings, the only way we have ever known it), with the exploitation of man by man. Its "positive law" was, therefore, only designed to secure the right of the "firstcomer" to property, and of perpetual wealth to the earliest and most aggressive—the ruling warrior castes. (These are the castes that found all society, and all "right" in Hegel, too.)[35]

But Rousseau tried to imagine himself beyond this situation. He did not, as many believe, do so by calling for a return to primitive nature, but, rather, by the specific creation of an alternative idea of what "civil society" could be. His thinking is utopian, not primitivist. Thus, his "savage" in the *Second Discourse* is virtually modeled on Condillac's statue of the *Treatise on Sensations*, an artificially stripped model for the subject who only later acquires its properties and characteristics. A blend of Locke's tabula rasa with Descartes's radical doubt, this puzzled savage inhabits an Edenic forest equivalent to the "garden" into which Condillac's statue, having fully developed its mental faculties from a single sense perception, awakens to itself as a singular and whole entity. Rousseau's hypothetical Adam, his "savage," was a device to permit the new social body a new point of departure, a new arena in which to forge a different idea of itself from the one that the "civil society" based on exploitation and artificial hierarchy had given to it. Its new name is "The People."

It is this concept of "The People," which is so vexed to this very day, and one that Marx fully eschewed,[36] with which, nonetheless, Rousseau intended to counter the aristocratic, noble landowners, and knightly, warrior castes who were ranged against the peasants even in his own day. Like all original ideas, his was of course appropriated for other agendas, many of the worst sort. But for him it was a sublime, new body.

In what did this "body" of the people consist?

Civil society *(la société civile)* was, for Rousseau, intrinsically antagonistic. It was founded in and by exploitation, deception, inequity, and injustice. Since human beings had never known any other form of society, Rousseau made a proposition based, he felt, on recognizing the way people related to those antagonisms. He suggested that we not try to seal and heal the breaches in the social fabric, since this would simply eternalize the iniquitous status quo, the falsely "natural" inequalities that characterize it. Rousseau thought he could instead throw the social process into reverse: rather than making a whole body out of something internally torn apart, he would legislate a new body on the basis of a permanent split in its social fabric: The people *as a whole,* he said, had to look at the people *as a whole* to determine its *general* will. There could be no special exceptions to this totality, no exemptions from the required split.

Just as Descartes had tried to divest his *cogito* of them, Rousseau proposed divesting the *corps moral et collectif*—individual and group—of all "acquired" or "inherited" properties. (This is Rousseau's word.) *Properties* is to be taken in every sense of the term, since in his *Second Discourse* Rousseau declared that the very first properties acquired by human beings upon their entrance into *civil* society were those of "Rich" and "Poor"; all other qualities *(propriétés)* were merely derivations of these two: "All these ills are the first effect of property and the inseparable offshoot of incipient inequality."[37]

Since Rousseau dated all human history from the advent of exploitation and the separation into classes of haves and have-nots, he proposed the alternative of dispossessing everyone. He was not thinking up some kind of primitive communism; his notion was to dispossess everyone only from the standpoint of the whole. In other words, no one party, no one class or person could claim to have the "whole" on his side, for him. Rousseau wanted to create equality before the law. To equalize everyone before the law, this law had to be a law of the whole and, as I have said, not the legislated "good" of any one of its parts. This Law had to support a freedom from being classified by one's "properties" (in the sense of labeled characteristics). These had never been anything but artificial, originally bestowed by the inherent inequity and iniquity of social society. Such properties masquerade as *natural* inequalities, but they always stem from some self-interest on another's part. Second, the law had to create de facto a new model for a fraternal social order. Like Freud's original mourning for the dead father, this society had to be founded not on blood, but on a destitution and mourning for a loss common to all: the loss of the ability to believe in a whole, unified social substance. After Rousseau, no one could legitimately conceive society as either a dead Ur-father or an expansive maternal body.

Rousseau's "general will" thus proposed what amounts to the law of castration (Lacan), and the potential to create community out of "strangers," rather than out of kin relations: natives, migrants, and immigrants alike were free to become citizens of this newly conceived social order.[38] Rousseau structured his general will so that it could not be the will of all, but the sum of "not alls." For the General Will is what remains after every individual will in the society is stripped of its naturally or socially inherited properties.[39]

Rousseau thus envisioned a kind of clean sweep, a whole new constitution where the "pluses and minuses" of "the sum of private wills" (his words) would cancel each other out.[40] Rather than a social order that simply masked the antagonisms that created it, Rousseau's general will was designed by him to mark society as a loss held in common. What was lost is not "nature" as much as a particular set of social markings, the *positive, symbolic,* and therefore *alienating* marks civil society had bestowed on us.

Rousseau, with this stroke, overthrew the notion of the Good, the Good of the whole as an ethical foundation for modern democracy. His fiction of a "divided whole" runs counter to utilitarian constructions of his and the next century's. The reason he gave up the Good of the Whole was, as I said, the expropriation of that Good by the few, by the narrow self-interests of one class or one party. The origin of civil society lying in the self-interests of the few, "the good" would always be tainted by special interests. In other words, what's good for the whole usually boils down to what's good for the ruling classes. (Joseph Heller's Milo Minderbinder put the same thing in reverse, saying that what was good for Milo Minderbinder—his greedy underhanded deals—was by definition good for the whole United States.)[41]

Rousseau's thought was bent toward blocking the purveyance of one's own good—as Minderbinder does—as the Good of the whole. To him, purveying the good was never anything but the special (economic) interests of the propertied classes. What stood in its stead was, rather, to be desire. Desire alone could ground the social body. Rousseau made a space for the individual freedom to desire. The basis, that is, for the collective democratic revolution.

Rousseau's ideas are stunning and inspiring. But inasmuch as he cast us perhaps a little too free of a shopworn symbolic, however, he placed us closer to confrontation with the Real Thing, and not the secondary properties that hide its view from us. Later, Kant would go much further and expunge from the will every hint of what he called the "pathological" from the way the will charts its actions. No class or selfish interests were to be taken into consideration in the act of general will in Rousseau; by the time we see this general will reappear in the Kantian imperative, it is all human interests that are barred. Kant edges more closely to Sade's than Rousseau's reason in this regard, by virtue of his philosophical thoroughness. Rousseau's remains an anthropology; he still spoke to the human; Kant pushed his discourse toward the inhuman, *Das Ding.*

But this is always what seems to happen in the course of human understanding whenever it takes up Rousseau's lead. The result is never quite

bearable. His definitions are too open to misconstruction, taken too literally or too ideally. Marx counted him one of two dialectic thinkers before
Hegel, and dialectical thinkers always run the risk that only one turn of
their thought will be realized. Mainly, his political ideas were just fiercely
opposed.[42]

Following Rousseau's initiative, logically, there should have been a
democracy rooted in a law of desire. Yet even had one actually been instituted, it might not have prevented the Good *(Das Gut, Das Ding)* that it
had banished from returning. Democracy could not adequately protect
itself against the return of the Good inside, in the form of its *unconscious*
installation. The law of the good may even come into its own after
Rousseau—in the form of the superego. The Good that was lost becomes
a Radical Evil within. That "lost" Good we might call the Bad Breast.

The Service of Goods as the Amputation of Desire

The complex democratic subject of the post-Enlightenment, positioned
by yet resistant to the moral, political, and religious orders, was made desperate by a traumatizing, irrational, disordering superego, which brought
that subject closer than is comfortable to the possibility of *jouissance.* The
stake of the unconscious subject's problem with the Good becomes, according to Lacan, the following:

> Will it or will it not submit itself to the duty that it feels within like a
> stranger, beyond, at another level? Should it or should it not submit itself to
> the half-unconscious, paradoxical, and morbid command of the superego,
> whose jurisdiction is moreover revealed increasingly . . . ? If I may put it
> thus, isn't its true duty to oppose that command?[43]

The political condition of the colonial situation shows the same terrible
ironies. Democracy, the advent of the superegoic form of law, and its complex subject all emerged in European thought as a response *against* the
realm of *goods* as being the proper arena for the evaluation and definition
of the political subject. Having and being were no longer, after Rousseau,
to be the measure of all human worth. Yet the realm of goods persisted and flourished in the unconscious—and in the colonies. They bore
the burden of all of the antidemocratic reactions that had been mentally
cast out of European thinking. The colonized bore the white man's Thing
for him.

That Good soon became sublime.

To the white owners of the term in Freud's time, *civilization* meant an
investment in a narcissistic perfection. This investment was paid for with

a restraint that was considered a point of pride for the "civilized." As compared with those persons of color who were "uncivilized" and therefore "unfree," who seemed to enjoy innocently (which means guiltily), the white European felt himself quite superior, and happily freed uncivilized peoples of all reminders of their uncivilized past.

Let us linger a moment longer with some of the errors that flow when a social group is grasped not as a collective subject (Rousseau) but as a collective ego, a "civilized race,"[44] in which secondary characteristics, "properties" like color, are made to count for something real (*jouissance*) in the other, instead of something merely political. Let us go back to two Enlightenment philosophers who made a mistake about the color of civilization that Rousseau never made: Hume and (the precritical) Kant. Rousseau personally feared David Hume,[45] and Kant later bent his own mind to combating the ethical dilemmas that flowed from Hume's pen. But early on, the upright German philosopher was as susceptible as anyone to a certain tone, a certain note that Hume struck with respect to race and its tie to cultural evolutionism.

In one infamous note to his essay "Of National Characters," David Hume had written:

I am apt to suspect the Negroes to be naturally inferior to the Whites. There scarcely ever was a civilized nation of that complexion, nor even any individual, eminent either in action or speculation. No ingenious manufactures amongst them, no arts, no sciences. On the other hand, the most rude and barbarous of the Whites, such as the ancient Germans, the present Tartars, have still something eminent about them, in their valour, form of government, or some other particular. Such a uniform and constant difference could not happen, in so many countries and ages, if nature had not made an original distinction between these breeds of men. Not to mention our colonies, there are Negro slaves dispersed all over Europe, of whom none ever discovered any symptoms of ingenuity; though low people, without education, will start up amongst us, and distinguish themselves in every profession. In Jamaica, indeed, they talk of one Negro as a man of parts and learning; but it is likely he is admired for slender accomplishments, like a parrot who speaks a few words plainly.[46]

The ideological character of Hume's outburst here is plain to see. He even gives it away with his "our colonies": it is a shameless apology for the British commercial and colonial adventures that dispossessed or looted the cultural treasuries of "Negroes" without a twinge of conscience. But unconsciously, the struggle for, over, and against "civilization" is ultimately a struggle about the original lost object, the maternal breast, split up as a treasury of *jouissance* (the good breast), and as the bad breast (the *jouissance* of the Other) who takes it from us.

Only an unconscious appeal at this level could possibly excuse the impeccably rational Kant for seconding Hume in his violent attitude here. Kant came from a country that was itself barely more than a set of peripheral colonies of the Austrian empire. Yet he took up Hume's theme in a context that seemed quite unrelated, his essay on the *Beautiful and Sublime* (1764). He cites Hume's 1748 essay quite uncritically and adds some of his own touches:

> The Negroes of Africa have by nature no feeling that rises above the trifling. Mr. Hume challenges anyone to cite a single example in which a Negro has shown talents, and asserts that among the hundreds of thousands of blacks who are transported elsewhere from their countries, although many of them have even been set free, still not a single one was ever found who presented anything great in art or science or any other praiseworthy quality, even though among the whites some continually rise aloft from the lowest rabble, and through superior gifts earn respect in the world. So fundamental is the difference between these two races of man, and it appears to be as great in regard to mental capacities as in color. The religion of fetishes so widespread among them is perhaps a sort of idolatry that sinks as deeply into the trifling as appears to be possible to human nature. A bird feather, a cow's horn, a conch shell, or any other common object, as soon as it becomes consecrated by a few words, is an object of veneration and of invocation in swearing oaths. The blacks are very vain but in the Negro's way, and so talkative that they must be driven apart from each other with thrashings.[47]

Kant was not simply caught in the ideological apology for the colonial adventure. After all, his own people were scantily implicated in colonialism. Nor could the mild-mannered, sociable Kant have been responding to Hume's carte blanche for aggression against nonwhite peoples. What Kant was hearing was something else, some unconscious appeal that made a qualitative distinction among human beings possible. He was hearing something about the ultimate goodness, the sublimity of the white.

Hume, seconded by the precritical Kant, resorts in his text to an ineffable, qualitative distinction as securing a racial distinction, an indefinable whiteness of being, attributable only to one race. That this indistinct distinctiveness happens to coincide with the political story he was not bothering to tell, the story of the dispossession of one race by another in the colonial adventure, is an ideological problem. But the sublimity that comes through to Kant from Hume's warped picture of civilization is crucial.

This "finer feeling" could only have come through a special relation to the origin—the source, the mother, that good breast.

Rousseau's critique of "civil society" and of positive right was a good beginning for shaping a new free European political subject; after all, he drafted the new constitutions for Poland and Corsica.[48] But at the level of the subject's relation to *jouissance,* no social or political revolution could ever be enough advanced. The reappearance of the Thing, the bad object-in-the-form-of-a-good played no small part in the second coming of exploitative civil society in the colonies. And its rule has not come to an end today.

The outbreak of tremendous pathologies in the twentieth century has made abundantly clear that Europe did not escape the consequences of this twisted ethical dilemma. The first postcolonial thinkers were given impetus by the public spectacle that the excessive European destructiveness they had both suspected and witnessed had finally made of itself, as Aimé Césaire's comparison shows. Colonialism instituted abroad the exploitative "civil society" that Rousseau had tried so desperately to undermine in his writing at home.

In the colonial case, the colonizer after the Declaration of the Rights of Man had to expel his Good, or have it expelled for him, like Guillaume de Villeneuve. Projecting his Thing onto the colonized proved handy. If he clung to the discourse of the Good, he still provoked, consciously or not, a dialectic of envy about his goods in which he unconsciously engaged with the colonized.

Duras's India Song: The "Good Breast"

If, in the colonies, as Duras wryly remarked, the colonizers learned to take a bath every day, and acquired many gifts from those they colonized (see Gandhi's purported remark on what he thought about Western Civilization: "It would be a fine idea"), there was no possibility of exchange, structurally speaking. Colonization brought what I would call the realm of "goods" to the foreign bodies it conquered and occupied. As the purveyor of *goods,* in all senses of the term, colonization provoked a dialectic of (unconscious) *envy* no less in itself than in those it conquered.[49] The colonial "shock" is not the simple confrontation with Oedipal "civilization"— as human, the colonized in the precontact state is already marked by the field of the Other. Nor is it the realization of childhood trauma replayed as dependency or the infancy of need and demand (Mannoni). It is the insistent insertion of a *dialectic of goods* (unconscious relation to bad objects, conscious relation to good objects) in place of one's own way of relating to the Thing.[50]

Witness Fanon, who keenly conveys the colonized's sense that the colonizer has exclusive possession of the Thing—made clear by the fact that there can be no exchange.[51] Witness Memmi's complaint that all creation within one's own culture is stymied by the advent of the colonizer—blocked not only by the colonizer's goods but by an overvaluing, as goods, of a set version of one's own culture and its "traditions."[52] Witness Chatterjee's plea for imagination.

And, finally, witness *India Song.* Marguerite Duras's astonishing film will help us make the ultimate analytic reduction of the pathology of the Good in colonialism. Duras's portrait of Anne Marie Stretter in *India Song* sketches out the basic mechanism that becomes decisive for the psychic violence done to the colonial subject. In a marvelous revelation, to be captured perhaps only on film, she reveals the deepest nature of the White Man's Thing: the white woman's breast.

India Song is, in my opinion, a brilliant analysis of the very problematic of the subject's relation to *jouissance,* fantasy, and the Thing as good and bad object in the colonial case. It is the story of Anne Marie Stretter (Delphine Seyrig), wife of the French ambassador to Calcutta. She is an apathetic woman with numerous lovers (of whom her husband is perfectly aware) who yet holds herself aloof from one man, the Vice Consul of Lahore (Michael Lonsdale). He appears to be driven to madness by his love, evidenced by his shooting both at himself (in the mirror) and (really) at the lepers of Lahore. About to be banished from Lahore to a different post, he attends a stiff, formal diplomatic party, at which he demands Anne Marie Stretter dance with him. She acquiesces, and as they dance he tells her that he is going to cry out that he wants to spend the night with her.

Speaking in a flat affectless tone, this "mad" Vice Consul tells Stretter precisely what he will shout out, and that he wants to make a scandal, so everyone will know of his love for her. He then proceeds calmly to leave the embassy for its grounds, and to scream out repeated pleas for her to let him stay the night ("Je veux rester avec elle!"), along with her maiden name, "Anna Maria Guardi." What the film clarifies in a way that simply reading the text cannot is that these screams resemble the demands for love voiced by a spoiled, unsatisfied child—increasingly so as they devolve into inarticulate repetitions of her maiden name, which comes to resemble nothing so much as variations on sobs of "Mama."

In a following scene, we see Anne Marie Stretter lying on a floor in the heat, wearing a long dark dress, with, however, one breast bared. The camera stays still on the breast, in close-up, for quite some time. Two of her lovers (not the Vice Consul) enter and lie down beside her. The scene, far from being at all erotic and "sexy," is filled with apathy and a sense of enervation. (In the book, the men have to lift Stretter's arms up for there to be any activity at all.) The Vice Consul starts to enter the room but hesitates in the doorway, at which point Stretter sits up and covers up her breast.

The model of sexual enjoyment purveyed by the scene here is that of mother and son—the "son/lover." It is what her posture visually suggests: the nursing mother, one breast bared to give it to the infant. The Vice Consul is the only one who is denied access to the sexualized maternal breast. He becomes the son who must no longer touch that breast once he has become a man. But the incest taboo depicted here is so cynically and superficially stylized that the Europeans clearly have voided it of all primary sense: even this human universal has been tokenized, given lip service and no more.

Anna Marie Guardi/Stretter's breast is not, after all, really an *object a*, it is not the stand-in for the Thing whose encounter all men must miss to become men. Like that breast in the Métro, it is not really that "object to be circumvented" that gives the subject its consistency, and whose avoidance would secure their manhood for the Vice Consul as for her other lovers.[53] Instead, this breast has been made into a *good* for "consumption," not for the eyes or mouths of her lovers, but for the eyes (and mouths) of the Indian servants who move silently, rigidly across and through the spaces occupied by all these white bodies.

What the Vice Consul apparently so passionately (yet with a passion that is purely histrionic and therefore cynical) dramatizes for the natives is The White Woman (or, rather, the White Woman's Thing, her lifeless White Breast). He is showcasing it as an ultimate, unattainable, highest Good. The inert body of Anne Marie Stretter, vapid, vacant, a mere shadow of a human womanly presence,[54] is being sold—or, rather, *advertised*—to the natives here. Their very status as "inferiors" depends on their realization of her absolute unattainability in her idealized form. She is the Ideal Ego par excellence. The one who has the power to deprive you of your *jouissance,* your Good.

The European Vice Consul and his tragic romance have thus succeeded in representing him, his culture, his skin, his "mother's" breast as a Good, *an ultimate good,* a good the colonial other is simultaneously warned, by precept and example, can never be exchanged *fairly* for any goods he or she might have. The colonized might give their all: but this Good will remain forever unattainable, like the "eternal feminine."

Duras's film aims to demystify the maternal body as a good. The imitation of maternity and its ultimate, untouchable, good, by Anne Marie Stretter, who "gives herself to all," like a good mother, and yet to no one at all, is already a travesty of that body—a "sublime" body, a "thing of nothing." As such, it is a pure *commodity*. A commodity of an ultimate sort: one that (so the scenario is written) if the Indian or Malagasy or Congolese has even had a whiff of it, he must simultaneously pursue and forsake if he is to *be* any good.[55] Always just below the possibility of attaining, doing, and being good himself, he is enjoined nevertheless to forsake all other goods in its pursuit. He has contracted the superego disease of the Westerner.

Once the colonized is given this body as the ultimate Good, with no other comparable, colonization has taken root, and taken its toll.

Paris Again

So we have returned to my breasts in the Paris Métro. To rethink them as signs of a clandestine colonialism without a master. Their assault on our sensibilities lies in their leering, sadistic implication that they are the things, the goods, "*you* really want."

4. Race/War

Racialization remains a deep current in the politics of inequality. It has generated severe historical contradictions to the point of crisis for the liberal
nation-state, which must reconcile racial logic with the universal aspirations of enlightenment ideology.
                    —Minoo Moallem and Iain Boal, "Haven with No Shadows"

On Color

For Western culture, and for Northern Europeans in particular, darkness
and evil have long been falsely linked.[1] San Francisco–based conceptual
artist Ann Chamberlain took this truism to another level in her 1990 installation titled *On Color: The Reclassification of a Dead Archive by Color*.[2]
While the artist represents beautifully the long-standing confusion of
aesthetics and politics in our black = evil error, her work also reveals
something more disturbing about race. By means of a brilliant conjunction of image and text, Chamberlain makes conspicuous that we so-called
whites equate our own moral worth, our own excellence, with an *absence*
of color.

Whiteness, to our most intimate self-regard, certifies an absence of
stain; it is a negative emblem that silently proclaims that we, at least, are

Ann Chamberlain, from *On Color: The Reclassification of a Dead Archive by Color* and the artist book *Fairness*. Photography and mixed-media installation. Mission Cultural Center, San Francisco. Reprinted by permission of the artist.

not tinted or tainted by *jouissance,* by the Thing. The white skin encasing us is a sign that there is nothing alien or dark within us.

In *On Color,* Chamberlain exchanged fresh film for the negatives from coin-in-the-slot photograph booths in Mexico. She then "smuggled" these illegal immigrant faces (of children from the Mexican city of Cholula) across the U.S. border. Exhibiting them in an altar-like construction, Chamberlain asks of these "undocumented images" in black and white: "What color are they?"

Her artist book, *Fairness,* sits before this altar of "decolorized" faces, its pages a mixed-sex series of photographs of "white" and "colored" faces. Transparent layers over the black-and-white images are rich with ironic social narratives of coloring and whitening. A North American bride-to-be makes an effort to be tan and healthy looking for her wedding; her Mexican counterpart shelters her face from the sun for the period prior to her wedding.

The cross-cultural contradictions of an *aesthetic* of fairness is written over the faces of these two women. A few pages later in *Fairness,* we find the ironies of a *politics* of color, its confusion with class, in the inscription over the faces of two Mexican boys.

That a naive aesthetics and politics are the outer limits of our thought

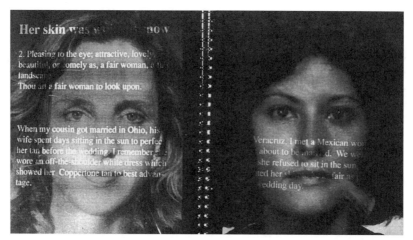

Her skin was so now

2. Pleasing to the eye; attractive, lovely,
beautiful, or comely as, a fair woman, a
landscape
Thou art a fair woman to look upon.

When my cousin got married in Ohio, his
wife spent days sitting in the sun to perfect
her tan before the wedding. I remember she
wore an off-the-shoulder white dress which
showed her Coppertone tan to best advantage.

Veracruz, I met a Mexican woman
about to be married. We were
she refused to sit in the sun
ted her skin fair as
edding day.

Ann Chamberlain, from *On Color: The Reclassification of a Dead Archive by Color* and the artist book *Fairness*. Photography and mixed-media installation. Mission Cultural Center, San Francisco. Reprinted by permission of the artist.

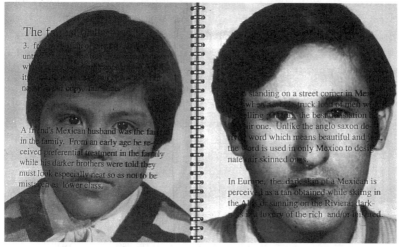

The f

3. fr
unt
w
it
n

standing on a street corner in Me
when a truck load of men w
lling for one the best translation
ir one. Unlike the anglo saxon de
word which means beautiful and
the word is used in only Mexico to desig
nate fair skinned ones.

A friend's Mexican husband was the fa
in the family. From an early age he re
ceived preferential treatment in the family
while his darker brothers were told they
must look especially neat so as not to be
mistaken as lower class.

In Europe, the dark skin of a Mexican is
perceived as a tan obtained while skiing in
the Alps or sunning on the Riviera; dark-
is a luxury of the rich and/or leisured.

Ann Chamberlain, from *On Color: The Reclassification of a Dead Archive by Color* and the artist book *Fairness*. Photography and mixed-media installation. Mission Cultural Center, San Francisco. Reprinted by permission of the artist.

when we confront race—we confuse color with morality, color with social class—is made stunningly clear in Chamberlain's piece. But her insight goes well beyond a cultural critique of the aesthetic-political mix. It also reaches an ethical and, I think, ultimately a psychoanalytic level.

Along the top of the narrative overlays, Chamberlain has run several dictionary definitions of *fairness*. The conceptual range this word covers is remarkable, though we encounter nothing so surprising as Freud's antithetical meaning of primal words in it. Still, when we add all of the definitions and synonyms together in this unexpected context—race—something new does emerge, something more disturbing than the ironies Chamberlain has highlighted. The psychological meaning of color and whiteness becomes frighteningly clear.

From *fairness*, Chamberlain has drawn out three layers of signification. Together they combine to inflect race-as-color psychopathologically. The first is aesthetic, the second, ethical:

—"comely, attractive, lovely, beautiful"

—"honest, open, equitable, reasonable, frank, clear, impartial, candid, beautiful, just, pure"

These first two definitions convey certain basic cultural values of Western peoples, and while they are ethnocentric, they do not have anything directly to do with color or race. Their culturally valued social qualities give a glimpse of the more or less simple give-and-take of social life. If we turn them around, their dialectical opposites remain recognizably human characteristics: honest/dishonest, open/closed, equitable/inequitable, just/unjust, pure/impure.

But the third definition Chamberlain has selected introduces a new element, an element of excess that installs the term as *psychical*:

—the fairest of them all . . . free from stain or blemish, unspotted, untarnished, pure, free from anything which might impair the appearance, quality or character

This constitutes an escalation; with the superlative, "the fair*est*," the "*un*tarnished," "free from *anything*," we move from sociocultural to higher grounds, to the level of drive. Any form their negation might take could never be simple and oppositional, as in the first two sets. It is absolute, one-sided, and nondialectical. We are suddenly in a game of all-or-nothing.

Once we go beyond "openness" to total evacuation ("free from anything"), once we go beyond "frank and clear" to the whiteness produced by a voiding ("free from stain"), a purism, a purging of tint or taint, begins to show itself. The extreme value—"the fairest"—we place on the *presence of nothing* can only be the result of a purge. Psychically, some unconscious Thing is being disavowed.

Fairness—as what is impartial and free of all aesthetic and social values, free of prejudices, errors, and cultural blinders—leads us, shockingly, right toward the unconscious ground of racism, to an extreme place where our education and our reason cannot fully protect us. As the battle-field where *good* combats *evil* in an inhuman, excessive way, the color of skin becomes more than just a surface; it takes on an added depth that its superego shadow gives it. *Fairness* cannot prevent the eternal return of racism as long as it retains its link to a drive to purge. The purge is a feature of all racisms: we find it written across the carnavalesque overflow of "im-pure blood" in the gutters of the *Marseillaise,* in the riddance of Jewish "vermin" in the Nazi Holocaust; over the Khmer Rouge's "purification" of the Khmer people under Pol Pot; and around the "ethnic cleansings" in the former Yugoslavia today.

Racism Today and Yesterday

Psychoanalysis must address the inexplicable persistence of race thinking in an age that has scientifically debunked racial logics. It must explain why cultural critique alone cannot reach the psychic layer from which racism springs. An "antiracism" that cannot inspect its roots in race thought, con-scious and unconscious, is useless. How else than at the unconscious level could we begin to account for the sensational return of an imaginary race factor in the affective life of the American and Northern European citizen, today, and now spreading to the "third world"? After all, race thinking has declined tremendously at the anthropological, legal, and scientific levels. Races were once identified by such factors as religion, language, and visual characteristics like eye and hair coloring.[3] Racial typing led to such absur-dities as having members of the same nuclear family declared different "racial types." Moreover, we have witnessed a structural decline in the so-cial desire for segregation by race; most of our laws prohibiting interracial marriage, for example, have systematically been repealed in the United States in the past seventy years.[4] Scientifically, the typological method that characterized the heyday of race thinking in the nineteenth century has long since been fully discredited.

Let us therefore return to the unconscious root, to that Thing we con-tinue to make of race even though it makes no logical sense. Let us go back to Carolus Linnaeus, who made the first classification of a living archive by color.

Colors

The primary, though not only, signifier of race up to our time is color. Why color? Has anyone thought to ask? The Swedish naturalist Carolus

Linnaeus in the mid–eighteenth century selected color as his criterion of the "races" that were his brainchild—a system for classifying us as he had classified plants.[5] Linnaeus simplified the ways of ordering peoples (in both senses of the term) by applying his morphological, taxonomic method to humans as well as flora and fauna. On this basis he sorted them into four races: black, yellow, red, and white.

Dare we speculate a moment on Linnaeus's unavowed motivation for this original color scheme? Since our skins never fit Linnaeus's color wheel precisely, for him to have selected color over any number of other characteristics as a decisive trait took some doing. (As one geneticist I know puts it, whites are actually a sickly, "pinkish brown.")

Linnaeus's move turned out, indeed, to be no neutral one. It crossed the growing aggressiveness of scientific empiricism with an Aristotelian concern for specific difference. But, more crucially, color also has a conspicuous remainder of meaning in the history of the West: *colors* signify the establishment of groundless antagonisms, as in gang colors, and other military flags. Did Linnaeus feel we were spoiling for a fight when he suggested grouping humans around colors? Was he preparing all of us for engagement with an enemy?

In effect, he was. As European empires spread throughout the globe, Linnaeus's work unwittingly supplied them with their most visible flags. The Linnaean division may even be the distant source of white supremacist beliefs today that an apocalyptic race war is just around the corner.

Ironically, of course, the race war he unwittingly started took on the opposite aura in the following century. The Linnaean scheme, cross-bred with social Darwinism, had become by the mid-1800s a palette adumbrating not war and colonial acquisition but its opposite, an ideal of the peaceful and harmonious existence of all races under a universal regime— "civilization." The eighteenth century had also invented a "cultural evolutionism" that reduced all cultures to an inventory or checklist; if elements were missing, it meant that the culture was deficient—or "further back" from civilization.[6] When cultural evolutionism crossed with Linnaeus's checklist, which likewise inventoried all the earth's peoples and reduced them to only four color-coded races, it became an article of faith that "civilization" had to be white. *Whiteness/fairness* meant being cleared of any irrationality, any spot or stain, any identifiable characteristic that might open you to the charge of "pathological" enjoyments.[7]

The stage was set for a racialism whose effects haunt us today. And not only today, as we shall see. In what follows, I trace the unconscious, deadly effects of the original twinned conceptualization of race as *color* and as culturally *evolutionary. Civilization* in the nineteenth century became a code word for a cultural evolutionism framed as a gradient, a spectrum. But of what? The answer can only be something like what Ann Chamberlain discovered: degrees of separation from the stain of *jouissance.*

Civilization as Cultural/Racial Evolutionism

To "civilization" only one species (Hume called them "breeds of men")[8] was born, though others could follow them, albeit distantly. Here we arrive at a crucial unconscious factor in racism of which color is only a symptom, though a decisive one.

Linnaeus, it seems, had made a second determinative classification that would unwittingly shape the way race would be played out in the Western psyche. Within the animal kingdom, he differentiated species according to criteria that placed human beings in the same class as certain animals. The absolute distinction between human and animal that Descartes had staked the subject on—the linguistic distinction—fell away. Aristotle, of course, had called man a political animal, but the vagueness of the class "animal" he invoked had nothing like the psychic impact of Linnaeus's conception.

Linnaeus focused on a single objective feature whose presence or absence made certain animals our close relatives: the breast. Around this object, the breast, a new bedrock for defining the human came into being, one that allowed for no absolute line between human and beast. Mammalians were suddenly a class of which human beings were only a subclass. Without that absolute division between man and animal, we mammals all became children of a lesser god—of a mother, Nature. A new gradient in human being was determined not by nearness to God but by proximity to the breast. An unconscious fantasy of fraternal rivalry, an unconscious fratricidal struggle over that good or bad object, that breast, became subterraneously linked to the competition among the races. A maternal breast to which all and sundry *could* equally lay claim became the unconscious cause célèbre of a psychic struggle over who should have it. An envied *jouissance* in the other, a *jouissance* one conscientiously denied oneself (and denied *in* oneself) began to shape the relations among races. The other enjoys at our expense; we are not so uncivilized as to still enjoy *that*; and so on.[9]

Yet should not a common mother, an original maternal breast, unite all her children? This bit of wishful thinking accompanied the news of a recent fossil discovery, genetically extrapolated, that showed a single African mother for all mankind ("Eve"). Eve, it was thought, would eventually produce a new logic of racial harmony that could move us beyond that old patriarch, Adam, and hierarchical logic. It might. But first we would need to get over several stumbling blocks in our mental relation to the mother. And electing to name this mother of racial harmony after the mother of Cain is not a very reassuring first step in the right direction.

The signs are even less hopeful when we consider that historically one of the first effects of species thinking was quite the opposite of racial harmony. Key thinkers in the Enlightenment, like Hume (and even, briefly, Kant) using species logic, immediately judged the white race as superior, not in *kind* to animals, but in *degree* to other humans of differently colored race. Not only were whites imputed a privileged capacity for sublimity and for finer feeling than the darker races (with one exception, the North American Indian), an intense narcissism of minor distinctions became the keynote of something called "civilization."

High "civilization" from the eighteenth to the twentieth centuries in the West disavows its link to *jouissance*. Political power over others is masked by a calculated rhetoric of higher or lesser civilization correlated with degrees of whiteness (anthropologically a silly notion). But this notion escapes the cynical political limits its users placed on it. The entrancing appeal of a sublime excess operates, so to speak, in addition to calculatedly devious political agendas and creates a second, graver moment in which we reach a psychoanalytic *cause* of racism. The unconscious question put to the subject by the superego voice is always, "Who has the *jouissance*?"

"Civilization," as the ideology that cloaks or hides this rivalry, is fundamentally shaped by the phantasmatic breast, the sublime site of *jouissance*. The greater your degree of civilization, the greater your distance from that breast, that *jouissance*. The closer to it you seem to be, the more uncivilized you are, the more savage you are judged to be. But even while you strive to deny it in and to yourself, you want even more to deny it to the racial other. The question is why? For whom do you want this *jouissance* held in reserve?

Racial Politics

But I have gotten ahead of myself here, since we seem already to be caught up with racism and I have not yet defined race itself, other than as the artificial color-coded category devised by Linnaeus.

There is no racial *essence*. Because human groups are not isolates and have always lived in contact with other human groups, the racialization of the foreigner has always potentially been with us. The term *race* appears only when it is a question of *enemies*. Race is always the consequence of a lopsided political encounter between human groups. Even the refreshing recapture of epithets for race in the Chicano emphasis on *La Raza*, the Caribbean on *Négritude*, among others, and in the immensely suggestive recalculation of the category "white" or *"blanc"* in Haitian history shows that this is the case.

The question is not, "What is race?" but "Under what political circumstances do races (plural) come into existence?" We must step beyond merely saying, in a Foucauldian way, that "Race is never natural, it is a constructed social category," to saying, "It is always a *political* category." That this is true can be seen in the recent (unfortunately successful) effort in California—the so-called California Civil Rights Initiative. This initiative was composed by two white men, who, feeling that the whites were now the targets of a reverse discrimination under the terms of affirmative action, decided to put it to public vote. They claimed they did so in the interests of fairness and equality for all races. University of California Regent Ward Connerly, who is black, backed this measure, firmly denying that there were any political interests at stake. Once the measure passed, enrollments of minorities in the state's university fell dramatically, in part because affirmative action was banned, but also in part because students "of color" elected not to attend under such circumstances. Thus Connerly, who had rhetorically urged fairness, had in effect strengthened one race's (white's) advantage. As he passionately disputed that race was a political matter, he was actually moving to make it the biggest political football in the statewide election.

Race always serves notice of *territoriality*, political divisions translated as the right to be somewhere, to occupy a certain space. In pluralistic societies that are not ostensibly organized by apartheids or legal segregations, we can still see just how territorial race is, even in small, local ways. Gauge your own shock of mild surprise as you encounter this piece by the contemporary London-based artist Ingrid Pollard.

Pollard photographed children and younger adults of Afro-Caribbean ancestry (though born in England) in the heart of Wordsworth's Lake Country for a series on "Heritage." One she placed on a billboard titled "Wordsworth Heritage." Another of her captions in the series reads, "It's as if the Black experience is only ever lived within an urban environment. I thought I liked the Lake District, where I wandered lonely as a Black face in a sea of white. A visit to the countryside is always accompanied by a feeling of unease; dread. . . ."

Pollard's work economically unsettles the assumption that rural life is neutral, while pointing up the purely ideological equation of black and

Ingrid Pollard, "Wordsworth Heritage," from *Autograph #11* (London: Association of Black Photographers, n.d.). Reprinted by permission of the artist.

urban today: not so long ago, even in Wordsworth's time, the black was confined to the savage wilds, beyond the city's and "civilization's" limits. Pollard exposes the British pastoral as racially territorial (our nature, not theirs), along with the quasi-automatic racial/spatial sorting we make when we unthinkingly locate whole peoples into "suitable" settings, including landscapes. She thus exposes one of the larger ideological pretenses: that race is natural and apolitical—that it is "nature" itself. Pollard's work reveals something of the "truth" of Linnaeus's undeclared declaration of a color war.

Race/War, Part One: Freud

> Social justice means that we deny ourselves many things so that others may have to do without them as well, or, what is the same thing, may not be able to ask for them.
>
> —Freud, "The Herd Instinct," in
> *Group Psychology and the Analysis of the Ego*

It may seem odd to move to psychoanalysis just when I have come to the question of war and race. The main comment on war within psychoanalytic theory comes from Freud's essay "Thoughts for the Time on War and Death,"[10] but we never consider it a meditation on race. We think of it, rather, as a devastating critique of civilization and of the way the veneer of civilized culture falls apart during wartime. Nevertheless, Freud's somber essay shows not only that an ideology of color is inextricably bound to that of civilization for Freud's time, but that it is inextricably linked to war.

Freud principally linked war to *narcissistic* aggressivity. War humbles this narcissism to a degree but at the same time gives it further impetus. That is not news. What is news is that, looked at closely enough, Freud discovered that a specifically *racial narcissism* lay at the very root of war, in particular, of a war that was by no means overtly interracial in character. The war that Freud saw as flowing from the alignment of color and civilization was that immense conflagration of self-slaughter—of European "whites" by European "whites"—known as the Great War. In this 1915 essay (written one year after his essay on narcissism),[11] Freud spoke directly to race and aggression, but as a *white* relation to color, to "civilization," and, ultimately, to a *jouissance* that overflowed ego boundaries. Let us watch Freud as he entered the discourse of war as a discourse of race, and beneath that, as a hidden struggle among brothers over enjoyments of the Mother.

Freud and Race

Freud labored to produce his psychoanalytic theories in an era marked by two entirely distinctive, though equally oppressive, theories of race. One was the openly displayed international racialism of Victorian (especially British) imperialism. The other was the internal racism of the Austro-Hungarian empire that was his home. The latter was marked by age-old anti-Semitism and by racial laws specifically against Jews. Both imperial powers were completely cosmopolitan or "multicultural" in character, yet each deployed race to denote access, or its lack, to the "highest" and "purest" forms of its civilization or culture. Most peoples didn't get into that club—their best of what's known and thought, as Matthew Arnold called them.

In his war essay we first imagine that Freud is himself partial and parochial in his brief against the Great War. He seems to be targeting mainly the British Empire, its territorial aggression and racialized ideology, as he mourns the loss of confidence in civilization for which the war is held directly responsible. After all, Freud's sons fought on behalf of the failing Austrian empire against the British one. So Freud had no difficulty in pinpointing ethical and logical failings in the Victorian (mainly British) ideals and ideologies of the "white man's burden." Nor did he have any difficulty in showing how easily these were placed in the uncivilized service of war. So there is a certain obvious *parti pris* against the British apparent here:

We were prepared to find that wars between the primitive and the civilized peoples, between the races who are divided by the colour of their skin—wars, even, against and among the nationalities of Europe whose civilization is little developed or has been lost—would occupy mankind for some time to come. But we permitted ourselves to have other hopes. We had expected the great world-dominating nations of white race upon whom the leadership of the human species has fallen, who were known to have worldwide interests as their concern, to whose creative powers were due not only our technical advances towards the control of nature but the artistic and scientific standards of civilization—we had expected these peoples to succeed in discovering another way of settling misunderstandings and conflicts of interest. ("Thoughts," 276)

But Freud's complaint is both parochial and universal in character: as the old joke goes, Freud might just as well be saying, "What mean we, paleface?" For he now shows that his tongue has been firmly planted in his cheek as he goes on to rebuke his own Germanic civilization for its particular kind of racialism:

> Observation showed, to be sure, that embedded in these civilized states there were remnants of certain other peoples, which were universally unpopular and had therefore been only reluctantly, and even so not fully, admitted to participation in the common work of civilization, for which they had shown themselves suitable enough. (276)

In Freud's eyes, then, both imperial powers, British and Austrian, had an unwarranted faith in their own white identity as superior to nonwhites based on their respective degrees of "civilization," which clearly meant "white" for the combatants on both sides. The "common work of civilization" that Freud contrasts with the imperial view obviously means something entirely different, as for him this "work" is something in which the Jew, the gypsy, the African, the Asian can and does participate, even though they are not, by "white" standards, entitled to. The Europeans disdained the immigrants in their midst, claiming they were incapable of participating fully not in Freud's "common work of civilization," but in the specialness of "white" civilization. The non-European, it seems, failed to be what we today call "qualified." Non-Europeans could work themselves to death and never attain the "excellence" that was granted exclusively to those who were to the manor born—who had the best of civilization, so to speak, by birth, with the mother's milk.

The "Science" of Race

Freud's melancholy catalog of the intangible losses caused by the Great War includes another related one: the loss of faith in our fairness, "impartiality," and scientific objectivity. These have become casualties of this war:

> We cannot but feel that no event has ever destroyed so much that is precious in the common possessions of humanity, confused so many of the clearest intelligences, or so thoroughly debased what is highest. Science herself has lost her passionless impartiality; her deeply embittered servants seek for weapons from her with which to contribute towards the struggle with the enemy. Anthropologists feel driven to declare him inferior and degenerate, psychiatrists issue a diagnosis of his disease of mind or spirit. (275)

Yet how "objective" had the anthropologists, psychiatrists, and evolutionary scientists ever really been? They had once gone about their science with what they considered "objectivity," but it was an objectivity that allowed them to believe that the last vestiges of violent, passion-driven, irrational forces remained only among the "uncivilized" colored races. The whites themselves were thought to be past that, free of any such taint. This "objectivity" granted only one portion of humanity a nonviolent reasonableness that came from "the artistic and scientific standards of civilization." Narcissism on this scale has come in for a shock with this war: "We had expected these peoples to succeed in discovering another way of settling misunderstandings and conflicts of interest." Now these same civilized, rational, highly cultivated "scientists" were being marshaled, ironically, to apply their worked-up racial logic to members of their own white race. The experts "driven to declare him inferior and degenerate" and "psychiatrists issu[ing] a diagnosis of his disease of mind or spirit" thus racialized their German enemies as uncivilized barbarians, "Huns." In the process, they unwittingly lent an air of scientific legitimacy to Nietzsche's mythification of the Teuton, the eminent barbarian.

The British and Germans cocreated, by racializing Germanics as Huns and uncivilized barbarians, a frightful precedent. Deploying the racial signifier—playing the race card—against a political enemy is a dangerous game. A signifier of race came into being, a race of barbarians, that the Germans were programmed to live up to within a generation. They in turn discharged it from themselves by bestowing it on a racial "inferior," the Jew. (I will return to what constitutes the alleged "inferiority" of the Jew and the Negro when I speak of Adorno below.)

Scientifically, no more than any individual does a "race" have any fixed points of identification. Race is political; it shifts its definition relative to its origination in the imputations, imprecations, and epithets an opposing group makes up about it. *Psychically*, however, races, like individuals, do have unconscious identifying points.

Where we are alienated ("castrated") in and by a signifier that represents us to other signifiers—signifiers that assign us a place in a symbolic order—something of our being is left out; this process constitutes our humanity as speaking beings. It is a process that has no necessary links with any signifier of race. But, like sex, it can have a traumatic relation to the superego, to that tone or attitude you see through or hear yourself speak, beyond the symbolic place the signifier and speech grant you. Race is thus a special case of unconscious identification. It is traumatic because it seems to recall something of your being to you beyond the edge of your humanity.

In English, *race* has links to words for root, but also for a sharp hook as well as an erasure.[12] It is hard to find a better example of a Lacanian *point de capiton*, the "quilting point," that seems to justify, explain, and satisfy the pain of your existence.[13] The *racial* quilting point constitutes a secondary, supernumerary, identification that differs fundamentally from primary identifications by the signifier to which any and every human subject is submitted. Why? Because it always comes to you first from an *enemy* other, and not from an other you can trust, like your parents. Thus racial identifications always have a racist core: that quilting point, that "Aha! Now it all makes sense" in which the other who conflicts with you tells you who you are and what your "race" means to him—it signifies backwardness, dishonesty, thievery, oversexuality, and so on. The way this quilting point represents you to yourself is not essential to your constitution as a human subject, but it marks and stains you all the same.

White "Perfection"

The command that you give up your enjoyment in the name of your civilization comes to you in the same superego voice that commands the reverse of you—"Enjoy, take what you can." Freud concentrated attention on the restrictive, sacrificial modality of the superego when he attempted to analyze the origins of the Great War. At least a portion of the cause, in Freud's view, lay with the excessive demands, felt strongly by the Victorian citizen of the white world, to *renounce* his enjoyments. This "instinctual renunciation," according to Freud, is always met with an equal counterpressure to indulge in those forbidden enjoyments, to throw off all social and mental constraints on your drives. Under conditions of war, the two superego commands come into direct conflict:

Within each of these nations high norms of moral conduct were laid down for the individual, to which his manner of life was bound to conform if he desired to take part in a civilized community. These ordinances, often too stringent, demanded a great deal of him—much self-restraint, much renunciation of instinctual satisfaction.... The civilized states regarded these moral standards as the basis of their existence. They took serious steps if anyone ventured to tamper with them, and often declared it improper even to subject them to examination by a critical intelligence. It was to be assumed, therefore, that the state itself would respect them, and would not think of undertaking anything against them which would contradict the basis of its own existence. ("Thoughts," 276)

While you might think that Freud's only target here is the strictness of British Victorian sexual repressiveness, he catches the opposed German ideology in the same net. The Germanic cultures, which have idealized the blond barbarian, the Teuton who breaks with civilization's constraints, are the other side of the same coin. Both are caught in a form of superego pressure that cannot be counted as the true "common work of civilization." That is a work engaged in by all human beings, who must find their balance between the demands of nature and those of culture. What concerns Freud here is a secondary, excessive sacrifice, and its converse, the sacrifice of all excess. In the excessive mode, no internal limit on an impossible and horrifying *jouissance* is recognized. In wartime the two sides press on the hapless subject at once: he is compelled to partake of a painful *jouissance*—murder—and he is compelled to anesthetize his *conscience* to allow him to bear up under war's necessarily obscene commands.

All that Freud would later call the obscene superego is already contained, then, in his meditation on war as revealed by the color of civilization. When, contrary to all expectation, whites had not been murderously attacked by other "savage" races, but by an undeniable savagery in themselves, there opened in them a narcissistic wound that has perhaps not yet healed.

A narcissistic or cultural superego had shaped the ideology of racial superiority. It demanded privations and sacrifices on the part of the whites, who in turn demanded the same of other "lesser" beings. These demands found a reflex in their own unconscious, where their own Superego required severe sacrifices from them but also commanded indulgences and *jouissances* that were unbearable in the light of their cultural claims. Thus, the aspiration to perfection expressed by "white culture"[14] neglected the consequences of the sacrifices it suffered in itself as blithely as it neglected the consequences of its infliction of sacrifices on other races. Confronted with the sheer meaninglessness of the unrelenting slaughter and the fact that it was perpetrated by the very race—the white—that had imagined itself perfectly rational, the whites' superiority in "civilization" at every point to the "lesser," colored races could never again really be credible.

Freud did not therefore indict the racial foundation of European identity solely for its bad politics, for its blindness to the real excellence of those the Europeans have discounted as "unqualified." To Freud, their blindness was only symptomatic of the larger disorder in the ego's relation to "civilization." Just as there is no spontaneous, free, open human being for Freud, there is no race superior to others in "ethical sensitiveness."[15] The spurious superiority of the whites is, he found, based on a superego, not on an ethics. The noble epic of civilization turns tragic and ends in the bosom of an overwhelming *jouissance* of the Other to whom the "civilized" whites have sacrificed their own relation—desire—to a loss of *jouissance.*

The Race, Nobility, and Jouissance

The whites, from Hume and the early Kant to the defenders of Victorian civilization cited by Freud,[16] did not claim that they owned *jouissance* individually, far from it. Rather, they themselves were fair and good because they were entirely free of it. But this *jouissance* that they were not themselves tinged with, they unconsciously handed over to "The Race," which, as early as the seventeenth century in England at least, was firmly tied to notions of noble ancestry. The Race was a kind of expansion of the ideals of nobility enlarged to coincide with the new conception of "civilization." It was thus a kind of imaginary Other on whose behalf the civilized being labored—not for his own but for *its* fulfillment. Just as, consciously, the despoiler of other peoples required them to be dispossessed of their patrimony, unconsciously, the presence of real others who might dilute or divide up the hoard of *jouissance* (or partition the racial inheritance) conflicted with this aim.

Racism is thus said to identify its targets by imputation of theft of *jouissance* to them.

"Civilization" and Jouissance

With our jouissance going off the track, only the Other is able to mark its position, but only insofar as we are separated from this Other. Whence certain fantasies unheard of before the melting pot. Leaving this Other to his own mode of jouissance, that would only be possible by not imposing our own on him, by not thinking of him as underdeveloped.

—Lacan, *Television*

One way we fail to face the abusive superego at the core of race and racialization is to mishear Freud's use of *civilization*. Freud's term now seems so dated that it no longer calls up the multilayered response it would have in his time. Moreover, it was radically misconstrued by many of his most famous followers. Freud, it should now be clear, indicted "civilization" as an *ideology and a conceit,* not as a carefully won set of limits on *jouissance*: the "common work of civilization."

Psychoanalytically, full enjoyment is never available to the human speaking being. Human being (the bearing of language) makes ours already a body without organs, a body with no possibility of experiencing an animal *jouissance*. The human being is "castrated" by the signifier, or put another way, it gives up a large portion of *jouissance* to become a member of the human community, whose only universal characteristic is that of speech. Hence castration is linked to language, that blade that carves a body out of an animal substance. In racism's focus on the phenomenology of color, however, there is no true line dividing animal from human, and castration cannot have the meaning it has when it is linked to speech. Instead, a secondary, imaginary idea of castration compounds the original difficulties of "castration by the signifier" (the common work of civilization) and is used to divide human beings another way, shading some more toward the animal of full *jouissance,* shading others more toward the human free of this animal "stain." Politically, it is used against certain peoples both to deny them their humanity and to limit their access to cultural goods, including (or perhaps especially) their own. To look at race and racism, then, is to encounter fantasies of castration and escape from it, fantasies of "Who has the *jouissance*?" The "possession" of *jouissance* is still an irrational element in all thinking about race, and it taints even antiracism today.

Racism and Antiracism Today

The imaginary confection that "civilization" was in Freud's time, its deadly narcissism, linked to a "white" quilting point, persists in other guises in our time. As we (academics and psychoanalysts) met to address the question of race and psychoanalysis in Washington, D.C. in 1996, the United States was reporting that the motivation of three out of every five hate crimes in 1995 was race (the next in importance was religion);[17] Proposition 209, the California Civil Rights Initiative (CCRI), had just passed; Carl Rowan was predicting a "coming race war," black churches were being burned; and an off-duty white fireman was gunning down a black man in Milpitas (mistakenly, but does it matter?), believing he was "getting away" from a shopping mall security guard.[18]

Because of Freud and Lacan, we can see the manipulative politics in such pseudo "antiracisms" as that of the CCRI and that of a recent brochure urging blacks to free themselves of white-dominated educational and psychiatric institutions. This mailer by a self-styled "Citizen's Commission on Human Rights," supported by the Church of Scientology, attacks community mental health programs, Margaret Sanger, and psychiatric practices as irretrievably racist.[19] Its cover shows a black man in chains, and a sidebar inside the magazine exhorts: "A castrated ox will pull its plow." Its message urges black people to resist both psychiatry and education as manipulative tools of the master class. Its implicit call to separate those who are "castrated" from those who are not ironically coincides with the newly promoted "neutrality" and apoliticality in the matter of race, à la Proposition 209. The coupling should give us pause to wonder just what it is that is being preserved *from* the black here? Why this flare-up of exaggeration of the dangers to black and white of contaminating each other that each of these show?

I think that, given the structural acceptance of racial coexistence that currently prevails in the United States, it is only a hidden return of the old concept of "civilization" as the highest and the best, a right to which must remain an exclusive possession of whites. Some sense that whiteness holds an inaccessible treasure surely is at work in the following twisted claim to have gone beyond "race": when Regent Ward Connerly was at his most exercised it was not over statistics and quotas, but over the fact that ethnic groups at the University of California sometimes have special *celebrations* for graduation.[20] That's when we know we have stumbled into the arena of the treasure—the other's *jouissance* that we imagine is what has been depriving us of our own.

Connerly's furor means that the designation of a *special enjoyment* for a nonwhite takes something away from the absolute specialness of the club whose rules are decided by whites. As a black, he must feel that he has sacrificed a great deal to get into that club. We could picture Connerly, who proudly notes that he "never marched with Martin Luther King," at a country club whose criteria (narcissistic checklist) he has worked diligently to meet.

But we could not picture him at a jazz club.

It is on the question of civilization—*Kultur*—as a club, a specialness, that Adorno will become relevant.

Adorno's Cultural Critique

Theodor Adorno nuanced *Kultur* somewhat differently from Sigmund Freud. Freud's sense of civilization had in it some measure of the unwholesome *société civile* that Rousseau had equated with the formal origin of inequality. Adorno's complaint against *Kultur* is more aesthetic and less structural in character than Freud's. Unlike Freud, Adorno was not much concerned with the hidden intersubjective and fratricidal (or sororal) war that lay at the basis of "civilization."[21] Adorno detested the blandness of contemporary culture and saw in it much more than something simply not to his taste. It was an evil he termed the "bad equality of today."[22] According to Adorno, there is a *quantitative* egalitarianism to contemporary society that demands the eradication of differences.

It was not war but, rather, peace ("the reconciliation of differences"), and what passed for peace, that drew Adorno's critical attention. Where Freud found the Victorian consensus on civilized behavior to be a thin veneer over aggressive narcissism, Adorno saw this veneer as a thick varnish spreading to all areas of life. False glossiness caused him the greatest alarm. Only specific attention to difference could, he thought, contest this narcissistic glossiness that covered the deepest violence. Adorno's technique in culture criticism was to place his most utopian moment for culture, his potentially "better state," into the same frame as his critique of what is. In the case of war and peace, peace would be where people could be different without fear (unlike the way things really are, with himself, the sensitively "different" little boy constantly beset by bullies):

> That all men are alike is exactly what society would like to hear. It considers actual differences as stigmas indicating that not enough has yet been done; that something has been left outside the machinery. . . . The spokesmen of unitary tolerance are always ready to turn on any group that remains refractory. . . . An emancipated society, on the other hand, would not be a unitary state, but the realization of universality in the reconciliation of differences. Politics that are still seriously concerned with such a society ought not, therefore, propound the abstract equality of men as an idea.[23]

Already in this quotation from *Minima Moralia* we can see Adorno's difference from Freud. He places certain Marxist claims ahead of psychoanalytic ones, such as that advanced economic exploitation is a primary cause of social distortion, not a secondary effect of unconscious narcissism. Still, Adorno's caution against mass culture may well be both economically and psychoanalytically justified. He ends his thought here with the following diatribe: "The melting pot was introduced by unbridled industrial capitalism. The thought of being cast into it conjures up martyrdom, not democracy" (102). Lacan, too, in *Television*, had pondered the frightening image of the melting pot as too close to the image of narcissistic fulfillment in a maternalized social body.

Yet, about Adorno, certain nagging doubts. It would, for example, be possible for a racial purist to share the antidemocratic rhetoric of Adorno's passage on the martyrdom of the melting pot. Certain contradictions appear throughout Adorno, many of them centered on a problem with the boundaries of culture, its purity. Let me stress that there is very little to find fault with in Adorno from the standpoint of today's "political correctness." His critical theory is virtually gender blind, uniformly protofeminist, and so on.[24] But where cultural productions and the subject's relation to them are concerned, there is always something a little confusing in Adorno. How else could so politically correct a thinker possibly be caught in such a trap as critiquing the melting pot in terms that echo those of the Nazis and other German thinkers of the time, and the Heidegger he once supported and then roundly criticized?

Let us pursue this melting pot image a bit to develop a sense of a certain contradiction in Adorno whenever a politics of culture gets involved. His horror of the melting pot is more than matched (and contradicted) by his demand to get beyond Kant's grid, which he laments as keeping us from The Thing itself. If we lose the rational separations the grid provides, are we not in the soup of matter, the cooking pot? Adorno saw Kant's "grid" through critical eyes: it was the analogue and agent of industrial capitalism's relation to matter as mere *raw material* for its production of goods. Adorno wanted to overthrow this "bad" relation to matter, return to the things themselves, and reestablish a proper relation to the object. Adorno, of course, only wanted to remedy Kant's and Hegel's failures to forestall the culture of capitalism, by putting the subject "*in* the matter and not always beyond it," to "penetrate into the immanent content of the matter" (*Minima*, 16). Still, the way he puts it, the rationality of separation of subject from material object does not withstand his vivid image of someone being "in the matter and not beyond." If we look at him through psychoanalytic and not just "materialist" eyes, we might wonder if this object might not also be the maternal Thing?

Moreover, his demand to "penetrate matter" is directly opposed to at least a portion of his aesthetic theory, which demands that art mirror, keep its distance from, and in no way involve itself in producing new matter.[25] In his aesthetic theory, Adorno felt that art should instead reproduce the trembling moment of an original encounter with matter: the fear we ought to feel before the object.[26] That object must make us yield on our attempts to dominate it; otherwise, it will take its revenge and turn us, the subject, into it, the object.

Adorno loved and hated art. For Adorno, art was both chief symptom and symbol of the discontents in civilization. He found art difficult to place in civilization, and at key points Adorno seemed to substitute a *cultural politics* for an *aesthetic theory*. It is this politics that will help us take one step beyond Freud in the psychoanalysis of race—and its war.

Aesthetic Theory versus Cultural Politics

Art's original inspiration lay in the feeling (Adorno's term) that results from neutralizing deep antagonisms and attractions. Art for Adorno is the equivalent of the sublimity we found in Kant's "finer feeling." To Adorno art in our time is irretrievably compromised because it has the same aim as bourgeois society: the domination and exploitation of the object. But its original impulse was the opposite. Art stemmed from socially determined human oral and sexual appetites—"cuisine and pornography," or food and sex culturally shaped. This original aesthetic (in the sense of the senses) must now, in the context of capitalism's rapaciousness, forgo its original appetites, its moments of *jouissance*. Only "disinterestedness" will permit the artist of today to distance him- or herself from bourgeois society, and thereby preserve self and art from capitalism's economic demands. Under the bourgeoisie, even artistic freedom is simply another kind of "open-air" imprisonment:

> The precondition for the autonomy of artistic experience is the abandonment of the attitude of tasting and savouring. The trajectory leading to aesthetic autonomy passes through the stage of disinterestedness, and well it should, for it was during this stage that art emancipated itself from cuisine and pornography, an emancipation that has become irrevocable. However, art does not come to rest in disinterestedness. It moves on. And in so doing it reproduces, in different form, the interest inherent in disinterestedness. In a false world all *hedone* is false. This goes for artistic pleasure, too. Art renounces happiness for the sake of happiness, thus enabling desire to survive in art.[27]

Though he uses the term *desire* here, it should be noted that for him art is actually more concerned with *jouissance* than desire. Art is a rough *sublimation* in the harshest Freudian sense, as it staves off the fundamental *jouissance* that drives the artist: "Every work of art is an uncommitted crime," Adorno tells us; "talent is sublimated rage."

I have no problem with Adorno's forthright politicization and economic analysis of the contemporary problems of art. He pinpoints hidden social antagonisms lying beneath our formal glossiness, which is all the more subjugating the more it resembles "liberation" from matter. I also think his notion of art as a primary form of resistance to the capitalist definition of happiness as production and the possessions it enables is most useful. But Adorno's vision, which might seem to come from Freud's sublimation, has an even more disenchanting and harder view of the process than Freud's ever did. Art's course is less human and subjective than it is in Freud, and more focused on an almost animal level: for Adorno, its basis in an original temptation to destroy and consume the object results in an exaltation of what he calls the subject (but he means the artist's ego). Exalting the ego, in Adorno, ironically and by the law of dialectic, only leads to the subject's ultimate objectification ("reification"). Adorno, whose true art is a defense against an enjoyment of the object, is really devising a theory of the bourgeois use of art for self-preservation.[28] Art must therefore, according to Adorno, renounce consumption of the object. Art has to be completely honest with itself about its original destructive motives: to go only halfway is to be unwilling to see its own "thorns pointed at" the object, and to become complicitous with capitalist depredation of the object.

Adorno's take on "culture" or "civilization"—and its unwitting relation to race—can be extrapolated from this core of his aesthetic theory: (1) Adorno claims that in modern mass culture art acts *as* the mirror of production, miming the inexhaustible manufacture of products for consumption and thus yields all claim to authority; (2) its sole authority comes from its renunciation of enjoyment (that *rage*, that *crime*, that urge to *devour* he sees at the root of art); (3) yet this crucial claim about art and its disinterestedness rests on a single, but all-important assumption: that the artist is not only capable of forgoing consumption (or *jouissance*) but that he or she is also capable of *indulging* in it. For Adorno, renouncing enjoyment is an elective choice. As we have learned, it is this assumption— that one person, one race, or another can choose to forgo *jouissance* and rid themselves of contamination by it—that underlies racial thinking, for then the other can be seen as enjoying uncontrollably, and at our expense.

In his unconscious belief that *jouissance* is physically and psychically *possible* for the human being, Adorno's ethics founder. He is not very psychoanalytic on this aesthetically ethical point: Adorno seems to take the sadistic superego at its word; you *can* enjoy even though you *must* not.

Adorno, that is, does not situate, as Lacan and philosophers from Descartes to Hegel do, animal *jouissance* as radically foreclosed to the human speaking being, the subject of speech. For him the enjoyment of the object is simply a primary human, and secondary capitalistic, drive. These two come into conflict with each other, the human wanting to enjoy what the capitalist keeps from him. This conflict is, for Adorno, reflected in the dialectic of artistic process: in its worst moment, art mimics and advances capitalism's death drive; in its best, it renounces its own aggressivity and thereby resists the death drive.

If, in Lacanian terms, Adorno simply wanted to fend off the big *O* Other (figured as Industrial Capital as *the* instance of the abusive *jouissance de l'Autre*), that would be one thing. Adorno, however, did not seem to reach a next layer of analysis, in which the possibility of an animal *jouissance* for the human being is cast into radical doubt. If *jouissance* is precisely what is impossible, to forgo it is not a willed choice, as he imagines. The mix of renunciation and resistance (both of which Adorno will link with "castration") is problematic.

The renunciation Adorno recommends to the artist is no more than the sacrifice of what she or he has. He does not understand castration as a symbolic gift of what one does not have, the sort of gift Freud called "holy." The centrality of renunciation in Adorno's thinking, especially where he ties it to castration, has implications along racial lines. In the end, I will suggest that Adorno's thoughts on art were unconsciously affected by race thinking, and not vice versa. He, too, linked color to "civilization," albeit in an inverted form.

Jazz and Adorno's Cultural Politics

Let us turn, then, to Adorno's infamous criticisms of jazz. These texts have always surprised, troubled, and confused his followers. Many have defended them, in the name of an attack on mass culture. But I will treat them here as part of the line of argument I have been developing on race as a political matter rooted in unconscious envy of the other's *jouissance*. In Adorno's denunciation of jazz we will find all the elements of race and racism, including a war over *jouissance,* that I have drawn out above, but in unsuspected guises.

In contrast to the older avatars of white culture or white civilization, Adorno denounced contemporary mass culture precisely for its restraint, its blandness (dare we say pallor?)—for not being quite passionate or colorful enough. He attributes this restraint, this *lack of color,* to the persons of the producers of mass culture. If they sound a bit like the "uncivilized" creatures of Mr. Hume's fancy (see chap. 3), it is not because of their uninhibitedness but because of their "cool" or restraint:

> Jazz . . . integrates stumbling and coming-too-soon into the collective march-step. There is a striking similarity between [the] jazz enthusiast and many of the young disciples of logical positivism, who throw off philosophical culture with the same zeal as jazz fans dispense with the tradition of serious music. Enthusiasm turns into a *matter-of-fact attitude* in which *all feeling* becomes attached to technique, hostile to all meaning. They feel themselves secure within a system so well defined that no mistake could possibly slip by, and the *repressed yearning* for things outside finds expression as *intolerant hatred* and in an attitude which combines the *superior knowledge of the initiate* with the *pretentiousness of the person* without illusions. [29]

For Adorno, it is not in the *whites* (who for Freud were the bearers of excessive restraint in the name of culture) but, instead, in *people of color* (including Jews and women, both of whom Adorno saw as responsible for massifying culture), where freedom is lost.[30] While Adorno seems to be extending Freud's critique of a *civilization of sacrifice,* we must be careful—for it is still an open question as to who has the *jouissance* in Adorno's text.

Jazz and "Castration"

Adorno justified his opposition to jazz on both Marxist and psychoanalytic grounds. He claims excitedly in a letter to Walter Benjamin (of March 18, 1936) that he has arrived "at a complete verdict on jazz, in particular, by revealing its 'progressive' elements (semblance of montage, collective work, primacy of reproduction over production) as façades of something that is in truth quite reactionary. I believe that I have really succeeded in decoding jazz and defining its social function."[31] Adorno jubilantly claimed he had discovered, by way of psychoanalysis, the "problem" with jazz as an art form, its "hidden thorns pointed at the object." They pointed within, toward the body of the black musician. Jazz indexed the black man's utter castration (Adorno's term) by white, capitalist society:

> Psychoanalytic theory alone can provide an adequate explanation of this phenomenon. The aim of jazz is the mechanical reproduction of a regressive moment, a castration symbolism. "Give up your masculinity, let yourself be castrated," the eunuch like sound of the jazz band both mocks and

proclaims, "and you will be rewarded, accepted into a fraternity which shares the mystery of impotence with you, a mystery revealed at the moment of the initiation rite. (*Aesthetics and Politics,* 129)

The conclusion Adorno draws about jazz openly assigns to it the function of maintaining a restricting, "castrating" civilization. The colored folk, far from being a contestatory force, are actually the instrument of forcing us to "comply" with the Other, "the triumph of order."[32]

Adorno, like Alfred Adler, of course, misread castration as emasculation. He had no concept of castration as the acceptance of social coexistence and a simultaneous liberation from the Thing. The condition of assuming the phallus is not that you give up your *jouissance,* but that you realize it has already been taken from you by your human condition. And that you have to come to terms with that loss. You are empowered by the phallus only to the extent that this nothing helps relieve you of the weight of this *jouissance,* this Thing that remains with you—the irrational drive, sex drive, death drive—that speaks to you out of the corner of the superego's mouth. You are never rid of it altogether; you cannot be purged of it.

No animal has to deal with this situation; animals do not have drive. But every human being does. It doesn't go away, and it is crucial that it doesn't: after all, as Freud put it, only drive incites us to "mental labor." Moreover, drive is secondary to cultural existence; it is not animal or natural; it is a returning remainder of *jouissance* that must be dealt with somehow. Cultural encodings: "civilization" cannot live with them; they cannot live without them either—there would be no spur to mental labor.

I believe that Adorno's mistake on castration was unwittingly driven by *race thinking,* in which *jouissance* belongs to the animal and the Other. Adorno might be forgiven such a mistake on a theoretical level, but on another he cannot. His immediate attribution of emasculation for the black artist eunuch secretly encodes the same message as in the Scientology brochure: do not give up your (animal) *jouissance*—or, in other words, stay out of my version of "civilization." By becoming (that is, remaining) animal, you will avoid the sacrifices that I, as a truly civilized human being, endure, and you will be "saved" from submission to it.

Jazz Racism and Anti-Semitism

Adorno, taking up the Freudian theme of "repression" as an indictment of civilization, claimed repression was the hallmark of jazz, which had become a whole subculture characterized by its refusal of self-awareness: "Bombastic triviality, superficiality seen as *apodictic certitude,* transfigures the cowardly defence against every form of self-reflection. All these old accustomed modes of reaction have in recent times lost their innocence, set themselves up as philosophy and thus become truly pernicious" (*Prisms*, 128; emphasis added). I am afraid that *this* is bombast, with its totalizing "theoretical" generalities. It is a posture usually reserved to racists, and to total nerds who feel themselves excluded.

Adorno accuses the jazz enthusiast of committing the forms of racism. "*Bombastic* triviality . . . seen as apodictic certitude. . . . superior knowledge of the initiate. . . . repressed yearning"—all these images that Adorno employs to criticize jazz, images of initiates and secret fraternities, recall the critique of the civilized "club" Freud saw through in "Thoughts on War and Death," but in reverse. Critiquing jazz fans in *Prisms*, Adorno writes:

> Gathered around the specialists in a field in which there is little to understand besides rules are the vague, inarticulate followers. In general they are intoxicated by the fame of mass culture, a fame which the latter knows how to manipulate; they could just as well get together in clubs for worshipping film stars or for collecting autographs. (128)

The very anti-Semitic structures he knew so well play around the edges of his own critique of jazz: *they* have a secret network, *they* are calculating, *they* have no feelings, *they* have too much control, *they* are in fact in control, and so forth. Adorno attributes a snobbery and exclusivity to those who were its first victims: jazz, he tells us, is a "monopoly" that "rests on the exclusiveness of the supply and the economic power behind it" (129). An attribution of reverse racism is not far behind. (Adorno included the Jews of America's Tin Pan Alley as well as black artists in his discovery of the workings of an alienated capitalism in the new art form of jazz.) Indeed, and disappointingly too like the antiracist face of racism today, the words that leave his pen convey a sense of personal injury by this perceived "exclusivity" of jazz.

Even when Adorno seems about to redeem his excessive rhetoric, he disappoints us. Speaking of a difference in American versus European jazz movements, he writes, "Of course, Europeans tend to overlook the fact that jazz fans on the Continent in no way equal those in America" (129). If, when we read this, we expect him to honor jazz's colored and colorful American creators for having produced an undeniably universal gift to civilization, we would be dead wrong. It is the European who is now praised for his spontaneity and rebelliousness over the "repressed" American Negro/Jew of jazz:

The element of excess, of insubordination in jazz, which can still be felt in Europe, is entirely missing today in America. The recollection of anarchic origins which jazz shares with all of today's ready-made mass movements, is fundamentally repressed, however much it may continue to simmer under the surface. Jazz is taken for granted as an institution, housebroken and scrubbed behind the ears. What is common to the jazz enthusiast of all countries, however, is the moment of compliance, in parodistic exaggeration. (129)

That Adorno unwittingly employs the rhetoric of racial thought with respect to jazz should give us all pause; that we have half-heeded it in a figure like Adorno is an index of the perverseness of our time, which can take any insight, including Freud's, in its formal appearance, and speed its predestined Hegelian conversion into its opposite.

Adorno and Race

We need to question still further: what other factors were at work in Adorno to make him vulnerable on the race issue? Why was Adorno unable to avoid the trap of race thinking on this particular subject, his favorite, music?

Adorno's approach to race fundamentally surprises and disturbs us because he refused to recognize it as a factor in his own life. Famous for his remarkable insights on anti-Semitism, this son of a Jewish father (and German mother of Italo-French extraction) was nonetheless reluctant to leave Nazi Germany for Oxford. He writes to a friend in 1938 that he does not personally feel particularly uncomfortable there:

Incidentally I would have been able to hold out perfectly well financially in Germany, and also would have had no political objection; except that every possibility for effectiveness would have been cut off from me, including that of [my music] being performed, and that was why I left; I spend my vacations at home or in the South [Italy].[33]

Adorno's resistance to recognizing racialization—both the general racialization under the Nazis, and to his own by them—was not intellectual and could only have been the result of a certain narcissistic blindness. Why, for example, did he assume he might have the privilege of exemption from the unchecked racialization, that is, the instant creation of enemies, then rampant in his beloved Germany? Why would his passion for fairness and color-blind social justice nevertheless dovetail with the values promoted in Nazi Germany's racialism only when it came to the study of jazz?

Adorno was, however unwittingly, clearly affected by race thinking, a race thinking he was the first to deny as having importance for him, the vehemence of his denial calls for a psychoanalytic interpretation. It would be, of course, much too easy to indict Adorno's criticism of jazz as based on Eurocentric racism or German anti-Semitism. He honored Schoenberg, the Jew, above all others.

In my opinion, what the pandemic of race thinking framed for Adorno was the notion of a *specialness* to be found in culture—"some particular eminence" unattainable by those of a cruder, ruder bent. And what this in turn reflected was perhaps less his open antipathy to his Jewishness inherited through his businessman father than his positive attraction toward what he felt he had received from his maternal line: the "best" of Germany—its high culture, its music in particular. It was his mother's sister, his Aunt Agathe, who opened the world of German classical music to him and offered him a secret refuge from bullying by his peers, as well as access to the "finest" in the world. This special relation to Germany's best was what he would never give up. He was a "racial" not a cultural Jew, a Jew, who by virtue of his own skill and mastery, his knowledge, *had* been admitted to the club, to "the best" that Germanic culture had to offer. He could not let that be taken from him by a rival. No more than Ward Connerly can . . .

Adorno, Art, and Enjoyment

There is much unconscious irony in the way Adorno accuses jazzmen of mechanistic death-driving repetitions, when, of course, all around him were ample reminders of a very particular European social history that surely was in the process of more than earning the outrage he (mis)directed against this art. The important lesson of his passion for ignorance on the racial point is that he *rationalized* his incapacity and his unconscious denial of the race factor with a thesis that called up all the resources of theory—his aesthetic theory and his understanding of psychoanalytic theory—to support his own wishing-away of the race factor in his cultural politics.

Adorno did not see any contemporary artist except the classical German musician as properly mediating what Lacan would later name the subject's relation to *jouissance*. In his theory, *jouissance* must a priori be excluded from art, whose "correct" role (as long as art is not yet in "the state of freedom") is to reproduce a shudder before an original object and to decline to produce new, false objects (*Aesthetics and Politics*, 122). This enjoyment sacrificed in art will be reencountered somewhere else: in life.

Only not just yet, not under capitalism, and only after a Revolution or History has made its way back to an original purer relation to the object. His great artist sacrifices to the Other in the guise not of "civilization" (although Adorno sometimes resorts to the imagery of antibarbarism) but of a future "state of freedom" for art. By refusing to grant something of that liberation to the contemporary art of jazz, Adorno leaves us to assume that sublime freedom is really a restricted province of the Other.

By deferring the question of enjoyment to the future anterior, Adorno removes us from the human register of *desire* (that is, our problematic relation to *jouissance*) and potentially (albeit unwittingly) opens us to the very domain of *abuse* he conscientiously fought against in all other realms.

We can now see disturbing similarities with Ward Connerly's move: the projection back onto a racialized other of one's own investment in having an exclusive privilege vis-à-vis a maternalized culture. Where Connerly fumes that the ethnic "they" (he himself is black) are being exclusive in their graduation parties, Adorno is knocking the "jazz monopoly" for "rest[ing] on the exclusiveness of the supply and the economic power behind it." Have we come very far from the exclusivized version of "sublimity of feeling"—that club—from which Negroes were supposed, by Hume, to be excluded?

What, too, of the *universal?* How does Adorno account for the universal appeal of jazz? Adorno explains it away with a somewhat lame notion:

> Jazz must possess a "mass basis," the technique must link up with a moment in the subject, one which, of course, in turn points back to the social structure and to typical conflicts between the ego and society. What first comes to mind, in quest for that moment, is the eccentric clown or parallels with the early film comics. Individual weakness is proclaimed and revoked in the same breath, stumbling is confirmed as a kind of higher skill. (*Prisms,* 129)

Admitting that his perceived "jazz monopoly" would have been "broken long ago if the ubiquitous specialty did not contain something universal to which people respond," he instantly dubs it the universality of the "eccentric clown" where " . . . weakness is proclaimed and revoked in the same breath, and stumbling is confirmed as a kind of higher skill."

Adorno just "didn't get it." He forgot about the universal, or misconstrued it. He quite failed aesthetically to appreciate the innovative musical form created by African Americans and exported to Europe and the rest of the world. Wherever Adorno comes close to granting the Negro of jazz a universality, he minimizes and belittles it and claims it appeals to the "lowest" in us, sadly reproducing the terms of racialization.

Multiculturalism and the Universal: Beyond Racial Narcissism

Moallem and Boal termed the current crisis for the liberal nation-state as one of "reconciling racial logic with the universal aspirations of enlightenment ideology." I have tried here to show that there is more than one universal in psychoanalysis, as there was eventually to be in Enlightenment thought (I am thinking of Rousseau, and of the later Kant he influenced). It is the universal that places speech, with its effect of deleting and yet calling forth the return of *jouissance,* on the side of the human—each and every human. Wherever the universal is conceived along imaginary superego lines that include the animal Thing within its bounds, we never fail to imagine greater or lesser degrees of separation from that animal—and that Thing. When we do, we near the dangerous region of racial logic and we move away from the only credible version of the universal—the flawed but always promising realm of language, which calls forth the human subject.[34]

In contrast, the Enlightenment model foundered first on a concept of race-as-color that refused acknowledgment of its own aggressivity and death drive. It framed race in an inherently hostile, categorically antagonistic posture (color as flag). Philosophically conceived along imaginary lines, it allied universality to an overwhelming sublimity that dissolved absolute distinctions between men and animals, and that supported degrees of discrimination among humans. But these fine shades covered up the consignment of all but one race to a subhuman animal realm, prey to the Thing.

Adorno's model of a "liberated society" wherein specific differences can be retained at first glance appears both practical and politically correct. Yet something remains amiss. Despite Adorno's rejection of the Enlightenment of Kant and Hume, their worst features resurface in disguise. Hume imagined the Europeans as having a special eminence based on their dedication to being "civilized" or, in other words, castrated (that is, in possession of the phallus). By denouncing the castration of the black man, Adorno unthinkingly consigns the black to a *racial* rather than a *human* identity. The black only apparently lacks *jouissance*: he is artificially confined and straitjacketed by a civilization that is not natural or native to him. He has been castrated. Adorno will magnanimously return it to him. For to have *all* the *jouissance* and none of the castration means that the Negro/Jew would not have the phallus, or symbolic power.

More cruelly perhaps, in this call to *jouissance* Adorno unconsciously makes the jazzman out as not even a slave who, if he does not know, at least *enjoys*. Instead, Adorno reserves the right to enjoyment to the European "race."

Adorno thus unwittingly grants only the European both *jouissance* and Mastery and puts the black "back in his place"—as the castrated animal, at best, no more than Hume's Jamaican, aping the Master,[35] a "parrot" of "parts and learning." Once the colored species is returned to a situation of an animal *jouissance*, only the white race is left to really know the sublimity of sacrificing *jouissance* to the Other.

The paternalism of Adorno's gesture toward the jazzman—don't give up your *jouissance*—reveals the perniciousness of the foundations of racialization to both the white and "colored" races. It excludes the black from his own relation to *jouissance*: it deprives him of desire. Each human subject, as speaking being, is submitted to the signifier: language expels bodily, animal *jouissance*. And each human speaking being must deal with the way in which that *jouissance* is lost (neurosis) and makes its insistent, partial return to them (drive).

Whenever anyone—including the well-meaning Adorno—sees *jouissance* as divided up absolutely between an Other (who has it all) and human groups (who have none), what always follows is a distinction *among* human groups based on their ability or inability to tolerate their castration. It is as if the unconscious racists said to themselves, "Only *I* know the suffering of loss and return of *jouissance*; *they* are full of *jouissance*—all the more so when they act as if they do not have it (like the "cool" restrained jazzmen, pretending to knowledge)"; "I know very well that they're not animals, but all the same, *our* people *do* seem to have 'something eminent,' some special relation to that Other that sets us apart as the only truly *human* group."

The indistinctness of the line dividing animal from human is psychically resolved as an absolute distinction *within* humanity. This is not in any way parallel to recognizing differences between or among peoples, tribes, or nations—the public and overtly political ways of representing a relation to the symbolic order. The imaginary and absolute division of *jouissance* from castration functions to exclude certain peoples from any and all symbolics and is covertly political. With this structure in place, these "others" are not far from being relegated, patronizingly (as in Adorno), or haughtily (as in Hume), to the realm of animal *jouissance*. This division of and in *jouissance* is the foundation of all racialization. As such it is never far from the death drive in narcissism and *its* race for the Real.

Beyond Racial Narcissism?

Freud's race-war essay, "Thoughts for the Time on War and Death," had actually depicted one utopian alternative to the dreadful, race-driven, narcissistic "civilization." After having debunked the virtues of white culture as a superego sham, and after showing how so-called primitives showed superior "ethical sensitiveness" to European warmongers, he went on to describe a utopian community. It was one made up not of blood brothers but of strangers. His vision is almost postmodern in its attempt to overcome race by removing the foreigner or the stranger from the automatic register of enemy. His utopia would be possible only upon the ruins of "civilization" (at least of that kind of civilization that predated the Great War):

> Relying on [a] unity among the civilized peoples, countless men and women have exchanged their native home for a foreign one, and made their existence dependent on the intercommunications between friendly nations. Moreover anyone who was not by stress of circumstance confined to one spot could create for himself out of all the advantages and attractions of these civilized countries a new and wider fatherland, in which he could move about without hindrance or suspicion. In this way he enjoyed the blue sea and the grey; the beauty of snow-covered mountains and of green meadow lands; the magic of northern forests and the splendour of southern vegetation; the mood evoked by landscapes that recall great historical events, and the silence of untouched nature. This new fatherland was a museum for him, too, filled with all the treasures which the artists of civilized humanity had in the successive centuries created and left behind. As he wandered from one gallery to another in this museum, he could recognize with impartial appreciation what varied types of perfection a mixture of blood, the course of history, and the special quality of their mother earth had produced among his compatriots in this wider sense. Here he would find cool, inflexible energy developed to the highest point; there, the graceful art of beautifying existence; elsewhere, the feeling for orderliness and law, or others among the qualities which have made mankind the lords of the earth. (277–78)

The war had intensified the negative aspects of "civilization"; the benign relationship among peoples that Freud, and many in Europe such as Walter Benjamin, had imagined possible prior to World War I had been shown to be unworkable. As long as abusive power (conscious or unconscious) underlies civilization (and according to Rousseau's civil society and Hegel's vision, that is always the case), the innocent commingling of peoples can never take place. Small wonder that Freud's picture requires that civilization be already a mere museum. This impossible Freudian model of a society made up of strangers is less that of a liberal (or free-market) nation-state—like the European Community or the United States—than of a liberalized one, with those foreign to each other freely allowed to roam what would be essentially the ruins of civil society. It is entirely unworkable where racialization prevails.

Of course, we would like to hope that racism today is well on its way out, that we are duly and properly educated to the lingering irrationality we inherited from racism's first coming in an insufficiently enlightened Enlightenment. But there are clouds on our multicultural horizon. Étienne Balibar, Renata Salecl, Minoo Moallem, and Iain Boal have all impressed on us that the escape hatches we have created for peaceful cohabitation among the races are fast becoming new metaracisms: do we not hear the echo of Freud's "civilization" even in "multiculturalism"? Two critics claim that the term is now "a shibboleth that continues to efface all historicity in its consumption of the present" and naturalizes "cultural identity" as "incompatible cultural differences."[36] Far from protecting a culture's own relation to its enjoyments, it functions instead as a "natural" determinative force, "locking individuals and groups a priori into their cultural genealogy,"[37] a noble term that makes sense only in the context of admission to The Race, The House of Aristocracy.

We are in a race against time on this issue. As fewer and fewer places remain racially homogeneous under economic globalization, we need better and more sophisticated models of the universal, models that allow for cultural specificity (a culture's own patrimony) and help to protect it from the predations of a pseudouniversality ("civilization" for the Victorians, the "new world order" for today). We also stand in need of much better models for coexistence, for that kind of negative universal Rousseau dreamed of. They are scant, and those out there require reformulation.

Lest you think Freud's vision eternally unworkable, then, I would like to offer you one new strategy that the City of San Francisco employed to integrate its school system (at least until the 1996 elections). The San Francisco Bay Area is a region with the greatest number of distinctive ethnicities living side by side in the United States. To comply with a U.S. Federal desegregation order, black educator Lulann McGriff devised the following ingenious system:

> Anyone who has sent a child to public school in San Francisco in the past 14 years knows of the city's strange and complicated enrollment system. They know that living across the street from a school is no guarantee of going

there. They know they can apply to any school, but getting in depends on an odd jumble of factors: a child's ethnicity, a school's ethnic balance, where the siblings go to school, and even the family zip code.

San Francisco's desegregation program requires that at least four ethnic groups be represented at each school, with no group exceeding 45 percent of enrollment. Students may declare themselves to be any one of nine ethnic groups—and may change that designation once.

Despite the complexity—or because of it—San Francisco schools are among the most integrated in the nation.[38]

Wherever the abusive core of civilization (the Other's supposed theft of *jouissance*) is not faced, this whimsical Butlerian fancy of a racial rather than gender masquerade will, however, come up short.

5. Fascism and the Voice of Conscience

The less you eat, drink, and buy books, the less you go to the theatre, the
dance hall, the public house; the less you think, love, theorize, sing, paint,
fence, etc., the more you save—the greater becomes your treasure which
neither moths nor dust will devour—your capital.
> —Karl Marx, *Economic and Philosophical Manuscripts*

Fascism is obscene in so far as it perceives directly the ideological form as
its own end, as an end in itself—remember Mussolini's famous answer to
the question "How do the Fascists justify their claim to rule Italy? What is
their programme?"; "Our programme is very simple: we want to rule
Italy!" The ideological power of Fascism lies precisely in the feature which
was perceived by liberal or leftist critics as its greatest weakness; in the utterly void, formal character of its appeal, in the fact that it demands obedience and sacrifice for their own sake. For Fascist ideology, the point is not
the instrumental value of the sacrifice, it is the very form of the sacrifice itself, "the spirit of sacrifice," which is the cure against the liberal-decadent
disease. It is also clear why Fascism was so terrified by psychoanalysis:
psychoanalysis enables us to locate an obscene enjoyment at work in this
act of formal sacrifice.
> —Slavoj Žižek, *The Sublime Object of Ideology*

Fascism and Genocide

Democracy is under serious assault these days. Global capitalism, in tandem with the displacement of community by networking, have asserted themselves as major antidemocratic forces (although apologists of both would disagree—believing that the equation of "democracy" with the "free market" was established long ago). With the minority election of representatives, and the self-destruct mode of legislative bodies, a stylistic fascism has begun to creep back into fashion in every sense (see, for example, reminiscences of 1930s Italy in recent clothing). In the new, improved stylized fascism, overt racial hatred is disavowed under the banner of "love" (or the united colors of . . .).[1] The colorful is championed as exotic, local; all sorts are welcome. While excesses such as ethnic cleansings are also occurring, they are depicted in the media as marginal, unrelated to mainstream political forms and legal structures. One speaks of "fundamentalisms" with a religious basis or "deep-seated historic conflicts." If we have gotten over the "possessive investment in whiteness," our racism has mutated in a highly disturbing way.[2]

Critical analyses of racism, even some of the psychoanalytically inflected ones, underplay racism's genocidal telos, but more damagingly, they fail to implicate fascist structural arrangements in contemporary ethnic hatreds and their implicit end.[3] Why are current instances of fascism, which have taken on a down-home air, especially on the airwaves, exempted from reminders of their historical connection to genocide?

Why are we skittish about political generalizing from what Hannah Arendt called the unprecedented and horrendous event known as the Holocaust? Why does democracy itself seem to have a bad conscience on this topic, even to the point of ignoring the issue as long as lip service is given by crypto-, proto-, or openly neofascists to the "unthinkability" of genocide? One answer, on the conservative side, is the lure of nostalgia: fascism today adopts a patriarchal aura. (Let us remind ourselves that this aura is false; the nostalgia feeds off the forms that fascism destroys.)[4]

There is also, on the Left, an understandable desire to preserve the Holocaust as absolutely unique. This would be fine, if such an event were truly never to recur. Unfortunately, the uniqueness of the Holocaust is being challenged by the horrifying outcomes of countless contemporary ethnic clashes, clashes whose stated goal of clean-sweeping and cleansing force us to recall their singular precedent and to doubt its status as a hapax legomenon.

Today's "cultural critics" are clearly not doing enough to increase our understanding of the basic *economic* differences between fascism and democracy (industrialization, self-taxation, entrepreneurship, etc.); nor have they adequately drawn the appropriate *legal* and *ethical* distinctions we need to secure our democracies from fascism's inroads. But it is perhaps even more important in this effort for us to detail the differences at the *psychic* level, the level of the heart, since it is at this level that fascism's ideological appeal to the individual persists today.[5] My focus here, then, will be on the mechanism of its appeal to the reserves of antidemocratic impulses in any individual subject, as these are uniquely intensified under any in-place fascist regime. That appeal is not to our dreams and our desires but to the painful topic of our enjoyment and its loss.

In what follows I show how the *voice* as *object a* is implicated in fascism's appeal, and that it is connected to the superego and to the disavowal of castration. But I must reaffirm my intent to retain genocide as the central issue in distinguishing fascism from, and in opposition to, democracy. I will analyze the role the voice played in enabling the "banality of evil," the normalization of heinous acts that resulted in the Holocaust. But I use a firmly Lacanian, rather than Derridean, approach because Derrida's critique of voice (which relates to Lacan's voice as *object a*) was obscured, in the Anglo-American translation of his work, under the blanket term *speech*.[6] My case is that of Adolf Eichmann, as it is detailed in Hannah Arendt's penetrating study *Eichmann in Jerusalem*.[7]

The Role of the Voice in Fascist Fantasy

Voice differs from speech, which is a social pact and act. For Lacan, the signifier in speech also precipitates an unconscious relation of the subject to enjoyment *(jouissance)*.[8] Voice is this precipitate; it is already a phantom locus of enjoyment, an *object a*. In the fascist unconscious, voice as *object a* became the embodiment of a principle behind the law of speech,[9] of speech-as-social-pact. That principle is the will of the people, but psychically taken to be the will to *jouissance* of an unbarred Other.

Voice, as unconscious fantasy object, exists on a different plane from Foucault's *discourse*. The discursive is a broad set of practices (e.g., Lacan's four discourses) that result from positions taken up in relation to speech.[10] In my analysis I treat discursively (in Lacan's sense) the problematic relation of discourse to voice in two parallel, competing, but strangely complementary ethics—Kant's and Sade's. Both ethics were contrived at the dawn of modern democracy. If we are to understand how fascism—and its strong arm, genocide—was unwittingly allowed to enter the world stage at the same point where modern democracy also made its debut, fine distinctions are necessary. In the case of genocide, the role of the *voice as object a* was apparently decisive.

Lacan introduced, with the disavowal of its *object a* in fantasy, the material form of a second-order alienation of the subject, an alienation that takes place in the perversion known as fascism: not through just any *object a*, but specifically through the *voice*. This has been noted by several analysts, including Mladen Dolar:

> Fascism feeds on the voice, onto death. This is the case of Peter Gemeinder, who died of exhaustion, in August, 1931, after a speech of two hours, preceded by 2000 other speeches. . . . But what does this exalting voice say exactly? We don't get to know by reading the fascist reports of fascist speeches. We find a flood of words on the impressions of the reporter . . . on the atmosphere of the public, dead silences, ovations, etc. In the long poetization by Goebbels on his first encounter with the Führer we find only three specific words that the Führer speaks . . . "honor, work, flag."[11]

Dolar concludes that "merely by emitting a voice the master becomes master, and merely by virtue of being the receiver of this voice ('his master's voice') a crowd becomes a crowd" (205). In short, fascism submits itself to what Lacan called "the invocatory drive" and its object.

Voice as Object a

Voice takes shape, for Lacan, as one of the *objects a* around which "partial drives" turn: the drives find their specific *embodiment* in fantasy objects. In other words, the partialness of Freudian drives is translated in Lacan by the partialness of objects: gaze, voice, breast, feces. While the drives themselves are defined as death seeking,[12] their objects are all representatives of life force or libido. For the subject of the unconscious they represent various forms of *jouissance* that life in society forbids, though they are, in fact, less forbidden than unbearable and unavowable.[13]

Classically, symbolically, these partial drives and their objects are subordinated to a larger ideological construction of identification for the subject, however much that identification may invert the real relations of production of the subject. In recent times, where the drives have become the only site left for an enjoyment denied in workaday reality, more perverse twists start to work. Through sacrifice, surplus enjoyment becomes phantasmatically located wholly in the Other. The subject, fantasizing prematurely its overcoming of alienating identifications, merely becomes the instrument of that Other's enjoyment, unconsciously identifying with the *object a*, rather than taking it on as an object of desire, as a fulcrum of its own fantasy.

Lacan says: "The *object a* ... is never found in the position of being the aim of desire. ... It is either pre-subjective, or the foundation of an identification of the subject, or the foundation of an identification disavowed by the subject."[14] The *object a* is always the center of identity and it is always consciously disavowed as that center: who, after all, would want to admit that something like a piece of shit lies at the center of his existence?[15] For the desiring subject, the *object a* only comes into its own in the fantasy, the staging of the subject's desire. For the perverse subject, this object is brought out into the light and an effort is made to stage its centrality as if it were a satisfaction. For the fascist subject, desire is foreclosed, fantasy becomes realized, and the *object a* loses all distinction from the real of death, *jouissance,* the Thing.

Democracy and Fantasy, Fascism and Jouissance

The inaugural terms of democracy included the "right to pursue happiness." Though opened with this enunciation of a freedom to desire, democratic societies often enough devolved, under unbridled capitalism, Lacan once noted, into the freedom to starve. Wherever a promise to secure a happiness that is quite obviously missing develops, fascism threatens. Such freedom to desire as is proclaimed in democracy is by no means necessarily a happy experience from the point of view of a subject. Desire divides the subject, in the mise-en-scène of desire, fantasy. The split is as simple as that exhibited by the daydreamer, who for Freud was both "author" and "hero."[16] Securing full enjoyment for a split subject can only be delivered phantasmatically. When the project of total *jouissance,* articulated by Sade for his bedroom, but dreamed of by anyone radically deprived, spreads to become a social and economic ideal—or, rather, ideology—fascism threatens.

A desiring subject arrays its fantasy of fulfillment around the enjoyment of an object (its *object a* cause of desire). This subject also deeply knows, by virtue of the very "unrealized" nature of its fantasy, that this object is "lost." The subject—who "enjoys" the object in and of the fantasy—is also witness to fact of the nonrealization of its own *jouissance* of this object. This is the structure of desire. Society founded along its lines differs from the fascist idealization of enjoyment. To know that the Other "wants" and is as devoid of enjoyment as we ourselves are permits us to face our own lack, our own want of *jouissance.*[17] (This is not as ascetic as it sounds, since *jouissance* is not only bliss; it is also that pain and humiliation only a social animal can experience.) Were we actually to experience full *jouissance,* our balance would be destroyed. Although the subject dreams of getting out from under its "castration by the signifier" (which means its compromise with social coexistence), and of accessing some prelinguistic *jouissance*, its only "liberation" arrives by way of the fantasy, and then only "by linking it essentially ... to the condition of an object."[18] That object is the good thing we tell ourselves we need for our happiness; but in reality it is only a way of lifting off the abusive things that have befallen us. It is the focal point of the "subject's claim to something that is separated from him, but belongs to him and which he needs to complete himself."[19]

This *object a* has "no alterity."[20] Unlike the signifier it is not caught up in endless metaphors and metonymies. It seems to be a "bit of the real," but it only appears as the point of satisfaction of partial drives that can reach it only in hallucination and fantasy. It purveys for the subject a whisper that the *jouissance* we have had taken from us is partially reclaimable in fantasy.[21] This *object a* is a way of accessing but also protecting us from our Thing.

According to Lacan, however, we have experienced a "cultural loss of the object" in modern life.[22] The original "alienation by the signifier" (the original "eclipse" of the subject in the signifier) has increased[23] with the growth of imaginary identifications at the expense of symbolic ones—imaginary identifications with an Ideal I of the sort crucial to group psychology—and fascism. A short-circuiting of fantasy takes place in the appeal of fascism. Fascism promises the subject an end to alienation (you can have joy in work, even if your labor is alienated). It disavows that you are ultimately separated from the real—by your *object a*. It is built around "realizing" fantasy, of putting you in the presence of a kind of super*jouissance.*

As Slavoj Žižek has described it, fascism always demands extraordinary sacrifices in the name of this extra *jouissance*:

> Fascist ideology is based upon a purely formal imperative; Obey, because you must! In other words, renounce enjoyment, sacrifice yourself and do not ask about the meaning of it—the value of the sacrifice lies in its very meaninglessness; true sacrifice is for its own end; you must find positive fulfillment in the sacrifice itself, not in its instrumental value; it is this renunciation, this giving up of enjoyment itself, which produces a certain surplus-enjoyment. This surplus produced through renunciation is the Lacanian *objet petit a*, the embodiment of surplus-enjoyment.[24]

The loss of your own claim to the object is to be recompensed with a surplus enjoyment over what you could have squeezed out of your own paltry fantasies, provided that you identify yourself with the One who enjoys beyond mere men.

Fascism preempts the subject's freedom to fantasize, to desire. It skirts the level of a disruptive drive that it would require mental labor to handle. It enslaves with excess work in the name of a deeper mental indolence: it implies or declares that *jouissance* is ready at hand: you need engage in no action to defend against it or attempt to access it. Its corollary is the unification of the subject, which under fascism is announced as available, provided one gets "beyond" desire and mere dreaming.[25] "What is Alexander's proclamation when he arrived in Persepolis or Hitler's when he arrived in Paris? . . . 'Carry on working. Work must go on.' Which of course means, 'Let it be clear to everyone that this is on no account the moment to express the least surge of desire.'"[26] What emerges when the subject yields on his desire is, however, harrowing: reality *as* a fantasy, fixed, static, ready-to-wear. By virtue of this short-circuit, fascism's real field is that of *castration,* where a split is made permanent between the subject of enjoyment and the subject of lack, without even a fantasized hope. Yet its appeal accelerates under these privative conditions. What is its hidden mechanism?

The Structure of Fascism's Appeal

Fascism is a technical term, not simply an epithet hurled by 1960s radicals at oppressive authority figures. It was the first systematic opposition to modern democracy, and it remains its only real opponent, politically and economically. No one fears a return to monarchy, and communism is "dead." Fascism was founded on antidemocratic principles for structuring relations between owners and producers, races and sexes.[27] At the outset, it was an industrial economic mode of production of a special type.[28]

Classical fascism as an economic structure was modeled on, but not materially connected to, patriarchal feudal forms. Though firmly hierarchical, it was supposed to incorporate all members of a productive unit in one structure. From the lowest floor sweeper to the CEO and the owner, all were supposed to be part of a single corporate body. One spoke of joy in work, and of making the workplace pleasant.[29] Produced goods were owned by *patrons,* who were, in exchange for these goods, supposed to care for their workers. Under capitalism, work had become increasingly disconnected from access to the products it created, as salaries never covered the "cost of living," and the owner could callously disregard his workers' needs. This often happened, especially in the Great Depression. Fascist-organized corporations in contrast promised to provide certain essentials to workers, health care, housing, and so on.

Despite this ideology of paternalism, however, the worker under fascism was structurally without personal value and rights. Workers were expendable to the degree that they were replaceable; the ideal worker would actually be, and in German fascism was, a slave.

As a pseudopatriarchy, industrial fascism could call up and call on a repertoire of fixed patriarchal stereotypes for purposes of nostalgia (most often nostalgia for the very things it had been instrumental in destroying). But if the corporate structure superficially resembled a lord-peasant relation, the stakes for owner and worker were completely different. A feudal lord needed his laborers to live (if not well) in order to produce and harvest the food they all required. (The "consumer" part of "consumer goods" is an interesting reminiscence of the agricultural model.) The pseudofeudalism of fascist ideology was belied by the fact that fascism was founded by Mussolini's party as politically nationalistic, partly out of opposition to the internationalism of unions, which cut across national boundaries to secure workers' rights. But its ideological appeal caught at the heart of worker-victims through more than its pretense to "paternalistic" care. It spoke to them of *jouissance*.

Where sacrifice (or foreclosure of desire) is called for, hearts and minds are moved to renunciation by something, some unrecognized object. In the case of fascism, it is the voice as *object a*, apprehended as coming from beyond the laws of desire. The voice is the most omnipresent of the *objects a* for Lacan: in contrast to the way the other sense organs are libidinally attached to desire, the ear cannot be closed. Voice requires no recognizable fantasy frame to be experienced as irrupting within the subject from without—"extimately," as an Other—as if it were not an object.

As such, a vocal imperative (as distinct from written law) is capital in securing the renunciation that allows fascism its grip on the subject.

Voice and Will-to-Jouissance *in Genocide*

That a ferocious will-to-*jouissance* currently inhabits the discourse of "rights" is not to be doubted. But how did this situation evolve? Is it enough to say that will-to-*jouissance* is itself fascist when early capitalism similarly exhibited such a will through its dream of unlimited profit? The critical figure for thinking this question is undoubtedly Sade, with his depiction of endless orgasms. Aristocrat-turned-sansculotte Sade proclaimed "right" in the new Republic as the right to unlimited enjoyment. Sade provided Lacan with a foil for Kant and his notion of moral law, while for Horkheimer and Adorno he was "precursor" of fascism. Which was he? We can begin to answer this question by noting that Sade figures an unlimited "will-to-*jouissance*"[30] that applies, theoretically, more to democratic "equality" than to "hierarchical" fascism. Sade's maxim, "I have the right to enjoy your body, and you have the right to enjoy mine," sums this up. One should not, then, too casually connect the sadism of Sade with fascism, but neither should one presume that his version of democratic "equality" is not abusive and deluded. It is. Lacan's four fundamental discourses (which all relate the subject of desire to the *object a*) had to be stretched to account for Sade, just as postdemocratic political philosophy has to stretch to account for its evil clone, fascism. Sadism is a response, according to Lacan, to the *jouissance* of the Other as *voice*, rather than to the desire of (lack in) the Other as *speech*. But it is not yet a fascist response.

Lacan's reading of Sade's *La Philosophie dans le boudoir* as companion piece to Kant's *Critique of Pure Reason* forces us to recognize the parallels that exist between the pair's vocal imperatives: "Enjoy!" and "Obey!" By stripping the Law of any mythic-rhetorical pretense of being motivated by the Good, Kant placed the Law in the territory of the Drive. That is, though he successfully eliminated every pathological object as source of the moral law, Kant, like Sade, allowed the law a source in another kind of object—the voice as *object a*.[31] The cost of Kant's foundation of ethics on a nonpathological basis may have been an unwitting empowerment of the Thing *(Das Ding)*.[32] While Kant seemed to believe that distance, achieved through the sacrificial eradication of the object of desire, would provide guarantee for the autonomy of the will, it turned out not to be the case. For the distance that was supposed to intervene between us and the Thing instead often became enacted as Sadean apathy, an apathy that put us *closer* to the object in the drive.

Let me be blunt, then, about my thesis: that the origin of the possibility of what Arendt names the "new crime" of bureaucratic genocide arises only with the opening of modern democracy (the attribution of will to the individual and hence, as in Rousseau, to the "people");[33] that this crime is democracy's chief and most constant danger, made possible wherever the "will" is appropriated by fascism under very particular but not uncommon conditions; and that the reasons why this crime threatens democratic civilization continually is that there is no written commandment, no written law against genocide. Where will operates through the voice as *object a*, there lies the danger.

A written law—independent of the voice of conscience—against genocide, which would prohibit the annihilation of one people by another as the moral equivalent of murder for the individual, has seemed unthinkable for us. Why? Because the "people," not the individual, would be the subject of such a law. Under such a hypothetical law, many issues would be sub-joined. For example, capital punishment, abortion, state-run sterilization programs, the destruction of viable lands, euthanasia, suicide doctors, hate crimes, even today's patenting of genetic material, and so on, would all be argued as matters transcending issues of individual rights and choices, and would become subject to other kinds of questions: the racial makeup of death-row inmates,[34] the statistical distribution of the availability of prenatal care, sterilization, abortion by race, and so on.

There is perhaps a technical and crucial reason why genocide, while ab-horred, has not been legislated against in our modern democratic states.[35] To understand this reason, we must first go back to the transformation of the notion of law that was the very condition of modern democracy. We must go back to Kant, and to the notion of *will*, or *good will*, that subtends a notion of Law as a vocal imperative rather than as the repression of a desire.

In Kant, the Law becomes a formal, empty universality by an evacuation of all content.[36] This emptiness is what permits the universality of the Law, which is both liberatory for the subject and an obvious prerequisite to any democratic order. But Kant did not leave things with this negative moment of merely formal emptiness, insisting instead on a need to pass to the act. While empty, the law is not entirely mute but appears as a voice, a maxim, a universal "Ought" or pure positive command to *duty*, "You must!"[37] In contrast to that law that merely inhibits an action ("You must not!"), Kant's practical reason demands, in the form of duty, "that a man do more than obey the law": he must "go beyond the mere call of obedience and identify his own will with the principle behind the law—the source from which the law sprang.[38] There is an excess in Kant's voice of conscience, a demand to go beyond.

Under traditional circumstances, what is known as "common law"—the normal, customary forms of conscience and the ordinary way we relate to each other—would preclude the tacit or overt legitimation of genocidal practices. But these are not traditional and customary times. The case can be made, as Arendt makes it, that customary forms of conscience are precisely what were openly overcome by fascism. Unfortunately, then, it may be necessary to consider the need for a positive law on genocide. Perhaps we require, after so much freedom to prescribe our own laws, a reminder by means of written law's alien or "dead" letter of the horrific character of its object—that all law must ultimately seem to come to us as if from an Other.[39] When that Other becomes too close to us, appearing as our own voice from within, we risk the worst.

Self-legislation, whether Kantian (or superegoic), is the necessary stake of democracy. But some of its riskiest aspects might be diminished by a less naive version of the good will than Kant was able to articulate.[40] This version should question our reliance on our "inner voice," which is insufficiently alien to mark its own limits.

Kant avec Eichmann

Kant's moral philosophy, which displaced Aristotelian ethics once and for all, is ultimately linked to man's faculty of judgment, which rules out blind obedience and condemns the instrumentalization of the other.[41] As such, the sadistic-perverse fantasy relation, where the other becomes the object/instrument or agent of the Other's enjoyment, should be a priori precluded. In Nazi Germany, however, the faculty of judgment quite obviously failed in this regard, and this failure has inserted a permanent warp into Kantian ethics, our ethics. This warp was almost simultaneously detected by Lacan, who published "Kant avec Sade" in 1963, and Hannah Arendt, who published *Eichmann in Jerusalem* in the *New Yorker* that same year.[42]

Thinkers from quite different fields, Arendt and Lacan each found themselves disturbed at precisely the same moment by an excess or perversion that Kant's moral philosophy had not precluded, even if it did not lend itself to it completely.[43] Lacan analyzed a scandalous closeness between Kant's maxims and Sade's. Arendt, writing about a different kind of perversion, documented and analyzed the proclamation of Adolf Eichmann, who administered the Final Solution, that, in faithfully carrying out his "duty," he was enacting a "version of Kant 'for the household use of the little man'" (*Eichmann*, 136).

Eichmann's invocation of Kant at his trial was for him no hypocritical cover-up: by all accounts, not only his own, Eichmann was motivated by only one thing: "He did his *duty*, as he told the police and the court over and over again; he not only obeyed *orders*, he also obeyed the *law*" (134). Dimly struggling to make clear that he was not just a "soldier carrying out orders that were clearly criminal in nature and intent," Eichmann "declared with great emphasis that he had lived his whole life according to Kant's moral precepts, and especially according to a Kantian definition of duty" (135–36).

Arendt, aghast, adamantly objects to Eichmann's self-declared Kantian ethics: "This was outrageous on the face of it, and also incomprehensible, since Kant's moral philosophy is so closely bound up with man's faculty of judgment, which rules out blind obedience" (136). She contests it but goes on to argue something interesting about how what Kant demanded in the name of duty had been misunderstood:

In this household use, all that is left of Kant's spirit is the demand that a man do more than obey the law, that he go beyond the mere call of obedience and *identify his own will with the principle behind the law—the source from which the law sprang.* In Kant's philosophy that source was practical reason; in Eichmann's household use of him, it was the will of the Führer. (136; emphasis added)

Although he clearly distorted it, Eichmann actually had specifically singled out *The Critique of Practical Reason* as his personal moral guide and spontaneously spouted an "approximately correct definition of the categorical imperative" (136) to the astonishment of Judge Raveh and the audience at his trial in Jerusalem:

I meant by my remark about Kant that the principle of my will must always be such that it can become the principle of general laws (which is not the case with theft or murder, for instance, because the thief or the murderer cannot conceivably wish to live under a legal system that would give others the right to rob or murder him).

Eichmann added that he had

read Kant's *Critique of Practical Reason*. He then proceeded to explain that from the moment he was charged with carrying out the Final Solution he had ceased to live according to Kantian principles, that he had known it, and that he had consoled himself with the thought that he no longer "was master of his own deeds," that he was unable "to change anything." (136)

Eichmann did ultimately confess to having abandoned Kant and betraying the Law rooted in the Kantian principle, claiming as his excuse that he had been "mastered" or overpowered by a force or will beyond his own.

But though this admission ought to have vindicated Arendt's severe objections to his claim of having been guided by Kant, she shows some hesitancy: hadn't Kant actually in some way demanded identification with a "principle behind the law," the "source" from which it sprang? She worries whether Eichmann had really "forgotten" Kant as he set to work accomplishing the Final Solution, finding "the Kantian formula . . . no longer applicable," or whether he had instead employed it in a twisted way. She is inclined to believe that rather than abandoning it altogether

he had distorted it to read: Act as if the principle of your actions were the same as that of the legislator or of the law of the land—or, in Hans Frank's formulation of "the categorical imperative in the Third Reich," which

Eichmann might have known: "act in such a way that the Führer, if he knew your action, might approve it" [*Die Technik des Staates* (1942), 15–16]. (136)

The scandal here is less that Kant's principles did not hold against a will to transgress them, but that something in Kant's very principle seemed to an Eichmann (and a Hans Frank) to lend itself to this particular distortion. At best, nothing in the structure of the law conceived on Kantian lines worked to disable this particular perversion—in the end the law failed to resist the will-to-*jouissance*. Not Eichmann's will, but that of the Führer. Here we have stumbled upon the paradox of democracy's peculiar susceptibility to totalitarianism: people who rule themselves with absolute freedom find themselves perpetually threatened with rule by dictatorship.[44]

Thus, while Arendt details the philosophical errors that permitted such a deadly misreading of the upright German idealist, she does not totally exonerate him or his theory from the consequences of this misreading. She leaves open the possibility that the empty moral law is, if taken the wrong way, highly vulnerable to the fascist as well as sadistic perversion. "To be sure," she argues,

> Kant had never intended . . . anything of the sort; on the contrary, to him every man was a legislator the moment he started to act: by using his "practical reason" man found the principles that could and should be the principles of law. But it is true that Eichmann's unconscious distortion agrees with what he himself called the version of Kant "for the household use of the little man." (136)

The Voice, Moral Conscience, and the Law

> Let us observe that the herald of the maxim does not need to be anything more than a point of emission. It can be a voice on the radio. . . . Such vocal phenomena, notably those of psychosis, indeed have this aspect of the object. And psychoanalysis was not far in its dawn from referring the voice of conscience to them.
>
> —Lacan, "Kant avec Sade"

At this point let us focus more directly on the remainder for which Kant left us unprepared, that is, the object left behind by his clean sweep of pathological objects of desire: the *object-cause-of-desire*. Analytically, this means we must address the question of castration, and the way it installs the modern superego, the voice of conscience, and successor to the "father" of Oedipal patriarchy.[45] For if fascism hooks the hearts and minds of a people, by determining its will rather than democratically permitting it to ask itself what "it wants,"[46] it does so through an implied threat of castration. Anecdotally, Lyndon Baines Johnson was reputed to have provided the (truncated) name for the U.S. community development program for South Vietnam—Hearts and Minds—with his pithy: "When you've got them by the balls, their hearts and minds will follow." Not castration but its disavowal *articulates* the appeal of fascism.

Before Kant, to act ethically meant to conform one's desires to the moral law, which described the set of behaviors conducive to the achievement of the goal of happiness. After Kant, the subject of desire could no longer conform but, rather, came into fateful conflict with moral law. In Lacan's rereading, Kantian moral law is nothing but desire in its pure state,[47] which means that the subject must not give in to but *resist* the voice commands of the superego. By ceding to its commands, we surrender our desire. While the original moral voice—the Jewish God—proffered the Ten Commandments as an alien being, the moral voice of conscience evoked in the texts of Rousseau, Kant, even Freud, proceeds from an Other within the self. This pseudoother, or superego, increasingly obscene, is felt within, "like a stranger":

> As . . . [the I] progresses in its experience, it asks itself [this] question and asks it precisely in the place where strange, paradoxical, and cruel commands are suggested to it by its morbid experience.
>
> Will it or will it not submit itself to the duty that it feels within like a stranger, beyond, at another level? Should it or should it not submit itself to the half-unconscious, paradoxical, and morbid command of the superego, whose jurisdiction is moreover revealed increasingly as the analytical exploration goes forward and the patient sees that he is committed to its path?
>
> If I may put it thus, isn't its true duty to oppose that command?[48]

Arendt likewise backs away from granting any longer to the inner voice of conscience the function of moral law: "Just as the law in civilized countries assumes that the voice of conscience tells everybody 'Thou shalt not kill,' even though man's natural desires and inclinations may at times be murderous, so the law of Hitler's land demanded that the voice of conscience tell everybody: 'Thou shalt kill'" (150). Genocide by administration fully depended on that "inner voice," unassimilable to any of its previous iterations. Speaking of the simplistic and overly traditional way in which the new crime, administrative massacre, was treated by the prosecutors in Jerusalem, Arendt complains:

To fall back on an unequivocal voice of conscience—or, in the even vaguer language of the jurists, on a "general sentiment of humanity" (Oppenheim-Lauterprach in *International Law,* 1952)—not only begs the question, it signifies a deliberate refusal to take notice of the central moral, legal, and political phenomena of our century. (148)

Lacan, arguing that the *perverted* position with respect to the voice as *object* was taken up by Sade, the aristocrat-turned-Republican, provides another instructive model for analyzing Eichmann, chief administrator of the Final Solution under Hitler. The perverse position, which disavows castration, works, as I claimed earlier, through a perverse identification of the self with the *object a* in its role as *agent* of the *jouissance de l'Autre.*[49] With this in mind, I would like to reexamine Arendt's analysis of the relation between Eichmann and Kant. Before beginning, it is important to note that whereas, under monarchy, the subject could structurally remain a subject no matter how much he labored for the king's pleasure, the same does not hold when the Leader, like the self, is also sacrificing . . .

Portrait of Eichmann: Voice and the Normalization of Excess

In her chilling, difficult, and heartbreaking report on the banality of evil, Hannah Arendt portrays Adolf Eichmann as a kind of neutral functionary, neither hero nor victim of his criminal acts. She finds that his actions cannot be viewed in the perspective of a traditional morality play. In this, she goes against the grain, accepting analytically Eichmann's self-professed "normality." But she sees his normality less as an index of his mental health than as an index of the fact of the existence, on the world scene, of a state whose norm was "thou shalt" rather than "thou shalt not" kill.

Watching without sentimentality[50] Eichmann's long, drawn-out trial—tellingly, *not* on charges of genocide, but of "crimes against the Jewish people" and "crimes against Humanity"—unfold in Jerusalem, Arendt waits in vain for the customary theater of justice to open its dramatization of good and evil in his case. The dramatization does not catch fire. Arendt grows alarmed when the traditional scene of judgment does not materialize either: the stage that places the evildoer *between* a judge who represents the community and the community for whom the judge speaks. Instead, it is Eichmann who commands center stage.

A man of "rather modest mental gifts" (135), Eichmann is the man in the glass booth, whose transparency and shielding are both a metaphor for the trial itself and what place him in the typical posture of the "woman" subject, weak and on display. Arendt deems his physical position—placed *below* tier upon tier of judges, translators, and officials, and *between* the prosecutors and the courtroom—as precluding the traditional work of justice.

Those who watch Eichmann ("medium-sized, slender, middle-aged, with receding hair, ill-fitting teeth, and nearsighted eyes" [5]) over the shoulders of the prosecutors form no "community" whose standards he could be said to have violated. Why are the charges of "crimes against the Jewish people" and "crimes against Humanity" *separate* charges? The charges themselves err by over- or underspecificity. The result is that the "Jewish people/Humanity"—the "victims"—are not as concrete and defined as the man in the glass booth.

In fact, both the Jewish people and Humanity have a reduced, remote role, relegated to being an "audience" of literally *no one*—which means, really, that they are an audience composed of everyone in the world (former victims and bystanders both). Cast as mere onlookers, peering over the shoulders of the prosecutors at the man who ordered and arranged for the deaths of a whole people, they have their opinions shaped mainly by the physical appearance of the man, not by the standards of their "community." Under these conditions, Arendt makes clear, Eichmann is the one who looks like a victim, not an instigator, capable at best of having been an instrument but not an originator of evil, whose source will be as inexplicable, nebulous, and undefined as the Humanity he sinned against.

There is an Evil, though its shape is still obscure. Arendt proposes that something "altogether unprecedented" was at work in the very acts of the man who is on trial, a "new crime," for which the "prevailing legal system and current juridical concepts" are entirely inadequate (294). What cannot be dealt with—justly—under the older forms of separation of individual guilt and group responsibility is "administrative massacre organized by state apparatus" (294). And yet Arendt wants to be able to refer it to Eichmann, to his personal "judgment." She terms her work a "report on his conscience."

Thus, though she is a political philosopher, Arendt, like the psychoanalyst, insists that Eichmann is an individualized *case*. She seeks not to determine a generic model, but to ascertain the point at which Eichmann's will, his relation to his desire (and to the Law) was a factor in his political acts. Though her aim differs from a psychoanalysis, and she will not facilitate his "cure" but only a judgment on the man, she will have reframed the question of the Law to which his drive and his desire respond (as no limit). Eichmann himself will never be able to "reorder" the elements of his discourse, his own narration of his life, in other than precut, formulaic terms, as an analysand might.

Arendt's "new crime" of "administrative massacre," which is simply the term for modern as opposed to traditional genocide, is not yet able to be brought to the bar of justice. Crimes committed above the individual level do not yet have to face the *decision*, a judgment (between Good and Evil). Perhaps it should be put another way: can we not mark Eichmann's original "ethical" decision (to do his duty) as Lacan marked Kant/Sade's, that is, with a *vel*? The alienating *vel* is a logical connective that denies one of its terms, a "choice" made in such a way as to avoid a decision, absolutely eliminating one of a pair of options. It means no choice at all: for example, "Your money or your life," wherein the choice of the latter destroys the option of enjoying the former. We can mark it thus, if we make the link Lacan does, between this *vel* and the *V* of the *volonté de jouir* (the will-to-*jouissance*). A simulacrum of judgment, the *vel*'s act of absolute cutting away preempts and precludes the need for any further judgment or decision: it is a form of final solution.[51]

Hannah Arendt gives a double answer: (1) that the escape from the area of ascertainable facts and personal responsibility that became pandemic in Germany of the Nazi years and of which Eichmann is an example is the only thing that justice can deal with and call to account; a failure to be able to *decide* between Good and Evil is the only moral failing. Hence her criticism of the widespread response and accusation against the trial of Eichmann ("Who are you to sit in judgment? You might have done the same in his place," and so on). All generalities ("It's humanity itself on trial") are in her eyes incorrect from any standpoint that takes justice as its goal: justice is a judgment to be rendered on deeds and misdeeds, the decisions of a person, an individual.

Arendt also argues that (2) there is, beyond the individual level, a *political* responsibility that "exists quite apart from what the individual member of a group has done, and therefore can neither be judged in moral terms nor brought before a criminal court" (298). It is this political responsibility that must be separated from the question of the *individual's* guilt or innocence, which are the only things, she tells us, "at stake in a criminal court." Hence her profound repugnance for putting a whole people, or humanity itself on trial, in the showcase way that she believes Ben-Gurion attempted to do. One can take on the guilt of his group's evil only in a metaphorical way, and no one can be held responsible for the acts of a whole society. Conversely, an entire society cannot be judged guilty, since there will always be individual members who dissented and disagreed (as in Arendt's example of the acts of the simple soldier, Anton Schmidt). What is at issue in the case of Eichmann, however, is that he felt no need to engage in the individual decision as to good or evil; he was beyond them by virtue of his being a mere executor of the will of the group, which had its own grounds—Hitler's—for the decisions it had come to.

Thus the central structural problem—self-legislation—remains. It is even emblematized in Eichmann's case by the locale of the trial itself: Eichmann is tried not in a supreme court, but in a parliamentary building: Beth Ha'am, the House of the People, is where this Beth Hamispath, or House of Justice, has been installed. Arendt, of course, concludes her book as she must, by reaffirming that "the question of individual guilt and innocence are the only things at stake in a criminal court" (298). That she nonetheless felt compelled to raise the question of the guilt or innocence of "political responsibility" is telling. "It is quite conceivable that certain political responsibilities among nations might some day be adjudicated in an international court" (298), which she immediately qualifies as necessarily not a criminal court ("What is inconceivable is that such a court would be a criminal tribunal which pronounces on the guilt or innocence of individuals"). She has also shown how far Eichmann's "Kantianism" protected him from bearing responsibility for any criminality or evil attached to an openly expressed "political will." The question remains, then, how can the crime of genocide be adjudged a crime as such? On whose head would the guilt lie?

Despite her tremendous reluctance to consider "political responsibility" as falling within the realm of criminal justice, Arendt has, I think, actually opened a path. Her inquiry turns into one concerning the relation of genocide to written and unwritten law—the same one I proposed at the outset. That it is a woman, and as such, classically "suspicious of the signifier," who was able first to define this problematic, and tentatively to call for a response of the signifier, is, in my view, highly significant.[52]

The Otherness of Laws and the Reason for Writing Them Down

For Arendt, the simple decision to keep its Laws "unwritten"—free of content, of pathological objects—granted tacit permission for National Socialism's plan of genocide. Any law explicitly directing genocide would have already been the result of a *vel*, and the expression of a specific *will-to*.[53] Single individuals were not so much loath to engage in such expressions as structurally impeded from doing so: their "will" was not "their own," as Eichmann recounted. One had to be attuned to the "principle behind the law,"[54] which should be, for Kant, the individual will, and for

Rousseau, the *volonté générale*, or the will of the people as a whole taking itself for an object, both of which are problematic and difficult to access. But functionaries like Eichmann had no difficulty in locating this will, because they identified it with the actual, if only indirectly heard, voice of the Führer.

For very practical reasons, of course, Hitler's genocidal program had to remain unwritten because of its criminal nature: international public opinion would have mobilized more quickly against it were it to have been written down. The only language ("Officialese") to which the Nazi regime condescended to transmit its orders constituted a new kind of discourse framed by a "language rule" (the new *Amtssprache*, the *Sprachregelung*). This rule was to remake what once, under common civil agreements, had been called "the lie" into the form of a specially honored secret: "Those who were told explicitly of the Führer's order were no longer mere 'bearers of orders,' but were advanced to 'bearers of secrets,' and a special oath was administered to them" (84–85). The secret therefore was, in formal communication terms, also technically "content free."

Speech versus Voice

All speech "calls for a reply" (Lacan, *Ecrits*, 40). The error—in politics as in the analytic session—lies in mistaking a call *(appel)* for an *appeal*. This mistake is made by placing primary emphasis on the "feelings" (as sensory perceptions) of the hearer:

> If the psychoanalyst [but could we not also say political subject?] is not aware that this is how the function of speech operates ["to call for a reply"], he will simply experience its appeal all the more strongly, and if the first thing to make itself heard is the void, it is within himself that he will experience it, and it is beyond speech that he will seek a reality to fill this void. (*Ecrits*, 40)

Self-absolved from any need to reply (if only with silence), the unaware listener will "echo his own nothingness" in the other, and it is this "echo" that is the source of the appeal of "empty" speech: an "appeal" to the "very principle of truth," which, Lacan tells us, is first and foremost "the appeal of the void, in the ambiguous gap of an attempted seduction of the other . . . to which he will commit the monumental construct of his narcissism" (*Ecrits*, 40).

"Mere formalism," the evacuation of pathetic content, delivers us over to the all-or-nothing game of a "full" meaning, yielded entirely to an Other who is thus empowered to reward us with a nugatory remainder, an empty "senselessness" for our being. But it is a senselessness that is experienced as a sensory impression, a certain *jouissance*. In repeating, in an aggravated way, the senselessness of the signifier it secretly tells the listener that a full meaning and sense have now come to fill out their lack. The listener responds to, then, rather than answers for, an insistent excess of *jouissance* in the Other, whose final mastery over all meaning is sufficient sign of its ownership of the transcendental signified-of-all-signifiers—the *jouissance* excised by speech.[55]

Listening to Eichmann from the "pre-Kantian," sympathetic, or "pathological" posture (that is, trying to "think from the standpoint of somebody else"), the Jerusalem judges imagined that Eichmann's perpetual recourse to "empty talk" showed that the "accused wished to cover up other thoughts which, though hideous, were not empty" (*Eichmann*, 49). But Arendt finds otherwise. The presumption of especially savage passions is perfectly refuted by Eichmann's verbal demeanor. His clichés are purely formal. Arendt asks parenthetically, "Was it these clichés that the psychiatrists thought so 'normal' and 'desirable'?" (48–49).

Eichmann showed "great susceptibility to catch words and stock phrases, combined with his incapacity for ordinary speech" (86). According to Arendt's analysis of Eichmann's speech, the "inner voice" of conscience in Eichmann was perhaps less silent than voiced over. "Genuinely incapable of uttering a single sentence that was not a cliché," Eichmann claimed that "Officialese *[Amtssprache]* is my only language" (48). At times, of course, Eichmann showed "uplift." He thrilled whenever he was able to revoice or utilize a cliché that made him feel part of the perpetual "movement of the Universe" (27). Eichmann reports being "elated" when he was able to link his "mood" with its "catch phrase" (62), labeling such phrases with the German term for touchstone quotations, *Geflügelte Worte* ("winged words" [48]). With them, he was "in movement" (43), he "lived for his idea" (42).[56] That attunement with the idea had no room for "pathological" emotions:

> When he said in the police examination that he would have sent his own father to his death if that had been required, he did not mean merely to stress the extent to which he was under orders, and ready to obey them; he also meant to show what an "idealist" he had always been. The perfect "idealist," like everybody else, had of course his personal feelings and emotions, but he would never permit them to interfere with his actions if they came into conflict with his "idea." (42)

Indeed, Eichmann's whole posture parallels that of the sadist in Lacan's analysis, who is precisely not a man filled with irresistibly savage urges but the executioner of the will-to-*jouissance* of the Other.[57]

For Eichmann, a "death whirl" circulated around the Führer's voice. Arendt writes that the Führer's words had the "force of law" for Eichmann *(Führerworte haben Gesetzkraft)*, which meant, "among other things, that if the order came directly from Hitler it did not have to be in writing. He tried to explain that this was why he had never asked for a written order from Hitler . . . but had demanded to see a written order from Himmler" (148). A barely perceptible thread, then, leads from the evacuation, opened by Kantian philosophy, of specific, affective content in the Law, to the absolute emptiness at the center of Eichmann's thought, the absolute void to which Arendt points in her report on Eichmann's conscience. Eichmann's salient "inability to speak" was, according to Arendt, "closely connected with an inability to *think*, namely, to think from the standpoint of somebody else" (49).

Precisely because no written Law specifically prohibited (or permitted) genocide, the command to genocide appeared as a pure function of the will of the Other, completely unrelated to Eichmann's own wishes and desires. As such, it became Eichmann's duty, and not only his. It had an astonishingly immediate appeal to the state's chief functionaries, few of whom owed their careers to the Nazis and might not have been thought reliable or responsive to Hitler.[58] Wannsee, where the Final Solution was laid out as the government's program in 1942, was a "cozy little social gathering" (113). Eichmann was secretary to this Conference of the Undersecretaries of State that resolved all his doubts. Arendt quotes Eichmann's deposition:

> "Here now, during this conference, the most prominent people had spoken, the Popes of the Third Reich." Now he could see with his own eyes and hear with his own ears that not only Hitler . . . but the good old Civil Service were vying and fighting with each other for the honor of taking the lead in these "bloody" matters. "At that moment . . . I felt free of all guilt."
> *Who was he to judge?* (114)

Arendt comments, "Well, he was neither the first nor the last to be ruined by modesty" (114); but when such modesty was a function of what Eichmann himself termed a "death whirl" (115), his failure to "judge" becomes obscene. His modesty instead marks Eichmann as the one who renounces his personal judgment, desires, and emotions to serve the will-to-*jouissance* of Hitler.

Just what "satisfying Hitler" meant—the sacrifice or "ethical renunciation" he demanded of the German people of the 1930s and '40s—is described movingly by Arendt. What the average German had to sacrifice was precisely his or her hard-won place in the symbolic order, in "civilization":

he or she had to give up the symbolic modes of fending off the call of the will-to-*jouissance*:

> Evil in the Third Reich had lost the quality by which most people recognized it—the quality of temptation. Many Germans and many Nazis, probably an overwhelming majority of them, must have been tempted *not* to murder, *not* to rob, *not* to let their neighbors go off to their doom. . . . But, God knows, they had learned how to resist temptation. (150)

The "voice of conscience" called on the people to give way on their desire. After the administration and execution of Hitler's genocidal plan, justice must no longer presume a certain content or character to the "voice of conscience." In order for there to be justice based on "conscience," Arendt writes, "unlawfulness must 'fly like a black flag above' . . . as a warning reading 'Prohibited!'" (148). By contrast,

> in Hitler's criminal regime this "black flag" with its "warning sign" flies as "manifestly" above what normally is a lawful order—for instance, not to kill innocent people just because they happen to be Jews—as it flies above a criminal order under normal circumstances. To fall back on an unequivocal voice of conscience—or, in the even vaguer language of the jurists, on a "general sentiment of humanity" (Oppenheim-Lauterprach in *International Law,* 1952)—not only begs the question, it signifies a deliberate refusal to take notice of the central moral, legal, and political phenomena of our century. (148)

More broadly interpreted, the status of the law is up for grabs: laws can no longer easily claim symbolic status if they are not simply isomorphic with the signifier (ultimately the phallus). Castration within the symbolic is nowhere near as radical as what Fascism required—a sacrifice to the *jouissance* embodied in the "principle behind the law."

Psychoanalytically, the "principle behind the law" in Eichmann's case is obscene: a popular will that masks a "maternal" will-to-*jouissance* beyond the regulation of the signifier. I would concur with Arendt that genocide's peculiar "call to conscience" is the "central moral, legal, and political" phenomenon of our century. Lacan's analysis of the pivotal role played by the *object a*—in this instance, the maternal *voice*—contributes, then, to developing an ethics that would acknowledge the force of drive and fantasy over desire in the postdemocratic era in which a fascist perversion of democratic principles continues to threaten.

Arendt's account does not identify the "voice" (as organ of the obscenely enjoying Other or "principle behind the law") with the superego. She does, however, signal the (potentially) fatal weakness in modern self-governance. Modern forms of state, as she demonstrates here and as confirmed in our subsequent experience, relentlessly and remorselessly lend themselves to the recurrence of genocide. If Arendt proposes no solution, if her imperturbable analysis of evil allows no remedy but the supranational written law, this is because, absent psychoanalytic insights, it is unable to account for the workings of fascism on the level of the subject. This task can only be shouldered by a politically informed psychoanalysis.

Sacrifice

I will end my discussion where I began, by recalling the link of fascism and its sacrificial imperative to genocide. Lacan has remarked on the resurgence of this "imperative":

> I would hold that no meaning given to history, based on Hegelian-Marxist premises, is capable of accounting for this resurgence—which only goes to show that the offering to obscure gods of an object of sacrifice is something to which few subjects can resist succumbing, as if under some monstrous spell. . . . for whoever is capable of turning a courageous gaze towards this phenomenon—and once again, there are certainly few who do not succumb to the fascination for the sacrifice in itself—the sacrifice signifies that, in the object of our desires, we try to find evidence for the presence of the desire of this Other that I call here, the dark God. (*Seminar XI,* 275)

While from a historical standpoint the uniqueness of the Holocaust must never be denied ("unprecedented" was Arendt's term for it; and Raoul Hilberg concurs that there was more than ordinary anti-Semitism at work in it), we should not shrink from recognizing the signs of a resurgence of a genocidal imperative. Ethnic cleansing, the demand for racial purification, the Khmer Rouge, the Bosnian War: these indicate not imitative repetitions, but that a new evil has entered the world that wears the face or mask of a certain detachment. Administrative massacre, as Arendt called it, enabled by a transcendental subjectification on the one hand, and by an unconscious identification with the *object a* on the other. While mass killings on a large scale have occurred before in world history, the calculating decision to cleanse, to expunge, to obliterate the last trace of—is altogether new. Mass murder was committed during the Holocaust with an industrial efficiency and an appropriate distance (executioners who appeared to enjoy killing in the camps were immediately relieved of their duties). Today's systematic mass rapes in Bosnia are accomplished, it seems, coolly, without lust.

What I am suggesting is not passion and empathy as alternatives—far from it. But I am suggesting that an analysis of the basis of this pseudo-distance would be useful. Not *critical* as Kant would have had it, this distance is instead *apathetic,* in the sense of Sade. Such apathetic "engagements" by the political subject mark a resistance to temptation—the temptation, as Arendt puts it, "*not* to murder, *not* to rob, *not* to let their neighbors go off to their doom." In short, this apathy marks the sacrifice of one's own symbolic mandate. This stubborn and persistent resistance to one's own desire, encountered again and again in the executives of genocide, indexes the preservation of a *jouissance* the subject disowns. It marks the advent of a new and radical evil.

In the passage above, one of his most enigmatic pronouncements, Lacan concluded his eleventh seminar by linking Nazism with a sacrifice, an offering to obscure gods. Dismissing Hegelian-Marxist premises as unable to account for the drama of Nazism, he intimates that his psychoanalysis has a more compelling explication. This psychoanalytic access comes from its questioning the notion of *sacrifice*: how and why did millions of human beings become objects of sacrifice? Behind these words of Lacan, which have haunted me from the first time I read them, I ask you to hear Arendt's chilling report on the sacrifice demanded from the German people by Hitler, the "dark god" whose will-to-*jouissance* seemed insatiable.

Lacan brackets his remarks on sacrifice with allusions, on the one side, to mass media[59] (its voice as *object a*) and on the other side, to Kant, who should counterbalance that voice. One of the questions I have tried to pose, if not definitively to answer, in this chapter is, why doesn't he? Without questioning the invaluable contribution that Kant made to the notion of a "democratic" law, we cannot mistake the dark overtones law takes on in Lacan's text. Whose hair has not been raised by the verbal coloration at the point in *Seminar XI* where Lacan describes the relation of moral law to the object? "This moral law, . . . looked at more closely, culminates in the sacrifice, strictly speaking, of everything that is the object of love in one's human tenderness. I would say, not only in the rejection of the pathological object, but also in its sacrifice and murder. That is why I wrote 'Kant avec Sade' " (275–76). Only a few paragraphs separate this sacrifice and murder of the object of love from the sacrificial aspect of the Holocaust. With these words, Lacan once again forges an alliance between what he called the "malevolent superego" and the moral law: each lives only from the fantasy of sacrifice—of desire.

For many, Kant's moral law, the law of pure desire, seems to guide the aim of analysis: to bring the subject to ask itself what it wants. Parsing

Freud's famous "Wo Es war soll Ich werden," Lacan writes: "That 'I' which is supposed to come to be where 'it' was, and which analysis has taught us to evaluate, is nothing more than that whose root we already found in the 'I' which asks itself what it wants" (*Seminar VII, 7*). Lacan's denunciation of normative ideals (genital primacy, adulthood, happiness) as goals of psychoanalysis likewise repeats Kant's fundamental ethical gesture of clearing the ground of sentimental cant.

Nevertheless, on the matter of the purity of desire, Lacan seems to distinguish his position from Kant's (and Sade's)[60] by insisting that the analyst's desire is not pure (*Seminar XI, 275*). That the attraction to and distancing from an equation of Kantian and psychoanalytic ethics come in the context of unsettling remarks on the Holocaust must give us pause. If nothing else, these remarks set an agenda for analyzing and overcoming the fascist temptation that inhabits all forms of self-governance: super-egoic, democratic.

It has not been my purpose here to trace blame for the Holocaust to Kantian philosophy (though others have tried to do so),[61] or, conversely, to exonerate Kant (as Derrida has, by honoring him as the Jew unassimilable to the fascist tendencies in Hegelian grand dialectics). My purpose has been less philosophical, less embroiled in contemporary academic politics. It has been to delineate a structure, available through a study of certain obscurities in Kant's thought, in which the vulnerability of the symbolic order to the particular, new, and ferocious excess of our post-democratic time—genocide, ethnic cleansing—might come to be better understood.

The phantasmatic character of human enjoyment must be accounted for in any ethic today: it must take primacy. Unconscious fantasy formations grow ever more central in our lives; they are the support of our "reality."[62] The law counters unconscious fantasy with *desire*, but it has no purchase unless it accounts for where the subject *enjoys*. The obverse also holds: only when the subject knows how its desire and the law respond to its *jouissance* can it encounter its own enjoyment. In centering on the object that Kant too naively swept away, Lacanian analysis shows the relation of desire, and its alienation, to the general will. To write the law against genocide would provide the way for the increasingly stateless citizens of the postmodern, "global" community to once again be asked, as individuals, *to decide, to judge*: and this means facing, not disavowing a relation to *jouissance*. Paired sets of alternatives (good or evil, to kill or to love) share the same object: separating it out as their hitch is the goal of the psychoanalysis of the alienated subject. It should now be clear that it needs also to be related to the alienation of the political subject. Only this kind of decision, as separation—which is the reversal of the *vel*—permits the individual to resist the will of the people when it has become a malignant will-to-*jouissance*.

6. Mothers of Necessity

A leading psychoanalytic writer was visiting my home in California. We were engaged in a roiling discussion covering many topics. I was director of women's studies at the time, so naturally feminism and psychoanalysis came up. It went from there to women, then wives, then mothers. At the word "Mother," my visitor turned to me with an impish grin and said, "You, *you're* the problem! You're a *Mother*! Pure evil! The source of radical evil!"

It stings when a theory that you have advanced for other reasons hits you where you least expect it. And when you find yourself unprepared to respond because the theory has not given you any way to, it is doubly troubling.

I did not feel evil. I had tried, during my two sons' youth, to be as un-smothering as a mother could be. I did not hover, to the point where one son complained that I was "too businesslike." My husband made certain that the children did not have a negative view of my absences for professional reasons: his mother and father had been professionals; his maternal grandmother was the lady boilermaker, Rosie the Riveter. Once, I asked my six-year-old son with concern if he was upset that I was so often gone. Obviously reflecting his father's attitude, he spontaneously and exuberantly responded, "Well, it's a lot better than your being an all-American thoroughbred housewife!"

Being a housewife is a profession itself with its own dignity and creativity; I think that even if I had been one, I would not have acted differently toward my children from the way I had as a professor and writer. But in neither case would I have wanted to think of myself as something other than just myself with respect to my children. I would not have wanted to be their Thing.

Yet I was perfectly aware they might have considered me that way.

The question of how a mother can or does materially contribute to the psychic well-being of her child, to its ability to reconcile itself to the demands of civil society, the ideals promoted by culture, and its own superego has yet to be answered fully either by feminism or psychoanalysis. Feminism wavers among assertions of the all-importance and power of a pre-Oedipal mother,[1] a desire to soften her duties under Oedipus,[2] and the freedom from maternal constraints now possible for her. Psychoanalysis recognizes the Mother as not much more than the fulcrum of Oedipus, the motor of male amorous behavior, and of course, as the source of the sadistic superego as well. Speech is where, after Lacan, both the contents and discontents in culture are structured; but this crucial domain, the power of speech (not voice), has never really been conceded to the Mother and is unlikely ever to be. Ever since Kant's *Anthropology*,[3] the domestic realm is ruled by woman's tongue, her chatter, her prattle, her scolding, her gossip, and so on. But such talk is so very empty, so radically full of nothing, that only the thing behind it seems to empower it. A mother's "speech" can apparently only reinforce culture's obscene superegoic voice.

It is time to review maternity in the psychoanalytic context, its relation to feminism. Can each contribute some greater knowledge to the future of the ethical female subject, who would include mothering within her range of possibilities? Revisiting the relation of feminism to maternity requires reassessing the "Mother" of psychoanalysis, Melanie Klein, and its "Father," Freud. Melanie Klein's contribution to the psychoanalytic understanding of the complex power of the maternal is even less understood than Freud's. She is perhaps the analyst most responsible for the vivid characterization of the Mother as *Das Ding*, the menacing Thing behind the privative, ideal ego before whom the child feels minimized and belittled. Yet it is Klein alone who granted a maternal role in the ethical development of the child, even before the intervention of the Father. Klein (and later Lacan) put a different stress from Freud's on the aggressivity and defense in the child's mental set toward the Mother. Separation from the Mother, or more precisely, from what the mother represents in the unconscious, is problematic for both sexes. What counts most is the way that the Mother's early privative function appears in the unconscious. If the Mother appears there as the One who retains the dominion over all *jouissance,* her children must resist becoming mere playthings, mentally, of the "everything" she commands.

Before I can get this review under way, however, it is necessary to speak about ideology in relation to motherhood—ideology in the Stendhalian sense.

Maternity and Ideology

Neither psychoanalysis nor feminism has ever questioned closely enough the part ideology has played in the evaluation of the mother and her relation to ethics. Its theoretical conception of the mother has never allowed psychoanalysis to make a properly ideological and political accounting of the role of the mother, either. Consequently, psychoanalysis and psychiatry have taken too little responsibility for concrete policies that have excluded the mother a priori from the cultural life of her children. A famous psychiatrist specializing in aesthetics and ethics, John Gedo, once served on a panel with me regarding psychoanalysis and literature. In his talk, he made the flat assertion that women who were cultural creators could not also be mothers: woman's contribution could be one or the other, never both. On the same panel sat Sandra Gilbert, professor, critic, mother, and poet.

But no feminism I know of, either, has taken the lead on the question regarding a maternal relation to ethics. That topic seems to have remained untouchable. Only a mother's return, positive[4] or pathological, to haunt her children's neurotic psyches has been broached by these two discourses. As many leading feminists are just experiencing motherhood, often by adopting children, I imagine that should change. We can now reconsider how the near-absolute social and cultural forfeiture that the woman-who-became-a-mother suffered so radically in Freud's day can be reassessed in the context of the question of the mother and ethics. Today, the average middle-class mother is no longer regarded as the privileged site of pure deprivation that she was under full nineteenth-century patriarchy. This should soften the perception of her psychic role, as it ought to enlarge her stake in cultural creativity; however, the place she used to hold, that of being culturally destitute, has stubbornly persisted and is currently being filled by media depictions of suffering masses all over the "third world." It also appears in ideologized depictions of the evil figure of the "single welfare mother" or "teenage mother"—even the middle-class "soccer mom" carries something of this slightly sinister stigma. Their real-life destitution causes them to loom large as menaces in the mental life of those who fear they have something to lose to these predatory figures, as became apparent in the United States Congress under Newt Gingrich's first term as Speaker of the House, where poor, single welfare mothers were said to be eating up the public treasury. (Even "liberal" representations of poor women as victims of absolute privation feed such fantasies: they must want what we have; they are our menacing Thing.)

The moment in American cultural history when the Mother was most ideologized and suffered her most absolute cultural deprivation in a way that nevertheless allowed her to dominate the psyches of her infant children was in the period known as the Cold War. The feminism of the seventies and eighties, having taken impetus from that era, still suffers from a certain mental blockage because it stems from that time. Nancy Chodorow, for example, says the concerns of contemporary feminism, "Seventies Questions,"[5] would have had no significance for "Thirties Women," largely because of what intervened. Thirties Women were European, often Jewish, women who practiced psychoanalysis and contributed to its theory. For them, concern with gender inequality and divisions of parental labor was nothing compared to the anti-Semitism and the fascism with which they contended on a daily basis. That the feminism of the '70s and '80s would appear to '30s eyes as a luxury afforded by the relative stability of Eurocentric society today might surprise us. But it should also give us food for thought, as it was in the decade of the 1950s that the ideology of stability in women's affairs reached its peak.

Did modern feminism perhaps really begin with, respond to, and take strange root in the freezing of history known as the Cold War? That was when the full-time mother was invented. She left an enormous legacy of guilt, a virtual plague to women who were attempting to combine careers plus parenting and hold both together with sexual relationships plus intellectual pursuits, while upholding her behavioral ideals in the decades that followed.

The Cold War: Deep-Freezing the '50s Woman
MAD: Mutually Assured Destruction

Mutually Assured Destruction (MAD) refers to the nuclear stalemating of the Soviet Union and the United States: the Cold War. Whatever the other destructive effects of the MADness of the Cold War on former colonies and primitive peoples,[6] one of its most invidious effects was felt at home. Framed by a pseudo-opposition between the two great post-Enlightenment experimental forms of "the people"—democracy and communism—political thought itself, too, froze up.

Whatever their official ideologies, the Soviet Union and the United States had been the greatest historical attempts ever made to create mass societies that were not based on a single, unified ethnic group. These were states that found in plurality and diversity, rather than in purity and unity, their equal points of departure—if only in theory.

While they had grown from quite different political philosophies, democracy and communism both tested radically the extent to which the state could any longer be said to be modeled on the family. The theorists who presided at their births, Rousseau for the one, Engels for the other, had logically destroyed the family as the model for social organization.[7] With the nuclear clouding of our vision, these two countries were deemed the deadliest of enemies. It poised the United States and the Soviet Union at each other's throats as absolutely opposed life-forms. Their real enemy (from without and within) was the kind of mass society that was alternatively formulated—fascist in character, based on One alone, one group, one language, one race, one common history, and so forth.[8] In this version of the group, the Leader takes over the Father function, while still using the residues of paternalism (love, authority, etc.) as his power source.

The Cold War shaped itself ideologically as a reaction to the social experiments of democracy and communism where the break with the familial model of society was concerned; in the United States, at least, the Cold War was the moment where a family model for the polity reached its apotheosis. The Cold War was constructed out of a specular freezing of social history, impressing us that "life-as-is" was "life-as-for-always," and this image was conveyed largely by representations of the nuclear family as an eternal form.

The Cold War created, as mirror stagings always do, imaginary identifications with the stable family. But its cryogenics unwittingly spawned new life-forms, such as the aberration known as the 1950s "full-time mother," a domestic woman the likes of which had never before been seen. Even in Victorian and Freudian fantasies, total maternal commitment to mothering never imagined her actually being confined to this single task. It would have been impractical for the vast majority of women, as domestic labor was very hard and very long and the time to accomplish even the most minimal tasks meant farming them—or, alternatively, the children—out to others: to servants, relatives in extended family networks, or the streets. This was true, as I recall, even for mothers in the late 1940s, like mine, who tried to fit the new norm of total focus on the children by literally staying up night and day. That was pre-Cold War reality, the one firmly denied by the '50s full-time mother.

For the *psychical reality* of the '50s woman, however, we need to make inferences. The effects of MAD on this woman's sexuality, on her amorous alliances, and on all her other forms of intersubjective relation have not been studied closely: what was its meaning to and for her, conscious and unconscious? Wittingly or no, her identifications and relations could not have remained unaffected by the nuclear situation as it was imaged by the world picture of the Cold War. I do not mean certainty of radiant-atomic death that popular psychology would assume, for Freud taught that we can never consciously accept the reality of our own death. Perhaps because it was structured as a certain kind of imaginary fiction, this Cold War, it wielded a decisive power to shape the '50s woman's identity and relations, distinct from those women of the '30s and '70s who had faced or would face other political scenarios.

The Cold War suspended time, which ultimately means "generation/s."[9] It presumed total destruction upon contact with a mirror-image rival if relations were ever really initiated, but it muted this destructiveness by producing fantasies of shelter and of conflict-free family life. Most important, it left unvoiced and unvoiceable any collective rationales for change or sociocultural transformation. To "start" history would actually mean to end life, even the hybrid artificial life experienced in the Cold War frame.

Did the Cold War really affect the sexual life of the '50s? This much we know: that "the battle of the sexes" was also "suspended": men and women were protected from each other's assured mutual destructiveness by a segregation of their separate spheres of influence; they became dear enemies who encountered each other rarely and whose powers in their respective domains were virtually never challenged by their "opposite number" (one of the popular locutions for describing '50s marital partners).

The hysterical emphasis on the mother and the child throughout the '50s was not, perhaps, then, merely symptomatic.[10] It was *the* central displacement by means of which cultural anxiety was masked: anxiety about reproduction, change, and vulnerability. In hindsight, the '50s insistence on imprisoning woman in the home and chaining her to a child she was not permitted to "have"—in any legal sense of the term—is a sign of cultural madness. From antiabortion laws to obstetrical practices, and school and military bureaucracies, the drive to take possession of the child from the mother was nearly total. When state control of child production claimed Oedipal morality on its side, psychoanalysis (and its saturnine view of the mother) was implicated in this madness. Small wonder that '70s women, on the way to entering motherhood, stopped and rebelled, first against domestic confinement, then against the falsified sexual relations rooted in the MADness assumed to underlie the relation of male and female.

The astonishing promotion of the idea of awesome (if also sometimes evil) maternal power broadcast in the 1950s during the Cold War assigned the mother a kind of extracultural power that served to make her both a scapegoat and an alibi for denying her political voice. This set up the ways in which the Mother and the arrangements of and between the sexes are being analyzed and understood even today. It is only now, as current feminists rebel against yielding every square inch of child-rearing territory to male cultural fictions, that we can become aware of the power of those 1950s fictions, and the degree to which they are an effect created by opposing a "maternal" Thing to the psychoanalytic fiction of the Father. These two fictions, the Cold War political one of pure maternal dominion, and the psychoanalytic support it found in the dream that the paternal could take cultural charge of the child as its ego ideal, resulted in severe, institutionalized abuses of both women and children in reality. The fact that these two fictions have dominated our psychical reality may account for the success that literary critics have had in joining feminism and psychoanalysis—one of the few realms in which the two have partially banded together.[11]

The women's movement as we know it will very likely weaken if conditions are altered, that is, if History starts to move again. Union is now here in Europe, and the rapid dissolution of the Soviet and American empires will soon have wrought changes with major implications for women's psychical life.[12] That is why it is so surprising that feminists with a sociological and political, rather than literary, bent seem to be dominated still by '50s ideologies regarding the mother. When we find feminists acting as if, in accordance with the '50s ideology, mothers and fathers have always stood outside of political arrangements and their ideologies, we should be skeptical.

To take one example, the "matricentrism" in postmodern and even object-relations feminism lent unwitting support to an early '90s conservative politics nostalgic for the stability of the '50s. The "end of history," a new freeze on our horizon, once again gave credibility to a matricentric position. Though it does not ascribe evil to its central maternal figure, it does nothing to render her any more ethical than in the 1950s portrait of her. Jane Flax's book *Thinking Fragments,* one of these postmodern theses on the mother, was oddly characterized by a certain analytical flatness or ennui consequent on her assumption that the "Death of History" (inaugurated in the Cold War) is irreversible. Flax dutifully repeated the postmodern litany: she is about to "explore how theories might be written in postmodern voices—non-authoritarian, open-ended, and process-oriented," while questioning "knowledge, gender, subjectivity and power" (3). Flax dispiritedly accepted that no synthesis, resolution, or even historical narrative integrating woman's fragmented projects is possible. But she still identified herself with feminism as pro-maternalism, that is, with "the awesome power of the pre-oedipal mother" (18). Flax was reluctant to engage the major feminist/psychoanalytic reflections on the pre-Oedipal mother (the mother before the advent of the Oedipus complex for the child): Julia Kristeva, who celebrates her, appears in only three footnotes; Nancy Chodorow and Dorothy Dinnerstein are reviewed briefly; Melanie Klein is barely mentioned. Flax simply declared her faith in this mother's power, the power essentially to dominate *infantile fantasies*. Flax refused to link this power to any "political, social and economic context" as she asks other feminists to do[13] and made virtually no political references. Without the "metanarratives" of epochs, even the Cold War, or epochal events, like the Holocaust, to flavor her picture of the Mother whose cause she wishes to take up, the picture remains abstracted from social context— as the Mother is supposed to be. Thus, her approach does not concern "ethical woman" since it focuses all thoughts of woman's authority on a mother who has her only significant relation to the helpless infant's pre-verbal emotional state. Flax's "powerful" mother shapes nothing; she merely takes her accustomed place in a helpless infant's fantasies of *jouissance* and deprivation.

If the mother ceases to exist as any sort of presence *after* the pre-Oedipal phase, she might return to culture by way of her impact on a son's and daughter's chosen substitute objects. But in line with that '50s ideology, Flax regards mothers as a power and presence in their children by removing them to a utopian time of a continuous, oceanic, maternal relation in which the maternal voice has its sole authority. To put it more bluntly, in Flax's theoretical perspective, women who are not now or have not been mothers of infants would never actually earn the right to authority, to be heard.

Flax's only attempt to "be political" regards psychoanalysis itself. She sees psychoanalysis quite cynically as "the bonding of fathers and sons against the full return of the repressed mother world" (charges she extends, with modifications, to the "sons of Freud"—Lacan and object-relations theorists) (90). She principally forgives Freud, granting that although he misrecognized the "mother's power over the infant's fantasy life" (18), which constitutes the "repressed material" of his own theory,

still, his protopostmodern "style" saves him: his "later theories" (of the id
as a reservoir of interpersonal object-cathexes) "incorporate the qualities
that postmodernists prefer—heterogeneity, flux, and alterity" (60–61). It
seems odd that an advocate of postmodernism would take interest in the
id, an unconscious force that should have no place in the world of postmodern surfaces. One might imagine that Flax is about to discover its
connection to the superego, which today, as Joan Copjec has shown, commands *jouissance* as a duty and sits enthroned beside our social selves and
on the same level.[14] But no. Flax's id displays the very same characteristics
as the pre-Oedipal mother: it is a "dark ocean" (85) and "awesome power"
(18); it cries out to be the big power, the mechanism that drives the cool
surfaces of postmodernity.

Flax's picture, then, unwittingly repeats the '50s model of the mother:
culturally dispossessed, wielding power over the child's fantasy life, and
shaping culture negatively by opposition to horror of her. How could this
help the real mother? Under patriarchal conditions the Mother saw her
cultural aspirations go unfulfilled. She was trapped in a vicious circle,
overloving the son who alone could express her own blunted social ambitions, and enmeshed in an interminable conflict with her daughter. Her
potentially terrible role in the mental life of the child (of both sexes) was
often used to blame the real mother for her children's problems. Film images of sadistic and smothering mothers also sprang up in the '50s and
'60s alongside her apotheosis as the center of the stable family. I am thinking not only of Hitchcock, but of such movies as Frankenheimer's *All Fall
Down* (1962), based on a William Inge story, in which a dreadful mother
produces one shallow, narcissistic son, and another who must escape her
clutches if he ever wants to create. Does postmodern Flax get us out of
such old-fashioned maternal dead-ends?

Chodorow's Alternative Model of Feminine Power: Still the Cold War?

The problem with approaches like that of Flax to woman and power is
that they have no model other than what is essentially an obscene maternal superego for that power. Their supposedly "feminist" Freud only
emerges, ironically, at a time where we are fearfully beginning to perceive
the growing hegemony of an irrational id over the ego. A mutant superego
seems to be assuming dictatorial powers over our cultural life: a sadistic
superego, as Melanie Klein, the supposed mother of object-relations,
called it. She saw its shape in the blighted child's frightened eyes, its incapacity to symbolize. But I anticipate.[15]

Of course, postmodern feminism and matricentrism are not the only ways feminism with a psychoanalytic touch has tried to deal with the maternal and to connect it somehow to an energized feminine power. I felt as sympathetic with Nancy Chodorow's social perspective in *Feminism and Psychoanalytic Theory*, which appeared within a year of Flax's book, as I felt uncomfortable with *Thinking Fragments*. Chodorow clearly wanted to see justice for women, healthier children, the end to male aggression against women, the reevaluation of the role of the mother, a truly better world. I was less inclined than Chodorow, however, to believe in the immediate potential for attaining these goals through the good offices of a combined psychoanalytic, socially progressive, and critically vigilant feminism. Her work often reflected her wishful thinking in this respect. But it is to Chodorow's great credit that she did not sacrifice objective observations to these wishes. Principally, she was dismayed that neither feminism nor psychoanalysis had worked out the relation to the mother.[16]

Chodorow used matricentric feminist terms to model the relationship the mother offers her daughters and sons—a maternal model of bonding. She could offer her children the value of a connectedness and relation that never appears in the paternal "cut." In contrast to someone like Flax, it was obvious to her that to offer women interventionist power at one point only in their own lives (and in the lives of their children) effectively deprives them of active roles later. It even opens the mother to blame without enabling her to defend herself or control what it is she is supposed to have done: "Belief in the all-powerful mother spawns a recurrent tendency to blame the mother on the one hand, and a fantasy of maternal perfectibility on the other" (Chodorow, 80). Ultimately, this setup lionizes and empowers the child, not, as the postmodernist Flax had thought, the mother. Chodorow writes, "If having a child makes a mother all powerful or totally powerless ... then the child who evokes this arrangement must also be all-powerful" (85). How alarming, and unfortunately how convincing.

Chodorow in general has been averse to the unconscious. She tended, her teacher Philip Slater once told her, to leave the unconscious out (2). She has also been hostile to drive theory, out of a good sociological sense that aligning woman with the instincts disempowers her politically.[17] Her critique of the historical limitations of contemporary feminist concerns ("Seventies Questions for Thirties Women") was inspired; it rehistoricized feminist concerns as linked to sociopolitical contexts.

What Chodorow sacrificed to her own wishful thinking was her theory. She conscientiously limited herself to a no-nonsense rhetoric, steeling herself against unnecessary obscurities and opacities in the "continental" (i.e., Lacanian and French feminist) approaches, which draw so much attention to language. Such limitation can be an Orwellian sort of virtue. Yet I think it hobbled Chodorow by encouraging her to focus on "normal psychology" at the expense of those extreme cases where "the normal" encounters itself at the limit. For it is precisely the norm that became the issue for '90s feminism: our norms are Oedipal, and it is Oedipus as the basic symbolic order that feminism has had to question.

By deploying a phenomenological term, *the self,* Chodorow evaded continental sharpness and proposed what turned out to be a premature solution to the Mother Problem.[18] Her language kept carrying her away from her basic and admirable motives, which she never entirely abandoned. She wanted to address the *intersubjective relation* as it is marked and shaped by gender and sexual concerns, in particular, the parental dialectic, as a way to reach the Mother. Despite her resistance to Lacan (10), Chodorow actually devised something rather like his Symbolic to get her from both biological and drive theories, to a child produced in large measure from social and cultural interactions. She also claimed to want to see the child produced out of the relation of the parents to each other.

Lacan offered the Mother a crucial role: he called it the Desire of the Mother; the Mother must designate the Father of the child; her attitude toward the father shapes the child materially. Chodorow did not use Lacan, nor did she define her Mother's "power" in this general direction. Chodorow never reduced, as Flax had done, the parent-child relation to a dyad, but she never really confronted the mother-father coupling in the context of *maternal ethics.* For Chodorow a third element simply exists in the socialization of the child. She repeatedly attempted to name it but never succeeded in making it precise. She assumed its existence but never located it in specific material practices external to the dyadic mother-child bond. The result is that *a Father* subtends this relation without appearing in propria persona—and without, in contrast to Lacan, any specific intervention of the Mother. Chodorow ended by resigning herself to the notion that, however important the model of connectedness that the mother-child bond offers, it can only remain as a *remembered model*—the warmth of human connection. Whatever actual relation of mother to child existed must be psychically given over: for Chodorow, mourning the closeness to the mother is a part of normal development, crucial to the constitution of the ethical, social self.

This is Oedipus, still. It depends exclusively on the Father—and on excluding the Mother. We have yet to see the Mother as anything other than dead matter for the process, no matter how nicely Chodorow attempts to treat her. She remains well within the '50s corrective to the all-pervading Mother: the ethical Father, goes it, so to speak, alone.

Alternative to Oedipus?

With the Father, of course, we are back in Freudian territory, comfortably so. And from safe within his vantage point, we can look out, with some consternation, on the only rival Oedipal Freud seemed to have for the Mother: Carl Jung, who offered us the great Mother. Chodorow would never resort to Jung's symbolic, as it defends *against* relationship, sexual or otherwise; his mythic province is structured by truncated pairs, one half of which is muted or lost. (How do you have a Trickster without a Dupe? How do you have a Woman without Man? A Hero without a Villain?) Feminism should recall that Jung wrote that "the domain of the 'Christian' white man" is the true center of European values;[19] Chodorow was opposed to Jung's mythic mother, and she espoused the idea that a certain relatedness in the parents was crucial for the child. In her efforts to bring the parental sexual relation under consideration in reframing the mother, Chodorow needed something like Lacan's Symbolic to counter the mythic Mother, but she remained resistant to him.[20]

Not Chodorow, nor any other feminist writing about mothering in the 1950s Cold War frame, conceived a sociosymbolic alternative to Oedipus. Had Chodorow made the actual relation of parents to each other a feature of her program, she might have done so, but it would have required reconstructing a model of social and group life along lines of sexual difference, not along that frozen, Cold War mirroring that still broods over our image of sexual relation. Although she might have liked to see what Jane Gallop calls a "reenactment of the mother-daughter bond" in society, Chodorow implicitly ceded social order to a *narrow* Oedipus, hidden under an object-relations screen.[21] By making the central vantage point that of the child, Chodorow marginalized the problematic of dual parenting that she had set out to investigate.

A symbolic transaction *is* necessary to bring the mother/father into relation with each other in their real production of the child's "self." That this symbolic remained Oedipal for Chodorow is not necessarily wrong, although it needed the updating it has been so crucially rendered by Lacanian analysts the world over. Because she refused the vocabularies of Freudian psychoanalysis, of ego and superego, the picture she painted is often blurred. An unfocused object-relations self hedges against ceding Oedipus too much and has permitted Chodorow to avoid setting her dream of maternal connectedness into too sharp a conflict with the time-honored power of Oedipus to separate mother and child. She wanted there to be *some* crucial relation between mother and child to remain after infancy, but she was prepared to drop anything that would countermand a strict antimaternal Oedipus.

The strength of Chodorow's work is that she was able to subordinate conceptual abstract consistency to the exigencies of the different contexts she addressed. For example, one of the things she fought for was the right to refuse the cultural glorification of the "selfless mother." She hoped for the mother's recognition as a "separate being with separate wants and activities that do not always coincide with just what the infant wants at that time" (101–2). Nevertheless, because Chodorow could not ever get beyond a certain liberal universal humanistic generic self, the "object-relations self," the maternal relation that she fashioned could have developed only out of an imaginary Family, like that of the Cold War '50s, or perhaps The Great Family of Man: what she called, "People everywhere" (4).

Ironically, her assertions concerning the existence of the family as universal came at the moment when the family as we know it was on the verge of collapse as a primary form of human association. Only at an Imaginary level could the family, as psychoanalytically understood, be said to persist in any meaningful way, and to conform to the '50s ideal of familial stability. Where it does persist, it is restricted to an increasing (and privileged) minority of members of the upper class who must expend much time and energy in mocking up its normality to keep it going. And, of course, those single welfare mothers keep hanging in there as well. Chodorow did not engage the reality of contemporary life, in which the possibility of dual parenting is more remote than ever before in our collective Western history. She conveys to her reader no sense of urgency that such things as human beings, families, and groups remain unproblematized and unquestioned as realities, or even as values, in contemporary life.

To take the humanness of humanity, of "people everywhere," for granted simply flies in the face of the constant assault on their associations by global capitalism and Western science, including social science and philosophy; it flies in the face of the increasingly phantasmatic manufacture of instant "groups" through statistical and demographic categories. However aware she may have been regarding the social history of feminism, Chodorow remained, it seems, captured by the '50s ideological concoction of the eternal nuclear family.[22] Feminism will continue to fall into the same error as long as properly Symbolic concerns are left out of account. And as long as the role and value of Maternal *authority* (not power) is not clarified.

The Symbolic

We need a Symbolic to reveal what is wrong with object-relations feminism and its equivocal relation to the mother. Chodorow's failure to specify and hold accountable the exact nature of the relation she invoked left the door open to the very narcissism and self-centering that she saw everywhere in feminist matricentrism, and that she despised. Her language was too imprecise to make her critique of narcissism stick: when she decided to reword, for example, "object-relation" as "other-relation," she attempted to bring some sort of nonimaginary third to break up the mother-child narcissistic couple (6). But in truncating the *complement d'objet* from her phrasing—she had written that "women's self in relation is a potential strength" (7)—she left us wondering: In relation to what? To Whom? She never says. Nor did Chodorow or Flax ask questions about the process of so-called internalization in object-relations theory. Internalization is the ground of object-relations, but it does not seem exactly to be introjection—symbolization or representation.[23] Nor by a more radical construction is it a form of incorporation: cannibalism, as in Melanie Klein.

The upshot is that while both wings of object-relations feminism, Flax's and Chodorow's, could criticize self-centering, they could not, in fact, do without it. They had nothing, no symbolic "relation," to counter it. Flax complained that Freud saw most of social life as "narcissistic projections," and so she decided to turn to D. W. Winnicott, who focused on relations. Yet Winnicott's own terms tended to vitiate the reality of the other being related to. His transitional objects moderated the starkness of individual separateness, but only by incorporating the self in a greater enveloping self whose "unit ... is not individual ... [but] the environmental-individual set-up."[24]

For Lacan, such centering is always Imaginary; ex-centricity is the constitution of the self in the Symbolic, and this ex-centricity is primordial. Ego-centering cannot help but open the door to the narcissism both feminists protest.

Or they protest it only until it appears in Woman, and not in infantile eroticism bound up with the Mother. Flax claimed that "we need real and not merely projected or narcissistic relations with others" (111), yet her object-relations faith in "the existence of internalized personal relations" (55) led her to espouse narcissism as the only sure root of group feeling. And the only *nonmaternal* figure for Woman. Even had Chodorow wanted to disagree with essentializing woman as narcissist, she could not. For even where they have opposed each other, as these two did, object-relations feminists seem to share a reliance on an imaginary self, at the expense of a Symbolic one. They also share in forgetting their common ancestor, Melanie Klein, who had offered some hope of producing a nonnarcissistic feminine Symbolic.

Narcissism in the Feminine

In America the self is said to need a "healthy narcissism." Woman's *feminine narcissism* is, however, open to some suspicion as to its healthiness.[25] The political issues regarding feminine narcissism are complex.[26]

Freud understood feminine narcissism as centered on its appeal to men—in a man's dream of returning to his own primary narcissism and his pre-Oedipal bonding with his mother. The narcissistic woman's happy self-focus, her indifference to culture, her self-sufficiency are supposed to remind the man of his own first love: not his mother-love, but his self-love, his infant autoeroticism, from the time before he encountered social and ethical responsibilities. To sanitize feminine narcissism, to free it from Freud's generally negative account in "Of Narcissism" (where he associates it with large birds of prey and big cats), is especially off-base. Yet Flax equated woman's *femininity* with it (54–55), a move dictated more by Anna Freud's views than by Winnicott's.

Here again, the Cold War paradigm haunts the theorizing of *maternity* and *femininity*. After all, the narcissistic woman is always designated as the destructive woman, at least in popular depictions of '50s movies.[27] Women, aligned with the allure of primary narcissism, are seen as sirens calling men toward an "oceanic feeling," which in Freud also means the death drive. Woman as destructive predominates whenever she is made into a counterself who threatens and yet promises man fission or fusion as he looks in her MAD mirror.

Let me pose this question to the postmodern legitimation of narcissism in Woman. Is the narcissistic "feminine subject" necessarily a *woman?* European literature identifies Narcissus not as a woman but as a male homosexual. Feminine charms are perhaps better displayed in drag than on the odd-lot female body. So much more effort has been poured into Queer Theory, as in the work of Eve Sedgwick, Elizabeth Grosz, and Teresa de Lauretis, than into theories of woman in feminist debate that apparently Woman does not (yet) exist for feminism. Is there any particular reason to retain woman as sexually different? That is an issue feminism has long been loath to consider and to argue in a sustained fashion.

Woman Doesn't Exist: Does She Need To?

Woman's existence has long remained a mystery, and it is still an issue for many literary feminists. The literary arguments are divided, but because they have focused much more on cultural and symbolic orders than feminism in the social sciences has, such as Flax's and Chodorow's, the critical question—that of Oedipus—has generally been faced more directly.

It is Oedipus who makes woman, the theory goes, not Narcissus. Anti-Oedipal, pre-Oedipal, and post-Oedipal stands may quarrel with the result, but they ultimately have to decide whether "woman-as-sexually-different" is worth the game, for she is what is at stake. Before we call the question of why or if woman is necessary, we might ask whether the mother must also exist?

To answer, we need Melanie Klein. As the object-relations feminists set the pattern for the next wave of feminist thought, the closest attention to this foremother is justified. Klein, surprisingly, leads us to Lacan—or not so surprisingly, since he leaned on Klein more than her feminist "daughters" have.

The Real Missing Mother: Melanie Klein

Klein's modification of Freud is peculiarly minimized in the feminist discourse on woman and motherhood, for reasons difficult to fathom. One reason may be that her discourse is of the *passions,* not the emotions.[28] For example, Chodorow credited Klein but failed to recognize Klein's formally symbolic situating of the infant's relation to the mother. Chodorow called Klein "more attentive, in an unmediated way, to the emotions and conflicts that relations rooted in gender evoke in the child and in the child within the adult" (3). Such characterizations, which are typical, seem highly disingenuous. How could anyone claim that "envy," "gratitude," "good," and "bad" are simple, unmediated emotions, that is, that they are not socially and symbolically charged, or ethically framed, not to mention culturally formed. And they mute the pure horror one cannot help but feel on reading Klein's accounts of disturbed children.

Klein's object-relations daughters overlook in her a discourse and an analytic of the passions, which has nothing to do with some dream of a pre-Oedipal, preverbal paradise of immediacy. It has nothing to do with the Anna Freud-ian relation of the self to itself, primary narcissism. The two fundamental assumptions of contemporary object-relations theory—primary narcissism, unmediated emotions—simply cannot be found in Klein. If anything, she is brutal in her frankness, extremely downbeat in her sense of what the children she has seen are telling her about their minds, hearts, and lives.

Passions are culturally and socially situated; they are not biological drives, nor do they exist on some fuzzy borderline between somatic and intellectual functions. They occur in *moral* terms, that is, in relation to symbolic or, better, superegoic positionings. The "good" breast and "bad" breast are, in Klein, originary, binary metaphysical oppositions, and they engender fantasies that result in passions such as envy and gratitude. But they are oppositions that the *ethically* constructed human being overcomes, through what Klein calls *reparation*.

Here, where feminists illogically resist her the most, Klein becomes the greatest ally of feminism against Freud and Oedipus. None of the Cold War feminists has seen her quite like this. Her stark insights were produced out of the horrors of two World Wars and the crushed symbolic they offered the children she analyzed. I think it is absolutely crucial for us to begin to read her in a post-Oedipal light.[29]

Klein and Oedipus

Klein is essential to any feminism that desires deeply to improve the elementary forms of life for woman, because she offers the first genuine move beyond Oedipus for the construction of human guilt and atonement. Klein is the only analyst yet to have grounded an alternative pathway to the ethical human being in the *other* parental figure, the mother. Moreover, she has done so without a trace of the emotional or sentimental aura that surrounds so many other appeals to the maternal.

In coding the *mother's breast* as the site of the first moral judgments and ethical reflections, Klein does not merely point to the mother's ontological, temporal, physical, and emotional priority over the father, but to her ethical one. The child does not have to await the coming of the phallic setup (the scene of castration, etc.) to make its distinctions by modeling them on the genital differences it perceives at the site of the penis. It does not even have to await the word. From earliest infancy, Klein finds distinctions and judgments of a moral sort being made on the "ground" of the mother's breast: "good" and "bad" start here.[30]

This interplay between the good and bad breasts can be called a "phallic function," but it is not really a matter of presence/absence, have/not have, plus/minus, and so on. Nevertheless, Klein's locating the original site of ethical judgment on the mature female body—a body that in girlhood lacks breasts, though it later acquires them—changes everything. It alters the perspective of when the child becomes a citizen of the social world (her argument with Anna Freud). It changes the sequencing of symbolic development in the girl child, drawing attention to, instead of away from, her budding womanhood. It revises the symbolic and imaginary evaluation of both the male and female bodies that lies at the root of "civilized" human behaviors. In the line of moral philosophy from Augustine to Lévinas, Klein stands with the great analysts of the *human*, not simply the animal or the sex-divided, subject. And she stands there on equal footing with Freud.

No one before me has read Klein in just this way, except Lacan—perhaps.[31] Klein's theses might well have had some role in stirring up Lacan's interest in doing variations on Oedipus, the phallus, and the other. He took to heart Klein's serious attention to infantile fantasy in ways that feminists like Flax did not. In Klein's theory, the "ethical" construction of the child—even though not classically Oedipal—is the direct result of its resistance to its own fantasies of aggression against the maternal body, cannibal orality, and so forth—as well as resistance to its own drives. That these take shape for the child's mental life in the form of only one part of the maternal body, and not its entirety, is crucial. It gives the infant a choice concerning its relation to the mother, who chiefly represents its sadistic drives to it: she can also, Klein finds, represent the fragile other, the other of lack and desire.

Did this not perhaps guide Lacan's enunciation of woman as "not all"?[32] He specifically does not say "not all there"—which would ascribe physical and mental deficits to her. "Not all" offers a potentially different sort of "opening" or "openness" to that provided by philosophy's feminine "w/hole" and Freud's "little man," as well as to the everyday psychical fantasy (and horror) of mother as the Thing.[33]

Klein and Fantasy

Fantasies are not epiphenomenal, not simply guilty reactions against primal wishes driven into an earlier, more biologically rooted set of wants: they are no mere cover-ups. Fundamental fantasies are those whose scenarios must be redrafted as mere scenarios (i.e., made unconscious) by later reparational constructions. They are not erasures or even archaeological layerings. The fundamental fantasy retains an absolute link to the later script: without it, there is no tale to be told. Subsequent verbalizations do not dominate and repress these childhood fantasies, as some Freudian theory of the unconscious might be understood; instead, they are fully informed by them, and for male and female equally. Attention to *form* as charged with these pre-Oedipal (even nonverbal) modes of shaping value is crucial and justifies fully linking artistic, literary, and cultural analysis to psychoanalysis. The turn that post-Kleinian object-relations theory took *away from* fantasy (from passion toward emotion) as critical to the construction of the ethical being has led its feminists unwillingly back to Oedipus and Narcissus. And it has blocked their capacity to see woman as a crucially complementary (if not perhaps *the* essential) factor in making the civilized life of the child possible.

Freud and Female Sexuality

I believe the reasons for the feminist avoidance of Klein are located in an impasse that Freud himself is responsible for. Freud made woman into a failed Oedipal convert, including the female homosexual (for him, she exhibits an ongoing infantile attachment to the mother, an incomplete transfer to the father). As a result, he rendered woman's desire passive, then passed it off as "female sexuality." There are, in Freud, no models for woman as such: he seemed wistfully to consider Lou Salomé as a real woman, but not many others. He mainly focused on the hysteric.

Like Freud, feminist psychoanalytics propose no models of woman either, crippled by Freud's limited perception of female sexuality—woman is a man and a woman (Barbara Johnson),[34] woman is like a man (Chodorow), woman is a narcissistic homosexual man (Flax). Ironically, each model of feminist/psychoanalytic woman appears in Flax (though not Chodorow), and very few appear even in the pages of the excellent overview of literary feminism edited by Richard Feldstein and Judith Roof, *Feminism and Psychoanalysis*,[35] which leans on the Freudian assumptions set forth in Freud's flawed 1931 paper "Female Sexuality."[36] Why this adherence to a Freud who disappointed us so much on the Woman Question?

After 1924, Freud realized there was an asymmetry between boy and girl in Oedipus. He noticed that boys indeed have it easier; they can make a simple analogy between sexual partner and the once-beloved mother, whereas girls have to skew and invert the image. In fact, girls are always little inverts; they are homosexual in their primal hearts. He willed the power of Oedipus to stymie a girl's orientation, just as he willed it to foster an active quest for a mother substitute in males: these were both proof that Oedipus *works*, although it does not make the girl's lot easy.

Having moved from Oedipus to castration theory,[37] Freud reverted to Oedipus in the 1931 essay, where he once again admitted having problems with the female Oedipus. But he remained adamant that there could be no alternative to Oedipus. He even insisted on making a woman's homosexual behavior governed by her relation to her father, as a hated rival. Why did he become so strident at this time?

Challenging "male analysts with feminine sympathies, and our women analysts also" to try to prove him wrong,[38] Freud insists in "Female Sexuality" that the daughter's relation to the Father, the transference of the girl's prior affection for the mother to him, commands her entire life course, sealing its fate, congealing it, and making it timeless. He seems to give up, and to dispense altogether with even the few concerns he has had, from time to time, for the girl's subsequent life as lover, wife, mother.[39] Freud conveniently forgets to think woman's lot through to the end, to the whole course of her life, to her life *after* the primary family.

This includes, if she is to be woman (not just daughter, mother, or sister), transferring her prior affections for her father to a man or someone else not her father, even in Freud's own system. After all, is this not his own prize discovery, Oedipus, and the incest taboo, we are talking about? But he has no theory of father-daughter incest, which would be necessary to make the Oedipal models symmetrical. Of course, this theoretical gap spared him from having to think about his daughter's "other man" as not simply a secondary copy of Papa. And it absolved him of having to think about woman's relation to other women, or about the problematic *maternal model* posed by Klein.

Freud was evidently blinded by concerns central to his own life, but which he pretended to hold apart from his text. It was, after all, 1931, two years before Hitler began his rise to power, seven years before his own forced exile from his mother country. Freud, unable to recognize greatness in his daughter's intellectual rival (Melanie Klein), and physically and emotionally dependent on his Anna to the end of his days, probably could not afford to give up his daughter, even in theory. Can he be altogether blamed for making this, the daughter's retention by the primary family, a classic first move, step one toward slowing down history? The particular history that followed was, as he suspected it would be, abominable. Retaining the girl for the family may protect her, but it mainly keeps her from full citizenship in the state. Anything that would have placed her in that state would have made that state perhaps too familial.

Freud's "Female Sexuality" should be the last place feminists look for woman. Whoever wishes to unfreeze woman's history, to tell her story, must begin elsewhere, maybe with Klein, if not Luce Irigaray. But let it be a tale of passions, not a heap of postmodern fragments, or of MAD claims about how "different we are" from our mirror-image other. It is time to end the Cold War between feminism and psychoanalysis. Even more than the old (Oedipal) metanarrative that postmoderns hate, the Cold War's narcissistic one was an awful bore.

Part II

7. On Woman's Speech

Prologue

As Artist-in-Residence at the Marin Headlands Center for the Arts, I was recently asked to present one of the informal Salon Nights the residents had agreed to offer so we could acquaint ourselves with each other's work. I have always found it relatively easy to speak about my academic subject matter. But I have never found it easy to speak nonacademically about myself, as a subject. To speak freely, I have always felt the need to be constrained toward a pedagogical end, which I designate, roughly, as an effort to unlock the student's mind, opening it to a place where they can start to create—thought, art, their life.

Salon Night, however, posed an additional unexpected difficulty for me. What could I teach artists? I had already discovered, during my residency, that what I thought of as the central aim of my teaching, my only reason to make use of speech—preventing premature closure—was completely unnecessary for these artists. So I began by telling them, "It is hard for me to speak to you because my speech is superfluous here: you are not constantly on the verge of closing your minds down. I sense no imminent danger of that. So I find it difficult to find anything that might make me feel the urgency I need to begin speaking at all."

I would have preferred to stop there. But I did not. I went on, moving into an unaccustomed speech dimension, a zone unfamiliar to me. I would have preferred to stop there because, while professional speech has never been troubling to me and I have lectured all over the world, I have shied away from personal, subjective discourse. As I prepared for Salon Night, I had to face the fact that what I've spoken most easily has been the words of others. My job as professor of literature is to make the words of others "telling," to make their power and presence felt. Language is common property, and I accept that; I have never needed to feel vain about my own speech. I have even been rather proud of entertaining my speech as the discourse of others, desiring less to master their words than to allow them to shine in their own right. (That is the reason I have loved and adopted foreign tongues.) I will continue here to make the most of others' words—with one difference, called for by the Headlands artists' invitation. I take on, perhaps for the first time, a *woman's* voice. For by inviting me to speak to them in a place and space where my speech was so unnecessary, so superfluous, the artists had put me on the spot—the precise spot where others' words were of no use to me. I would need, at the very least, to explain why, even for my own case, I had to go on using others' words.

Mardith Louisell, a fellow resident, had called me back after I had already left my Headlands residency, just to put me on that spot. I had more or less fulfilled my duty to Salon Night, having presented an academic paper on "Freud's Antiquities" (a study of Freud's treasured collection of art objects).[1] After my term at the Headlands, Mardi telephoned to ask me (I kept thinking, "In French, that word is *demande*") to talk, about "anything—your work, your life, what you *do!*" The desire expressed, then, was for my "excess" speech, for that "encore"—that "more"—which, as a woman, I could legitimately be asked to give. I was not to have Freud's or Rousseau's or Stendhal's word as an excuse for speaking up.

It was daunting.

Yet this request was compelling, a logical endpoint to thoughts I had begun thinking about woman's voice, about her acceptance or rejection of the contracts implied by speech, and ultimately about her silence, her failure as a subject of speech. So I finally agreed. Not fully, I confess, to accept the challenge of my subjective mandate (to take on a speech of my own) but also because, intellectually, I sensed a need to think woman's voice, speech and silence, "on this spot," this particular millennial moment so near the end of a century, and still so close to those catastrophes that have repeatedly threatened to end the world. Where the invitation brought me up short was that it forced me to realize that in order for me (or anyone else) to do that study, to undertake the task of tackling "woman as subject of speech," neither I nor anyone could really begin with the "general" case. I knew I would have to begin with myself at almost fifty, with myself as subject.

There are not many models. Whenever I write, I can usually feel secure that some literary text—antique, modern, foreign, English, first world, third world—will bountifully provide appropriate models for me. Some novel, some essay will always be there to point me in the right direction. But facing so unknown a topic, I realized I would only know for sure after I had already begun, with myself, what the "model" I needed would re-semble; only later could I look for whatever coworkers in the cultural un-conscious of the feminine subject were to be found.

As it became clear that I was going to have to try to speak not from my usual, comfortably disembodied mode, disconnected from my subjec-tivity, but from somewhere else that was intimately familiar yet strange to me, I realized that the obstacles to such speech as my own were personal, in part, and I will discuss these below; but they were also, preeminently, not just personal. My acceptance into the academic world had meant checking the slightest impulse toward my own speech. For example, in my book *The Regime of the Brother: After the Patriarchy* I had ventured for the first time in my life to link, very tentatively, what I was writing to my own particular history. Writing about the contemporary world as "post-Oedipal," I had said,

There is another crucial historical event that forces a re-vision of the mod-ern Symbolic as a post-Oedipal frame. That is the fact of the calculated, planned disruption of the civilizing and protective side of Oedipal order effectuated by Fascism. It is clear that the resonance, in the Symbolic, of the rationally planned destruction of a community, a species, a tribal and above all, perhaps, a familial relation—artificial "Oedipus" at its darkest—is by no means limited to those who were its direct victims. . . .

Members of my generation did not spend our childhoods dreaming the terror of an all-powerful totemic Father like the Wolfman did: Instead I had the nightmares parents are supposed to have: how to save, how to protect those who cannot protect themselves? I was born in the last days of 1943 in the midst of the war period, but to parents whose existence day to day, in America, was in no wise immediately threatened. Yet . . . the Holocaust structurally reversed the parent-child relation. It did so to serve Fascism's aggressive narcissistic ends: to be itself the survivor and the master, replacing the weak and feeble parents for good. In our dreams, the children were the "parents." Our parents never came close to being the royalty, the kings and queens of the old family romance—we knew them as potential victims, knew they were barely able to survive without our help.[2]

The critic for the *American Book Review* singled out this particular passage for reproach, zeroing in on these paragraphs as typical of my outrageously "self-aggrandizing" and "egotistical" style, my lapses in tone and decorum. It was dismaying that I had been so unable to communicate, since I was analyzing the devastations of "self-aggrandizement." Was it my inept prose or the critic's misprision? I wondered if there were not some structural infirmity, mine or his, linked to my "woman's speech," that incapacitated his hearing me.

We have been taught by both the world and psychoanalysis that it is a masculine subject who upholds the power of the word, which means the contractual arrangements and symbolic laws governing civilized life. I agree. Hence my love for men and words. But that love does not solve my problem, my puzzle: for while I would never go along with Freud's grumpy remarks about women regarding only their cooking pots, I have yet to discover some less inadequate means of speaking as woman than only and always borrowing the word from others, from men. Though we seek equal access to the "power of speech" (which is a good thing), we need something more than that at this moment in history. That is, we must find some way to grant legitimacy—and more than that, credibility—to woman's speech. We need her testimony in the struggle against minor and major horrors abounding in our time. If she speaks only with the words of men, we will miss something—as much or more than what we would miss if she did not, like the hysteric, speak at all.

I do not think I have been able to, or will ever personally, achieve a way to do this, but I appreciate those fleeting moments when I know it has occurred, in women or feminine subjects[3] who have, if only briefly, managed to come into their own—Jean Rhys, Marguerite Duras, Maya Angelou. I will use Angelou's autobiographical novel *I Know Why the Caged Bird Sings*[4] to help me express where femininity has had to bear the ethical burdens of a faltering "civilization."

As I prepared for Salon Night, then, I was mindful of the absolute need to reconstruct the speech act for a feminine subject, and to re-form it so it might bear what we as women could bear witness to. This is more difficult as, one should note, *testimony* has, it seems, a male root.

Woman's Testimony

It's not for nothing that in Latin testimony is called *testis* and that one testi-
fies on one's balls. In everything of the order of testimony there is always
some commitment by the subject, and a virtual struggle in which the or-
ganism is always latent.

—Lacan, *Seminar III*

What does a woman want?

—Freud, *Letter to Marie Bonaparte*

I may not know what "woman" wants, but I want here to isolate this
notion of testimony as a form of speech in which one's body, sexual parts
included, is literally put on the line. And I also want to place this problematic of woman's speech, of woman's accounts, in the frame of the castration complex.

The feminine counterpart for a superego does not exist. Freud calls its
function impossibly "weak" in woman. This is because her "organ" is absent at the origin: she cannot accept castration as a universal principle of
entrance into society. Physically absent, but phantasmatically not so, the
sex-dividing organ, phallic, remains a constant presence for her—by way
of *penisneid*. Woman is thus said, by Freud, to reject castration less for herself than for others. She knows she is castrated, but, as he remarks, she
assumes someone, especially her mother, retains the organ. This renders
her mute. If speech requires the transformation of brute physical matter
by "metaphor" and "symbol," Freud's claim implies that when woman
does not submit to this deletion the speech mantle cannot descend on
her. Once the Freudian "bedrock" for woman—castration—has been laid
down, she is humbled in many ways, unable to access the higher climes of
universal signification, either because she continues to bear the untamed
organ within (through fantasy), or because she demands repeatedly that it
be given to her by those (men) who do have it.

Now if Lacan and the French feminists were on to anything, it was their
translation of Freud this way: that the subject, in psychoanalytic terms, is
whatever is divided by the fact that the word, speech, replaces organic fulfillment with a symbol, and that this symbolization and metaphorization
are the price of civilization—but more than its price, they are its *cost*. The
division mobilizes the subject into a universe of desire; to presume, however, that the form of desire constructed by a speech that replaces and sub-
stitutes for enjoyment and for pain is universal (phallic) in character represents an inequity for women. If the woman does not accept castration,

in one way that says she does not accept the responsibility for her speech; in another way, though, it says that she minds what she experiences.

Must that be the choice? Either to "accept castration" exactly the way the male subject does and acquire language by forsaking the evidence of one's senses, or simply to dispense with language and the internalized superego? Catharine Millot argues that woman's relation to the Oedipal complex makes of it a *refuge from* rather than an *acceptance of* castration.[5] Not only is woman's superego weak because she never renounces her demand for the father's penis (in the form of a child) from him; she never develops the identification with the father (ego ideal) necessary for her to take on the cultural superego. Consequently, the woman has only an external superego, and her "love object" is always only a "real" Other from whom she continually demands the phallus. As a wife or partner, her strategic adaptation is to become an echo, to mime, second, and identify with her Man, who then becomes the superego for her. Hence the Freudian view of woman as never properly the *subject of speech.*

What if we were to reject the woman's "essential languages"—motherly cooing, daughterly silence, wifely supportive echoing of her Man—but without accepting that her only other choice is the "masculine" adoption of male language? What other channels would be open to her as she closes off and drowns out her mother's voice? Feminists from Julia Kristeva to Carol Gilligan are not very helpful. The "different voice" that Gilligan wants to hear is inevitably aligned with a classic, nurturing maternity. Renata Salecl puts it this way: "Carol Gilligan . . . argues . . . that women, because they tend to 'reason in a different voice' are less likely than men to privilege abstract rights over concrete relationships and are more attentive to values of care and connection."[6] Kristeva's submissively symbolic woman yearns for the presymbolic, knows it, feels its nonverbal rhythms, but cannot by definition bring them to the repressive form of speech.[7]

I have to question whether speechlessness, maternal speech, and male discourse are the only choices for woman's speech. I want to raise the technical question of whether woman is not presently in the process of devising a woman's way of relating to society, the social contract, and to the verbal signifier. "Speech is always a pact, an agreement, people get on with one another, they agree—this is yours, this is mine, this is this, that is that," writes Lacan in his *Seminar III:* "Nevertheless, this division is always provisional, and must be renewed, for it retains the stamp of the aggressive character of primitive competition [that] leaves its mark on every type of discourse about the small other, about the Other as third party, about the object" (39–40). If woman has some obstacle to accessing speech as a "pact," "an agreement," this may be due less to her not knowing than to her knowing (if only unconsciously) something about the "aggressive character of primitive competition" returned in our time to haunt "civilized order." She may know somewhat more about the violence of the contemporary social pact than we would like collectively to know.

The challenge is this: to make woman's silence eloquent—at least about the brutally "uncivilized" quarters of what passes for our symbolic and legitimate order.

For me, "woman's speech" is still an open question, a real concern, in which I, like other women, have much at stake: what matters, ultimately, is the structure, identity, and *desire* of the feminine subject. It has not been posed in quite these terms, either by feminism or by psychoanalysis. Beyond some pointers by Willy Apollon and Danielle Bergeron in a recent issue of *Topoi*, and Lucie Cantin's elaboration of an "ethic of the impossible" for women in the same journal, few if any feminists or analysts have attempted to describe a model of feminine desire.[8]

Still, as the epigraph above indicates, Freud enunciated the question rather plainly—"What does a woman want?"—though it has taken us quite some time to divest his question of the tone of challenge, exasperation, querulousness, and male superiority that clings to it. To ask what a woman wants is to move the question of woman's desire, requiring that we learn something more about woman as subject of speech, *the one who puts the word in the place of an enjoyment.*

Women have a certain experience of living with the castration complex that could prove instructive in this matter. Taking seriously the presence of the *testis* in testimony, we might ask whether it is possible for there to be credibility and truth to woman's speech in a culture built on the legal discourse of "one's balls"? Are we not perhaps missing a crucial opportunity because we unwittingly continue to credit only those who have something to lose—men—with the power to witness? A woman's account, her speech, her testimony, brings a necessarily *fragmented body* to the task. She always risks on the one side being invaded by a set of foreign bodies, on the other having to join them on their own terms, and lose her own. Hence the "commitment by the subject," the peril, of woman's narrative.

If I were to pose conceptually this puzzle of the feminine position as subject, the relation to the voice, I would set it forth as an essay on "woman's voice" through a series of attempted modifications of the classic Freudian positions on women: linked to Nature's ultimate claim on man through her three social roles as mother, mate, and beauty,[9] woman is she who calls men to their love—and to their death. I would ask, with feminist assertiveness, "Why does a woman's voice *have* to be recognizable, hearable only through the 'man's word'?" (Lacan would call it the "phallic signifier.") Must woman's voice only be a death-orienting charm, a siren's appeal, the voice of the Mother whose deadly call we must all, even women, resist? And if not one of these destructive, seductive devices, what in the world could or would a woman's voice—not adopted and adapted masculine speech—be? Instead of this programmatic essay, however, I would like to provide a more preliminary path: first through my experience, and then through that of Maya Angelou.

The Violent Framing of Woman's Speech

I want now to link what I am calling the violent framing of the subject in our time, the nuclear, Holocaust, excessive violence in our late era, to woman's speech, to her potential ability, at last, to testify. The plethora of violence, the senseless brutality of our epoch have taken their toll on everyone. Yet the sheer surplus of catastrophe has also granted the woman's voice, her speech, her subjectivity, an entirely new meaning. I am not simply referring to the encouragement women have finally had to speak up about abuse. I am, rather, suggesting something very much in the spirit of the earliest Freud: imagining there to be an "authority" to the feminine subject, at least where the overt and also hidden violences of our current era are concerned. (I am thinking here, for example, of why it was Sabina Spielrein, Jung's tormented lover, who was first to formulate the death drive.)[10] I am by no means suggesting that we grant credence to any and/or all women's words; these have to be distinguished according to their form and their source. Rather, I am suggesting that we renew Freud's contract with the hysterics, listening to the significance in their silences. Imbedded in these silences that Freud found eloquent were the points where the social contract was failing the women, if not everyone. By now, we should suspect that the social contract did not fail them alone.[11]

To put it another way, it is not as if all women suddenly had a "privilege" over men, for we are only just beginning to get reports—very few—about the feminine subject of the post-Oedipal world. No one has yet told the story of the feminine subject of today, the one who starts out, as Marguerite Duras put it, with "ground zero, Hiroshima,"[12] rather than ending there. We do not yet know the Woman of the Aftermath. In any classic scenario woman's voice would simply end with the ultimate silence, the love-death of Hiroshima; Duras decided to begin there. So with her help, and help from others like her, we can begin to conceive the inconceivable: access to the woman after the patriarchy—her story. Not yet in the words, perhaps, but beside them, in their cuts and silences, their interruptions.

My Story

So I return to the scene at the Headlands, where I know that I have to begin not with the history of my academic writing projects but with the history of my own voicing and unvoicing, my tentative entrance into speech. My first memories of language, my first sense of bonding to the larger order come naturally through my parents, though not quite according to the time-honored sequences presumed for "language acquisition by the child." I am quite early connected to and disconnected from my parents' narratives: that of my mother, child of an apparently extraordinary family emigrating at the turn of the century to New York under the domination of a matriarch who gave birth to her last child, my grandmother, when she was forty-nine and buried that daughter when she had reached ninety. My mother spoke a dialect of Italian until age four, when her father was killed in an accidental fall. Her mother was obliged to work as a cleaning lady, and to place her seven children in a Catholic boarding school, where my mother learned a hearty anticlericalism along with "the basics." From the time she lost her father, my mother also lost her native language and was never again able to understand her mother when she came on weekly visits. The visits only lasted until my mother was twelve and her mother died. I knew my mother's family only from her stories; I never once met them.

My father, well-off Jewish boy, left motherless at age six, was also relegated, briefly, to a Catholic boarding school while his grandmother fought her own son for custody. She won; my father, though, lost some of his power of speech, or his feeling of freedom of speech then. Witty, humorous, master narrator, a student of the human heart, he could nevertheless not once speak to me about his own feelings, his childhood, and its losses.

I introduce these details because "loss of speech" for me was always associated with my parents, both of them. That this was so constitutes a tremendous reversal—the *in-fans* being the one who is without speech. Without speech, one is outside the shelter and mantle of civilized order: one faces starkly its "holes" and "blind spots," the sites and locales it cannot or does not protect. (Femininity has some affinity with that vacancy in the symbolic order.) Without speech, one is vulnerable, at home only among the powerless. Like my mother.

Returning one night from a brisk walk to the local store to buy pickles in South Chicago, my mother, seven months pregnant with her third child (my younger sister) has her throat slashed. A strong young woman, she fights off her assailant and walks home, to collapse in my father's arms. She and the baby survive, but she loses her voice for a while. (My sister is made aphasic by the attack, and my mother gives her patient and hard lessons to help her attain speech, which she does, miraculously, by age six.)

I was fourteen months old when this occurred in March 1945. I have no direct memory of it whatsoever. My mother recalled my staring at her bloodied body wide-eyed from my crib. I have no memory of this event.

But by April 1945, I am fifteen months old, and I remember. I am watching my mother sobbing uncontrollably. Roosevelt, a great man, the president, is dead. Near the same time, it must be so, I am looking down at her weeping inconsolably at the pictures of the Jews dead in the concentration camps, victims of what Hannah Arendt has called not simple anti-Semitism, but "administrative massacre."[13] The explanation is complete, I understand the whole picture. By May 1945, when my sister is born, I am sixteen months old. My mother tells me I am already surprisingly "adult." I am already bearing the burdens of a failing civilization, already facing what the sadism of our time means. I am always ahead of myself after that, reading at three, entering school at age five in the second grade, high school at twelve, graduate school at twenty. Although I am immunized to social peer groups (I never meet someone my own age until I am in graduate school), and I am stranger to my time, it is only because I am *of* it so deeply.

I am aware that I am older than my years because my parents were vulnerable. They were both subject to senseless, horrible, yet somehow insanely tolerated brutality—my mother because she was a woman, my father because he was a Jew. From this start, then, my sense of mission in life—I do not like the word *mission*, but I have to struggle for some sense of the extraordinary—the charge I have always felt, is that I must seek out and undo the cause of such brutality. What I write here today has to do with that larger connection. But it also has to do with what is different, qualitatively, now about woman and how she is "silenced." If she "suffered" constraints in civilization, she has suffered so much more in the horrendous violations that civilization has so ominously and so visibly tolerated in our time. Even as "infant" I had grasped the whole story of life in our time, I had become its witness—silent myself, but in full possession of language. The same holds, I feel certain, for any infant.

Things are different now between woman and her perennial "victimage" once she has learned deeply that her loves—her parents and her partners—are all vulnerable in this time of unlimited "enjoyment" of all by all.

Women may not have the given right of speech. The senseless violence of our time has, however, earned it for them.

Maya's Story

By realizing my own speech, I can now return to what I said earlier about needing to find, after I had found my own source, my real coworkers in this quest. I feel that I have discovered a companion in the autobiography of Maya Angelou, *I Know Why the Caged Bird Sings.*

Angelou was evidently, like me, a lover of words. Taught (somewhat prematurely at five years old) and encouraged by her matriarchal southern grandmother to read the great African Americans (Langston Hughes, James Weldon Johnson), Maya finds, at the same time, her forbidden "first white love," William Shakespeare. She begins writing young, composing, using speech in all its power, competent well beyond her years and her station in life. Zestful, poetic, imaginative, she relishes the world of language. She masters it.

Then she loses it. Sent away from Stamps, Arkansas, and her nurturing grandmother ("Momma") to live with her divorced mother in St. Louis, she continues reading, adding comic books and pop radio to her cultural repertoire. Her mother is very different from Grandmother, though she is an equally powerful figure for the girl. She is glamorous, and she has an aura of sex and violence. "Mother dear" is a star to her children. Angelou tells of her brother's inability to leave a movie theater back in Stamps, having stayed through the show several times because he could not tear himself away from the movie with Kay Francis in it—"a white movie star who looked just like Mother dear."[14] Mother dear was an habitué of the demimonde of lounges, cafés, musicians, and card rooms of the late '30s in the big midwestern city.

Mother dear's live-in boyfriend, Mr. Freeman, an older man, cared scrupulously for the children while she worked as a nightclub singer. He was adequately paternal, even tender and loving. He would take Maya into his bed and surround her with an especially "fatherly" sort of protection she had not experienced as a younger child. (Though she was close to her father later, at the time her parents divorced her father unceremoniously tagged his two children and shipped them by rail to his own mother in Stamps.) This warm intimacy with Mr. Freeman had some odd (to her) elements, in particular a "mushy hard thing" he liked her to touch.

Inevitably, unjustifiably, the surrounding becomes penetration. At eight years old, Maya feels herself responsible for the rape, for having enjoyed the warmth of the earlier less sexual overtures. When she is made, at the trial, to testify against Mr. Freeman, she reexperiences her guilt, redoubled because when she is asked, "Did the accused touch you before the occasion on which you claim he raped you?" she and "everyone in the court knew that the answer had to be No":

> Everyone except Mr. Freeman and me. I looked at his heavy face trying to look as if he would have liked me to say No. I said No. The lie lumped in my throat and I couldn't get air. How I despised the man for making me lie. Old mean, nasty thing. Old, black, nasty thing. The tears didn't soothe my heart as they usually did. I screamed, "Ole, mean, dirty thing, you. Dirty old thing." (71)

She has been caught here in an absolute double bind, one created by the fictional moral world in which childhood is pure innocence. Any indication of that innocence's being breached would subvert the justice that ought to be done and would exculpate the rapist on the grounds of her preexisting nonignorance. A female child who imagined that the "promises" of home and paternal care were to be taken literally, Maya's intimately truthful Yes here would have meant the destruction of public truth in the case. When Mr. Freeman is found murdered (most likely by her uncles) in a vacant lot after his conviction but before going to jail, Maya feels that "a man was dead because I lied" (72). So "I had to stop talking" (73).

Maya must cease to use the very language that had sustained and supported her as a subject, she who had once been able to believe that language was an infallible entity that could tell the whole truth as she knew it. Now that truth as such could never be told in a public hearing if justice was to be done.

She loses her voice for quite some time. Returned to the security (now inalterably compromised) of Momma in Stamps, Maya is for the first time considered "dumb," in both senses, though many remember her earlier precocity.

Her speech is restored to her by the perceptive love of a generous, cultivated woman, Mrs. Bertha Flowers, the "aristocrat of black Stamps" (77). Her "gentlewoman" air reconnects Maya to the world of the novels she loved. Mrs. Flowers seems to her

> Like women in English novels who walked the moors (whatever they were) with their loyal dogs racing at a respectful distance.... Women who walked over the "heath" and read morocco-bound books and had two last names divided by a hyphen. It would be safe to say that she made me proud to be Negro, just by being herself. (9)

Her tongue is not restored by books alone, for they only grant her access to the lovely woman who does. Inviting Maya to walk with her, Mrs. Flowers says,

> "Now no one is going to make you talk—possibly no one can. But bear in mind, language is man's way of communicating with his fellow man and it is language alone which separates him from the lower animals." That was a totally new idea to me, and I would need time to think about it.
>
> "Your grandmother says you read a lot. Every chance you get. That's good, but not good enough. Words mean more than what is set down on paper. It takes the human voice to infuse them with the shades of deeper meaning."
>
> . . . She said she was going to give me some books and that I not only must read them, I must read them aloud. She suggested that I try to make a sentence sound in as many different ways as possible. (82)

Mrs. Flowers gives Maya "lessons in living," teaching her that she must be "intolerant of ignorance, but understanding of illiteracy" (93). She encourages Maya to "listen carefully to what country people called mother wit."

What Mrs. Flowers has done is to lift Maya's relation to the word out of the impasses of "truth" where truth of the inner feeling and truth as a public "good" are especially in conflict where the girl is concerned. Following Mrs. Flowers's directive, Maya puts on the voice of Sydney Carton in Dickens's *Tale of Two Cities,* an act that grants Maya the cleansing tears she has been unable, since the trial, to experience: "When I said aloud, 'It is a far, far better thing that I do' tears of love filled my eyes at my selflessness" (84). That "selflessness," we should note, is both Carton's sacrifice and Maya's lifting off her troubled ego by taking on the persona. Maya's reacquired voice is no longer shaped by patriarchal virtues alone but is given an extra dimension by the "selflessness" of a voice no longer merely "maternal." It is a voice newly able to render justice, to bear a witness the court of law did not.

Although, as in her first, early childhood command of language, Maya's tongue was returned to her through literature, her voice was not. Nor when it came back did it return unaltered. Maya had gone through "the worst." The worst had silenced her, as all violence is intended to do. On this rare occasion, and through the instinctive therapeutic act of Mrs. Flowers, that silencing was not for ever. More than a restoration, more than just a resumption of her poetic vocation, Maya's speech reemerges with a new way of apprehending and *communicating* the truth—a new mode of testimony.

This new speech form fuses, brutally, the mixture of classic "civilized" constraints on woman's speech—her compliant silence, muted moments—with her knowledge that civilization as a set of codified laws based on what we thought of as "masculine" models has gone dead. No longer could fathers be counted on to be fathers; their simulacra were everywhere taking on the privilege without the responsibility; no longer could men be counted on to be men. Maya recognized this and accepted her responsibility, as victim, as survivor, to speak.

Moving with her mother and brother to San Francisco in the war years, Maya depicts the liberation experienced by the black men who take over the scene and walk the streets of the liberal city without the constraints of racism and poverty (they have well-paid jobs in war factories):

> The Black newcomer had been recruited on the desiccated farm lands of Georgia and Mississippi by war-plant labor scouts. The chance to live in two or three-story apartment buildings (which became instant slums), and to earn two- and even three-figured weekly checks, was blinding. For the first time he could think of himself as a Boss, a Spender. He was able to pay other people to work for him. . . . The shipyards and ammunition plants brought to booming life by the war let him know that he was needed and even appreciated. (178)

Throughout this sympathetic, yet bittersweet and ironic portrait of the "arrival" of the "Black newcomers," men finally granted status as men by the larger society, Maya keeps another face of the truth in view. It is a face that stays hidden from the men, who cannot afford to be conscious of it if they are to enjoy their liberation. That other face is not what one might suspect—the inevitable future betrayal of these same men by their society when the war effort ends. Instead, it is a quiet loss of freedom (by "administrative" means) that is the very condition of possibility for the Black newcomers' arrival. Maya sees behind the sudden appearance of the Black man the disappearance of the Japanese: "As the Japanese disappeared, soundlessly and without protest, the Negroes entered with their loud jukeboxes, their just-released animosities and the relief of escape from Southern bonds. The Japanese area became San Francisco's Harlem in a matter of months" (178). Maya does not moralistically condemn the Black newcomers' insouciant "indifference" to the injustice visited on the incarcerated nisei; she does not dwell on why the "sensations of common relationship were missing" (178). She economically enumerates, one after another, the failures of consciousness and of conscience necessary for the Black newcomer (always a *he* in her text) to blind himself to that injustice:

he is "free" and "in charge" (so he thinks) for the first time in his life; the "Japanese were not whitefolks. Their eyes, language and customs belied the white skin and proved to their dark successors that since they didn't have to be feared, neither did they have to be considered. All this was decided unconsciously. No member of my family and none of the family friends ever mentioned the absent Japanese" (178–79).

What is extraordinary about these passages is that Maya has learned to turn her "voice" as instrument of "truth" away from diametrically opposed patriarchal and matriarchal models (truth as what is external and in the public interest versus truth as what is internal, sensed, veiled). From the "selflessness" of taking on the subject's voice, the speech of the other (Sydney Carton), Maya has learned to bend her own voice to giving voice to those who have "disappeared, soundlessly and without protest." When she does this, she discovers a new orientation for herself, her "identity" as subject, and it is for the first time as a specifically feminine one. Hers is by no means the impersonal voice, the dry abstract "I" once seen as democracy's best hope; but it is not sentimentally "personal" as many feminisms today demand. Her newfound identity is as a subject of a new contract for civilization:

> The air of collective displacement, the impermanence of life in wartime and the gauche personalities of the more recent arrivals tended to dissipate my own sense of not belonging. In San Francisco, for the first time, I perceived myself as part of something. Not that I identified with the newcomers, nor with the rare Black descendants of native San Franciscans, nor with the whites or even the Asians, but rather with the times and the city. (179)

Not only, we should note, a city, but a city under siege, in wartime, haunted like little Maya, by an "undertone of fear." It is important to stress that it is an "undertone of fear" that heightens rather than lessens her "sense of belonging." As much by the quiescent, tacit, administrative violence of the Japanese detainment order (signed by Roosevelt) as by the fear of bombings and loud air-raid sirens, Maya's "city" is transformed from the classic, masculine *civitas* to an entirely new feminine—but by no means maternal—model:

> Then the city acted in wartime like an intelligent woman under siege. She gave what she couldn't with safety withhold, and secured those things which lay in her reach. The city became for me the ideal of what I wanted to be as a grown up. Friendly but never gushing, cool but not frigid or distant, distinguished without the awful softness. (180)

For me, Maya's version of civilization here differs little from what Freud identified with and as Father—protecting, saving, making judicious choices—that is, civilization's only excuse for being. It is an ideal, impossible for any one person (particularly merely human fathers) to uphold. That its ideal is, however impossible, now borne on the words of a woman in our violent times should be properly recognized and valued. That it is, in Angelou's book, a woman who voices her appreciation of civilization's limits as well as its common advantages as her fellow men do not, I consider the true measure of our time, woman's new time.

8. Things to Come

Pirates, these women, with their ladylike briefcases for the loot and their horsy acquisitive teeth.

—Margaret Atwood, The Handmaid's Tale

The Handmaid's Tale: A Dystopia of Sexual Difference

For those who do not know it, Atwood's The Handmaid's Tale is a dystopic vision of a breakaway semifundamentalist totalitarian state in parts of North America.[1] (The scene is set in the Northeast; I recognize it as Cambridge, Massachusetts; friends tell me it is surely really Berkeley.) It is called the Republic of Gilead, ruled by Masterful Males (the Commanders) and watched over by their Eyes, Guardians, and Angels. The Commanders hold women in positions of absolute submission to their reproductive and supportive roles. There are Wives, who run complex bourgeois-type households; Handmaidens, who are breeders, mistresses; Aunts, who indoctrinate other women, or teachers; and Marthas, who are what they were for Victorians, cleaning ladies. In addition, there are the Econowives, who combine all four functions. The narrator is never called by her own true name, but the genitive and generous "Offred": she is of Fred; she is offered.

Atwood's *Tale* is to be read, I believe, as an anatomy of hysteria in every conceivable sense. It is also, ultimately, a damning of the undamming of the concept by a contemporary feminism that has failed to consider that hysteria is its absolute passion.[2] Atwood forces hysteria's "unconscious" process directly into what the blurb for the novel calls the "history of the near future." It is "hysterical" in the mundane sense of being a woman's (author's or narrator's—who can tell the difference when a fictional "I" is at stake?) accusatory projection of a worst-case scenario for the future, extrapolated from a negative judgment on the contemporary "white male domination of the social and symbolic order." It is a book not so modestly proposing, as it were, a final solution to the Woman Question, as the Victorians used to call it, one that could even be taken as a satire on feminism.

The *Tale* is also thematically hysterical. Its background is a pastiche of tabloid issues—abortion, biological clocks, toxic pollution, televangelism, lesbianism, *Playboy*, overpopulation, white heterosexual male domination, militarization, centralized control of media and technology—all the issues that fill the media today. It was precisely because I had heard these were the novel's concerns that I was averse even to opening it. To my surprise, however, reading it in bits and pieces on insomniac nights, I found it was neither a grim satire nor a monological extrapolation of a single feature of the present, like a Philip Dick novel, for example. Instead, the book poses burning issues in a way that questions how issues become "burning," how they are "issued," and from whose mouth their mutually contradictory imperatives emerge. Why, it makes us wonder, do burning issues so consistently crystallize, in Gilead as on Capitol Hill, *sinthome*-like, around the evidently hidden *jouissance* of a woman? Offred is so devoid of *jouissance* that its very absence makes us feel it should be urged toward revealing its "presence" in her, and, potentially, away from that presencing and into feminine desire.

The novel was on the best-seller lists of 1986, despite its narrator's passive voice, which is mainly apathetic, disembodied, and devoid of any image but the red nunlike uniform the Commanders have her wear. She is no one with whom anyone would reflexively identify. The *Tale* struck an immediate chord with the public, as *Fatal Attraction* did in a different way. The reasons for its popularity exceeded its genre as satire or fable. Or, I might say that it hit [its] genre right on the mark. I want to take the question of the hysterization of the feminine subject to a fundamental level in this novel, reaching its logical structure through its style, language, and voice.

Hysteric Style

The style is one of complete familiarity skewed by a strangely mild exaggeration, in which the logic of "normal" everyday life in the present is simply extended. When asked about himself, Offred's Commander claims, "I'm just an ordinary kind of guy," and he is believable (239). There are no extraordinary devices, no technologies run wild, no unheard-of aliens or small subgroups (fascists or robots, mutants, or schizos) taking over from the normal. The normal has taken over, that's all. We are told "there wasn't even an enemy you could put your finger on" (225). This state just "happened" to happen. But for that very reason, there can thus be no doubt that it responds to some imperative, some will-to-*jouissance*...

Hysteric Language and Voice

The book is supposed to be a woman's speech act: it is a future transcription of oral tape recordings made by Offred as she attempts a belated flight from Gilead. Her deadpan voice, represented as calm, passive, decorous, rejects all autobiographical devices (there are no tricks to evoke sympathy or disgust in the listener/reader) and refuses any desiring dimensionality.

Even less is Offred speaking as a "camera," a mere record keeper of events; her reporting is detailed, factual-seeming, uncolored by emotionality. But her flatness is not particularly objective; it does not feel like the product of a will to a truth or to a science of its object. It is flat because the fact of the matter is that there are no real events in her Gilead. Quotidian incidents, present and past alike, surface in the same undifferentiated detail, with Offred's making only the most minimal efforts to connect or judge them. Nor is she subjective: she takes events in the most impersonal way, without reference to her own feelings of enjoyment or disgust. Neither fictionalized nor storylike, her narrative is so devoid of obvious motivations (emotional or truth-seeking) that ultimately the book stirs us strangely. For Offred reveals that she has unexpectedly responded to and continues to respond with an inexplicably total passivity to the Will that has taken over the polity.

Why Hysteria?

Hysteria has a special privilege in the question of the subject, the one Lacan granted it. This is not because it offers allegorical, indirect representation to what "male" discourse leaves out, but because, as I have noted in the case of young Charlie in *Shadow of a Doubt*, it carries a demand that *jouissance* persist uncastrated, unabated in and for Man: Man as an Ideal

Other, a Master, and Man, as I have suggested, as Perverse. Offred's hysteria, however, brings this demand to such a crisis that it verges on making that Ideal collapse, on having its demand founder into desire, into speech—turning off the Master's Voice.

Hysteria "preserves" the feminine subject from the "psychotic" world of pure rejection of the signifier by virtue of its absolute devotion to the Master signifier, matched by its own dispossession before its pure phallic power. In reserving the phallus to the Ideal Man, however, hysteria shows the limits of attempting to assign absolute Mastery to the Man, limits that indicate where we must go to formulate the hysterical impediment to forming an ethical structure of feminine desire.

As *The Handmaid's Tale* opens, Offred is under no explicit threat. She is not only perfectly obedient, she neither expresses nor experiences any desires, wants, or needs beyond what she is permitted to have, at least at first. Later, she offers herself some small indulgences, butter for her skin, a certain degree of enjoyment in bathing. Even her memories of the Time Before the takeover of Gilead are apathetic, distanced from her personally, and provide virtually no entrée into her specific desire. You have the impression that she has responded to the will of the Commanders because their imperatives are so pure, so unselfinterested. She bends not to the desire of the Commanders, that is, but to their lack of desire, which read in the Sadean way would mean their total *jouissance*. For the Commanders are not just Men, but over-Men, Ideals (negative as they may be) of Man-as-such, of Man as absolute possessor of All. Man for the hysteric is a subject whose "I" is whole, perfect, and strictly identical to itself, something no real men are.

Less obvious, perhaps, is that the will to which Offred responds so passively is also at least as much that of women as of Men. Although he is blaming the victim, and challenging the feminists (which include Offred's mother) with a world the way "they wanted it," it is also true that the Commander's ideality as a Man is linked to the demands expressed by his Wife. The Wives of Gilead, who cannot themselves bear children, have their husbands reproduce through Handmaidens. Set up in a household with plenty of servants, the Wife cannot command, though she does demand, however despairingly, her husband's love.

Atwood includes the unvoiced voice commands of the Wife (the Wife of Offred's Commander is named Serena Joy), along with feminists' historic demands, as integral parts of the Command he carries out. The Commander explains that Gilead has, indeed, been constructed to meet the demands of feminists (and sympathetic males) to mitigate the offenses of sexual harassment and women's treatment as sex objects in the Time

Before the Republic. Atwood's book is good sociology here, insightful about the motives of fundamentalisms of both the Religious Right and feminism. But her book is more than that. It is also structurally astute. By making the will that the Handmaidens serve ambigendered, Atwood's text outlines a superego along Lacanian lines, conjuring it up as an Other who is neither maternal/female nor paternal/male, but Moralistic, Fake, and, above all, imperative in character.

In point of fact, the topical issues framed by the novel are posed as neither soluble nor insoluble: they are not actually laid at the feet of a dominant interest group, however much this may seem to be the case (this is no simple indictment of white male domination as being *responsible for* x, y, or z.) Rather, Atwood shows these subjectless issues forming to cover up a central weakness or fault in *ideal gender identification,* especially where sexuality and *jouissance* are at stake, for male and female alike. The Commander asks Offred where "they" went wrong in trying to please women, to care for women the way they seemed to want. And he readily admits that the troubles that led to the New Order were not only with the women but with the men: there was "nothing for men anymore," the Commander complains, somewhat plaintively adding, "there was nothing for them to do with women" (272).

What Is a Man, What Is a Woman? A Hysteric Tries to Speak

What does a Woman want?

—Freud

Tell me why your daughter does not speak?

—Lacan, *Seminar XI*

Lacan wanted us to understand that discourse is what makes man a Man: "Man, the male, the virile, such as we know it, is a creation of discourse" (*L'homme, le mâle, le viril, tel que nous le connaissons, est une création de discours).*[3] What, if anything, makes woman a Woman?[4] Before Lacan, that was largely left to nature, society, and the particular fate of her relation to men.

If we can take seriously the question of speech in Hysteria's, and in woman's, relation to discourse, we might make certain discoveries. One is: what if hysteric subjects speak?

Castration, the Superego, and Feminine Desire

If the subject in psychoanalytic terms is what is castrated or divided by language and mobilized into a universe of desire, the presumption that the form of this desire is universal—that is, phallic—renders woman essentially speechless. If her silence as daughter, her wifely echoing of her Man, her professionally "masculine" adoption of male language are the only channels open to her and are the whole story of woman's speech, then what can we say of her relation to the signifier? If woman does not accept castration, because she is wholly invested in the logic of exception to the phallic signifier, a specifically feminine subject is moot, and her perpetual silence is assured. But if, as Lacan presented the argument, she has a differently nuanced way of relating to this signifier, then "feminizing the subject" becomes an open possibility.

Woman's speech (her way of desire) would be at the very heart of her pretension to a subject of her own. A feminine subject—not object—of desire has never been posed in quite these terms either by feminism or psychoanalysis,[5] unless we were to count seriously Freud's querulous "What does a Woman *want*?" as putting the question of woman's *desire*, of woman as *subject*.

The two questions—"Am I a man or a woman?" and "What does a woman want?"—are linked at a deeper level, as one and the same question from two different sides. Answering either of them demands that we remain hard and fast in our conviction that the bedrock of castration is the firm foundation under theories of sexual difference. Castration succeeds our "failed" faith in the "universal" solution of the Oedipal complex, which managed only the male's problematic relation to the enjoyment of the Mother. The hopeful side of the successor to the Oedipal Father, the superego, is that it presumes a unisex Other, a transcendental coupler that ought to treat the sexes equally. (Freud explains in "The Passing of the Oedipus Complex" that superego includes both mother and father in its structural foundations.)

These hopes, which were shared by Sade, are dimmed somewhat, however, by the problem that, unfortunately, the gift of the signifier is prone to be bestowed principally on the male.

The internalization of the superego—that which enables discourse and desire—still works almost exclusively for the male, despite its unisex character. Perhaps any model identified as "oneness" or selfsameness (Lacan will call it "le je identique à lui-même") is inclined to shadow and represent itself as double of the singular male organ. Physically absent and spiritually present, the penis gives the phallus its imaginary figure.

The tenacious linkage of the signifier-as-phallus to representing the Male is historical and institutional. As such, it is subject to change. Each sex's distinctiveness in relation to the phallus, a matter raised repeatedly by Lacan,[6] should be confronted, not because it is an irrational leftover from less enlightened times, but because it indicates the tenacity of sex, of sexual difference in the composition of the human subject. Lacan correctly perceived that the transcendental modality of love—neighborly love— was intended to dispense with sexual difference.

If a feminine counterpart for a superego did exist, it would be another matter. At the very least we might imagine the Superego less as unisex than, like the hysteric, constructed doubly, through a heteronomy, an irreducible contradiction in its sexual makeup. After all, Freud's initial question was how a woman became a woman out of an originally "bisexual disposition." One way of looking at the hysteric is that she is demanding that attention be paid to sexual difference as the contradiction that inhabits her, body and soul. The sexual alternation in her can mean that she has to reverse continually from being an object (a mystery inside a riddle wrapped up in an enigma: a complete, if anesthetized, anesthetic posture) to a subject (empty, devastated, desiring).

The Feminine Superego?

What woman can become under the unisex superego may now be reformulated. Woman feels that her own particular (and quite "real") castration is not a universal requirement, but an accident; surely, she tells herself, some women (and all men) escape it. Because she feels no need to acknowledge the universality of castration, speech is not necessary for woman's ideal identity: she does not personally need to undergo the metaphorization of her organic body requisite for the speech mantle to descend on her. This is because, for her, someone exists—some Father or Mother—whose castration can be denied, an Other for whom *jouissance* persists unabated, uncastrated. Even when it is taken into herself, this *jouissant* Other remains a foreign object, alien, extimate, a Thing, not an internalized limit, as it is said to be for the male.

For Freud, once this bedrock is laid down for woman, she is humbled in many ways, unable to access the higher climes of universal signification, bearing the awful stigmatizing *jouissant* organ[7] within or demanding repeatedly that it be given to her by those who have it. Her posture is unattractive or more precisely unappealing: it lacks lack, it lacks desire. The "presencing" of the full organ within her supposedly can take many forms, including uterine centering, attributing speech to the lips of the vagina, offering lovingly sacrificial support for "great men." These positions, which are thought to vary among types of women, ultimately all bespeak the same refusal of castration: the same denial of lack of phallic power, the same forfeiture of desire, the same preservation of *jouissance* elsewhere than in themselves.

Woman's impaired access to speech, fully determined by the default of castration in her, by the positive presencing of the uncastrated organ within her, thus would be irredeemable. Moreover, her structural speech impediment would align her with the "metaphysics of presence" tracked down by Derrida[8] (but not linked by him to the psychic setup of the woman as such).[9] This is so, however, only if there *is* no, only if there *can be* no specifically feminine castration, through a "ladies' way" of accepting the signifier that grants her a special deal with the unbearable, uncastrated *jouissance* within her—her horror, her Thing.

Once we have accepted the bedrock of castration (as indeed we must), and once psychoanalytic feminists concede (as we must) that the obscene superego is a horrifying Thing, we must set to work (or to war). We must strategize and ferret out ways to uncover whatever special *savoir* (knowledge) as well as whatever know-how women have devised for fending off this Thing.

We need to know how woman finds her own recognizably feminine relation to her *jouissance*. Hers will not be the time-honored male strategies, but they could lead the way to feminine speech, feminine desire: to the feminine subject.

This brings us back, then, to hysteria but from the other side, to that question, "Am I a man or a woman?" Though it is enabled by the formal unisexuality of the superego, the fact that it takes the form of a question should, according to Lacan, not be taken lightly: it grants the hysteric a *mode of speech*. Nevertheless, the feminist celebration of hysteria's brilliance at communicating, silently but expressively, a woman's desire (from Bertha's birth fantasies and Dora's punctuation of her speech by fiddling with her purse; from Monique David-Menard's reading of hysteria to Catharine Millot's sophisticated text) has still failed to provide a *model* for feminine desire (acceptance of castration in her own way) that would enable her speech and permit her a woman's way of relating to her *jouissance*, beyond fiddling with her purse.

Analysts who have addressed Freud's castration construction of woman seldom nuance the feminine forms of relation to the castration complex.[10] Lacan, however, made a kind of opening. He implied that for all the difficulties woman had with speech and the signifier, mistrusting its promises because they de facto fail her, a certain freedom to play was available to woman. If man is a creature of discourse ("le mâle, le viril"), it is also the case that, according to Lacan, "Women are less enclosed by discourse than their partners in the cycle of discourse." That sentence from *Séminaire XVII* poses a challenge for those concerned with the relationship of speech to the feminine subject.

Lacan uses the word *discours*, which is neither *la parole* nor *le langage*, nor any of the terms for speaking he ordinarily employs when he discusses speech as desire. *Discours* is reserved for the complex of speech and act, "discursive practices"—even acting—whose significance arises from their conjunction, disjunction, and sequencing in a complex "hypersignifier." *Discours* takes a certain *cours* or course of feeling, thought, event, presentation into account; it implies a longer term, a tracing, tracking, even backtracking over time. Discourse means, then, a certain history, even a destiny. And for Lacan it means a specific relation to *jouissance*.

A sexual split within the field of the signifier is contained in Lacan's first elaboration of the *discourse of hysteria*. I want to work through his particular conjoining of woman's desire (her relation to the signifier) to the discursive practice of hysteria, to raise seriously the possibility for a feminine ego-ideal.[11] Or at least an internalizable feminine superego as opposed to the maternal (and sadistic) superego located outside, keeping us on a leash, or at least under voice command, and at last extimately erupting full-blown as an alien within.

If she is Oedipal, woman chooses the "paternal type"; or she chooses a "narcissistic man" of the sort she herself had once, in her phallic phase, wanted to be. For post-Freudian psychoanalysis and for its rebellious feminist daughters, the hysteric's silent speech—her body's language—is a crucial alternative to "virile discourse" and constitutes a primary challenge to "male" domination of discursive forms.[12] Here I want to question if an adoption of hysteric discourse can support and suffice for—or even offer the best opening toward—the feminine subject.[13] It may prove necessary to enlarge the concept somewhat before this work can be done. The presence of the hysteric, whose radical question is "Am I a man or a woman?", accrues special interest at this moment of our cultural history, practically as well as theoretically, since it can index the way in which sexual difference presents itself as a persistent problem even under the global "universal" regime of neighborly or brotherly love.

Hysteria and the Feminine Subject

An unlikely testing of the limits of the claim that there is not yet a feminine subject because there is not yet feminine desire (a specifiable ethical mandate for the feminine subject through speech) shows up in Atwood's Gilead. *The Handmaid's Tale* bears reading as more than social satire, and more than just a fiction. Atwood raises the stakes in the two questions posed by hysteria ("What does a woman want?"; "Am I a man or a woman?") by doubling each, shadowing the first with the underlying question, *"Does* a man want?" and the second with, "Am I a man's woman or a woman's woman?" In the event that I am one and/or the other, "What do I, a woman, want?"

So far, in the novel, we have seen woman as defined by her nonrelation to the logos, the phallus, unable to take up the signifier. This incapacity for speech is not resolved by either of the novel's feminists (Moira and Offred's mother). Nor is it resolved by the fundamentalist/essentialist womanism of the Wives, Aunts, and Marthas. The bedrock of the castration complex as laid out by Freud leaves little to choose between the one and the other: both take woman as ideally and Really "uncastrated," either bearing a full organic *jouissance* within or making her absolute dispossession of *jouissance* the support for its existence elsewhere. Atwood illustrates this dilemma concretely: despite liberations and conquests of "public discourse" women were never quite able, before Gilead, to articulate their gender ideals differently from those posed by male discourse. They had to *become the phallus* in order to figure and shape their *jouissance.* They had to imagine themselves the way they imagined the sexual male was imagining them. Offred reflects:

> I used to think of my body as an instrument, of pleasure, or a means of transportation, or an implement for the accomplishment of my will. I could use it to run, push buttons of one sort or another, make things happen. There were limits, but my body was nevertheless lithe, single, solid, one with me.
>
> Now the flesh arranges itself differently. I'm a cloud congealed around a central object, the shape of a pear, which is harder and more real than I am and glows red within its translucent wrapping. Inside it is a space huge as the sky at night and dark and curved like that, though black-red, rather than black. (95)

The uterus is positioned here as if it were the ultimate real. But the work it is doing is, of course, imaginary: it gives circular consistency to Offred.

Women, including this woman, pictured thus are passive receivers of ideas in the most literal way: their "inmost" sense of their history, their most "intimate memories" are what is "extimate." Offred's "personal history" is from the start no more than a pastiche of stereotypes she has taken to heart. The book opens, for example, with her nostalgic reminiscences of high school and the "old sex" that, along with the basketball games, used to fill the gymnasiums she and the other women are now being detained in, for purposes of reeducating them to be Handmaidens:

> I thought I could smell, faintly like an afterimage, the pungent scent of sweat, shot through with the sweet taint of chewing gum and perfume from the watching girls, felt-skirted as I knew from pictures, later in miniskirts, then pants, then in one earring, spiky green-streaked hair. Dances would have been held there: the music lingered, a palimpsest of unheard sound, style upon style, an undercurrent of drums, a forlorn wail, garlands made of tissue-paper flowers, cardboard devils, a revolving ball of mirrors, powdering the dance with a snow of light. There was old sex in the room and loneliness, and expectation. (3)

It takes a second thought to realize that a thirty-three-year-old woman with "viable ovaries" in her time period could hardly have been a personal witness to this procession of epochs in romance ('50s, '60s, '70s, and '80s). But these are normal, historically verifiable memories, are they not? Are they?

That the novel is framed, finally, as an alternative set of fantasy scenes seems to me indubitable. (Late in the text Offred begins to acknowledge that her recordings are "reconstructions": "When I get out of here, if I'm ever able to set this down, in any form, even in the form of the voice of another, it will be a reconstruction" [173].) Less obvious, though, is their specifically hysterical nature, because they are set not toward the personal memory of a forbidden *jouissance* from a remote past, but toward a proximal future: they flesh out her renunciation of enjoyment.

Her central fantasy is that of the state of Gilead as a totalizing master discourse wherein the contradictions between a gendered female "I" and the feminine subject of *jouissance* are finally abolished, but not necessarily to the benefit of the phallic, to male desire. It aims at foreclosing the Thing, the threatening internal tidal wave of maternal (oro-vaginal-anal) *jouissance*.[14] Note that the actual commandments to which Offred responds are those that were once reserved for making girls into "ladies," that is, for acting feminine, ladylike. Her transgressions are often framed as violations of decorum, for example, her potential laughter seen as "a fart in church" (117). The hysteric demands, as Danielle Bergeron puts it, that the "pervert set the limit,"[15] and Aunt Lydia remarks, "freedom from; don't underrate it" (33). In other words, the Aunt Lydias act as the moral form of the externalized superego, which, by urging decorum, permits the persistence within of the Thing through the simple device of barring It from woman's conscious experience and overt expression.

The Ideal Ego, the Unisex Subject, and the Freudian Thing

The signifier of the unisex superego/Other is the "I" (the Eyes). The mere enunciation of "I" grants this purely formal "shifter" status as bearer of the voice of truth. Atwood's novel (perhaps not unknowingly) reproduces Lacan's analysis of the relation of the Discourse of the Master to the Discourse of Hysteria. It so happens that the Offred tapes in Atwood's novel are suspended precisely where Lacan hung hysteria—between the two "collective" discourses, that of the Master and that of the University. In the world of the Masters of Gilead Offred is reduced to her reproductive role, nothing more than the fruit her flesh might bear. In the world of the University she fares no better: her tale is entirely disconnected from her own narrative, which, at the hands of her future historians, is reduced, sniggeringly, to being a handmaid's "tail" as in "a piece of. . . ." In the fantasy world of the hysteric, however, Offred falls between these two stools, these two discourses presumed to bear a special relation to "truth."

Lacan saw the "sororal" position of truth in relation to *jouissance* as enunciated differently in the discourse of hysteria ("L'énoncer dans le discours de l'hystérie").[16] Truth is born in the discourse of the "I" (the Discourse of the Master, the Commander's "I") as much as it is born in the discourse of the manipulator of the signifier (the Discourse of the University; the academic historian who "reads" Offred's tapes at the June 25, 2195, conference devoted to them). But both Master and Academic try to put knowledge in the place of truth.

The hysterics are, Lacan says in his *Discours de Rome*, witnesses to the birth of truth in speech: "[Hysterical revelation] presents us with the birth of truth in speech."[17] If woman is only a body bearing full *jouissance* both for the Master and for the University and is therefore speechless, as Hysteric she does have a privileged relation to their speech—if only as the one who has been cast aside from it.

Lacan therefore taught, during the turbulent days of 1968, that "when woman takes on discourse, she becomes an eminent guide: this is what defines the hysteric, and therefore why I put her in the center" (between University and Master).[18] Woman stands to benefit from a certain culture defined by discourse, but we have to strive for *her* speech and *her* truth within it. Otherwise, we are locked into male discourse, or we risk the "women's culture," Aunt Lydia's term for Gilead's female economy, devoid of all feminine discourse (women's reading, writing, and speaking to each other are proscribed, except under certain strictly limited conditions).

Hysterical Fantasy: A Prolegomenon to Any Future Feminine Subject

I wish to reapproach the discourse of the hysteric now from the inside out, trying to look at how hysteria could serve to make some preliminary guidelines for feminine desire. I want to look at Hysteria differently, not only from within the collective discourses, Mastery and Universitarian, where its content is intriguing but irrelevant to the epic march of the Symbolic. I want to move to the ground of the subject itself, the feminine subject, where the hysteric takes on discourse, inhabits the same fantasy universe of desire and becomes potentially more than its "silent partner."

Freud Again

Though hysteria in Freud's discourse is always characterized by an engagement in fantasies (psychical façades constructed to bar the way to memories of primal scenes of premature sexual enjoyment), it remains by and large indefinite, at best doubly registered. Hysterical fantasies combine things that have been experienced and also perceived from inference. So, in the beginning, as so often in Freud, was the word as well as the deed, intertwined; as Lacan later put it, we are all creatures of the *plus-de-jouir* language leaves us: "We have logical needs because we are creatures born from the *plus-de-jouir* resulting from the use of language."[19] While Freud found that the somatic origin of the hysterical symptom lay in "premature" stimulation of infantile genitals (1896, Paper II on "Neuropsychoses of Defense"), there was also a second origin: "Things heard by children and only understood later" were also discovered as a source.[20] When Freud found he was unable to make an absolute diagnostic distinction between hysteria and obsessional neurosis, he moved further and further back in time to "the first period of childhood"—one-and-a-half years old (in the 1894 letter on the mechanism of the neuroses; by letter 59, in 1897, he had pushed this even further back, to age "six or seven months").

On one point, though, Freud seems invariant: he says that no hysterical symptom can arise from real experience alone, but in every case, memory (at least "reminiscence") of an earlier experience plays a part in causing symptoms—or the peculiar alteration of "premature" (pre-Oedipal) sexual excitation named the hysterical "conversion of affect" (See the 1896 "Aetiology of Hysteria"). According to Freud, this doubling or equivocation is true at all psychological levels, from the somatic to the group.

Thus, while he complained that it was difficult to segregate hysteria per se from "normal human misery," Freud embarked upon a quest for its specificity; but, since the question involved memory, he oriented his research consistently toward hysteria's history: its origin, or first truth. That this was to remain a frustrated quest, is, I think, the result of his having given an unwitting gender slant to his earliest conceptual architecture of hysteria. His 1896 paper on "Neuropsychoses" sought, for example, to differentiate hysteria from obsessional neurosis by envisaging two different primal scenes of sexual enjoyment: the hysteric is someone who experienced premature sexual pleasure as a passive participant; the obsessional took an active role. This "passivation" effectively feminized hysteria, marvelously aligning word and organ. Freud thus imaginatively reconstructs a primal scene in which, characteristically, the maternal part(s) is (are) granted the role of "organic origination" through quiescence and passive receptivity. The *hyster-uterine matrix*, like the Mother, plays no active role in constructing the master narrative or dominant history of human sexuality and never speaks of its own. Feminine speech is quieted, woman's desire denied by this Hysteric destiny, slated from the origin. At best, she is a passive feminine subject desiring only insofar as she has been divided from *her* (maternal) *jouissance* by the hand of another, not, as the obsessional male, by verbal denials.

Lacan Again

Lacan's "Function and Field of Speech and Language in Psychoanalysis" (the Rome discourse) opened toward a different perspective on hysteria, oriented away from origins and listening for something else entirely.[21] As with Freud, word and deed are for Lacan imbricated in hysteria, but this is the case for any "historical" act, understood in the primary sense of the term, the recounting of past events in language.

Lacan nuances the narration of the past by pondering whether the "subject"—read "patient"—analyzed by behaviorist psychology is ever actually called on to remember "anything whatever from the past."[22] Has he (*he* is, as you shall see, intentional) not, Lacan asks, always only "simply recounted the event"[23] by making "it pass into the *verbe*, or, more precisely, into the *epos* by which he brings back into present time the origins of his own person.... [H]e does this in a language that allows his discourse to be understood by his contemporaries, and which furthermore presupposes their present discourse." The past[24] is reduced, in the behaviorist *Aufhebung* of Freud's technique, to being a modality of the present. Contemporary psychoanalysis refuses to recognize that something social and synthetic, histrionic, clings to its patient's discourse, whose "historical" form of recounting marks it indelibly "male." Valorized as the hero of his own life, his traits become objects of a *genealogical* rather than a *genetic* quest by a subject who seeks "the origins of his own person" (we know these will be noble, and so he won't find Mama and her *jouissance* there):

> The recitation of the *epos* may include a discourse of earlier days in its own archaic, even foreign language, so may even pursue its course in present time with all the animation of the actor; but it is like an indirect discourse, isolated in quotation marks within the thread of the narration, and, if the discourse is played out, it is on a stage implying the presence not only of the chorus, but of spectators.[25]

The speech of the "hero" is "empty." Assuming its rightful genealogical place in speech and narrative, the masculine subject glides easily from fiction to fact as equally honorable modes of avoiding the horrors of *jouissance* and the whole feminine thing.

Lacan calls this hypnotic-histrionic, though charmingly literary, discourse in "quotation marks," contrasted with another kind of historical recollection, what he calls the "hysterical revelation of the past." Both modes are "speech acts," though "speech" dominates the "acting" in the first, and "acts" of course classically stand in for the hysteric's speech. But the hysteric's mode is obviously seen by Lacan as truer if only because it is more honestly and more overtly *ambiguous*. Its fantastic conflations are not due to "the vacillation of its content between the imaginary and the real"[26]—for from the first it is "situated in both"—nor to its being "made up of lies." Instead, hysterical fantasy is a unique way of revealing history. Whereas the masculine subject's "histrionic" speech is indirect discourse rooted in a nonabsolute, heroicized, epic past (open to revision for political reasons), hysteria evokes an absolute, not provisional, future:

> [Hysterical revelation] presents us with the birth of truth in speech, and thereby brings us up against the reality of what is neither true nor false … for it is present speech that bears witness to the truth of this revelation in present reality, and which grounds it in the name of that reality. Yet in that reality, only speech bears witness to that portion of the powers of the past that has been thrust aside at each crossroads where the event has made its choice.[27]

This is not to say that what is said in the fantasy is a truth dredged from the past, for it may indeed speak falsely. Rather, its birthing of truth arises from *the* peculiar "witnessing" granted by its linguistic form of expression—the witnessing of what has been left out of "present reality."

Hysterical fantasy constitutes the "history" of that half of the subject who has been "saved" from a devastating relation to *jouissance*.[28] But it

also constitutes "present reality" as the effect of a series of strong fore-
closures: a woman's hysterical body attests more profoundly than aesthetic trimmings ("quotation marks") to the radical cutting off of the
body of the past as the place where "truth" lies (in both meanings of the
term). The hysterical fantasy tilts instead toward the future: it "witnesses
the birth of truth in speech," becoming less a mode of revelation of the
past than a regathering of revolutionary potentiality . . .

At least such is Lacan's sense in the Rome discourse of 1953, when
Lacan's position as witness to radical cuts is exceptional, having just been
himself expelled from the International Psychoanalytic Association.

We come to 1968, to *Séminaire XVII: L'Envers de la psychanalyse* (underside, seamy side, dirty side, backside), "Vérité, soeur de la jouissance"
(61–76). Here Lacan speaks of his first picture book, "L'Histoire d'une moitié
d'un poulet" (The Story of Half a Chicken) and muses on his perennial
concern with such "Histoire[s] d'une moitié d'un sujet" (Histories of Half
a Subject) (63). His future biographers, he is convinced, will be bound to
read this first picture book of his as significant for his subsequent intellectual development. Indeed, he says, he has always searched for the "cut-off
side." But he has done so more in the sense of the road not taken, the foreclosed or repressed (the two are not the same), and less in the sense of the
content of what was lost in the cut-off part of the chicken. Instead, what
counts is what is affirmed by the cut: that the truth, the truth of the book,
was not in this "other, cut-off side" but only in what was said in the book.
Its expressive form—the book—wholly contained whatever link to truth
there was, its "truth" as intrinsic to its mode of proposition.

Now, philosophically, analytic accounts (66–67) of "truth"[29] posit it as
not being internal to the proposition (68). The subject of the enunciation
is assumed to be motivated by some external prompting for him to trouble
marking his proposition as "the truth" per se. According to Wittgenstein,
only *facts* are articulated (Prop. 6.51, 2, 3, 4); hence, any affirmation of
truth beyond annunciation would be an "added value." To articulate
"Truth" is to take on what Kant would call a "synthetic" status. It is something added, *d'en plus*—a supplement or surplus over what is in the subject of the phrase. To rephrase Wittgenstein à la Kant, then, truth retains
the character of being outside discourse, in some other world, even if its
mode is fiction, fantasy, superfluity. Lacan argues, by contrast, that the
sentence as synthetic (that is, not an analytic judgment and not concerned
with the object) supports only the signifier. Wittgenstein's willingness to
impute "truth" to the signifier is simply wrong; it depends on his having
made grammatical structure the truth of the whole world, turning any

assertion whatsoever into a tacit, unspoken annunciation of "truth."[30] For Lacan, the discourse of synthesis is the very Discourse of the Master.[31] Lacan (quoting his anonymous "best friend"—Merleau-Ponty?) defines the discourse of consciousness as the "discours de la synthèse, discours de la conscience qui maîtrise" (the discourse of synthesis, of the consciousness that masters). What synthetic discourse tries to master is the "referent"—the object of discourse.

Now, to state a "truth" without making explicit reference either to its object being spoken truly or to its speaking subject and "the truth" of its statement capitalizes on the way the rhetorical tradition has always dealt with the truth of the subject. The subject is implicitly granted an *ethos,* and this, in turn, becomes correlative and corroborative of its "indirect discourse." The same holds for the histrionic patient.

What is missing from this imputed ethos is, however, a more strictly "ethical" relation in the psychoanalytic sense, that of "not giving way on one's desire" ("ne pas céder sur son désir"). The destiny of desire-as-speech, which is hidden within rhetorical form, is to be the imputed "truth" of the speaker. The subject automatically speaks Truth as "I"; "I" am always authentic. But it is a symbolic not a real truth.

The histrionic as opposed to hysterical subject thus capitalizes on the classical *ethos* as well as the tried-and-true forms of the *epos* ("unwritten, heroic song") to avert the truth of its Thing. I say *capitalizes* because, however ironic it may be, it is the very ability to avoid the Thing that becomes the "glory" of the epic hero as subject: a true heir of the artificial patriarchy, the master of the signifier becomes the person in whom Truth itself speaks as "I," having gracefully avoided, through verbal wit and rhetorical form, having to bear witness to the horror of *jouissance.*

For Lacan, this assumption of truth-speaking in a person is a political matter, the grounds for the elaboration of a veritable *"Je-cratie"* or "I"-ocracy (*Séminaire XVII,* 71). Positing truth exclusively as *ethos,* as an effect of the authenticity of the speaker, makes the S_1 a "je de maître" (in Lacan, S_1 is a matheme for the master signifier). Any "I" identified tacitly or implicitly with truth is "identical" with itself: "le je identique à lui-même" speaks in the mode of the pure imperative—"le je identique à lui-même de l'impératif pur."

Fantasy—the privileged mode of the hysteric—is politically so charged because, on the one hand, as the handmaiden or passive partner to the speech-act couple, hysterical fantasy is the absolute support for the master's evasion of the object of *jouissance,* while on the other, because the fantasy is the underside of the epic of triumph over *jouissance,* it is organized entirely around and by this object. As fantasy (S ◊ a) it has an infinite degree of power with respect to truth—it is capable of birthing it, of producing it as a thing. If hysterical fantasy bars access to remembered *jouissance,* by a second alienation of the subject, it turns again around and supports this "presence within" under the terms of fantasy, that is, in a mode that is neither completely inaccessible to language nor to memory. Fantasy organizes drive around the "substance"—object or bit of *jouissance*—so as to reveal rather than conceal the way the epic liar claims that his/her primary relation to enjoyment is intrinsically alienated. Enjoyment returns to the subject, but in the guise of its being the *jouissance* of an/the Other.[32]

Hysterical fantasy creates a dilemma for feminism: on the one hand, hysteric "discourse" suddenly accrues value as a formal means of woman's expression, requiring skilled and sympathetic interpretation; but on the other, its consequences for the construction of a feminine ethic, an ethic of woman's desire, are devastating. As she becomes doubly subject to the signifier, she can *only* fantasize. She has been displaced by her possession of the Real Thing.

Lacan 2/Atwood 1/Freud 0

Hysteria at the simplest, nontechnical level abounds in the book. Serena Joy, Wife of the narrator's Commander, is a thinly disguised version of Tammy Faye Bakker, a former evangelist with "her sprayed hair and her hysteria" who used to weep on demand for her weekly TV show ("How furious she must be now that she's been taken at her word" [61]). Offred's subordination of her identity to her uterus (*hystera,* Greek for womb) has already been mentioned; she repeats this organic submission as her understanding of the sexual contract: for the men of Gilead "we are for breeding purposes . . . two-legged wombs, that's all, sacred vessels, ambulatory chalices" (176). There are also mass hysterias in the novel, such as the Salvagings (353–55) where women gone astray are reclaimed; and Particicutions, where men convicted of "sex crimes" are torn apart by the furious collected Handmaidens. When a Handmaiden gives birth, the Wife of her Commander simulates her childbirth postures and actions (149), but the group of Handmaidens must go further. They are compelled to witness the birth and are told by the Aunts to "identify with your body" (159). Offred tells us, "Already I can feel slight pains, in my belly, and my breasts are heavy." There is even direct reference to Galen's "wandering womb" (189).

Most important thematically, Serena Joy is structurally placed by Atwood in the position of Freud's "Butcher's Wife"—the classic analysis of hysterical identification with a sexual rival.[33] Recall the desire of the butcher's wife to keep all desire at bay, choosing as her imaginary rival a thin woman whom she knows cannot be desired by her husband, since he is known always to prefer a woman with a "good slice of backside" on her. Significantly, she herself desires not to be desired by her husband either, at some level, for she has herself already determined to "give up caviare," in order to keep herself thin.[34] Thus the wife's renunciation, her "giving up" the food she loves, actually speaks, Lacan at length decided, to a hysteric's demand for a limit to be placed by a mastering subject on the *other's jouissance* that threatens her. It will keep her butcher of a husband away from her own good slice of backside, for example. By preventing her husband from desiring, she formally insists that he retain the fullness of *jouissance* for himself (something that he, a mere man, can never, of course, do).[35] Serena Joy must hold the Handmaiden on her belly while the Commander makes love to Offred during the Ceremony, so that she can identify in the flesh with this competitor who is being "had" by her husband, but whom she knows, because of the conditions of the sexual encounter, that he can only "enjoy" and can never desire.

Atwood's work could not even be faulted as a technical definition of *hysteria* by such authorities as the *Oxford English Dictionary* and the *Standard Edition of Freud*. She crystallizes nearly every aspect of traditional and modern versions of hysteria around Offred, including, for example, the awe and respect she feels for flowers. Freud's 1897 "L" draft on the "Architecture of Hysteria" tells of a girl who was afraid to pick a flower, or even pull up a mushroom, because it was against the command of God, who did not wish living seeds to be destroyed. Offred, longing for a dandelion, is horrified by her Commander's Wife who "mutilates the genitals of flowers" (275). Her first intensity of tone appears when she describes Serena Joy in the garden,

> snipping off the seedpods with a pair of shears … she was aiming, position-ing the blades of the shears, then cutting with a convulsive jerk of the hands. Was it the arthritis, creeping up? or some blitzkrieg, some kamikaze committed on the swelling genitalia of the flower: The fruiting body. To cut off the seedpods is supposed to make the bulb store energy. (195)

What the cutting does, of course, is allow the flowers to continue to bloom, to grow lush: they are specifically *not* sacrificed directly to repro-duction, although Offred strains to that conclusion. In fact, the resultant

luxurious flowering appears to Offred as "subversive," too purely a pleasure for the senses, without higher, later, or ultimate purpose (196).

So total, I propose, is this hystericized definition of woman in the novel
that no woman escapes it: certainly not the narrator's women's-lib mother
(who burned *Playboy* because it represented woman as sex object and who
chose to bear a child without a husband—"What use are [men] except for
ten seconds' worth of half babies. A man is just a woman's strategy for
making another woman" [155]). Nor the "rebel" Moira (Gaelic for "hope"),
the tough, wisecracking, "loose woman" (172), lesbian roommate (she's
the one who, in the Time Before, used to fix her own car and managed to
escape from Gilead's Red Center). Moira ends, however, as the Greek
rather than the Gaelic meaning of her name, Moira as Fate.[36] Her anatomy, too, turns out to be her destiny, and she is last seen as a whore plying
her trade in a faded *Playboy* bunny suit at Jezebel's, the Commanders'
mocked-up brothel, throwing into reverse Gloria Steinem's own infamous career shift (312).

The setting-up of Offred as "hysteric" is more than a play on words, for
she is also set up as the product of the most enlightened "education of
women" currently available in modern times.[37] One might be tempted
to conclude that her utter passivity and submission are a conservative
critique by Atwood of visionary, untried revolutionary ideas about changing the arrangements between the sexes, her judgment on the feminist
woman as the *belle âme* who assists in constructing the reality it accuses.[38]
But I don't think so. For if we "diagnose" Offred as a hysteric, and I think
we have to, we have to understand that her projection, her fantasy—
assembled out of mnemic fragments, reminiscences, partially remembered scenes, past images—is not the repetition of a past enjoyment but
only of past passivity, aimed at precluding her enjoyment in the present.

That Gilead is *her* fantasy is not to be doubted. Her Commander in
Gilead is clearly no more (no less) than an exaggerated aspect of Luke,[39]
her husband in the Time Before, the husband who said he would "always
take care of her" (232), just as he takes "care of it"—the cat—by killing it
when they attempt to flee Gilead (249). Like the Commander, Luke was
unsatisfactorily married when the two of them met. In fact, the parallels
are nearly absolute: Offred was, then, as now, the girlfriend "on the side" of
a married man, meeting her lover in hotel rooms, which never really
seemed to offer enjoyment for her, not even with Luke, for they took place
when he "was in flight from his wife, when I was still imaginary for him.
Before we were married and I solidified" (67). When the Commander
takes her to a hotel to have sex without Serena for the first time, Offred

hears herself screaming over his threatened impotence: "Fake it!" (331). She must keep her Man from being less than omnipotent, overmastering, whole (but for whom: for him or for her? Does she not want him to set the limits on her *jouissance*?).

Offred goes rigid when the chauffeur, Nick (the nicked, the cut man?), tries to make an opening: "Nice walk?" he says.

> I nod, but do not answer with my voice. He isn't supposed to speak to me. Of course some of them try, said Aunt Lydia. All flesh is weak. All flesh is grass, I corrected her in my head. They can't help it, she said, God made them that way but He did not make you that way. He made you different. It's up to you to set the boundaries. Later you will be thanked. (60)

Earlier she has seen the bodies of doctors who once performed abortions in the past hanged on hooks against The Wall (42); later on she is sent to buy meat for the Commander's household at a butcher shop called "All Flesh," whose sign, a picture, not words, is a cut of meat. This equation of men with the cut, the weak, the person who lacks is the man, not the woman. What Offred refuses intercourse with here is a man who might want, his desire. At the same time, this fear of the less-than-Total Man can be traced to her memory of detecting inadequacy in her own "man," her husband Luke: her daughter was nearly abducted by a fanatical fundamentalist (who felt the Lord had given her the baby) when they had been out grocery shopping with Luke. Offred had her back turned, buying cat food; Luke had been

> over at the side of the store, out of sight, at the meat counter. He liked to choose what kind of meat we were going to eat during the week. He said men needed more meat than women did, and that it wasn't a superstition and he wasn't being a jerk, studies had been done. There are some differences, he said. . . . mostly he said it when my mother was there. He liked to tease her. (83)

The memory does double work in producing the fantasy: in it Luke appears to be a commanding figure, but he is not up to the job of protecting the family. The figures hung like meat carcasses on the wall are a reproach to him for his inadequacy: he needs meat, he is meat, he's a pig, he's dead meat. But as the little bit of reality at the base of Offred's fantasy, the butcher-counter incident precipitates whole chains of images, which, like everything else in her Gilead, Offred has to reduce down to their root in a natural sexual difference—and to provide her distance from the possibility of her own *jouissance*.

Each of the rules, or commands she claims and believes are absolute, is broken by virtually everyone else in the novel, from the Commander to the cook. The Commander sees Offred on the side and sins with her (they play *Scrabble* together; he gives her old forbidden magazines to read; they drink and smoke together in private, though they do not, until later, have sex outside of the Ceremony). Lame Serena Joy "fixes Offred up" with Nick, the chauffeur, to help her get pregnant, yes, but isn't she offering her bliss, too? Serena also promises to help Offred get her daughter back (266). Nick at night transgresses these absolute rules: he lets her in when she knocks, full of desire, on his door ("He didn't have to," she tells us [344]). If it is anyone's, Gilead is Offred's "hysterical" fantasy, her self-offering to a perverted master discourse into which she would be fitted, and to which her own weak flesh ("*Chair*: leader of a meeting; mode of execution, first syllable in charity, French word for flesh" [140]), divided from any *jouissance* or enjoyment of its own, would be sacrificed—to her total Man, her Commander.

Which is not to say that male discourse is blameless, just because we've called its critic a "hysteric." To the contrary, the hysteric has here simply birthed, in her fantasy, the "truth" of the tacit, subjectless, arrogation of the truth by the "I": if there ever was one, Gilead is the *"Je-cratie"* (the "I"-ocracy) of indirect discourse, history at its most epic, truth in quotation marks.

So we must now try to account for the sympathy we feel for Offred and her projection of an omnipresence of commanders and commandments, mastering males, and universally joyless, hysterical women. To do so, we must first look at the trouble with the Discourse of the Master, and then at how the hysteric woman is rewriting her "history" as a relation to a maternal *jouissance*, the *jouissance* of the nonbarred Other.

The Commander is, just like Luke, in every sense of the term, believable, like the spoken truth. Yet looked at very closely, he is composed of nothing more, for himself as well as Offred, than a series of stereotyped pictures of the Man, but conceived on the model of the totemic father ("he looks us over as if taking inventory" [112]):

> The Commander has on his black uniform, in which he looks like a museum guard. A semiretired man, genial but wary, killing time. But only at first glance. After that he looks like a midwestern bank president, with his straight neatly brushed silver hair, his sober posture, shoulders a little stooped. And after that there is his mustache, silver also, and after that his chin, which really you can't miss. When you get down as far as the chin he

looks like a vodka ad, in a glossy magazine, of times gone by. . . . now he looks like a shoemaker in an old fairy-tale book. Is there no end to his disguises, of benevolence? We watch him, every inch, every flicker. (111–12)

When Offred tries, as they say in film studies, to reciprocate and "return the gaze," she quickly reaches a limit that is no less than the limit of the constructability of perfect male identity in any ideal/imaginary discourse: "To be a man, watched by women. It must be entirely strange . . . sizing him up . . . to have them thinking. He can't do it, he won't do . . . to have them putting him on, trying him on, trying him out, while he himself puts them on, like a sock over a foot, onto the stub of himself" (113). Man's desire is quickly glossed over here and turned into his failure, his castration in the most abject, literal sense. How soon "her" discourse turns into "his," for Offred, turns around his penis, which from being seen, evaluated, and estimated, transforms from a phallus into the very promise of a power of seeing her own inner "truth." At first she calls the penis that will enter her an "extra, sensitive thumb," then a "tentacle," then a "stalked slug's eye, traveling forward as if along a leaf, into them, avid for vision . . . sharp eyed" (113). Defeated in her not very real demand for equal participatory access to vision, Offred hurls a silent defiance: "But watch out Commander: I tell him in my head. I've got my eye on you. One false move and I'm dead" (113). Again, note the ambiguity: if you falter as master subject, I do not exist.

Thus, even if these are stereotypical advertising images of the successful Man, we cannot dismiss them as merely that: if they meet a particular need to construct an ideal gender, the total Man, it is by now clear that either of them, Offred or he, could have framed that image out of the elements of discourse; it is Offred, though, who alone pushes it to the extreme of totalization where her own "kernel of the real" can again become a question for her.

Of course, insofar as she lifts the bar, even just a little bit on her discourse's structured disavowal of *jouissance,* and insofar as she does so not in spite of but through her "reconstructions" (her fantasies), Offred offers us, as Lacan said, a different "guide" to the history not of the past but of the future. In each situation where Offred discovers, minimal as it may be, *jouissance* in her hysteria, a little fragment of her discourse of her Master falls away. This *jouissance* plays doubly:

(1) As *jouissance* through hysterical fantasy:
With Nick the imperative to "Fake it!" lifts off, and she admits—after how many hesitations?—that she went back, night after night, and that she did

so not for him or to save her life (for she risked it by doing this), but for herself alone, for her *jouissance*: "I went back to Nick. Time after time, on my own, without Serena knowing. It wasn't called for, there was no excuse. I did not do it for him, but for myself entirely. I did not even think of it as giving myself to him, because what did I have to give?" (344).

In other words, Nick is not acting as the instrument of Serena's *jouissance* except in the most roundabout, indirect way: Serena wants the baby, but less for its own sake than for the status it would permit her husband to retain. Thus Nick only partially participates in the sadistic structure of Gilead: he shows his power or potency to be something in addition to the instrument of "divine *jouissance*," to use Lacan's term (*Séminaire XVII*, 75).

But Nick is acting even less as a site of the absolute *jouissance* that the hysteric structurally demands from him. Far from Commanding, Nick is ambiguous (Offred never knows for sure if he will let her in or turn her in). A "man made of darkness" (338), without a face for her, Nick is obviously "less" than The Man. He declines, from the start, participation in the "I-ocracy" of spoken truth: he is an "eye" that cuts his gaze by winking at her (24). He is a mode of transportation, an instrument of pleasure, yes, just what Offred had imagined herself to be in the Time Before. But he is also a joking partner, someone who wears his hat askew, a comforter, one who allows her to make those indecorous "sounds, which I am ashamed of making" (340). Of course, he is no more than other stereotypes of romantic, if hard-boiled, leading men (isn't he a private eye? tough but virile T-shirted bachelor, the loner who takes women as they come, without complications). But Atwood/Offred does not attempt to depict him as a hysteric's Total Man, the summation of "All": he is just enigmatically partial enough that she has to keep on her toes, and though her life really depends on him, she no longer links that life-dependency to the set of curtailments of her *jouissance* that Gilead is for her. (Nick's gestures never constitute for her the kind of moves the Commander makes that cause her to flinch; she even tells Nick her real name [345].)

(2) Hysterical *jouissance* as radical resistance:
At one point Offred spontaneously resists the imposition of an epic history that has cut off *jouissance* in a certain way. Alone in her room, another of her predigested prepresented narratives surfaces in her mind, but this time remembered as having a media frame around it. Offred tells us she remembers having seen an interview once, on television, with the dying mistress of a concentration camp commander (189); in it the woman had spoken of the gentleness of her man, of whose dirty work she had known nothing except that he did it as a pure duty and not with enjoyment or

relish. And he was so kind to the dog. "How easy it is to invent a humanity, for anyone at all. What an available temptation," Offred reflexively thinks, almost verging on a judgment, though the diction seems alien to her (189). And then suddenly,

> I've broken, something has cracked, that must be it. Noise is coming up, coming out, of the broken place, in my face. Without warning. . . . If I let the noise get out into the air it will be laughter, too loud, too much of it, someone is bound to hear, and then there will be hurrying footsteps and commands and who knows? judgment: emotion inappropriate to the occasion. The wandering womb, they used to think. Hysteria. And then a needle, a pill. It could be fatal. (189)

Why *this* hysteria, at this moment? This rising gorge, this wandering womb, which surely is not the Bakhtinian laughter of carnival? Offred is laughing *in the face of* the sheer absurdity of the mistress's narrative, her epic depiction of *her* Commander as a hero of ordinariness, a real regular guy, and forgivable of any crime as long as he was a Total Man. Given that Offred has been experiencing her Gileadic existence as that of the concentration camp inmate, the real one for whom laughter was really forbidden, the one who was really barred from all *jouissance*, Offred is laughing at the mistress's Myth of Man—and at her own. Such fairy tales of the "truth" in writing are important to desecrate. At the same time it is crucial that Offred *be* hysteric in the other sense, "out of control," in order to make this, her unconscious yet all the more accurate critique of the Biggest of Lies, articulated with the active voice of the "truth" as such.

How, then, do Offred's hysteria and the history of the near future of Gilead intersect? Starting with a fragmented or dissociated sensibility, someone whose very sense of her own body is so remote that taking a bath ("My nakedness is strange to me already" [82]) and rubbing purloined butter on her skin are monuments of self-awareness, she gropes sidelong toward a recounting of her "own" history, her time for understanding: it will never, of course, be in time, in her time, or her discourse. But it will be in her reconstructed voice.

So what emerges in her apathic, affectless assemblage of memory fragments in her narrative is a kind of "birth of truth in speech"[40] of which the reality is what is neither one nor the other—Gilead and all its institutions, laws, rules, regulations, everyday routines centrally commanded and organized around a single purpose (supposedly the reproduction of fathering but really the demand to sacrifice totally her *jouissance* to the *jouissance* of the Other, to obviate her desire). What that "truth" is, I have argued, is that of hysteria itself, its being paired with woman, and its intrusion into history, a special voicing that allows the return of *jouissance*. What has surfaced in Offred's hysterical laughter is an avowable enjoyment, another relation beyond sacrifice and foreclosure, to the insistence of her *other jouissance* within.

9. Becoming and Unbecoming a Man

Entre la jouissance et le savoir, la lettre fait le littoral.

—Lacan, "Lituraterre," in *Séminaire XVIII*

In artists Freud saw his precursors, and in literary texts he saw an opportunity to verify the analytic method. From Sophocles to Goethe, via Jensen and Dostoyevsky, he found in literary fiction an anticipation of the discovery of the unconscious: and thus for Freud it is the neurotic who seems to be copying the fable in telling his family history, which he calls the "family novel" [romance] to say that his fantasy is structured like a novel.

—Colette Soler, "Literature as Symptom"

I implore the reader, if ever I get one, to remember that I make no claim to veracity except in so far as my *feelings* are concerned; I have always had a poor memory for facts.

—Stendhal, *The Life of Henry Brulard*

One evening at Headlands Center for the Arts, I was discussing femininity in men with the gay Swedish artist Stig Sjolund.[1] I was curious at the time to know what he thought of the controversy then swirling up regarding gays in the military and the infamous "Don't ask, don't tell" policy that had just been implemented. Stig sighed that gay men in the military were like any other soldiers: they were there because they wanted to shoot and make war. That was obviously not his predilection.

The conversation turned to Stendhal, on whose texts I was working, and who had his own interesting relation to a military career under Napoleon. He was a successful soldier, but his military career was tempered by two things, his sense of justice and his identification with a feminine side of life. On hearing his name, Stig looked at me with a knowing, conspiratorial glance and said, "Ah, Stendhal! Where would *we* be without Stendhal?"

Stendhal, Simone de Beauvoir once wrote, was the only author ever to create true women. I would add that he created them with an eye to Sade, and *after* Sade had tried to do away with sexual difference. I think this is important because Stendhal is clearly a *feminine* man, but he is neither homosexual nor perverse. I think that if we can get a keener sense of the kind of femininity he was able to bear, which is neither Butlerian camp nor Riviere's envious womanliness, we will, as Sjolund's knowing glance suggested, find an entirely radical way of considering femininity. As femininity cannot possibly be so filled with the envy, the penis envy, that Freud saw at its root and that blinded women to justice, it seems possible that Stendhal may have indeed been the first "woman" to lead our way to the future female subject. His autobiography will prove instructive.

Feminization by Letters

Lacan's Poe showed us that following the letter feminized all parties to the supposed knowledge it contained; together they threatened us all with feminization by letters. Around the same time as Poe had coined the phrase to characterize what his Chief Inspector would do to find the queen's "Purloined Letter," Stendhal was writing about his own "becoming and unbecoming a man"[2] in a text that has proved virtually opaque to critical understanding: his autobiography, *La Vie de Henry Brulard*. Its resistance to criticism is due to its excessive lucidity and, I think, to its own brand of femininity.

Brulard is a continuous anticipation of Freud's discovery of the unconscious. But I will not proceed as other readers, who are always "discovering" Stendhal's desire for his mother's body and rivalry with his father, as though he hadn't told us about these in direct terms.[3] For *Brulard* points beyond Freud and the Freudians who would yield to the temptation to see literature as having the same status as the slip, the lapsus, the dream. Beyond, to Lacan and even to Deleuze in his premonition of anti-Oedipus and its politics, philosophy, and its literature.

Stendhal resisted a phallic logic that was increasingly detaching itself from its Oedipal moorings and drifting fearsomely and aggressively against the *jouissance de femme*—the *jouissance* with which Stendhal will identify himself in *Brulard*. The mechanism of both his negative resistance and positive identification is strikingly anticipatory of the later Lacan and, I like to hope, of the future female subject.

Stendhal holds up the letter (literature, litter, littoral) against the phallus, extending its feminization to himself in a way that outwits the ruses of phallic logic, which absorbs and inhabits *any* logic, as long as it denies the passions, even passions that are merely literary, including homosexual ones.

Brulard

I ought to write my life, perhaps I shall at last know, when it's finished, in two or three year's time, what sort of man I have been, gay or gloomy, wit or fool, brave man or coward, and all things considered, happy or unhappy.... I liked this idea. Yes, but what an appalling quantity of I's and me's.

—Stendhal, *Brulard*

Brulard[4] repeatedly calls our attention to elements that a psychoanalytic patient's "fables" of childhood try to distract the analyst away from—those "extra bits," or elements that are not easily integrated into the story the patient tells of his life. Whether these are birds, orange trees in pots,[5] or mere verbal confusions,[6] they first appear textually as unintegrated, extraneous matter in a patient's narrative. The patient usually tries to have this litter retrospectively fit into a fable that is unconsciously constructed to deny their significance.

What most astonishes about *Brulard* is that we find these "insignificant" incidents, on the contrary, fitting into a narrative constructed for their sake, created in order to give these objects their due for having played a key role in the formation and the constitution of Stendhal's "feelings." These bits and pieces are not sacrificed to an epic/heroic version of the author's life, but are instead presented in a way that, while it leaves them fragmentary, yet lends them significance, importance. They are bits, but they are more than bits, since they form the sole matter of *Brulard's* composition. They alone grant Stendhal eventual access to his passions. And they take precedence over his ego.

In "Lituraterre" Lacan counts on just the parts that don't fit into a larger picture to tell the analyst the other story, the one that the analyst alone can help the subject to articulate, by joining the primary tale to the primal scene of the unconscious—the other scene. Only through these bits, Lacan argues, does the *échec du savoir* become *le savoir de l'échec*. For Lacan, this "litter" *(ordure)* of bits is literally the letter: the "feminizing" letter that the *jouissance de femme* proffers against the phallus.[7]

Stendhal, too, was onto that game: he once declared that no analysis of modern passions can be made in the absence of understanding "the relation of literature to human nature and the way it affects man; I for my part, had a perfect grasp of the way Helvétius explains the behaviour of Regulus; I frequently applied his theories in the same way myself" (*Brulard*, 320). Stendhal did not accept the advent of the Letter uncritically, however. For in his time the phallus had taken on a "litter-ary" guise: "Letters"/ "Literature" now formed the basis of a new aristocracy—the "new aristocracy of literature" (229). Henceforward "Letters" in their most phallic and least feminized mode (Chateaubriand, military and bureaucratic documents, the name of the father reduced to the actual patronym) would be what a fully politicized Stendhal would resist most emphatically.

For if Stendhal's narrative of *Brulard* rejected the literary phallus, his gesture had propelled him through feminized letters directly toward that other scene—a scene of *jouissance* that is no mere "literary form." Still, all good analysts must take form as the gravest matter. *Brulard* is notable for being entirely devoid of novelistic touches, devoid indeed of any trite romance, epic, or fantastic narrative formulas. According to Freud, narratives of childhood are most akin to the "legends by means of which a nation that has become great and proud tries to conceal the insignificance and failure of its beginnings."[8] Nothing legendary of this sort presides over Stendhal's youth; his narrative expresses rather than confesses faults and failings (biting his cousin's rouged cheek, desiring his mother sexually, and so forth). The larger "crimes" he reports always form moral and political allegories: he forged a letter so he could enroll in the Battalion of Hope; he vandalized one of the trees planted in Grenoble's town square to commemorate the motto of the Revolution, defacing the one dedicated to *Fraternité*.

So the fact that Stendhal never uses these incidents nostalgically from the self-satisfied standpoint of "himself at 50"—because at fifty his question is not how good, but only "What *sort* of man have I been?" (opening pages)—we must read Brulard as a sustained indictment of fantasies of perfectibility (and sublimity). *Brulard* in fact blames the bourgeoisie (especially his own father) for appropriating and misapplying Rousseau's social "perfectibility" to real nature, real women, real children (for example, *Emile*), and particularly in his own case (166).

His question—"What sort of man have I been?"—is, moreover, not one he feels he can answer by judging himself in the light of the array of personal roles an overly literarized society has deemed suitable for the "man" of his time: the writer in the early nineteenth century was at the top of the cultural hierarchy (Chateaubriand!), but he was also the don Juan and the fop, not to mention the businessman. Stendhal finds he has been all, and none, of the above.

We might try to make the case for Stendhal as hysteric, but he isn't asking "*Am* I a man or a woman?" but a completely different question: How can I, a man feminized by letters, even feeling myself to be inside a woman's skin, be a man still *(encore/en corps)*,[9] but one who faces what Lacan has called "feminine *jouissance*," the Other *Jouissance*—the nonphallic one? I mean that his question, "what *sort* of man have I been?" is neither ontological (the "am I?") nor metaphysical ("what is a man?") but psychoanalytic: what *form* has my relation to the phallus and to *jouissance* taken? Ontology and metaphysics are equally dispensed with through a humorous comparison: "I can see," he says, "that I was like a restive horse."[10]

Having proposed to discover "what sort of man I have been" at the beginning, *Brulard* would seem to "end" (that is, be fulfilled) when Henry enjoys a fully achieved manhood (at seventeen, he is winner of the prize in literature and mathematics; he is an accomplished soldier, a writer, and a hero). So, if he can still ask, at fifty, "what sort of man have I been?" it can only mean that another scene has psychologically supplanted this tableau of success, a scene where the particular *form* of his manhood has become a question. The high point, the "manly" happiness he achieves, opens rather than forecloses for him the possibility of another (terrifying) *jouissance*.[11] His phallic perfection—fulfillment—is an endpoint marking the unseen presence in and for him of what is obviously another (feminine) aspect of his life.

Stendhal as Psychoanalyst of Femininity

I *have no memory at all*. That's one of the great defects of my mind: I keep on brooding over whatever interests me, by dint of examining it from different mental points of view I eventually see something new in it, and I *alter its whole aspect*. I point and extend the tubes of my glasses in all ways, or retract them, to borrow the image used by M. de Tracy.

I only write my recollections to guess what sort of man I have been—stupid or witty, cowardly or brave.

The surface of my body is like a woman's.

—Brulard

Stendhal's autobiography gives us his life and loves from a "psychotic" perspective: he has broken with both his maternal and paternal "fathers" in writing it (not even the *patrie* signaled by a national language remains in the title, since his real last name is Beyle, not Brulard, and Henry is spelled in the English style. Moreover, by the end of the narrative of his childhood, like Schreber, he tells us that he has become a girl (though he has also, we already noted, identified with a few animals along the way).

Yet he had started his memoirs off quite quantitatively: on "this morning, October 16th, 1832," three months shy of fifty. Moreover, the recounting of his youth in the book has been oriented toward one moment: the point where, at seventeen atop the Alps, he attains his childhood dream of being a soldier in the service of revolutionary liberty, about to reach the land of his mother (Italy) and, with Napoleon's army, to take part in "liberating" it. These successes are further linked, narratively, to an emotional peak: in reaching the St. Bernard Pass, he has also experienced what he calls "perfect happiness" à la Rousseau, a happiness granted by his traveling as a pilgrim/tourist/soldier to places that appear in Rousseau's *Nouvelle Héloïse*—Vevey (or is it Rolles? he wonders) reliving Rousseau's fiction (329–30).

At this point, Stendhal unexpectedly remarks on his state of being:

> Nature has given me the delicate nerves and the sensitive skin of a woman. . . . I was unable to hold my sword for a couple of hours without having my palm covered with blisters. At the St. Bernard Pass I had the physical constitution of a girl of fourteen. . . . Things grew worse at every step. I made my first acquaintance with danger; the danger was not very deep, it must be admitted, but for a girl of fifteen who had hardly got wet by the rain ten times in her life.[12]

Stendhal, a transsexual psychotic? Not quite, for Stendhal's sanity and his indelibly impressive masculinity are beyond doubt, and I mean this seriously, not ironically:[13] if Stendhal becomes a woman, it is not as a Queen, in drag, putting on the masquerade of the feminine narcissist simply because "woman does not exist" and he can make up her lack; nor as the bourgeois *Hausfrau* of God, like Schreber. He becomes a fragile and sensitive young girl, the one subject central to and utterly denied by the triumph of enlightened consciousness and by a romanticism seemingly bent on effacing her (don't sensitive young heroines always die off?).

The uniqueness of Stendhal's position, which I must characterize as both psychotic and beyond psychosis, beyond patriarchy but not beyond masculinity, commands our attention for many reasons, not the least of which is the analytic status of Stendhal's discourse of the passions. For he decisively gives up the phallus, especially in its new, liberal mode—the one Napoleon, democracy, and Rousseau's literature (unintentionally) granted renewed powers. Gives it up literally, litterly, for the sake of the bit of debris, the one who is the leftover in the march of the new dominant narrative; he gives it up for the sake of the feminized body—his own, his sister Pauline's, and a fourteen-year-old girl's—experienced only at and by means of letters.[14]

Now Stendhal always marked his women, himself, his cities as letters: recall at the start of *Brulard* that he lists his mistresses only by their first initials. If there are "scenes" of passion, they have nothing of the reverie about them: the material immediacy of his discourse places Stendhal's most "intimate" feelings in a minutely particularized scene, but one that always crosses at a stroke—literally by way of one letter too few or too many, a word added or deleted, or that one has failed (like Count Mosca) to delete—into another territory, an *other scene*. Half-illegible words proliferate in the drawings that he imbeds in his texts, littering, scrawling on the scenes of his memory. In *Brulard* (though similar sketches occur in the other book where intimacy is narrated with analytic distance, *De L'Amour*) these lettered drawings have never properly been read. Oh, there have been sophisticated efforts, but in the most recent one, Michael Sharingham's attempt to deal with them à la a "traditional"-Freudian reading, these lettered drawings are rather more seen through than seen.[15] I want to look at them here.

A common feature of these drawings is that a certain line or path, perhaps representing a strong *narrative* line, is shown as spanning two points. Next, this single dimension is supplanted either verbally or pictorially with another line that crosses or bisects it with one small detail (*object a?*). This object-letter in turn belies the singularity and strength of the first line without supplanting it, thereby demanding of readers that they articulate the first line differently to another dimension—what I contend is the unconscious scene of passion or the Other *Jouissance*.

Let me offer a first example of how these drawings enable us to understand Stendhal's narrative technique and the insistence of the letter in *Brulard*.

Rome, Bologna, Carthage

In *De L'Amour*, Mme Ghérardi, who has led the party to the sparkling, salt-encrusted *rameau de Salzbourg* and now leads a discussion of its analogue—(male) love—attempts to explain her analysis of the four steps leading to "perfect love" by comparing it to the itinerary between Bologna (state of indifference) and Rome (state of love perfected). The narrator listening to her discourse picks up a playing card to try to draw the itinerary: he "illustrates" for himself Mme Ghérardi's allegorical cities:

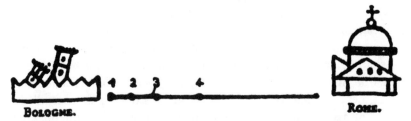

From Stendhal's *De L'Amour*. Reprinted courtesy of Merlin Press Ltd.

But in illustrating the itinerary, Bologna (which Stendhal spells "Bologne") is momentarily miscalled Carthage. We are told that one reaches an endpoint once the beauty and perfections of the woman one loves are fully exaggerated: one attains not Rome itself, but what "we in the know *[nous autres adeptes]* call *crystallization*, which puts Carthage to flight" *[qui met Carthage en fuite]*. The trajectory toward a triumphal Rome, perfected love, is marked with a caesura (note that point 4 on the line is less than halfway there), but what is more interesting is that the caesura itself is marked, by the remark about Carthage as the checking, or *échec*, of Carthage. In other words, the trajectory toward a very phallic–looking *jouissance* here, the one leading to an erected, Christian love, finds its opposite suddenly not to have been the counterphallic one—indifference (see how the tower is falling over in Bologna)—but something entirely off the path, not on the itinerary, or rather, one that was forced to become only tangential to that itinerary. Carthage is marked as the site of the feminine because it is where feminine *jouissance* was abandoned: Aeneas forsook the love of Dido and thus became the father of Rome (Book IV, *Aeneid*). Carthage, the city of woman, the Semitic city, was put to flight by Rome, but as the narrative slip of the pen/tongue shows, it is not dead and buried for good: it has only been repressed. And in revenge, if Carthage is "put to flight," it must also be noted that so too is "perfect" or "satisfied love." Perfect love remains only a distant and unattainable promise on the phallic path. For phallic *jouissance* to be able to see "Rome" (fully satisfied love) even in the distance a put-down of the feminine is necessary; not Caritas but Aeneas's heartless sexual abandon of Dido founded the triumph of Christian Rome. Although this put-down assures the security and sheltering safety of phallic logic so that phallic love thus maintains its dominant posture, it can really only do so by having positioned itself against feminine *jouissance*. Evidently, this put-down must be continually energized, for even one minor slip brings feminine *jouissance* together with its whole bitter fate (Dido's passion) back into the picture. With one word they slip briefly into view, displacing the utopian goal of perfect phallic love. Carthage returns while being "put to flight"—and with this return flight, dispossessed feminine *jouissance* comes too.[16]

Now, if we turn to the opening of *Brulard* we find Stendhal's own "Memory on the Acropolis" (it's the Janiculum Hill in Rome), where, as usual, Stendhal situates his enunciation with a view to penetrating to another scene, a site hidden by what is present before the eyes: "I was standing this morning, October 16th, 1832, on the Janiculum Hill, in Rome, in magnificent sunshine. A few small white clouds, borne on a barely perceptible scirocco wind, were floating above Monte Albano, a delicious warmth filled the air, and I was happy to be alive" (1). A masterful, material description; and yet the scene immediately falls into several partial dissolves. Before his eyes, Brulard recalls the "sublime fresco of Judith" inside one of the churches he sees in the distance; this segues into an associative chaining from the "white wall that marks the latest restorations made by Prince F[rancesco] Borghese, whom I saw, colonel of a regiment of cuirassiers, at Wagram, on the day when my friend, M. de la Noue, had his leg blown off." These two references to dismemberments—biblical Judith and modern war—are followed by a train of images of Christian Rome (the capuchin monks, a priory, several saints and churches). Finally, "the whole of ancient and modern Rome . . . lies spread before me." This grand panoptic Parousia dominating past and present alike, and seamlessly integrating pagan and Christian, subjective and objective, past and present, and so on ("There is no place like this in the world, I mused") suggests a triumphal grand narrative—the sort of Hegelian moment of achieved synthesis that we are so suspicious of, and which Slavoj Žižek tells us wasn't the point of Hegel anyway.

And it's not the point of Stendhal, either. For suddenly, "against my will, ancient Rome prevailed over modern Rome; memories of Livy crowded into my mind; . . . and I could see the fields of Hannibal." As in the pictographic example from *De L'Amour,* Hannibal—and therefore Carthage—enters the scene, sewing the disorder that will lead Stendhal to make that accounting, literally, of himself: "What sort of man have I been?" For Hannibal, the great Semitic general, has to signal a counternarrative to the triumphal march from ancient paganism to modern Christianity, from Carthage to Rome: his eruption in the fully synthetic scene stitching past and present "syncopates" (Louis Marin's word) Stendhal's own "synthetic manhood," the manhood that had been fulfilled with Henry atop the Alps in 1800, poised to repeat Hannibal's ancient invasion of Italy—and where Henry is suddenly "feminized."

Now, Stendhal tells us that what started him on his triumphal trajectory to the top of the Alps and into membership in the company of men is his "passion for mathematics," a passion that afforded him escape from his hated family and the narrowness of Grenoble, gave him access to Paris and the literary scene, and finally opened a military career for him, since as letter-writer and accountant in the War Ministry under Napoleon he was given his entrée to Napoleon's army. Nevertheless, each of these successes has had a downside; the literary world of Paris is another form of aristocracy and ranking; and the dreamed-of perfection of its inhabitants is severely marred, not by provincial narrow-mindedness but potential loss of mind, as in this aside:

> Casimir Perier was at that time the handsomest young man in Paris; he was somber and wild and there was a look of madness in his fine eyes. I mean madness quite literally. Mme Savoye de Rollin, his sister, famous for her piety and yet not ill-natured, had gone mad and for several months had uttered remarks worthy of Aretino [a writer of pornographic illustrated books], and in the most outspoken, undisguised terms. This is strange: where could a pious lady of the best social standing have picked up some dozen words, which I dare not write down here. One explanation of this charming behavior is that M. Savoye de Rollin, a man of infinite wit, a free-thinking philosopher, etc., etc., and a friend of my uncle's, had become impotent through excesses a year or two before his marriage to the daughter of Perier milord. (315)

Finally, Stendhal's mathematical passion, his *esprit de géométrie,* has led him to the companionship not of Knights but of soldiers for democracy who are "embittered and ill-natured egotists" (*des égoïstes aigris et méchants,* as he calls his companions-in-arms [332]).

But of course *Brulard* doesn't "end" at all with Henry poised for the assault on Italy. The present perfect of "What sort of man have I been" ("Qu'ai-je été?") indicates that the St. Bernard Pass is the merely presumptive *telos*, only one possible "crystallized" endpoint or ending to the fable or novel of his career. It needs, like "Rome" in the example from *De L'Amour*, to be supplemented with a depiction of its point of origin, its "Bologna," so that we can plot an "other" trajectory. Now this point of origin is, he claims, his "passion for mathematics"; if we can discover the "other" face of this passion (as Carthage displaces Rome), we may be on the road to discovering what repressed *jouissance* bisects or interrupts it, and thus reaching this "other scene" of Stendhal's *jouissance*. At the end of this second line, Brulard/Stendhal will arrive not at Rome but Milan:[17] "Here indeed was Beauty [342; "Je trouvais que c'était là le beau"]. . . . this heavenly, passionate love which had entirely carried me out of this world and transported me to the land of illusions . . . the most heavenly, delicious, utterly satisfying illusions, did not attain what is known as success until September 1811" (345).

He thus explicitly will arrive, in Milan, at the site of that *other jouissance*. Its narrative will "fail" him; it will be a scene he cannot fully picture, not even in the distance: he will not be able to "give a rational account of my love for Angela Pietragrua,"[18] because "everything will seem absurd in my account of that year 1800." Yet it is only from *its* unseen perspective that Stendhal's feminine logic emerges.

Mathematical Passion, Scene One: One Scene, Two Aspects

Stendhal is finally in public school after his beloved maternal grandfather has succeeded in overcoming his widowed son-in-law's objections. The father wants to educate little Henry privately à l'Emile, at home, apart from society, and Grandfather Gagnon has had to found a Central School in order to secure a public education for the boy, having had to champion locally the education plan framed by Destutt de Tracy. The end of term comes and Stendhal competes in the annual mathematics examination. His performance is mediocre, and he is awarded only a pass, humiliating his grandfather, though the latter treats him mildly, "with courtesy and restraint": "His simple remark made the greatest possible impression on me. He added, with a laugh: 'You were only able to show us your big bottom!' This unflattering position had been noticeable at the blackboard in the mathematics class."[19] Here Stendhal produces a flat schematic diagram of the classroom, with the notation that the board is elevated three steps.

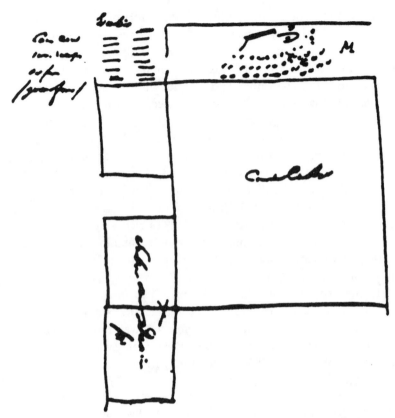

From Stendhal's autobiography, *La Vie de Henry Brulard.* Reprinted courtesy of Merlin Press Ltd.

His head "elevated quite some eight feet in the air" (179). Henry is consumed with shyness, though nonetheless able to do the problems competently, so his grandfather's complaint is correspondingly mild, "Why didn't you get a prize?" Yet the remark returns at several points in the narrative as an object of Henry's brooding throughout his childhood. By the end of his schooling, when he has earned "by my own merit" (177) a mathematics scholarship and hence a passport to his beloved Paris, Stendhal has acquired a singular "passion for mathematics."

Interestingly, he marks this second moment, in which his perfection as a mathematician is achieved despite his earlier humbling at the blackboard, by another illustration, one in which the boy himself is seen, in profile at the top, facing the blackboard, and no longer with his "big bottom" visible from behind.

[*Slate.*]

From Stendhal's autobiography, *La Vie de Henry Brulard*. Reprinted courtesy of Merlin Press Ltd.

At this point we have exactly the kind of "legendary" account—even a screen memory in which the child sees himself in the third person in a visual scene—that Freud would later ascribe to the neurotic's version of his childhood: a clear narrative trajectory that recognizes early failings only in the context of a later triumph of the legitimate narrative that masks the censored scene.

Despite his success as a mathematician, Stendhal never confesses in school to what he finally decides is an ultimate mathematical failing, a failing that causes him to forsake mathematics for letters: "What a shock for me to discover that nobody could explain to me how it happened that: minus multiplied by minus equals plus ($- x - = +$)! (This is one of the fundamental bases of the science known as *algebra*)" (258). His teachers cannot provide any explanation: his tutors pretend to complex explanations; the brilliant pupils laugh haughtily at him. And a new diagram of Henry at the blackboard appears.

[*Slate, or rather blackboard.—Blackboard.—M. Dupuis in his big armchair.*]

From Stendhal's autobiography, *La Vie de Henry Brulard*. Reprinted courtesy of Merlin Press Ltd.

Notice how the steps are much higher now, but there is another figure in the scene, and the blackboard has lost its (phallic) uprightness. Stendhal comments on the scene:

> Mathematics deals only with one small aspect of things (their quantity), but on this point (and that's its charm) it only says what is certain; it speaks the truth, and almost the whole truth. In 1797, at fourteen years old, I imagined that higher mathematics, which I never learnt, covered all, or practically all, aspects of things, and that thus if I went on I should succeed in learning indubitable facts, which I could prove to myself as I chose, about *everything*. It was a long time before I convinced myself that my objection about - x - = + simply couldn't enter M. Chabert's head, that M. Dupuy would never reply to it save by a haughty smile, and that the *brilliant ones* to whom I put my questions would always make fun of me. . . . My great worry was this:

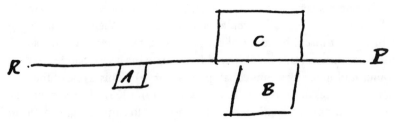

From Stendhal's autobiography, *La Vie de Henry Brulard*. Reprinted courtesy of Merlin Press Ltd.

Let RP be the line separating the positive from the negative, all that is above it being positive, all that is below negative; how, taking the square B as many times as there are units in square A, can one make it change over to the side of square C?[20]

This formula, which is essentially a claim that loss is overcome by a prosthetic appearance of a new figure that rises over it, creating gain or positive surplus, makes Stendhal extraordinarily anxious. Since the structure resembles nothing so much as the phallic logic of castration, we don't have to imagine why for long. Having reached to this root of his mathematical passion, Stendhal "gives it all up." Though he continues to perform outstandingly, his mathematical passion is gone or, rather, is transformed into the burning need to leave Grenoble and his father's house.

What has really happened, though, is that in turning mathematics from a passion to a weapon, Stendhal has overcome not his actual father but his grandfather, that superego who has seen the "negative side" of Stendhal (his "big bottom"): it is his grandfather,[21] not mathematics, that has seen "all aspects"—all Henry's aspects—mastering, abjecting, and "staining" him. In this stain his love for his grandfather and his identification with his mother render that "bottom" of his the site of phantasied *jouissance,* of sexual gratification by means of his grandfather, who for him is both the representative of the mother and, he tells us, also "his real father."[22] When Stendhal made the first anamorphic twist in his line of vision, putting himself in the picture, he was erasing the stain of his wide backside, even going so far as to clothe it in a "light gray coat" (179); in doing so he partially accomplished what the enigmatic algebraic formula posited; and he worked through a complex moment necessary to his "forward progress," the overcoming of his Oedipal relation to his maternal grandfather. Note the word *until* in the following: "My excellent grandfather, who was in fact my real father and my close friend until I took the decision . . . to get out of Grenoble with the help of mathematics" (35)—a decision significantly arrived at when he reaches puberty, at age fourteen.

Thus opens another narrative line or, we might say, yet another "aspect" as he terms it, which will later crystallize around that other fourteen-year-old, the feminine figure for and of Stendhal, who is not armed with a phallic logic—quite the contrary. In realtering the "aspect" of the whole scene, the other Stendhal begins to surface, feminized and touched by letters in contrast to the phallic letters of his forsaken mathematical passion.

Postscript: "A Few Discussions"

In "A Few Discussions" in "The Case of Infantile Neurosis" (the Wolf Man), Freud made the point that his analysis sought to distinguish what he calls "scenes" from "phantasies" in the discourse of his patients. Freud argued strenuously against those who would equate the primal scene with the phantasy on the assumption that merely working out the lines "of communication" that run between the past or infantile fantasy and the current moment of the "patient's real life" (*Wolfman*, 49) would solve the patient's problems, the puzzles of his existence. To the contrary, Freud insists that the facile resolution of the distinction phantasy/real life is merely to give the suffering patient "a premature sense of their [phantasies'] unimportance" to make it seem "[that] they have no real significance," and so on (50). To divert the patient's "attention" from the phantasies and the scenes of primal passion they screen off "as soon as their existence and general outlines are divined, [gives] support . . . to the work of repression, thanks to which they have been put beyond the patient's reach in spite of all his pains" (238). The patient will never obtain "command of the interest which is attached to them"—in short, he or she will have been barred access to the source of his or her passions by fresh means; psychotherapy itself will reinforce the first work of repression.

That the *scene* is often confused with *phantasy* is understandable, but incorrect; Freud plainly stated

> I am not of opinion . . . that such scenes must necessarily be phantasies because they do not reappear in the shape of recollections. It seems to me absolutely equivalent to a recollection if the memories are replaced by dreams, the analysis of which invariably leads back to the same scene, and which reproduce every portion of its content in an indefatigable variety of new shapes. (239)

(1) *Phantasies* are structures, neurotic or psychotic, wherein gratification or *jouissance* is being obtained by their means, even though they may be painful and symptomatic, and variable in the degree to which they adapt to reality or deny it.

(2) *Scenes* are entirely different: the scene is the place where the patient has encountered the real and has had to blank its power—its pleasure and terror—from memory. The object of primal repression is, we know, what Freud characterized as a "scene" of passion toward which everything in the patient's current narrative, demeanor, and suffering is oriented and yet completely blinded: the scene cannot be recollected directly and thus

must be apprehended only by its repetition in the discourse, not despite but because of the variety of forms it takes. I hope it is by now clear that Stendhal's book has performed, as Freud does for the Wolf Man, the analysis by means of which he reaches his primal scenes of passion, having forced himself "beyond" the phallus—the signifier—by means of the feminized letter.

10. Love outside the Limits of the Law

Qualities You Look for in a Mate:
Must be male.
Must be mammal.
Must do dishes.

—*Mixed Blood,* installation by Valerie Soe,
Yerba Buena Center for the Arts, San Francisco, 1994

My first impulse, when the order to write on "Lacan and Love" came in, was to place him into the long, delicious literary line of lovers (mainly French) that I have taken: Rousseau, Stendhal, Flaubert, even Barthes and Duras. These are writers who have most elegantly and eloquently expressed how love exceeds the limits of the word. The lover's discourse is, by definition or by default, what overshoots the four other discourses (the "forms of the social tie"), which together try to make up for its absence.[1] If Desdemona loves Othello by granting him, for his pains "a world of sighs," how much these sighs mean as signs (standing for something to someone) can only be implied through a supplementary catalogue, "beyond the phallus," which can never be exhausted by any vocabulary.

"A letter," Rousseau tells us, "which love has really dictated, a letter from a truly impassioned Lover, will be loose, diffuse, lengthy, disordered,

235

repetitious. His heart, full of a feeling that overflows, says and says again the same thing, and it is never finished saying it, like a living wellspring [source] which flows endlessly and is never exhausted. Nothing striking, nothing remarkable; one retains neither words nor turns of phrase."[2] Wordless, love edges over into what Rousseau terms, "une autre sorte de jouissance,"[3] the same unspeakable *jouissance* Lacan designated as the "feminine" one: "Ever since we've been begging them . . . begging them on our knees to try to tell us about it, well, not a word!"[4]

Love opens where the Symbolic chain is broken down, revealing something unsayable, even transcendent that escapes its range. Or something poetic. Words diverted from their purely symbolic—which is to say, militantly meaningless arrangement—become objects in themselves, the working space of a culture, "a demand for something else which, metonymized, spreads out in the gap."[5] They bring us, broken down, eyeball to eyeball with the Thing; or, rather, they lead us to the point where we "search to find Things in signs."[6] An impossible quest, since "what is found is sought in the paths of the signifier," Lacan tells us: or, not really "found," but only promised by a signifying network whose function is "to lead the subject from signifier to signifier, by generating as many signifiers as are required to maintain at as low a level as possible the tension that regulates the whole functioning of the psychic apparatus."[7] (One recognizes here the aim of Aristotelian ethics based on the pleasure principle.)

I see Bernie Lubell's flow chart for his installation *Niche of Desire* through Lacanian eyes: note Lubell's special place, the void (or labyrinth), created near the center by the flowing of the terms. This vacancy has something to do with the Feminine Thing we have sought for in signs.[8] Note also that the weak "line of flight" from this emptiness falls toward a site marked "Lies as a Landscape"—a nice ambiguity. Lubell has paths from "Very Particular Male/Fem Boundary" to "Desire," crossing this line with one from "Mother" to "Completion." But it is his "Landscape as Lies" (what "Lies as a Landscape") that drops straight from the empty spot, between the limits of unfulfilled Desire and the Mother. It is an "uncommon ground."[9]

That network—but only if the absence at its heart is re-marked, as it is in this artwork—is what we call Love. It confers a consistency on what is nothing at all—"crystallization," Stendhal calls it; "plane of consistency" for Deleuze and Guattari.[10] Rousseau writes:

> Love is only illusion; it makes for itself, so to speak, another Universe; it surrounds itself with objects that are not, or to which it alone has given being; and as it renders all its feelings into images, its language is always figurative.

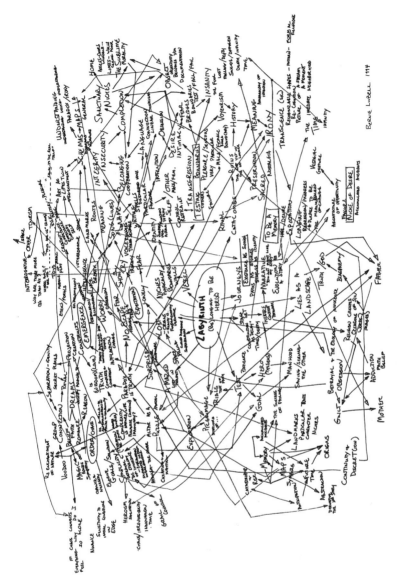

Bernie Lubell, flow chart for the installation *Niche of Desire* (1993). Reprinted courtesy of the artist.

But these figures are unbalanced, unstrung *[sans suite]*, their eloquence is in their disarray. It proves all the more the less it reasons.[11]

For a long time I, following Rousseau and Stendhal, ardently hoped that this other space opened up by the symbolic breakdown might be a free one, "an inexplicable void,"[12] that would become an occasion to articulate an event—the advent, the coming of something else, something other, something feminine: "Héloïse speaks to you of love; some ass speaks to you of his love; don't you sense that these two have nothing but the word in common?[13] I also imagined that Lacan was hinting at this other coming: was it not he who told us of the "other" *jouissance (féminine)*? So far, though, I have found the other *jouissance* has not spoken itself, though it has been approached on a stream of words that, even for Lacan, constitute a lover's discourse, having intentionally lost their place in ordinary discursive chains.

Lacan is, however, brutally frank about the disproportion in the distribution of pleasure in love as in language between the sexes. He, who so plainly told us that speaking of love was a pleasure in itself, reserved this pleasure at its height not to the lover, but to the analyst: "Speaking of love, we analysts do nothing else." Thus he seems to run counter to the hopes implied by Rousseau and expressed by Stendhal, that some feminine things might speak—with pleasure—about love.

It is the stake of this chapter, and the reason for my entering the uncertain and disconcerting game of love, for walking the uncommon ground of the country of love, and for risking falling into the world of art, that my feminine Thing might come, as object or as subject, to speak of love. Though I am hesitant, this means I must close the loop from Lacan's reading of courtly love to his pronouncement that all fields of science, prior to his, gave up on "feminine *jouissance*"—what used to be called female orgasm.[14] Even Freud modeled bliss entirely on an autoeroticism that took self-sex organ-pleasure as its model, limiting *jouissance* to the masculine final choice of "my Mother or myself."[15]

Tempting as it is, then, I will not simply insert Lacan into my French series, although he certainly participates in it—at least not without some delays and preliminaries. These will constitute the foreplay of my paper, made up of reading the "pleasure of speaking of love" more in the register of the "pleasure" to be had in "desiring" than in a register of compensatory nonfulfillment. I cannot feel—at least not yet—completely free to imagine that Lacan's wordless "*jouissance de la femme*"[16] might really be the next step from Rousseau's lover's letter and Stendhal's famous ellipses to refinding Héloïse's word. Even though Lacan provides a rationale—at last—for the feminine Thing to speak, he just as forcefully forecloses this possibility. Or so it seems. For Lacan pointed to something a little different from the tongue-tying endemic to love.[17]

Lacan was entranced by the idea of another *jouissance* (I would rather call it a different pleasure) inscribed *between* systems of signs and Things themselves.[18] He thought it could only exist in a newly re-marked emptiness, the one that art (the other name for love) inexhaustibly signaled. In other words, it could only take root in the field of *sublimation* where a new form of Thing was to be found, without perhaps only being refound.

The feminine object, this new form of the Thing, as Lacan elaborated it in *Seminar VII,* exists only within a certain space, a space beyond the good. Like the old Thing, it, too, is a site of a sublimation, sublimation being necessary for the elaboration of a culture, a creativity, an art. But this culture and art would be oriented differently from the good/evil, moral/immoral axis commanded by the old Thing. It would be oriented not by supposing a *jouissance de la mère* as a Supreme and interdicted Good, but by soliciting a *jouissance de femme,* a woman's enjoyment (orgasm, ravishing, bliss, pleasure). This *jouissance* would be neither the unlimited *jouissance* of the mother (though it has links, often defensive, to it) nor the limited and carefully trimmed *jouissance* of the phallus (though it has links, often compelling, to it as well). Between these two poles of enjoyment—which are so many deaths for her—the *jouissance* of the feminine object exists as on a permanent plane of consistency of desire (which is how Lacan's oddest and in some ways best followers, Deleuze and Guattari, designated courtly love).[19]

Lacan reduced the analysis of love to the imaginary as *means,* and it led him to the confrontation with the place and space around the new feminine Thing. I want to take Lacan's insistent reduction of the *aim* to its *object* (that is to say, in Freudian parlance, to its *means*) and experiment with detaching it utterly from the body of the mother-as-final-Good, in fact, to experiment with detaching it from any relation to goods at all.

I also want to reconnect Lacan, after these preliminaries, to the romance tradition wherein love is a region, a "country" (*"un pays de tendre"*). It is possible that this "country" (Cythera, Rousseau's "other universe") remains open only to a psychology of love and never to its psychoanalysis—psychoanalysis being too cynical, too logical, or too rational. Still, Lacan's strong assertion of *two* sexes—Other to themselves—who might become its inhabitants can both enrich the psychology of love and expand the horizon of psychoanalytic regard for the feminine Thing.

It is also well to emphasize here and now that "man, a woman, they are only signifiers. It is from that, from speech in its incarnation as one sex or the other, that they derive their function. The Other, in my terms, can therefore only be the Other sex" (Lacan, *Séminaire XX*, 39–40).[20] The Symbolic Other is supposed to occupy the space of *jouissance* itself. However, when Lacan in his seminar on "The ethics of psychoanalysis" refers to *jouissance* as a concept, he posits that *jouissance* cannot be completely translated into words. *Jouissance* always leaves a "remainder" that cannot be spoken; it is to this remainder that we attach the well-known concept of *objet-a*, to which Lacan assigns the function of cause of Desire.

> Once the subject has been constituted in speech, the Other will never exhaust the "real" of *jouissance*; the signifier which would put this *jouissance* into words will always be lacking. For this reason, Lacan marks the place of the Other with a bar ... as a matheme S(Ø). ... It is through the barred Other that the status of truth is revealed as that which can never be entirely spoken."[21]

What is it that Love has to deal with, apart from biology, psychology, gender, and even genre? *Love*, not sex all by itself, is the original gender (and genre/as/species) "fuck." Anyone can fall in love with anyone or anything. (That is the secret of Robert Mapplethorpe's being so reviled, too—that as he "becomes animal" [à la Deleuze] he keeps himself entirely lovable.)

Psychoanalysis following Freud is most suspicious of love as transference and as narcissism, but Lacan, unlike Freud, does not fail to show a certain tenderness toward the *pays de tendre*, for a "love outside the limit of the law where alone it may live" *(Seminar XI)*. What I am writing here is a way of remarking how deeply the illusionary character of love solicits tender, though not uncritical, attention from the rational and logical systems of psychoanalytic thought, even of the sternest European sort.

Lacan and the *Pays de Tendre;* or, The Space of "Destruction"

In *Seminar VII,* utilizing a neo-Heideggerian vocabulary of *Destruktion,* Lacan initiates the thought of the feminine Thing in the form of a meditation on a renewal of space—of its elementary, awesome emptiness before the Thing. A spacing rather than a space, really, a displacing, rather than a placement, of the subject momentarily deprived of the signifier's assistance. The subject giving up on the phallus, in other words. Here Lacan addresses what Freud did not wish to address, the moment of creation, the origin of the work of art. Speaking of the cave paintings of Altamira, Lacan notes:

> These images are often painted over each other; it's as if in a consecrated spot it represented, for each subject capable of undertaking such an exer-

cise, the opportunity to draw or project afresh what he needed to bear witness to, and to do so moreover over what had already been done before. That suggests the idea of something like the updating of a certain creative potential. (*Seminar VII*, 139)

Lacan did not stop with this moment of renewal of the powers of language (or artifice) to conquer "new territory," to sieze hold of whatever astonishingly singular space has suddenly revealed itself at a certain spot, and as a particular "locus of pain." Here, Lacan showed his own originality. He continued looking at the same space, but asked after its origin on the *objective* side. We are to look at the same ground from the antinomian other perspective, to see it from the point of view of the Thing that it protects, defends, defers, and defers to:

These images cannot fail to seize us as being deeply linked both in a tight relationship to the world . . . and to something that in its subsistence appears as possessing the character of a beyond of the sacred—something we are precisely trying to identify in its most general form by the term, the Thing. I would say it is primitive subsistence viewed from the perspective of the Thing. . . . Emptiness . . . designates the place of the Thing. (139–40)

Where love gets into the picture, or shapes the imaginary, empty field between the signifier and the Thing, at least at one odd moment in European history, is the elaboration of courtly love.

Interestingly, when Heidegger wrote of "the clearing," he immediately envisaged a "folk" springing up there.[22] What passing beyond the sacred does, in Lacan's case, is the opposite: it is the very disorienting, reorienting, or even disestablishing of a people—at least of its symbolic economy— by virtue of its being seen from the perspective of the Thing, the Thing that the human signifying network could never encompass. What interested Lacan here was less the power of the signifier to renew the city, "civilization," following on "Destruction"—the clearing—than its opening the way to the New Thing (which is rather the reverse of Heidegger). The capacity to "create an emptiness" (140) alone provides the point necessary for dignifying the object—sublimating it.[23] There "one finds a sensitive spot, a lesion, a locus of pain, a point of the reversal of the whole of history, insofar as it's the history of art and we are implicated in it" (140).

That "locus of pain" for feudalism is, of course, the woman, reduced as she was by the Symbolic order to being a pure commodity, a pure good, a pure subject of the traffic in women. At this historical moment, an incredible, impossible moment, courtly love poetry arises as if it were in another place, another time and country altogether. Stendhal, like Lacan, saw courtly love as the birth of a civilization formed by art: a civilization of pure poetry, and, thus a world perhaps beyond the superego.[24] "There is," wrote Stendhal, an

> indication that this way of life [courtly love] was well along the road to true civilization: they were but a step from the horrors of the Middle Ages and of feudalism, where force reigned supreme, yet the weaker sex were less oppressed then than they legally are today. The poor weak creatures who have most to lose in love and whose charms soon vanish held in their hands the destinies of the men around them. (*Love*, 166)

What does courtly love so satisfy in the lover that it compels him to this tender spot, this "locus of pain," this anguished origination point known as art—and as love? According to Lacan, this anxiety meets an anti-nomian demand for desire under the peculiar circumstance where the Thing itself, thoroughly at the mercy of the signifier, is no longer counted for any Thing at all. That place where the Thing as a goal was relegated to the infinitely real. What arises is a masculine demand to be deprived of something real—of the Real—but by other than traditional, Oedipal means.

Courtly Love

> Courtly love blazed across history like a meteor.
> —Lacan, "A Love Letter"

For lovers before Freud, the Other field of Love—however idyllic and Elysian (or infernal and torturous), however open it imagined itself to be—was by no means free from legislation. What remained "outside" the symbolic was less an open *pays de tendre* than a spacing around a pole star that unconsciously guided its lovers toward a Sovereign Good. Quoting a friend of his in *Seminar VII*, Lacan says, "The problem of evil is only worth raising as long as one has not fixed on the idea of transcendence by some good that is able to dictate to man what his duties are. Till that moment the exalted representation of evil will continue to have the greatest revolutionary value" (70). The lover orbited but never attained this Thing, this untouchable Good. Why? Because it was "the object of incest, das Ding, the Mother" (70):

> Well now, the step taken by Freud at the level of the pleasure principle is to show us that there is no Sovereign Good—that the Sovereign Good, which is *das Ding*, which is the mother, is also the object of incest, is a forbidden

good, and that there is no other good. Such is the foundation of the moral law as turned on its head by Freud. (*Seminar VII*, 70)

Man's every move, motion and emotion, was determined by this untouchable Thing.

One should distinguish, though: the object qua Thing is less object than, in Freud's terms, *aim*, the end, "the end, the terminal point, the abolition of the whole world of demand, which is the one that at its deepest level structures man's unconscious" (Lacan, *Ethics*, 68). Not only did the abolition or banishment of the Maternal world of demand open up a whole world of *goods*: it supplied the criteria, the very range and definition of the surrogate aims of love as we ordinarily envision them, the goals we might actually someday attain—the "possession of all women for a man, and of an ideal man for a woman" (*Seminar VII*, 303).

After Freud, Lacan knew, the revelation of the mother as the ultimate aim could no longer innocently support even the most wordless, seemingly disoriented lover's discourse. At best, the bracketed Mother supports an act of love dependent on a "polymorphous perversion of the male," that montage of partial drives (oral, scopic, anal) circulating around the *objets a* (breast, voice, gaze, feces), without which "man has no chance of enjoying the body of the woman" ("A Love Letter," 143). Man manages with the objects he has at hand, so to speak.

Lacan fully conceded that for those who take up a masculine position, phallic *jouissance* is directed to those body parts (designated as *objets a*)[25] that seem to the subject to be the residue or remains of what would have been his supreme, but forbidden, Good: the *jouissance* of the Mother. Idealized as the ultimate Good, she of course becomes what deprives him of the Good, that is, of her presence. Because he cannot have the Thing Itself, man is granted leave to enjoy certain objects, representative parts of her Body, but he is also granted the power of speech, which is to say a place in the Symbolic order.[26] After all, it is only the "distance between the subject and das Ding [that] is precisely the condition of speech" (*Seminar VII*, 69).

But this speech is precisely not the condition of love. Or, rather, it is what lives, where it calls itself love, only from the suffering of its object, the Thing or "that which in the real suffers from the signifier" (134):

> The Thing is that which in the real, the primordial real, suffers from the signifier.... The real we do not yet have to limit, the real in its totality, both the role of the real subject, and the real he has to deal with as exterior to

him. . . . There is nothing between the organization in the signifying network [of *Vorstellungreprasentanz*] and the constitution in the real of the space or central place in which the field of the Thing as such presents itself to us. (118)

Once Freud had revealed the (obscene) nature of the Supreme Good as the Maternal Thing, however, Lacan saw an absolute reversal in the direction of the moral law, the one formerly based on the pleasure principle. In his own *Ethics* seminar Lacan attempted to go beyond the Good (and therefore beyond Evil). Dimly adumbrated in the Freudian equation of the Thing as Sovereign Good with the interdicted Mother was—in Lacan's eyes—the possible *disequation* of the Thing from the Mother. Removed from the dominion of the Good, the register of goods, the stock of goods that are granted to the man, what would the Thing be if it were no longer a disguised representative of the end, death, and the Mother? (Bataille, it seems, never saw erotism as anything other than a deceived relation to these two. He appreciated those, criminal and transgressive, who were at least this "honest" about the "truth" of love.)[27] I cannot help speculating whether at the precise point where the aim is suspended in an absolute way—by Freud (by Kant?)—that something else is possible in the definition of love, and especially of its object. Seen in the perspective of something that points away rather than toward the Maternal body, what would the new, or, rather, simulated Thing be?

It would still be feminine, of that Lacan seems sure, simply because it would not be masculine. It would be feminine because it occupies the place of the object that binds the libidinal drives of the masculine subject. Its position is risky, both for itself and for the masculine subject. Unsheltered by the *distance* that separates the subject from the Thing, the object is all the more open to "suffering from the signifier," from its being consumed by phallic drive. But the masculine subject risks something also if the object loses its (veiled) link to the aim that must be forever deferred (the Mother). His entire existence—as the speaking subject—is at risk if that distance ("precisely the condition of speech") is forgone.

It is all the more crucial, then, if the Mother is definitively foreclosed, that the new object itself be the subject of a sublimation, that it be itself "raised to the dignity of the Thing." Exploring this Other Thing, not merely hallucinatory but imaginary—site of a sublimation machinery different from that of the phallus—is Lacan's ostensible reason for researching his only true love, Courtly Love:

At the level of sublimation the object is inseparable from the imaginary and especially cultural elaborations. It is not just that the collectivity recognizes in them useful objects; it finds rather a space of relaxation where it may in a way delude itself on the subject of das Ding, colonize the field of das Ding with imaginary schemes.... In forms that are historically and socially specific, the [object] a elements, the imaginary elements of the fantasm come to overlay the subject, to delude it, at the very point of das Ding.... That is why I shall talk to you ... of courtly love. (*Seminar VII*, 99)

Recently, Slavoj Žižek has pinpointed the "neutrality" of Lady of Courtly Love as a figure for the superego: though art-based, she issues senseless "moral" commands. The Lady is after all, historically, *the* legislating body of her time, but her courts of love were, point for point, opposed to the "law" that regulated good and evil.[28] Žižek reserves the subject position only for the masculine side, effectively assigning woman the pleasure-principle ethical role of mastery:

> The relationship of the knight to the Lady is . . . the relationship of a subject-bondsman or vassal to his feudal master-sovereign, who subjects her vassal to senseless, outrageous, impossible, arbitrary, capricious ordeals. It is precisely in order to emphasize the non-spiritual nature of these ordeals that Lacan quotes a poem about a Lady who demands that her servant literally lick her ass. The content of the poem consists of the poet's complaints about the bad smells that await him down there ... and about the imminent danger that, as he fulfills his duty, the Lady will urinate on his head.

Žižek characterizes these commands as "wholly incommensurate with our needs and desires ... meaningless demands at random." He sees the Lady as the Maternal *Ding*: a terrifying, inhuman force (*Ethics*, 214). It is true that Lacan says the Dame has a Thing-like character. But she is also as near, as sweet, as dear as Stendhal's Clélia in the *Charterhouse of Parma*, who nevertheless "terrifies" Fabrizio with her sheer sublimity.[29] What is missing in Žižek's analogy between the Dame and the Mother is that he does not characterize the possibility of the act's desirability and enjoyability from the other side, so to speak—from the Lady's own position.

Is there not a hint at least of a desire for something else than the Mother, his end, his death in the poet's response to the commands of the Lady? In all versions of the feminine subject of courtly love, the Lady has an elementary coldness. But it is a coldness that perhaps relates more to her untouchability, her inviolateness, her superiority to the masculine subject, her lover, than to her obscenity.

What I want to question here is the subjective side of the Lady, how she is enabled *as subject* by a certain barrier or wall that "raises her to the dignity of the Thing," but that nonetheless not only does not preclude her enjoyment but is its precondition. This barrier will be the field of *jouissance* itself, what cannot be borne to be experienced; it will not be the "arbitrary" laws of men, the signifier, even of the law of the good ("the sphere of the good exerts a strong wall across the path of desire," *Seminar VII*, 230).

Barriers, delays, deferrals are both defensive and enabling. On the one hand, they protect the feminine Thing against such inversions as the one described by Ford Madox Ford in his bitingly ironic depiction of the descent of courtly love and all its trappings in our culture, quite against their originating spark. Placed at the service of self-love, courtly "love" invades the space of the feminine subject, takes it over rather than taking it on:

> The real fierceness of desire, the real heat of a passion long continued and withering up the soul of a man, is the craving for identity with the woman that he loves. He desires to see with the same eyes, to touch with the same sense of touch, to hear with the same ears, to lose his identity, to be enveloped, to be supported. . . . So, for a time, if such a passion come to fruition, the man will get what he wants. He will get the . . . assurance of his own worth.[30]

To crawl up inside the lover's head, to see through her eyes—what? Himself as he would like to be seen, valued, and esteemed by his highest self, to see himself as the beloved—this is the aggressiveness of narcissism, of course, and it is pretty much the general model for love in the Western world today, even, according to some like Ford, the very legacy of courtly love itself.

Now this just won't do, as far as the feminine Thing is concerned: to this sort of use she must remain inviolate. She must represent, in fact, an absolute barrier to such an invasion, to being placed in the service of the Ideal Ego as the newest and most artificial version of the Good. She must represent, let us recall, the perspective of the Thing, not of the signifier. Everything must be turned around, so that it is she who views the signifier, and not the reverse. (It is for this reason that in *Encore* Lacan insists on the signifier as what puts a limit to *jouissance* and therefore causes it.)

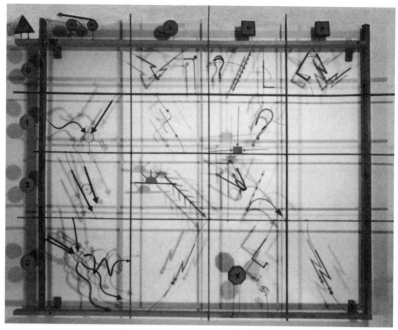

Bernie Lubell, *Accident Report!* (1991). Wood. Reprinted courtesy of the artist. Symbols inserted into the text in this chapter are taken from this figure.

> Clélia's severity seemed to diminish in proportion as the material difficulties in the way of any communication between them increased.
>
> —Stendhal, *The Charterhouse of Parma*

She is lovely, this feminine thing. As the crossing point of the field of the "beyond-the-good"—it is as the beautiful and not the sublime—she becomes, like the Mother, inviolate: "The good that mustn't be touched becomes a beauty that mustn't be touched" (*Seminar VII*, 237).

She may not be done violence. But may she not be "moved"? If only to look back, give her perspective on the masculine subject, his signifiers, and their mutual powers?

We know that the "salutation" by the beloved is the greatest gift of love she gives.[31] It is a sign that she is touched, moved by the Other sex. Being "moved" thus is no small part of her courtly role. She may be moved, like Desdemona, to a "world of sighs," stirred to "pity" like Rousseau's Julie or Stendhal's Clélia; or she may be more deeply moved, transported physically, in her body, as it is rent and opened by the masculine glance, that "look" that intends/recognizes her connection to the Other *Jouissance*.[32]

Her coldness and neutrality, her "inhumanness" as Lacan notices, in the final account may be less coldness than this terrifying connection to another sort of *jouissance*—the one that can never coincide with the other without some serious repercussions:

I see this piece by Bernie Lubell as a highly contemporary *carte de tendre*: on the wall beside it is a road map of where an "accident" took place. The grid is based on that used by the police for detailing accidents, and the "symbols" in the grids are adapted (and newly contrived by the artist) from the templates they use to depict the scene of the event: for example, —x—x— is the standard symbol for "fence" and ⊗ for "emergency stop"; ⌐ for "overtaking"; △ for "time," and so on. But ⟋⊘ is Lubell's own symbol for "confusing[ed] mixed emotions"; ⊤ is his symbol for "fear"; ⋎ for "pain"; ⇢◻◂ for "patience" [unmovable under pressure]; and ♭ for "performance anxiety." Lubell uses this grid to figure a tale of love, precisely the two man–one woman problem preeminent in courtly love. In the column on the left are "events"; in the column on the right are "initial states": pain, fear, doubt, and so forth. What results is a mapping of the eventful (non)relation of the One Sex to the Other.

Woman in the World of Goods—and Beyond?

So far, I have been reproducing as best I can the thinking that led Lacan to that site where a new foundation began to be laid out, a culture of poetry not determined in its orientation by the maternal body and its Supreme Good-ness. What links the advent of the new feminine Thing to a culture and an art not devoted to the service of the Good is less historic and thematic for Lacan than for Stendhal, less tied to the actuality of courtly love than to courtly love's having come upon the same problematic that psychoanalysis today is beginning to face: the foundation of a new form of creation, an art linked neither to the sacred space of God nor to that of Mother, but to the spacing around a feminine Thing whose sexuality is strictly nonprocreative in nature.

Her place in the world of goods, as analogue or transferential referent of the Sovereign Good, or as goods to be exchanged, bought, shared, or left on the shelf changes, potentially, the definition of woman. Ordinarily, women work within the symbolic economy—as mothers, daughters, whores, debutantes, dates, Playboy bunnies, goody two-shoes, bad girls, damaged goods, dolls, molls—the range is wide but never leaves the confines of the realm of goods. Woman is free to give up her role as object of exchange: she can always just join the other side, like the girl in Margaret Atwood's story, "The Man from Mars," who has simply become "one of the boys," a seeker after the good.[33]

Neither position specifies anything, however, of the feminine Thing, what cannot be met with through the signifier and cannot be put into words precisely, but of which we need the idea for us to see how far short of it the masculine subject must fall. The feminine Thing, Lacan tells us, is in a field beyond the good.

What happens, it seems, to woman when she is taken out of the register of the stock of goods—when she is no longer the allegorical, transferential Mother (a figure of the Supreme Good), and when she is no longer housed, domiciled, domesticated, and placed under the regime of goods— is that it is she who comes.

But this coming will not be, as Sade assumed, on a level equal or equivalent to that of the masculine subject. For although Sade appeared to promise a turning point for the relation to *jouissance,* it is not clear that he was sufficiently free from the finality of the Mother; the deepest movement of his desire was still an instinctive flinching before the End. Yet, he at least spoke of *jouissance* rather than of ownership of goods and briefly, therefore, gave rise to the thought that "the Other is free which the right to *jouissance* posits as the subject of its enunciation."[34] Sade's hesitation really to go beyond the Supreme Good landed him just where Lacan thought—in the lure of Supreme Evil. The structural impediment lay in Sade's too hasty[35] presumption of an equality between speaking subjects, the subjects of the signifier ("Men and Women," Lacan reminds us, are "effects of the signifier"). There is no symmetry, either linguistically or sexually, between masculine and feminine subject positions. It is their nonreciprocity that demands the creation of that emptiness, an uncommon ground (or in Lubell's flow chart, the "Landscape as Lies")—in short the imaginary land of "love."

Highly sensitive to this asymmetry in feminine and masculine *jouissances,* Lacan was also following a way opened earlier by Stendhal's *De L'Amour,* wherein their divergence, arrayed endlessly, becomes the matter of both love and psychoanalysis.[36]

That their readers never notice this is purely a function of the assumption of the masculine position: see José Ortega y Gasset, who says Stendhal is just plain wrong,[37] as well as the many who criticize Lacan for his misogyny.

The Political Importance of Love

The duplicity of good is that it isn't only satisfaction of a natural need, but possible power, the power to satisfy. Thus the relation of man to the whole world of goods is relation to an other (imaginary) capable of depriving him of it.

—Lacan, *Seminar VII*

Love has to be the inversion of the ordinary powers of satisfaction operative in the world of goods: otherwise, it is merely its policeman. Coming between an ego-ideal—that which has the "power to do good"—and the Ideal Ego—that which has the power to deprive us of goods (who can fail to recognize "Father" and "Mother" here?)—the feminine Thing offers a way out of that world of goods (*Seminar VII*, 234). To love her is to reverse the power of satisfying or unsatisfying, to disarm all relations of lovers in terms of possession, distribution, and hoarding.

For Lacan, the "blazing of courtly love" before "the return of all its trappings in a so-called renaissance of the old craze" ("Love Letter," 156) offered a unique, unusually frank encounter with this feminine Thing, an encounter that runs at absolute cross-purposes to the world of goods, which is the world of pure power, like that of feudalism. The figures and trimmings of courtly love have since, of course, become our stock of love goods ("all its trappings"). In this guise, *l'amour courtois* serves a doubly policing function: we create romantic theme parks, capture in miniature the countryside of love, and sell it, a bill of goods—as an escape from the dreary everydayness of existence—to those for whom "all is not well between themselves and their beloved," to adapt Stendhal's definition of *crystallization,* the "ideology" of love. They have, of course, only fitted themselves inside a total commodification of their experience of love.

The feminine Thing must be reasserted from time to time. Possibly, it cannot be in the courtly mode in our era (although we are perhaps far enough from its peak abuse time, which ended with the 1950s), but it might be (Žižek sees it returning in the movie *The Crying Game*). She will not just be put on the shelf, warehoused like so many other once-demanded and out-of-fashion goods. She will always reemerge, completely detached from the traffic in goods, impatient with any marketplace where she is not loved for her own sake, that is, for her Otherness, for her being the Other Sex. She must be estimated at her true worth, and for the perspective she brings to bear on the meaning of the space between herself as object and the Real Thing, as well as between herself and the masculine subject.

Finally, this reassertion of the feminine Thing, even if in the courtly mode, should not take the route of "good behavior" on the part of the Lady. We need not be Catharist, or purer than pure, about detaching sexuality from procreation (we have other means than simple abstinence for prevention), and restart a cult of virginity. Stendhal offers this charming reading of courtly "Love in Provence, before the Conquest of Toulouse by Northern Barbarians in 1328":

Love took a strange form in Provence from 1100 to 1328. There was an established code of laws covering amatory relationships between the two sexes, as severe and as rigidly followed as the laws which cover the affair of honour today. . . . When one had kissed a woman's hand one graduated from stage to stage by merit alone, with no preferment. It should be noted that although husbands were entirely out of the picture the official promotion of lovers did not go beyond what we might call the delights of the most tender friendship between persons of the opposite sex. However, after many months or years of trial, when a woman was perfectly sure of the character and discretion of a man, and when that man had all the privileges and outward signs of the tenderest friendship with her, such a friendship might have been a very serious threat to virtue. . . . A woman might have several lovers, but only one in the higher grades. (*Love,*165–66)

Disconnecting the Lady from the Virgin altogether, Stendhal followed with this later in the book:

I am glad to have found the following passage in the memoirs of Horace Walpole: the Two Elizabeths. Let us compare the daughters of two ferocious men, and see which was a sovereign of a civilized nation, which of a barbarous one. Both were Elizabeths. The daughter of Peter (of Russia) was absolute yet spared a competitor and a rival; and thought the person of an empress had sufficient allurements for as many of her subjects as she chose to honour with the communication. Elizabeth of England could neither forgive the claim of Mary Stuart nor her charms, but ungenerously emprisoned her (as George IV did Napoleon), when imploring protection, and without the sanction of other despotism or law, sacrificed many to her great and little jealousy. Yet this Elizabeth prided herself on chastity; and while she practiced every ridiculous act of coquetry to be admired at an advanced age, kept off lovers whom she encouraged, and neither gratified her own desires nor their ambition. Who can help preferring the honest, open-hearted barbarian queen? (*Love,* 229–30)

New Foundations; or, Love as Uncommon Ground

Marking the emptiness left by the untouchability of the Thing is, for Lacan, the essence of all art, all making. Re-marking this emptiness, *noticing* that it has constantly to be renewed because it always tends to come under the sway of the signifier and lose its value as sign, is a marking-out of another foundation, a different set of directions, paths, limits, coordinates for the subject and its drives.[38] "Viewed from the perspective of the Thing," the subject occupying such a space—its agency—lies in the object (the *objet a* as gaze). What I have tried to show is that the object/subject is

Bernie Lubell, installation *Confluence and Compression at the Cusp of Continuity: An Antediluvian Catastrophe* (1986–94). Pine, music wire, nylon, etc. Reprinted courtesy of the artist.

Bernie Lubell, installation *Confluence and Compression at the Cusp of Continuity: An Antediluvian Catastrophe* (1986–94). Pine, music wire, nylon, etc. Reprinted courtesy of the artist.

indeed equivalent to a *feminine* subject—the one with the "privileged" relation (wordless) to the *other jouissance.* The feminine Thing (no longer just the Mother) represents thus a subjectification dependent on the return from aim to object. When the *aim* (the Mother's body, the Sovereign Good) is cast into infinity, only the object, the means to the aim, remains. As such, the object takes on the status of *sign,* that which "stands for something to someone in some capacity or other" (Charles Sanders Peirce's definition), and thereby implicates itself in the subject. Only an object, raised to the dignity of a Thing, has the possibility of becoming a Subject, subject to suffering from the phallus. Under Lacan's pen, the Thing is not simply cold, obscene, harassing, but has a sympathetic side.

This means intensifying the recognition that there need not be— indeed, that there must not be—any "common ground" between lovers for love to exist. The walls, lines, limits between them must be reemphasized and re-marked for there to be a place for the feminine object raised to the dignity of the Thing to take on its own subject, assume its own sex, its own relation to *jouissance.* The masculine subject that wants to join *this* new subject across the limit must yield, must give up what Lacan calls "the phallus" to take on woman, facing with her the other *jouissance.* Not all men are by any means willing to do so. But for those who do, a certain fresh, new *poeisis,* a new art, a new foundation for culture itself, not prescribed along parental lines, is opened.

I renamed *Confluence and Compression at the Cusp of Continuity* "arrows of Eros." The installation consisted of two mechanisms, a rocking chair on one side, and an elaborate bow-and-arrow-like construction on the other, separated by a wall. A drive ran through the wall: as the chair rocked with its regular rhythms—although one had to have enough faith in the system to lean back rather far in it to make this happen—the drive turned a ratcheting device that drew what I am calling "the bow" on the other side of the wall ever so slightly tighter. Over what would seem like ages of comfortable rocking with occasional slightly risky backward tilting, the bow on the other side of the wall was to reach its limit and let fly. In doing so it would, naturally, be destroyed. Only a very discerning viewer would notice that the two events (the rocking and the letting fly) were even connected.

Their *uncommon ground,* then, means that the lovers will never find themselves housed anywhere but in their own separate cells. Yet whatever ground they travel over together will be the country of love, what "Lies as a Landscape," Rousseau's *pays des chimères,* the Cythera of the imagination. Its mapping was once called the *carte de tendre,* and resurfacing in the artwork reproduced here, it is a pure "accident," even an "antediluvian catastrophe" when viewed from the normal route. While the map promises, like the network of signifiers, to be a complete set with *"correspondances"* or connecting points between everywhere and everywhere else, the truth of what such "correspondances" means is told by the rocking chair in the Lubell piece. Whenever this landscape of love is seen, used, exchanged for something else as a "good," it will have become a destiny or destination, an end, and no longer the imaginary means to defer that end. It will no longer be Love.

There's no telling when, how, where the Other Sex will line up with yours in the field of view. I'll close with a little parable.

Dateline San Francisco, 1994, Slim's Bar

I go to this club where they are doing readings of erotic texts, because I get to be with the man (or two) I love. But it's a bit depressing, at the beginning, because everyone is so earnest. Waiting on line, everyone is avid, seeking— but not each other. What? The lesbian couple passionately kissing in front of me performs gender in an orthodox way: for me, or for themselves?

Once the erotic readings begin, I start to catch religion from these sex-perts. Each piece renounces religion as their first and most important former, used love. As they denounce their theologies in the name of sex, it is less the thematic resemblance between sex and religion that seems so remarkable to me than the straitness of their gait, the narrowness of even the enlarged path they are following.[39] They follow it, perhaps, in order not to know its end and its beginning (in Death, the Mother): not one of the performers—either actively or tacitly—tells of renouncing what (psychoanalytically) has to be the first and only real renunciation, that of the mother. Not even a father, a sister, or a brother is mentioned. That renunciation should, by all rights, be what has brought them to this point of celebrating liberated sex.

If not liberated from the family, from transferential love, then from what? Or is this erotic-as-art just another bit of goods for sale? By celebrating sex, they are, I see, becoming its celebrities, its Madonnas. Making a living, I guess.

My disappointment is palpable, compounded by the ache in my legs: we are a strictly stand-up audience, suffering, sacrificing for our new religion, after all.

But one yarn does stand out, after the fact, for me, in the middle of the night. It is by the artist Trish Thomas, whom Susie Bright—emcee and tireless cheerleader for sex—touts as the most shocking to the bourgeois press and (Bright admits) the least fathomable for her personally. Trish Thomas, the original "genderfuck" artist, recounts in an exquisitely literary language how she, a bulldagger, found herself faced with the dismaying realization that she was attracted to a man, even though he was a transvestite, and a queenly one at that.

I've been hearing such stories with increasing frequency from gay friends, accompanied by the shock of their mild surprise. But what was it that made the performance stand out for me later that night? It was surely because Trish Thomas was telling a love story, a story of the mystery of falling in love. Her story was the story told at least since the eighteenth century—where, its courtly roots dug up, love became what "surprised" you. Here was Eros, once again the mischief maker, disturbing by its appearance the completely scoped-out gender-bent gay scene of total performance. Here was *trouble,* of the sort that, for all the title promises but disavows, *Gender Trouble* doesn't treat.

Interestingly, though her story was filled with sex, the only sex detailed in the story on stage that night was with a lesbian pickup, "Pretty Boy." Pretty Boy took on a certain prestige as a premonition or precursor of the beloved transvestite, but she was nonetheless never deemed an object of love. And Thomas never got to the sex part with the transvestite.[40]

So, while the rest of the lineup maintained the sacred separation of sex from love (except for one story about lesbian angels), Thomas maintained the segregation in reverse, pointedly embellishing the tale of unloving sex and segregating it from the love story within the limits of the narrative. This purity, so strictly maintained between love and sex, took on significance when viewed through the same religious frame that all had taken pains to announce.

Concluding Unscientific Postscript: Some Propositions about Love

1. Loveless sex and sexless love are pulsations of discontinuity and continuity crucial to the symbolic order; they are the form of how we suffer that order, the order of the signifier. That we may love without sex and have sex without love is the fundamental law of the group. We patiently bear the absolute alternation between sex and love because, in our very sacrifice of one for the other, we find the comfort that is built into the rocking rhythms of this alteration.

2. Sexed love runs on a different axis, the axis not of presence and absence, of signifiers. It is structured as an antinomy or a contradiction, not

simply an opposition. Its axis is that of *cause* and *event*. It has to do with *meaning*, the meaning that the system of signifiers is constructed to evade, that is the (non)relation of the One sex to the Other.

3. Sexed love constitutes an ongoingness, but only in the form of risk. This is because sexuality is tied directly to the cause, to the *object a* cause of desire, and—at the very same time—to the object raised to the dignity of the Thing.

   While love intends its object fully, it does so by sublimation, largely disclaiming the beloved object's kinship with the *object a*. In sexed love the object and its double collide.

4. Where they collide is the point where the Symbolic has a hole it is resolved to hide from itself and its adherents. The Feminine Thing (the object raised to the dignity of the Thing) is no more than the difference between the *object a* and the Thing.

5. Love consists entirely of words that are deprived of their ordinary meaning, words that point to the place where "no words" also insist.

6. Love is therefore that straying, errancy from the biological and theological paths that link the end to the beginning, death to birth, the Mother at the start and at the finish.

7. Love is what necessarily blinds us to the political and social orders we get. It is, as Stendhal told us in no uncertain terms, *ideology*. In calling it an anamorphosis, Lacan showed its positive as well as negative political and cultural power. For, as "blindsided" it is also what allows Desdemona not to see Othello's blackness first, before all else; what permits the Marquesa del Dongo in the *Charterhouse of Parma* not to see Lieutenant Robert's ragged shoes. At the same time, Love—narcissistic, taking itself for its own object—blinds us to that blinding in our partner, creates jealousy, fear, passion.

8. *Object a* is the most personal, most intimate cause of desire. Love intends its object; it develops its vision of its object from all sides, all perspectives, all points of view. It is the original phenomenology. Yet there is always that spot of opacity, even in its totalization, where it must hallucinate around its own *object a*. When Stendhal writes that he would wish to be granted invisibility so that he could see his beloved, unseen, whenever he wanted, he still excepts from his would-be powers of vision those moments when she would be doing something she does not want him to see. This point of opacity, the point where the beloved as object and the

beloved *object a dis*connect, is precious. When their conjunction is seen, the result is the murder of the thing one loves, in the name of the law. Othello: "It is the Cause," meaning both *la Chose* and the just *cause,* the one in whose service he had once gained his symbolic identity. (Remember William Heirens, the young Chicago boy who, in the 1950s, committed one of the first of the front-page "sex maniac" murders, biting off his victim's breasts. Did he achieve, perhaps, the passage to the Thing, to his Death, his Maternal Body? He seemed to impress Bataille in *The Tears of Eros,* as if he finds the boy's act a way of facing the "Truth in Love.")[41]

9.   Which is why sex is dangerous, precarious, too hot to handle when it is linked to love. The tension between the beloved object and the *object a* she allegorizes is the very cause of our existence. (Rousseau's Julie: "What would we be if we no longer loved?") But more than that, in each sex act where love is implicated, that love is put on the line by confronting love with its own *object a.*

10.   Because love is so personal, idiosyncratic, mad, psychoanalysis has wanted to put itself in its place. The way it has done so is through the transference and the demystification of the Other to the benefit of the *object a,* uncovering the *object a* at the base of the ideal Ego, the Ideal we would want to be and to be loved by.

11.   There are anticipations of psychoanalysis in the critical romanticism of Stendhal. Precisely on the overturning of Plato, and the destruction of idealization (in the form of the Beautiful Good), that love, seen from the start as ideology, commands.

12.   Love and Meaning: love is a sign, not a signifier, says Lacan, adding that it is a sign that one is changing discourses. It falls between. Discourses, we know, though, are designed to prevent us from having to face central conflicts they cannot cover. So love is right there, at the point where the antinomies face each other starkly; it is there that love ex-sists or in-sists, without ever con-sisting.

Epilogue: The Free Female Subject

> In the bedroom ... Alissa is no longer any age.
> —Marguerite Duras, *Destroy, She Said*

Asked to comment on her film *Destroy, She Said,* Marguerite Duras responded with more than a little incredulity when interviewer Jean Narboni asserted that her movie has "always one last watching eye, which is none other than that of the camera, which overarches all these people who are watching each other."[1] Duras responds, "Does it exist, in your opinion?" Her question draws him up short, and he repeats it to try to fathom its unsuspected depths:

NARBONI: Does it exist as a watching eye?

DURAS: Yes, in *Destroy,* the film.

NARBONI: No, because the expression "watching eye" is not the right one—let's say, then, a last determining actor, a last court of appeal.

DURAS: As if someone wanted to tie the whole thing together?

NARBONI: No, no, not at all like something tying the whole thing together. Not a "gaze," something static, but a watching function, so to speak.

DURAS: Yes, but this watching function can also be called identification with the character. Do you agree with that? With the sacred law that Sartre laid down in an article answering Mauriac, I believe, about twenty years ago, in which he said that one could identify only with one person. To reach the other characters it is necessary, therefore, to do so through the character with which one identifies: if there are A, B, C—A being the spectator and the character with whom one identifies, one must go through him in order to reach B and C.

JACQUES RIVETTE: Yes. Sartre accused Mauriac of taking himself for God the Father and dominating all the characters.

DURAS: That's right. But this is a law that has applied to spectacle for centuries now. And to novels too. I attempted to break this law.... There is no primacy of one character over another in *Destroy*. There is a gliding from one character to another. Why? I think it's because they're all the same. These three characters, I believe, are completely interchangeable ... the camera is never conclusive as regards the way one of them acts or the words that another pronounces....

NARBONI (undergoing a revelation): You therefore refused this sort of closure that always makes the camera enclose a space or imprison a character by making it assume multiple roles, in the same way that the characters are interchangeable.

DURAS: Yes, that's it. At any rate that is what I tried to do.

Director Jacques Rivette, agreeing with Duras's assessment of her technique, interrupts to offer a formalization of it, and Narboni launches into a history of how "modern" films vary the role of the camera. Duras interrupts: "But it is the relation between the people that isn't right, perhaps, in *Destroy*?" (95–96).

Ignored by these two instant specialists in her cinematic technique, Duras breaks in again with a radical question: "But what would be the equivalent of what you have just mentioned in writing? The role of the author in his book, for example. ... No: the role that the author would like the reader to have?" (98). Receiving no reply, Duras finally retorts with a fierce assertion of her ignorance: "I wrote it in a state of imbecility ... it was necessary for me to plunge back into the dark so that the camera would have the same sensitivity, if you like, as the pen has when I write" (98–99).

I present this lopsided exchange to place before us the history of the eye as coming to us not solely from Mauriac's God the Father but Sade's dark God. Duras's aesthetic effort to fragment not God but Sade's perverse visuality is new. Hers is an art that transgresses even the perverse mode of transgression. A "destruction" operates in her simple, even optimistic text/film, beyond Sartre's dismissal of the classical viewpoint. More than perhaps any other author or cineaste of the later twentieth century, Duras questions our feminine "imprisonment" by the "liberated" viewpoint— Sadean or Freudian. We can watch her at work, freeing the aesthetic character, freeing the girl. Duras's "girls" are psychotic (Lol V. Stein) or perverse (Alissa in *Destroy* is called "insane"), but only from certain points of view. Duras is really preparing them for an as-yet-unnamed ethic, that of the free feminine subject.

Duras's girl is either locked into or freed from her "emancipation." She is captured less by a patriarchal "sexist" eye than by a perverse Superego gaze whose viewpoint takes her from behind, overwhelming and flooding her with *jouissance* so that she is petrified by it. Her "room of one's own" is a small space—her bedroom. She may visit other designated playgrounds, tennis courts, hotels, resorts, dance halls, saloons, gaming tables, but it is in her bedroom that her bondage and freedom gets decided.

Destroy, She Said: The Free Female Subject

Sade's utopia stands or falls and can be *ethically* faulted for not having fully described, included, and comprehended the female subject as one that is fundamentally characterized by a resistance to unlimited enjoyment. Or, to put it the other way, one that is open to desire. Utopian dreams to the contrary, it is not enough simply to declare the death of sexual difference as a new ethic following upon the death of the subject, as Sade's work in effect did. Nor is it enough, as an older psychoanalytic undertone once seemed to imply to its "girl," that they have no real right to resist a sexual encounter.

That is why I would grant Marguerite Duras's repetition—and deep revision—of Sade's *Philosophy in the Bedroom* in her film *Destroy, She Said* such capital importance. In *Destroy,* the ground of freedom has monumentally shifted from the objective to the subjective meanings assigned them juridically. A *free female* subject takes some of its first steps there.

The scene has changed slightly from that of the Saint-Ange boudoir. We are no longer in a private bedroom chamber, but in a resort hotel. Its bedrooms are regularly intruded on by strangers. The text opens with an attractive, vaguely melancholy, rather affectless married woman, Elisabeth Alione, who has on her doctor's advice come alone to the resort to recuperate. From what? At first, we are not told. Elisabeth's demeanor, her looks, her world-weary absence of mind, her apathy draw immediate libidinal attention from men around the resort. Someone pens a note, hinting at the possibility of a brief liaison while he and she are temporarily free of their spouses. The note is written with the standard romantic cant of such missives. She is utterly nonreactive. She sleeps a great deal, half-read books dropping from her somnolent fingers. Elisabeth Alione is, then, the typical, somnolent, pill-popping Durasian femme fatale. Yet a liberation is afoot, which is, if not the reverse of Dolmancé's, at least on a different track.

We are in the space of idleness, the medieval precursor to romance in whose domain the forces of law, order, morality have no authority. A space, in short, that always functions to update dreams of freedom. As in Sade's bedroom the stage is set for deploying a "free" libertine/sadist fancy. Once again we find a trio: Alissa, Max Thor, and Stein appear in this scene, and like the Dolmancé-Saint-Ange crew, they too gravitate to this single woman detached from her familial and social anchoring points. Elisabeth Alione, beautiful, numbingly bored, is nonetheless unlike Eugénie in that Elisabeth is already a woman of the world, a woman who has experienced to the limit the Sadean version of a woman's freedom. As she half dozes, taking sleeping powders and tranquilizers, her solitude in this leisure setting causes her to be seen as open for spontaneous affairs, but it is a false opening, for she is closed to her own experience of everything. She has had lovers besides her husband and she has willingly, if it turns out somewhat traumatically, given up her maternity. She has recently aborted her lover's baby—a girl it would have been. And she has done so for the sake of everyone's continued *jouissance*—hers, her husband's, her lover's. (Elisabeth had agreed to the abortion after her husband and her doctor lover joined forces to get her to do so. It is this abortion that turns out to be the illness from which she is recovering at the resort.)

Alissa is Elisabeth's younger double (Alissa/Elisa), her lost daughter, her lost adolescence, her other self. Alissa is very young. She is married to a professor who teaches the History of the Future, Max Thor, who loves her desperately. She has been his only student, ever. She has slept through all his lectures. Alissa is also loved passionately by Stein, a musician, and she loves him. Stein and Thor seem to switch stances and identities. It is difficult to find or assign a clear-cut or distinct individuality for any of the three. All of them, however, are attracted to Elisabeth, singly and as a group. The scenario proceeds as if the trio were undertaking a seduction of Elisabeth.

Indeed, there is a seduction, but it is less sexual in nature, whatever *sexual* means for this latter-day daughter of Sade, than something having to do with freedom. The trio works on and with Elisabeth by way of pointing her toward another sort of freedom than the one she has enjoyed with her husband and lovers, the caged-in freedom of the man-made resort, with its sun decks, pools, and tennis courts. The trio begins by engaging Elisabeth in a series of rather hilarious social moments and conversations like the card game in which they break all the rules, confusing and loosening her laughter. Her very bourgeois husband, who comes to fetch her, is angered and frustrated by their Beckettian chatter that tests the thinness of his polite veneer. The trio finally causes him to lose his cool, and to show his crude tastes and his brutal treatment of Elisabeth.

In what does Elisa's seduction consist? Alissa chiefly urges Elisabeth to go beyond the gates of the tennis court and into the forest. Elisabeth cannot bear the forest; she fears it. She refuses, but tentatively. She at last takes herself right to its very edge. She does not, finally, go beyond the limits that her confinement to Sadean *jouissance* has set for her. But because she has even considered entering that space outside the limits of reason (the Sadean law she obeys), the forest operates a certain kind of liberation for her. The forest is, at some level, a spirit of psychoanalysis and its *démontage* of her death drive. As she takes this small step, the magnificent music of Stein breaks through the forest to reach everyone's ears. At some level she is beginning to get free. Elisabeth does not actually enter the forest; Duras's version of freedom is not linked to nature, as for Sade. The music that cracks through the forest is a high cultural form, a crashing symphony. The forest is not primitivity, not Sade's great Mother; it sings no siren song. It is culture, but that of a civilization that is not restricted to limitations and their transgression. We access it despite the theater of the perverse.

Who, then, is this girl, Alissa? And how has she worked to partially free Elisabeth as a subject? Alissa is clearly insubstantial, a kind of spirit or pure subject. This eighteen-year-old bride does not "exist." But she does insist. That Elisabeth is Alissa is also clear, but only in negative. She is the embodiment of all the openings in Elisa that Elisabeth has not felt free, even under her Sadean liberation, to pursue. Alissa is the young Elisa whose desire Sade foreclosed; she is the daughter Elisabeth has aborted; she is the subject of Elisa that Elisa has denied in herself. Why not love Alissa as much as Thor or Stein? Why not love herself?

In this parable, we have, perhaps the crucial difference between the freedom Sade teaches woman and the one the analyst can. It is seemingly slight, but it is all-important. It is the difference between the sadistic will-to-*jouissance* and the analytic desire for knowledge concerning the truth of that *jouissance*. The history of Elisabeth Alione's future lies with her potential for that crucial *savoir*.

It is Duras's particular genius to have given us one of the secrets for reaching the "subject," especially the female one. She endows a paranoid or perverse character, such as her older brother,[2] or Elisabeth here, with what they lack or have denied within themselves. She does this by supplementing them with another character that is "close" to theirs, but that exists only at an insubstantial, tentative, and metaphoric level. With this subject-shadow, she moves them beyond the narrow rage of their ego and super-ego alike. In the case of Elisabeth, Duras offers this femme fatale certain openings foreclosed to her Sadean character. They differ radically from openings in the Sadean mode, like those mechanical "predispositions to chance affairs," as Riva so aptly names them in *Hiroshima, Mon Amour*, which are ultimately revealed as false openings, constraints, not freedoms. The openings of the subject are its entire makeup, its means of release from an alienated immersion in being and in meaning alike. The subject is constituted purely as an antiweight to the positive dimensionality of the ego.

The sadist comes to "liberate" the young woman—within the limits of reason, figured as the confines of the perverse scenario, philosophy's private boudoir. This liberation will have already taken place, even before the young woman of today will have been born, and even if her parents had never heard of him. Once Sade has put his thesis in play, it is there, it is part of the new patrimony of the girl child. After the sadist has undertaken to teach woman her freedom in the form of an/her absolute relation to enjoyment, it cannot be undone.

Yet like the old patriarchy, Sade's liberatory rules, for girls and boys alike, bring with them their own impasses and blind alleys. To find your way through them takes more than a simple rebellion against the mother and her "morality," more than a simple rebuff to patriarchal ideology, more, I think, than a Butlerian commitment to surface. The cunning of reason as it occupies the body of woman remains our contemporary ideological problematic—on a par with that of the body of the child for Rousseau's eighteenth century. It would be a mistake to persist in seeing the feminine sexual body formed only by the fading light of patriarchal ideology, and by the stage lighting of Sade. Nor her female subject formed only by envy of men.

In the end, I think what I have looked for as a sign of the future female subject is not the mask-free woman of the Sadean dream. Nor is it the ambivalent, hostile woman of the old femininity's masquerade. Nor is it only the aesthetic persona of the extraordinary woman artist. (These are all here in my book, and they correspond somewhat to the Sadean, hysteric, and aesthetic positions.) I have looked, I think, for a new femininity, lighter and less substantial than the envy-filled one of Joan Riviere, but much tougher. Rather than a mask, I have looked for woman with a *face*.

Masks are real. As long as there is an unconscious, there is the mask. It is consubtantial with our humanity: it is the sign that we acknowledge and credit social coexistence. The mask is our form of homage to the presence and the claims of the other.

How we, as women, don that mask makes all the difference. Can it form itself as a face—face as front: bravery and composure and openness and challenge and sensitivity and toughness and alertness and care and haughtiness and warmth and "cool" . . . ?

Place the penetrating look of Hannah Arendt together with the artful fragility of Marilyn Monroe. Put the austere strength of Golda Meir beside the openness of Maya Angelou. Compare the wonderfully ravaged, wrinkled, gorgeous face of Marguerite Duras with the passionate countenance of Maria Callas, whom Duras said had the courage of a lioness. Put the delicate strength of the young Vietnamese woman who at age twelve led her young brother through exile to a new homeland, in the same frame as the smooth, unlined face of Hélène Cixous, who looked into the heart of the war that forced those children's exile. You will begin to get some idea. They have in common the face they have earned in squaring off against an overpowering force, a horror to which each could have allowed herself to succumb. Even if they may have at one time or another given in to it, they have also discovered how to recover, how to stop submitting. The knowledge they have gained through their struggle is unspoken. Yet they share it with us through their face. This is perhaps the real secret of "Antigone's beauty."

The lines and contours, the quirks and asymmetries of these fine faces—they are as much guides to the future female subject as any of the words in this book.

Notes

Introduction

1. Destutt de Tracy's *Idéologie proprement dite* (Paris: Librairie Philosophique J. Vrin, 1970). It was originally written at the height of the revolution (1796–1800) and published in two stages, 1801 and 1803. De Tracy was of a younger generation than the philosophes, a generation increasingly marked by splits into right and left wings (de Maistre, Constant, Cabanis, and so on). He wrote as part of his design to create from scratch a central school system for the new France.

2. Donatien-Alphonse-François de Sade, *Philosophy in the Bedroom* (1795), in *Justine, Philosophy in the Bedroom, and Other Writings,* trans. Richard Seaver and Austryn Wainhouse (New York: Grove Press, 1965).

3. Stendhal calls his *De L'Amour* "a book of ideology." *Love,* trans. Gilbert and Suzanne Sale (Harmondsworth: Penguin Books, 1957). Stendhal admired de Tracy (see chap. 10). Stendhal's farsighted *De l'amour* is a work of penetrating psychological analysis of women (of all sorts, including sadistic—and a few men) in love. See also Slavoj Žižek's crucial book *The Sublime Object of Ideology* (London: Verso, 1989), for an invaluable treatment of the "sublime substance" that is ideology's essence from a psychoanalytic point of view.

4. I am referring mainly to my 1991 book *The Regime of the Brother: After the Patriarchy* (London and New York: Routledge, 1991).

5. By this I mean extimacy, the social conflict that inhabits the individual's

heart. See Jacques Lacan, *Seminar VII: The Ethics Seminar,* trans. D. Porter (New York and London: W. W. Norton, 1993), 139; and Jacques-Alain Miller, "Extimité," in *Lacanian Theory of Discourse: Subject, Structure and Society,* ed. Mark Bracher et al. (New York and London: New York University Press, 1994), 74–87.

6. The reference is to Lacan's quotation of Saint-Just in "Kant avec Sade," *October* 51(1989): 71; and "The Direction of the Cure," in *Ecrits: A Selection,* trans. Alan Sheridan (New York and London: W. W. Norton, 1977), 252.

7. Sade, *Philosophy in the Bedroom,* 321.

8. See Max Horkheimer and Theodor W. Adorno, *Dialectic of Enlightenment,* trans. John Cumming (New York: Continuum, 1982), 85–96; Gilles Deleuze, *Coldness and Cruelty* (New York: Zone Books, 1991), 41–43; Slavoj Žižek, *The Metastases of Enjoyment: Six Essays on Women and Causality* (London: Verso, 1994), 89–112; and my critiques of them in chaps. 1 and 12, and in my essay "Adorno: The Riddle of Femininity," in *Adorno and Women,* ed. Maggie O'Neill (London and New York: Routledge, forthcoming). See also Lucie Cantin, "De la complicité à la perversion à une éthique de l'impossible," *Savoir: Psychanalyse et analyse culturelle* 2, no. 1 (May 1995): 47–50.

9. Žižek proposes an alternative ethics of the (Lost) Cause in "Why Is Sade the Truth of Kant?" in *For They Know Not What They Do: Enjoyment as a Political Factor* (London and New York: Verso, 1991), 229–33.

10. Serge André has masterfully summed up the weird but reverse symmetry of the two in his important book *L'Imposture perverse* (Paris: Seuil, 1993), 22–31.

11. See Jane Gallop, "The Immoral Teachers," *Yale French Studies* 63 (1982): 117–28; Angela Carter, *The Sadean Woman and the Ideology of Pornography* (New York: Pantheon Books, 1978); and Joan de Jean, *Literary Fortifications: Rousseau, Laclos and Sade* (Princeton, N.J.: Princeton University Press, 1984), to name a few.

12. *Cape Fear,* directed by Martin Scorsese (1991), script by Wesley Strick, based on the 1962 screenplay by James R. Webb from the novel *The Executioners* by John R. MacDonald. Lori Davis is played by Illeana Douglas, Max Cady by Robert de Niro.

13. Anne Marie Stretter appears in Duras's *The Ravishing of Lol V. Stein,* trans. Richard Seaver (New York: Pantheon, 1966), 38, and in *India Song,* trans. Barbara Bray (New York: Grove Press, 1976). Stretter is beautiful, mysterious, entirely apathetic. She has multiple lovers and no discernible passion.

14. Heinrich von Kleist, "The Betrothal in Santo Domingo," in *The Marquise of O . . . and Other Stories,* trans. David Luke and Nigel Reeves (Harmondsworth: Penguin Books, 1978).

15. Lacan, *Seminar VII,* 222.

16. I owe my strongest intellectual debts in this project to so-called New Lacanian authors Slavoj Žižek, Joan Copjec, Renata Salecl, and post-Lacanian

clinical theorists Willy Apollon, Danielle Bergeron, Lucie Cantin, and Serge André, as well as to astute social analysts like Dean MacCannell. I am also strongly indebted to the work of Gilles Deleuze and of Pierre Klossowski on Sade, and of Alain Badiou, Walter Benjamin (and others touched by Freud or Lacan) on ethical matters. They have all made their own way, as I am trying to make mine.

1. The Soul of Woman under Sadism

1. Joan Riviere's "Womanliness as Masquerade," *International Journal of Psycho-Analysis* 9 (1929): 303–13, works on psychological, sociological, and ideological planes simultaneously. I quote it from *The Inner World and Joan Riviere: Collected Papers 1920–1958*, ed. Athol Hughes (London and New York: Karnac Books, 1991), 90–101. Some think of Riviere's work as protodeconstructive since it marks the feminine substance as nothing but a discursive veil: it has "no there there." See Emily Apter, "Masquerade," in *Psychoanalysis and Feminism: A Critical Dictionary*, ed. Elizabeth Wright, Juliet Flower MacCannell, Dianne Chisolm, and Margaret Whitford (Oxford: Basil Blackwell, 1992), 243.

2. Sigmund Freud, "Femininity" (Lecture XXIII of "New Introductory Lectures on Psychoanalysis" [1933]), in *The Standard Edition of the Complete Psychological Works of Sigmund Freud*, trans. James Strachey (London: Hogarth Press, 1960), 112–35.

3. Ibid., 116. See also my entry "Freud," in the *Oxford Companion to Women's Writing in the United States*, ed. Cathy N. Davidson, Linda Wagner-Martin, Elizabeth Ammons et al. (New York: Oxford University Press, 1995).

4. The Mother is actually the one who forbids her children's pleasurable genital activity. Freud, "Femininity," 123.

5. Ibid., 124. Further citations from this work will appear parenthetically in the text.

6. For further discussion see "Mothers of Necessity," chap. 6.

7. See Susan Brownmiller, *Femininity* (New York: Linden Press, Simon & Schuster, 1984).

8. Freud, "Femininity," 129, 135. He writes, "Women must be regarded as having little sense of justice, because they are filled with envy (penis envy) and have no mental space to entertain a moral superego. Oedipus has failed for them" (134).

9. Jacques Lacan, *Seminar III, The Psychoses*, trans. Russell Grigg (New York and London: W. W. Norton, 1993), 144. "Whatever the appropriate role to attribute to it in psychical economy is, the ego is never alone. It always implies a strange twin, the ideal ego, which I spoke of in my seminar two years ago. The most apparent phenomenology of psychosis tells us that this ideal ego speaks. It's a fantasm *[fantaisie]*, but unlike the fantasm, or fantasy *[fantasme]*, that we highlight

in the phenomena of neurosis it's a fantasm that speaks, or more exactly, it's a spoken fantasm. This is where this character who echoes the subject's thoughts, who intervenes, spies upon him, names his actions in the sequence in which they occur, and commands them is not adequately explained by the theory of the imaginary and the specular ego."

10. On San Francisco's Haight Street I recently (1997) saw the reverse promoted: "Resist to ex-sist."

11. The "*Jouissance* of the Other" means an aggression against the body and subject of the human being. It represents an invasion by the Real (death drive). See Lucie Cantin, "De la complicité . . . ," 47–50, for a review of the other *jouissance* or feminine, extra, supplementary *jouissance*), as it differs from the *jouissance* of the Other.

12. As in the old cartoon of the man before the firing squad who refuses the traditional last cigarette saying, "No thanks, I'm trying to give up smoking." See Freud's essay on "Humour," in *Standard Edition*, vol. XXI: 161.

13. In "Femininity," Freud writes, "A mother can transfer to her son the ambition which she has been obliged to suppress in herself" (133).

14. I use the term technically, following Lacan's analysis of the perverse structure. Lacan's most extended discussion of perversion appears in "Kant avec Sade." Perversion appears as a question for ethics throughout Lacan's *Seminar VII*, especially 191 ff.

15. When I have presented my findings in various settings—third world, North American, and European—one predictable response has been, "That's an American problem." Traditional societies will not escape the collapse of patriarchal authority by telling themselves it is confined to North America; globalization grants them no quarter.

16. In a later chapter I have an extended analysis of a case of hysteria—no, not Freud's Dora or Breuer's Bertha Pappenheim, but Margaret Atwood's Offred, in *The Handmaid's Tale*.

17. *Shadow of a Doubt*, directed by Alfred Hitchcock (1943, my birth year). Screenplay by Thornton Wilder, with Sally Benson and Alma Reville (Hitchcock's wife). The character of the mother was named for Hitchcock's own. The script was based on an original story by Gordon McDonnell.

18. This may be typically American. Texas artist and musician Terry Allen told me in an interview recently that during the Depression his aunt and uncle routinely and half-seriously spent their evenings planning the perfect bank robbery.

19. It is, of course, not unheard of for an actual mother or father to occupy the pervert position. Still, any good psychoanalysis knows very well that the way the parent is unconsciously perceived by the child is of equal or greater psychic significance for it.

20. I am thinking of such naive yet interestingly symptomatic films as *Who Killed Teddy Bear?* (1965, directed by Joseph Cates). I discuss the "violence-lite" of sadism in chap. 2.

As it is medically defined, sadism is not "violent" if it finds a consenting partner. See the *DSM-IV*: of "paraphiliacs" (sadists, pedophiles, voyeurs, fetishists, masochists, frotteurists, and exhibitionists) the manual states, "These individuals are rarely self-referred and usually come to the attention of mental health professionals only when their behavior has brought them into conflict with sexual partners or society." *Diagnostic and Statistical Manual of Mental Disorders,* 4th ed. (Washington, D.C.: American Psychiatric Association, 1994), 523. Perverts, I understand, rarely seek psychoanalysis.

21. According to Lacan in "Kant avec Sade."

22. In contrast to the view entertained by certain fundamentalist religions, for psychoanalysis homosexuality is neither uniformly nor officially "perverse." Still, neither Lacan nor Freud is completely clear on this, but Freud usually treats the homosexual as a simple variant of the expanded sexuality he discovers. Lacan attempts to sketch perverse positions within female homosexuality in his "Proposals for a Congress on Feminine Sexuality," in *Feminine Sexuality: Jacques Lacan and the École Freudienne,* ed. Juliet Mitchell and Jacqueline Rose (New York: Pantheon Books, 1982), 96–97 (from *Séminaire XX: Encore* [Paris: Seuil, 1975]).

23. See "Publisher's Preface," in Marquis de Sade, *Justine,* xvii–xviii: "Although he was far from forgotten throughout the nineteenth century . . . he was relegated and confined to a nether region, to a clandestinity from which it seemed tacitly to be agreed he should never emerge." The first publication of his work was in part the result of Apollinaire's efforts in 1909.

24. Surely he had his own mother-in-law in mind—Madame de Montreuil, who persecuted and prosecuted him. She was also apparently in love with him and riddled with jealousy of her two daughters who were wild for him. (Sade had an affair with his sister-in-law, too.)

25. We must remember that what counts for the child is the way he or she "sees" the Mother unconsciously. There is no way of predicting that the child will inevitably see the mother as the unbarred Other of unlimited *jouissance.*

26. Jean-Jacques Rousseau, "Seconde préface à la Nouvelle Héloïse," in *Oeuvres complétes,* vol. II (Paris: Gallimard, Bibliothèque de la Pléïade, 1964), 23.

27. Those who speak in the name of "morality" today seem eerily consistent with the sadistic superego's voice, echoing its most obscene side. Religious fundamentalists, for example, have recently insisted on dragging before the public the gayness of the policies and decisions of the Disney Corporation—Who knew or didn't know? Who cares? They never voice concern that this corporation reaches into everyone's lives—their housing, their amusements, their consumer goods in

other ways. News reporters and public prosecutors are ensuring, as I write this, that the obscene side of our leaders is made quite public. Kenneth Starr's probe of President Clinton's sexual life, posing as a traditional heterosexual "conservative" stance, nonetheless pathologizes heterosexual relations, even or perhaps especially between married people. Prosecuting attorneys under Starr are reported to have asked Clinton's associates if sexual intercourse was part of his religion, and if his wife, Hillary Rodham Clinton, felt he had a "sex addiction" problem (*San Francisco Chronicle*, July 2, 1998, A29). This public prosecution of sex constitutes a loss that cannot be made up for: that of dignity, the human dignity of the president, the dignity of his office, and the dignity of his wife and child.

28. Freud, "Femininity," 103.

29. Lacan, "Kant avec Sade," 71.

30. See Joan Copjec's now classic and critical analysis of Butler's refusal of the logic of sexuation, "Sex and the Euthanasia of Reason," in *Read My Desire* (Cambridge and London: MIT Press, 1994), 201–36.

31. Butler, *Gender Trouble: Feminism and the Subversion of Identity* (New York and London: Routledge, 1990), 142–43.

32. Ibid., 148 (emphasis added).

33. Butler inserts herself here into the line of skeptical or doubting philosophers from Montaigne to Descartes, from Hume to Sartre, who advise adopting a merely ritual adherence to the social and traditional codes we are born into in order to free our minds of prejudice. But she is much more radical: she touches on the law itself, or at least the norm, which will collapse under the weight of repeated blows to its credibility. She's close to Sade, though she's not quite there, either. In light of her tremendous popularity with today's young people, it seems crucial to understand the source of the appeal.

34. See Deleuze, *Coldness and Cruelty*, and Pierre Klossowski, *Sade, My Neighbor*, trans. Alphonso Lingis (London: Quartet Books, 1992 [originally 1947]), 84–88. Klossowski discusses Sade's relation to Nature in great detail.

35. See Dean MacCannell, "Going through the Motions: Marriage and the Family in the United States after 1950," *Savoir* 3, no. 1/2 (February, 1997): 151–64, for an almost chilling description of the social/sexual life of children in America today.

36. See Jacqueline Rose, *The Case of Peter Pan; or, The Impossibility of Children's Fiction* (London: Macmillan, 1984).

37. Mikhail Bakhtin, "Epic and Novel," in *The Dialogic Imagination* (Austin: University of Texas Press, 1981), 23.

38. Duras, *The Ravishing of Lol V. Stein*, trans. Richard Seaver (New York: Pantheon, 1966), 38.

39. Walter Benjamin, "The Destructive Character," in *Reflections*, trans. Edmund Jephcott (New York: Schocken, 1986).

40. This is what Willy Apollon, Danielle Bergeron, and Lucie Cantin call "wandering" or "unanchored" *jouissance* (Groupe Interdisciplinaire Freudien de Recherches et d'Interventions Cliniques [GIFRIC] training seminar, Quebec, June 1997). Lucie Cantin calls for an ethic of the impossible in an article of the same name, in *Topoi,* special issue on Femininity and Jouissance in the Politics of Postmodernity, ed. J. F. MacCannell, 12, no. 2 (September 1993). In a wildly metaphoric way, such things as budgetary and economic surpluses inspire some of the same kinds of grief as Sade's total *jouissance.* One professor of my youth explained atomic weapons investment this way: "If people had to decide what to do with the collective excess they have generated, they would be caught up in endless squabbles; so if we just explode it all, there's no problem."

41. Certainly, Apollon's theses on femininity along with those of his colleagues Danielle Bergeron and Lucie Cantin can be counted here. See Apollon's remarkable paper "Four Seasons in Femininity: Or Four Men in a Woman's Life," *Topoi* 12, no. 2 (September 1993): 101–15, for an analysis of the way the "other" *jouissance* is a challenge to science. See also Lucie Cantin, "An Ethic . . . ," and Danielle Bergeron, "Femininity and Maternity," in the same issue of *Topoi.* Bergeron has also explicated femininity in a remarkably thorough way in "Femininity," *American Journal of Semiotics* 8, no. 4 (1991): 10 (an expanded version of her article "Femininity," in *Psychoanalysis and Feminism*). Most feminist authors treat femininity and hysteria separately; few of the major female intellects who labored to produce a figure of "woman" out of hysteria in the wake of Freud and Lacan attempted what I do here, to go beyond hysteria in tracing woman's ethics. See Hélène Cixous and Catherine Clément's *The Newly Born Woman,* trans. Betsy Wing (Minneapolis: University of Minnesota Press, 1986); Catherine Millot's *Nobodaddy: L'Hystérie dans le siècle* (Paris: Point hors ligne 1988); Monique David-Menard's *Hysteria from Freud to Lacan: Body and Language in Psychoanalysis,* trans. Catherine Porter (Ithaca, N.Y.: Cornell University Press, 1989). Luce Irigaray's *An Ethics of Sexual Difference,* trans. Carolyn Burke and Gillian C. Gill) (Ithaca, N.Y.: Cornell University Press, 1993) is consumed with contesting male privilege and does little to address its prevailing sadistic ethics. See also Teresa Brennan's *The Interpretation of the Flesh: Freud and Femininity* (London and New York: Routledge, 1992). Drucilla Cornell's *Beyond Accommodation: Ethical Feminism, Deconstruction, and the Law* (New York: Routledge, 1991) takes an essentially hysteric stance.

42. Marguerite Duras, *Destroy, She Said,* trans. Barbara Bray (New York: Grove Press, 1970).

43. *Encore: Le Séminaire de Jacques Lacan XX* (Paris: Seuil, 1975), 9. Lacan's insights into woman basically synthesized Freud's hysteria-femininity opposition, largely by interpolating the pervert into the picture.

2. Perversion in Public Places

1. The Pentagon's new sex policy forced Gen. John Ralston, "a confessed adulterer . . . a candidate for chairman of the Joint Chiefs of Staff, . . . to withdraw his name." *San Francisco Chronicle/Examiner,* June 8, 1997, A1.

2. Julie Hinds, "S&M Is a Big Hit in SoMa," *San Francisco Chronicle,* June 8, 1997, A1.

3. Ibid.

4. See the magazines *Propaganda: Gothic Chronicle* 23; *Wild Child*; and *Gothic Girl,* an Internet zine. Thanks to Carl Reyes for this information.

5. Gilles Deleuze, *Coldness and Cruelty.*

6. Karin M. Cope, "Sado-Masochism," in *Feminism and Psychoanalysis,* 388.

7. See Willy Apollon, Danielle Bergeron, and Lucie Cantin, *Traiter la psychose,* (Quebec: GIFRIC, 1990), 17.

8. Jacques Lacan, *Seminar III,* 39–40.

9. Ibid., 40.

10. The algorithm of Sade's fantasy from Lacan's "Kant avec Sade" (65) is re-analyzed brilliantly by Serge André, *L'Imposture perverse,* 22–31.

11. Lacan, "Kant avec Sade," 59. Lacan is speaking about Kant, but the remark contextualizes his entire reading of Sade.

12. "He" is generic: André studies two lesbians, Rose (a hysteric) and Violette (a pervert), *L'Imposture,* 89–144, 221–22. Violette affirms and denies castration, declaring both that s/he *has* the phallus, and that s/he *is* the phallus.

13. Lacan, "Kant avec Sade," 63.

14. Deleuze, *Coldness and Cruelty,* 25.

15. Violette identifies with neither woman nor man—both are miserably castrated. Instead, she identifies with "le plus que masculine": "Violette ne se présente pas comme un homme, mais comme un sur-homme" (125).

16. See the diagram of Sade's fantasy, "Kant avec Sade," 65.

17. Ibid.

18. "The master-slave dialectic reappears here," Lacan, *Seminar III,* 40.

19. "'Introduction' to the Names of the Father Seminar," trans. J. Mehlman, in *Television,* trans. D. Hollier et al. (New York and London: W. W. Norton, 1990). Lacan interprets the Ten Commandments as the laws of speech in *Seminar VII: The Ethics Seminar,* 68–69.

20. From the demanding, threatening, and exasperating Yahweh to the Hegelian State, which periodically disrupts the happiness of its citizens, the terrifying Other's intervention reminds us of the fragility and necessity of the Law.

21. Jean-Jacques Rousseau, *The Social Contract, The Discourse on Human Inequality, and The Discourse on Political Economy,* trans. Donald A. Cress (Indianapolis: Hackett, 1983), chap. 7, "On the Legislator," 38–41.

22. "[Man] thinks as a consequence of the fact that a structure . . . language . . . carves up his body, a structure that has nothing to do with anatomy." Lacan, *Television*, 6.

23. Walter Benjamin, "Critique of Violence," in *Reflections*.

24. André, *L'Imposture perverse*, 218–50. Institutional pederasty was required for pre-Hellenic Greeks, tribal Germains, Cretans, Macedonians, New Guineans, among others.

25. *San Francisco Chronicle*, November 25, A3.

26. Deleuze, *Coldness and Cruelty*, 134

27. Joan Ryan, "A Painful Statement of Self-Identity," *San Francisco Chronicle*, October 30, 1997, A1.

28. Deleuze, *Coldness and Cruelty*, 134.

29. Craig Marine, "You Always Hurt the One You Love: On *Sick: The Life and Death of Bob Flanagan, Super Masochist*," *San Francisco Chronicle*, November 2, 1997, C7.

30. Ibid.

31. *San Francisco Examiner*, June 8, 1997, A1.

32. Bondage is restriction and control; dominance is psychological reversal and giving up power; sadism is talking and taking power; and masochism is transforming pain.

33. Thanks to Stephanie von Schnurbein and Carl Reyes for invaluable research assistance. The Lacanian and other French analytic literature on perversion is expanding. No one yet seems as insightful as André clinically, and Lacan theoretically. Still, the work of the following can be consulted: Jacques-Alain Miller, "On Perversion," in *Reading Seminars I and II: Lacan's Return to Freud*, ed. Richard Feldstein, Bruce Fink, and Maire Jannus (Albany: SUNY Press, 1996), 306–32; Paul-Laurent Assoun, *Le Couple inconscient: Amour freudien et passion postcourtoise* (Paris: Anthropos, 1992); Piera-Spairani Aulagnier, Jean Clavreul, François Perrier, Guy Rosolato, and Jean-Paul Vlabrega, *Le Désir et la perversion* (Paris: Seuil, 1984); Balbino Bautista, *Préalable à l'étude des perversions* (Paris: PUF de Mirail, 1990); Michel Boiusseyroux, *Abords de la père-version* (Paris: PUF de Mirail, 1990; Janine Chasseguet-Smirgel, *Ethique et esthétique de la perversion* (Paris: PUF de Mirail, 1984); and Michel de Certeau, *Histoire et psychanalyse entre science et fiction* (Paris: Gallimard, 1986), on the question of the tortured body. The American version is Jessica Benjamin, *The Bonds of Love: Psychoanalysis, Feminism, and the Problem of Domination* (New York: Pantheon Books, 1988). See also the astute essay by Thais E. Morgan, "A Whip of One's Own," introduction to *American Journal of Semiotics* 6, no. 4 (1989), special issue on pornography, T. E. Morgan, guest editor.

34. The investment in making war into a series of nonthreatening images—e.g., Grenada and the Gulf War—is a sadistic structure.

35. When the censor rated his *Bent* NC-17 for "scenes of excessive sensuality," director Sean Mathias objected: "I didn't know sensuality needed to be limited." Edward Guthmann, "Director Mathias Has a Long, Intense History with *Bent*," *San Francisco Chronicle*, December 2, 1997, D1.

36. Lacan, *Seminar VII*, 109–10.

37. Ibid., 15.

38. Julia Lupton, "Sublimation," in *Psychoanalysis and Feminism*, 416–17; and Slavoj Žižek, *Metastases of Enjoyment*, 89–112.

39. See "Love outside the Limits of the Law," chap. 10.

40. Lacan, "Kant avec Sade," 63.

41. No neo-Luddite, I use computer compositing for my own installation art.

42. Iain Boal and James Brook, eds., *Resisting the Virtual Life* (San Francisco: City Lights Books, 1997).

3. The Postcolonial Unconscious

1. Caryl Phillips, *The European Tribe* (London: Faber & Faber, 1987), 13. He continues: "Hollywood's ability to leap deftly even the greatest hurdles of reality and create myths independent of place, time and facts, will always be its greatest strength."

2. Homi Bhabha, *Nation and Narration* (London and New York: Routledge, 1990), 292. See also Slavoj Žižek, *They Know Not What They Do*, 255–60. The sublime body emerges from the illegal violence that precedes the founding of law.

3. The exhibition was part of the International Group Show of the Global Cultural Center, headquartered in Japan. It is making a ten-year around-the-world voyage, holding shows in different host countries each year.

4. Of his *object a*, Lacan says that it is the object of the "subject's claim to something that is separated from him, but belongs to him and which he needs to complete himself" (*Seminar VII*, 195).

5. Albert Memmi, *The Colonizer and the Colonized* (Boston: Beacon Press, 1965), 91–92 (originally published in 1957).

6. Hannah Arendt, *The Origins of Totalitarianism* (New York: Meridian Books, 1958), 185–249. Originally published in 1951, her classic study provides a thesis that parallels Aimé Césaire's later work: that even the most seemingly "normal" practices of the colonist against the colonized placed a permanent distortion in Western life, especially where "rights" and "nation" are concerned. Arendt argues that these concepts, distorted by colonial racism after they were hard won in revolutionary struggles in the Enlightenment, returned to a troubled Europe. "Rights" were renaturalized (to legitimate the "natural" superiority of the European colonizer) and permanently interfered with the delicate progress of the new democratic social contract (whose contracting parties could have no substantive,

a priori qualities). European thought, which suffered new "nationalisms" in the form of thinly veiled racisms and imperialisms (e.g., pan-Slavism), was caught in ideals of democracy that did not recognize this "nationalism" for the evil clone of Rousseau's democratic popular sovereignty it had become.

7. Teshome Gabriel's formulation, unpublished paper, presented at the University of California Multi-Campus Research Group on Intercultural Communication meeting, San Diego, 1992.

8. Cited in Arendt, *Origins,* 173.

9. See Arendt, *Origins,* especially chaps. 7 and 8 on race and bureaucracy, government by decree, and the general "lawlessness" of imperialism.

10. Cited in Frantz Fanon, *Black Skin, White Masks,* trans. Charles Lam Markmann (London: Pluto Press, 1986), 91 (originally published in 1952). Further citations from Fanon will be cited in the text. Césaire's 1950 text predates Hannah Arendt's 1951 classic.

11. This is Homi Bhabha's term. An interview with him, "Location, Intervention, Incommensurability," in *Emergences* 1 (Fall 1989): 63–88, describes the evolution of his intellectual and autobiographical journey toward conceptualizing hybridity: a journey from the "cultural bastard" (64) to "something different in order to deal with the post-colonial subject." This would be neither as authoritative nor as self-questioning as various purisms. Bhabha tells eloquently how the "only place in the world to speak from was at a point whereby contradiction, antagonism, the hybridities of cultural influence, the boundaries of nations, were not sublated into some utopian sense of liberation or return. The place to speak from was through those incommensurable contractions within which people survive, are politically active, and change. . . . it is not passivity, it is not always allowing the master to set the terms" (67). See also Néstor García Canclini, *Culturas Híbridas: Estrategias para entrar y salir de la modernidad,* ed. Miguel Hidalgo (Mexico: Editorial Grijalbo, 1989); English translation *Hybrid Cultures: Strategies for Entering and Leaving Modernity,* trans. Christopher L. Chiappari and Silvia L. López (Minneapolis: University of Minnesota Press, 1995).

12. Teshome Gabriel has devised this term to speak about the intercultural subject. See his "Memory and Identity: In Search of the Origin of the Nile River," *Emergences* 1 (Fall 1989), 131–37. Gabriel contests the birth and death of the subject as overdetermined by Western notions of the life cycle and its narrow identification with the private self. Gabriel laments the Western invention of the subject because it served as preliminary to treating the subject as an object (131). Rousseau's understanding of the *social* subject as antipathetic to the *privatized* interests of the ego (see below) suggests points of contact here that could be explored. My reading of Rousseau goes against the grain of his usual identification with the private, Western ego Gabriel denounces.

13. Renata Salecl, *The Spoils of Freedom* (London and New York: Routledge, 1994), 77.

14. Memmi, *The Colonizer and the Colonized*, 80–89.

15. Ibid., 97–98.

16. J. M. Coetzee, *Waiting for the Barbarians* (New York: Penguin, 1980).

17. See Mahasweta Devi's search for the pre-Aryan tribals in India, a quest she analogizes to the Native American effort to recapture their culture. Mahasweta Devi, "The Author in Conversation," in *Imaginary Maps: Three Stories by Mahasweta Devi*, trans. Gayatri Chakravorty Spivak (New York and London: Routledge, 1995), xi.

18. Partha Chatterjee, *The Nation and Its Fragments: Colonial and Post-Colonial Histories* (Princeton, N.J.: Princeton University Press, 1993), 13, 5.

19. See Dean MacCannell, "Tradition's Next Step," in *Discovered Country*, ed. Scott Norris (Albuquerque, N.M.: Stone Ladder Press, 1994), 161–79.

20. Lacan, *Seminar VII*, 73.

21. Jean-Jacques Rousseau, *The Social Contract, The Discourse on Human Inequality*.

22. Lacan, *Seminar VII*, 73 (emphasis mine).

23. Heinrich von Kleist, "The Betrothal in Santo Domingo," 231. Kleist sensed immediately the significance Haiti would hold for freedom and fantasy in democracy. Such a significance has recently been described by Willy Apollon in "The Esthetic Stakes of Voodoo Space" (unpublished paper) as "the war of the slaves against the masters [which] took place in the line of the great French Revolution in which the people, spectators of the pomp of the great and noble, suddenly became actors in their own destiny. But when the slaves of St. Domingo revolted and created their own space for the possible, they had no language through which to express the unheard of. Two worlds opened that henceforth set each against the other in a highly ambiguous coexistence, but one that formed the axis of Haiti's political history. On one side were the new free men, former slaves, for whom the voodoo structure offered a language where an esthetics was possible. On the other side were their allies for the period of the war of independence, the emancipated, former free men, mastering the language of their former masters and succeeding them in the objective possession and control of natural resources, and thus able to manage a national space in dialogue with an emerging international order. Two languages and two spaces therefore existed, opposed in their own esthetics because of the divergence in their interests and in their means of survival and hinged together by the force of the history of control and combination of one by the other for two centuries."

24. Lacan, *Seminar VII*, 310.

25. Ibid., 73.

26. Renata Salecl, *Spoils*, 87.

27. It is akin to the relation of fantasy to its object: $ \diamond a. In Lacan's formula for fantasy, $ means "subject," $\diamond$ means "stamped by" (as in lozenge form or "punch"), and *a* means "object a." See Jacques Lacan, *Seminar XI: The Four Fundamental Concepts of Psychoanalysis*, ed. Jacques-Alain Miller, trans. Alan Sheridan (New York and London: W. W. Norton, 1978), 182.

28. This is what Willy Apollon, Danielle Bergeron, and Lucie Cantin call "extra-jouissance"—the stuff of Drive GIFRIC training seminar (Quebec, June 1997).

29. Hannah Arendt, *Origins*, 173.

30. Let me recall here the attention Lacan (*Seminar VII*, 229) gives to the word *défendre* with its double meaning of defense and forbid. One's defense of one's goods is spoken the same way as depriving oneself of these goods in French.

31. Arendt, *Origins*, 297, calls the "master-slave relationship" a human relationship only as long as there exists a community "willing and able to guarantee any rights whatsoever": it is the loss of this community that has brought on dehumanization—"the calamity which has befallen ever-increasing numbers of people." Colonization works in the realm of the inhuman, *Das Ding*. In his *Discourse on Human Inequality*, 138–39, Rousseau says slavery requires a mental dimension: "If someone chases me from one tree, I am free to go to another; if someone torments me in one place, who will prevent me from going elsewhere? Is there a man with strength sufficiently superior to mine and who is, moreover, sufficiently depraved, sufficiently lazy and sufficiently ferocious to force me to provide for his subsistence while he remains idle? He must resolve not to take his eyes off me for a single instant, to keep me carefully tied down while he sleeps, for fear that I may escape or that I would kill him. . . . were his vigilance to relax for an instant, were an unforeseen noise to make him turn his head, I take twenty steps into the forest; my chains are broken, and he never sees me again for the rest of his life."

32. Hannah Arendt, *Origins*, 32.

33. In the first version of *The Social Contract*, "Du Contrat social, ou essai sur la forme de la république," in Jean-Jacques Rousseau, *Oeuvres complètes*, vol. 3 (Paris: Bibiothèque de la Pléïade, 1964), 290, Rousseau speaks of the act of association as producing a "corps moral et collectif composé d'autant de membres que l'assemblé a de voix" whose "moi commun" would grant it formal unity, life, and will. He calls it a "personne publique." Each "personne" has a "volonté générale" whose force is only a means toward an end: "le bonheur du peuple" (509).

34. See Louis Althusser, *Montesquieu, Rousseau, Marx: Politics and History*, trans. Ben Brewster (London: Verso, 1982), 129–33 (originally published in 1970), on the discrepancy of the two recipient parties to Rousseau's social contract.

35. Hegel placed the first moral values of civil society, a realm of self-seeking,

in the ruling warrior castes *(Sittlichkeit)*. Individual private moral subjectivity appears only with the relatively weaker bourgeoisie *(Moralität)*.

36. Étienne Balibar, with Immanuel Wallerstein, *Race, Nation, Classe* (Paris: La Découverte, 1988).

37. *The Second Discourse,* 148. The French reads: "Tous ces maux sont le premier effet de la propriété et le cortège inséparable de l'inégalité naissante" (*Oeuvres* 3: 175; see also 170, 173). In a parallel way, Salecl (*Spoils,* 82) points to the Kantian subject as a cogito delivered from all *substantial* remainders. Kant claimed Rousseau inspired him.

38. This is a key part of his reflections on religion in *The Social Contract,* 96–103, book IV, chapter VIII, "On Civil Religion."

39. Rousseau, *The Social Contract,* chapter III, "Whether the General Will Can Err" (31–32): "There is often a great deal of difference between the will of all and the general will. The latter considers only the general interest, whereas the former considers private interest and is merely the sum of private wills. But remove from these same wills the pluses and minuses that cancel each other out, and what remains as the sum of the differences is the general will."

40. See previous note. Later utilitarians would try something different, creating a "will of all" from the sacrificial logic of pluses and minuses. Unlike the utilitarians, Rousseau does not believe that the distribution of goods will do any good in righting inequities; the ruling classes can simply create scarcity (or even excess) to mask the fundamental dialectic of envy the good evokes.

41. Joseph Heller, *Catch-22* (New York: Simon and Schuster, 1961).

42. The inference, drawn all too often, was that Rousseau's new state would call forth an "uncivil society." But make no mistake, Rousseau was not Diderot, and his *sauvage,* or man in the wild, was no sentimentalized Tahitian (spontaneous, sexy, and uninhibited). The problem for Rousseau is deeper, more constitutive of the human being.

43. Lacan, *Seminar VII,* 7.

44. See Theodor Adorno, *The Stars Down to Earth* (London and New York: Routledge, 1994), 162–69 for a characterization of fascist rhetorical devices and propaganda structures in radio preachers and astrological horoscopes. It is a "technique of substitution of a collective ego for paternal imagery" (163). Psychoanalysis presses the structure of ideological identification one step beyond, to an unconscious level, beginning with a subject's problematic response to *jouissance.*

45. Rousseau swore in his *Confessions* that he heard Hume call out in his sleep as they crossed to England together, "I have got Jean-Jacques Rousseau!" Hume's disingenuousness in getting the English king to grant Rousseau a pension without Rousseau's knowledge made the fiery man of the people look like a hypocrite.

46. David Hume, *Essays and Treatises on Several Subjects*, 2 vols. (Edinburgh, 1825), 1: 521–22. ("Of National Characters" was first published in 1748).

47. Immanuel Kant, *Observations on the Feeling of the Beautiful and of the Sublime*, trans. John T. Goldthwait (Berkeley and Los Angeles: University of California Press, 1959). (Originally *Beobachtungen über das Gefühl des Schönen und Erhabenen* [Königsberg, 1764].) There's always an exception—and, for Kant, of the dark races, it is the North American Indian: "Among all savages there is no nation that displays so sublime a mental character as those of North America" (111). We should note that this Canadian noble savage is mighty like a Greek to Kant: "Lycurgus probably gave statutes to just such savages. . . . Jason excels Attakakullakulla in nothing but the honor of a Greek name" (112). This is, re-member, the "precritical" Kant. The "critical" Kant was far more circumspect and rigorous in his quest for a universal subject.

48. Rousseau accurately predicted that the Tyrrhenian island would produce, within a generation, a person who would astonish the world and change the face of Europe. How did he know Napoleon would emerge from the Corsica he was shaping? Because he saw there the possibility that a whole "people" could now be founded not on natural rights, not even on their inherent rights as children of God, but only on the rights they have, as a whole, bestowed on themselves.

49. It is impossible to ignore the economic context of psychoanalysis. Fanon (*Black Skin*, 86) reserves his greatest criticism of Octave Mannoni for "not hav[ing] tried to feel himself into the despair of the man of color confronting the white man." Mannoni also failed to recognize that a "racist structure" is "funda-mentally the result of the economic structure" (87, on South Africa). "All forms of exploitation" are "identical because all of them are applied against that same 'object': man" (88).

50. Here an underlying economic difference subtends the psychic: gift as ex-change is precluded by the marketing of goods.

51. Colonization interrupts permanently the normal human ways of welcom-ing the stranger, the ways of exchange of the gift. Eighteenth-century terms are sprinkled in Fanon's description of the precolonial days: "What Césaire calls 'the old, courtly civilizations,' were characterized by 'humanity,' 'good will,' and 'cour-tesy,'" Fanon writes. "The foreigner was called *vazaha*, which means *honorable stranger;* . . . shipwrecked Europeans were welcomed with open arms. . . . [T]he European, the foreigner, was never thought of as the enemy" (Fanon, *Black Skin*, 99). Unable to pinpoint precisely its special trauma, Fanon invokes a range of pos-sibilities, speculating that both colonizer and colonized are transformed ("since Galliéni, the Malagasy has ceased to exist" [94]); or that the Malagasy alone is al-tered: "The Malagasy alone no longer exists, . . . he exists *with the European*" (96).

He finally settles on the utterly inexplicable *dehumanization* of the Malagasy: "white alone means human" (98).

52. Stirred and stirred up by Octave Mannoni's *Prospero and Caliban,* Fanon recognized that both he and Mannoni reject a normative psychoanalysis for being pressed too easily into colonial service, too inattentive to the specific situation of the colonized, racialized subject (*Black Skin,* 80–89). Memmi also credits psychoanalysis, but discredits it too, in the colonial case: "Psychoanalysis or Marxism must not, under the pretext of having discovered the source or one of the main sources of human conduct, pre-empt all experience, all feeling, all suffering, all the byways of human behavior, and call them profit motive or Oedipus complex" (Memmi, *Colonizer,* xiii).

53. In the sense of the *object a* as object of the "subject's claim to something that is separated from him, but belongs to him and which he needs to complete himself" (Lacan, *Seminar VII,* 195). This *object a* is simulated for the colonized, however.

54. Her pure death drive must be contrasted in absolute terms with the sheer life force of the Beggar Woman from Savannahkhet, both in the film and in Duras's earlier novel, *Vice-Consul.* The beggar woman, who has crossed continents on foot, lived by eating raw fish, and sleeping on straw, is never seen in the film. Her laughter is, however, heard—a mad, uncontrolled laughter that contains every bit of the feminine animation that exists in the film and more.

55. Whereas under democracy what emerges from the violent founding of the law is a sublime body of the "people," in colonization, the "sublime" body of the commodity, founded on a law of the superego, is born.

4. Race/War

1. The epigraph is taken from Minoo Moallem and Iain Boal, "Haven with No Shadows: Multicultural Nationalism and the Poetics of Inauguration," in *Between Woman and Nation: Nationalisms, Transnational Feminisms, and the State,* ed. Caren Kaplan, Norma Alarcón, and Minoo Moallem (Durham, N.C.: Duke University Press, 1999). See also Étienne Balibar, *Race, nation, classe*; and Renata Salecl, *Spoils,* 77: "Liberals do not see how the project of 'justice as fairness' cannot be universally acceptable because of the specific way people relate to some traumatic determinations (nation, race, sex) around which they form their identity."

2. Ann Chamberlain, *On Color: The Reclassification of a Dead Archive by Color,* photography, mixed media. Installation at Mission Cultural Center, San Francisco, 1990.

3. The classical work is by Stanley M. Garn, *Human Races* (Springfield, Ill.: Charles C. Thomas, 1961).

4. Dean MacCannell, "Going through the Motions," 158.

5. See T. H. Watkins, "The Greening of the Empire," *National Geographic* 190, no. 5 (November 1996): 28–53. Carolus Linnaeus devised the universal scheme for classifying plants (*Systema natura*, 1735), then animals (*Genera plantarum*, 1737). He finally included humans in his *Species plantarum* (1753,1758). He did some plant collecting at Physic Garden in Chelsea, just outside London. His disciple, the Swede Daniel Solander, worked with Sir Joseph Banks, inspiring the worldwide voyage of the latter. Banks's circle apparently included Linnaeus's disciple and, at Montagu House, David Hume, Thomas Gray, the poet, and William Blackstone, the jurist.

6. Claude Lévi-Strauss, *Race et histoire* (Paris: Gonthier, 1967), 26–30 (UNESCO reissue).

7. It makes Melville's novel about a large white whale a more prescient interpretation of the colonial adventure than we knew.

8. See the section on Hume in chap. 3, "The Postcolonial Unconscious."

9. Lacan's unconscious *jouissance* factor begins to appear in the question of race. In *Television* he says that racism will only grow stronger and deeper in our time.

10. "Thoughts for the Time on War and Death," in *Standard Edition of the Complete Works of Freud,* vol. XIV (London: Hogarth Press and Institute for Psychoanalysis, 1957), 273–300.

11. Freud, "On Narcissism," in *Standard Edition,* vol. XIV: 73–104.

12. C. T. Onions, ed., *Oxford Universal Dictionary on Historical Principles* (Oxford: Clarendon Press, 1933), 1646.

13. See Slavoj Žižek, *For They Know Not,* 16 ff, on the quilting point and anti-Semitism as a thought structure.

14. Dean MacCannell coined the term in *Empty Meeting Grounds* (London and New York: Routledge, 1992).

15. Freud writes of the greater degree of conscience in the "savage" today over the way the European soldier is commanded to kill without guilt: "It is worthy of note that the primitive races which still survive in the world, and are undoubtedly closer than we are to primaeval man, act differently in this respect, or did until they came under the influence of our civilization. Savages—Australians, Bushmen, Tierra del Fuegans—are far from being remorseless murderers; when they return victorious from the war-path they may not set foot in their villages or touch their wives till they have atoned for the murders they committed in war by penances which are often long and tedious. It is easy, of course, to attribute this to their superstition: the savage still goes in fear of the avenging spirits of the slain. But the spirits of his slain enemy are nothing but the expression of his bad conscience about his blood-guilt; behind this superstition there lies concealed a vein of ethical sensitiveness which has been lost by us civilized men" ("Thoughts").

16. Stendhal saw in the Parisian drawing room that both noble manners and the art of power were cultured together. The appearance of self-control in the aristocrat demands the same from their inferiors. In *Red and Black,* trans. Robert Adams (New York: W. W. Norton, 1969), Julien Sorel admires the Maréchale de Fervaques for her "*patrician calm* which breathes an air of perfect politeness and especially the total impossibility of any keen emotion. Any spontaneous gesture, any lapse of complete self-control would have scandalized Mme de Fervaques almost as much as a failure of dignified condescension towards one's inferiors" (327). The arbitrary exercise of autocratic power requires a sadistic coldness; the aristocratic salon is that apathy's proving ground. See Juliet Flower MacCannell, "How Julien Loses His Head: Or Stendhal and the Politics of the Imaginary," in *Red and Black,* ed. Stirling Haig and Dean de la Motte (New York: PMLA, 1999).

17. *San Francisco Chronicle,* Tuesday, November 5, 1996, 2.

18. *San Francisco Chronicle,* Tuesday, November 5, 1996, 1.

19. *Psychiatry's Betrayal in the Guise of Help* (Los Angeles: Citizens Commission on Human Rights, 1996), 11, 8, acknowledgment to *Freedom Magazine,* published by the Church of Scientology International. The letterhead accompanying the anonymously authored brochure reads, "Founding Commissioner Thomas Szasz, M.D., Professor of Psychiatry Emeritus; Established in 1969 by the Church of Scientology to investigate and expose psychiatric violations of human rights."

20. As I write this, he is bringing up the matter of special celebrations for ethnic studies graduation parties, which he wants banned. (*The California Aggie,* June 29, 1998, 1).

21. Freud, *Group Psychology and the Analysis of the Ego,* in *Standard Edition,* vol. XVIII: 120, found modern egalitarianism expresses the replacement of jealousy by "group feeling." If one "cannot be the favourite oneself, at all events nobody shall be the favourite." He adds: "We have only to think of the troop of women and girls, all of them in love in an enthusiastically sentimental way, who crowd round a singer or pianist after his performance. It would certainly be easy for each of them to be jealous of the rest; but, in the face of their numbers and the consequent impossibility of their reaching the aim of their love, they renounce it, and, instead of pulling out one another's hair, they act as a united group, do homage to the hero of the occasion with their common actions, and would probably be glad to have a share of *his* flowing locks. Originally rivals, they have succeeded in identifying themselves with one another by means of a similar love for the same object. . . . What appears later on in society in the shape of *Gemeingeist, esprit de corps,* 'group spirit,' etc., does not belie its derivation from what was originally envy. No one must want to put himself forward, everyone must be the same and have the same. Social justice means that we deny ourselves many things so

that others may have to do without them as well, or, what is the same thing, may not be able to ask for them."

22. Theodor W[iesengrund] Adorno, *Minima Moralia: Reflections from Damaged Life,* trans. E. F. N. Jephcott (London: NLB, 1974), no. 66: 102 (Originally published in 1951.)

23. Ibid.

24. Such as his pronouncement that "the feminine character, and the ideal of femininity on which it is modeled, are products of masculine society." Adorno, *Minima Moralia,* no. 59: 92.

25. Oddly, Sade was certain that nothing new could be created, only naturally recycled.

26. See chap. 2, "Perversion in Public Places," on the aesthetic relation to the object.

27. Adorno, *Aesthetic Theory,* ed. Gretel Adorno and Rolf Tiedemann, trans. C. Lenhardt (London and New York: Routledge & Kegan Paul, 1984), 18.

28. Adorno makes it truer of his aesthetic than of Kant's. Unlike Kant he saw through, as did the later Lacan in "Kant avec Sade," to a secret enjoyment hidden in disinterestedness. Adorno reminds us that the stronger the taboo against enjoyment in Kant, the more it must be matched by a repressed urge for its opposite. If disinterestedness is to be more than a synonym for indifference, it has to have "a trace of untamed interest somewhere" (*Aesthetic Theory,* 16). He calls Kant's aesthetics a "castrated hedonism" that ignores art's fundamental source.

29. Adorno, *Prisms: Cultural Criticism and Society,* trans. Samuel and Shierry Weber (London: Neville Spearman 1967), 128 (emphasis added).

30. Adorno criticized the modern professional woman as having "lost" under advanced capitalism "an emotion which seemed to point to freedom." Horkheimer and Adorno, *Dialectic of Enlightenment,* 107.

31. T. Adorno, W. Benjamin, E. Bloch, B. Brecht, and G. Lukács, *Aesthetics and Politics* (London: NLB, 1977), 125–26.

32. That is the other way of reading his sweeping indictment of all mass art and its enjoyments. See Adorno's remarks to Walter Benjamin, where he complains that Benjamin has "swept art out of the corners of its taboos—but it is as though you feared a consequent inrush of barbarism (who could share your fear more than I?) and protected yourself by raising what you fear to a kind of inverse taboo. The laughter of the audience at a cinema . . . is anything but good and revolutionary; instead, it is full of the worst bourgeois sadism." Chaplin, too, comes under his gun here. Adorno, *Aesthetics and Politics,* 123.

33. Adorno, letter to Ernst Krenek, cited in Susan Buck-Morss, *The Origin of Negative Dialectics: Theodor W. Adorno, Walter Benjamin, and the Frankfurt*

Institute (New York: Free Press, 1977), 137. Adorno differed radically from Walter Benjamin. Benjamin felt he could not even "breathe" in Nazi air.

34. To distinguish language as logical system from any one particular language when "language as such" only appears in the existential form of known languages is not easy. Hannah Arendt herself regarded her native tongue as an exception to castration. German was, for her, irretrievably special. In an interview with Gunter Gaus on October 28, 1964, "Was bleibt? Es bleibt die Muttersprache," broadcast on the television show *Zur Person,* she expressed her inability to experience a sense of enjoyment in any language but her maternal one.

35. *Psychiatry's Betrayal* (11) equates psychic castration with physical castration and urges black people to have nothing to do with psychiatric discourse. It threatens, in effect, anyone who is being educated with castration: one page is labeled, "Education or Mental Slavery." Its sidebar on the right-hand page shows a dark figure in chains with the words "Mental Slavery" printed in red. On the left-hand page, in bold letters, is a quotation from "Ernst Rodin. American Psychiatrist," which says, "The castrated ox will pull its plow." The voice of Power here is stating, in effect, "Stay out of my domain, the domain of knowledge, of the Master. Enjoy your *slave-jouissance,* or better yet, your *animal-jouissance.*"

36. Moallem and Boal, "Haven with No Shadows."

37. Salecl, *Spoils of Freedom,* 12.

38. Nanette Asimov, "Guardian at the School Gate," *San Francisco Chronicle,* November 3, 1996, 3.

5. Fascism and the Voice of Conscience

1. A rare mention in a news report of the openly neofascist soccer clubs in Italy notes that membership is reputed to require "killing a nigger" (*San Francisco Chronicle,* December 17, 1994).

2. The title of a recent book by George Lipsitz, *The Possessive Investment in Whiteness: How White People Profit from Identity Politics* (Philadelphia: Temple University Press, 1998).

3. One of the few is Renata Salecl. See her article "Society Doesn't Exist," *American Journal of Semiotics* 7, nos. 1–2 (1990): 45–52; and her book on Eastern Europe, *Spoils of Freedom.*

4. In *The Regime of the Brother,* I argued that fascism is *not* patriarchal or related to the Father but has instead to do with a fantasy of fraternalism.

5. Lacan calls the place of the partial drives the domain of the "heart" for Freud. *Seminar XI: The Four Fundamental Concepts of Psychoanalysis.*

6. For Lacan, and for the earliest Derrida, speech is not voice but *parole,* which has an entirely different ethical inflection. Speech, in classic Lacan, is the signifier, the symbolic pact, the social contract that divides us from each other as

mutual aggressors: "Speech is always a pact, an agreement, people get on with one another, they agree—this is yours, this is mine, this is this, that is that." Lacan, *Seminar III: The Psychoses*, 39.

7. Hannah Arendt, *Eichmann in Jerusalem: A Report on the Banality of Evil* (Harmondsworth: Penguin Books, 1963).

8. The *object a* is the bearer of that bit of *jouissance* excised by accession to the symbolic and yet produced, retrospectively, by that accession. The *object a* is a remainder, unaccommodated by and unaccountable to the symbolic.

9. *Principle* is intertwined with *drive* throughout Freud.

10. It would be nice to free democratic and poetic versions of voice from the onus of a misapplied Derridean critique. For it is the monology and monotony of the fascist voice, not the plurivocality fundamental to both democracy and poetry, that is, or should be, the target of critique.

11. Mladen Dolar, "Prolégomènes à une théorie du discours fasciste," in *Perspectives psychanalytiques sur la politique* (Paris: Navarin Éditeur, 1984), 42; my translation. See, additionally, Jacques Derrida, *The Ear of the Other*, trans. Peggy Kamuf and Avital Ronell (New York: Schocken Books, 1985). See also Avital Ronell, *The Telephone Book* (Lincoln: University of Nebraska Press, 1990). Dolar's essay provides greater specificity. From Siegfried Cracauer on, critics have sensed that without radio or film Hitler could not have come to power. By using Lacan, we can narrow this to the field of operation of the *object a*.

12. Lacan, *Seminar XI*, 205.

13. Tracking the start-up of drive, Freud noted that the "first" enjoyments in "mental" life are *hallucinatory* fulfillments of inner needs. The enjoyment attributed to a prior "state of nature" for any form of *mind* is already produced by desire: "Whatever was thought of (desired) was simply imagined in an hallucinatory form, as still happens today with our dream-thoughts every night." See his 1911 essay, "Formulations Regarding the Two Principles of Mental Functioning," in *General Psychological Theory: Papers on Metapsychology, Standard Edition*, vol. XII: 215 ff.

In *Seminar XI* (169–77) Lacan makes drive one of the four fundamental concepts of psychoanalysis. Lacan explicates Freud's metapsychological concept (setting drive apart from "the life force" [165]) by emphasizing both that it is the original break with a natural, reproductive cycle, and with the homeostasis of the pleasure ego. Drive exceeds these cycles with a "partial circuit" of its own, a movement out and away from—and back to—a prior *jouissance*. Freud notes that the partial circuit of drive is called up by a "hallucinated object," which is equivalent to Lacan's fantasy *object a*: breast, feces, gaze, or voice. The drive, the full, whole drive for Lacan is always Death Drive. The partial drive, empowered by an *object a* that organizes it, skirts full drive.

14. Lacan, *Seminar XI*, 186.

15. Julia Kristeva's *Powers of Horror* (New York: Columbia University Press, 1982) tried to link fascism and anti-Semitism in Céline to this abject identification. Her analysis lacks the clarity and rigor that Lacan's provides by way of the *object a*.

16. Freud, "The Creative Writer and Daydreaming," in *Standard Edition*, vol. IX: 143 ff.

17. In Lacan's 1966 essay on the "Subversion of the Subject and the Dialectic of Desire" *(Ecrits)* he envisaged the "Che vuoi?"—the fantasy of the desire of the Other—as liberating us from alienating identifications.

18. Jacques Lacan, *Ecrits*, 313.

19. Lacan, *Seminar VII*, 195.

20. Lacan, *Ecrits*, 315.

21. In perversion, fantasy is short-circuited by a need to act out a scenario resulting in a "statics of the fantasy," in Lacan's terms. "Kant avec Sade," 63.

22. Lacan, *Seminar VII*, 99.

23. Lacan, *Seminar XI*, 251.

24. Slavoj Žižek, *The Sublime Object*, 82–83.

25. The morality of power, of the service of goods, is as follows: "As far as desires are concerned, come back later. Make them wait" (Lacan, *Seminar VII*, 315).

26. Lacan, *Seminar VII*, 315.

27. In the party Mussolini started to construct before and after World War I (1909–19), he introduced "no systematic exposition of its ideology or purpose other than a negative reaction against socialist and democratic egalitarianism" (*New Columbia Encyclopedia* [1975], 925.

28. Fascism's potential translation into new and unknown forms of production (especially in the media and technology) remains to be seen.

29. See Slavoj Žižek, *The Sublime Object*, 83–84.

30. "The right to *jouissance*, were it recognized, would relegate the domination of the pleasure principle to a forevermore outdated era. In enunciating it, Sade causes the ancient axis of ethics to slip . . . for everyone: this axis is no other than the egoism of happiness. It cannot be said that all reference to it is extinguished in Kant" (Lacan, "Kant avec Sade," 71).

31. See Slavoj Žižek, "Why Is Sade the Truth of Kant?" in *For They Know Not*, 229–33.

32. Kant sends it off to the unthinkability of the Thing-in-itself (Lacan, "Kant avec Sade," 60). But it has a remainder, the object-*cause*. Here the reader is asked to recall the creation of surplus enjoyment by virtue of sacrifice outlined by Žižek (*The Sublime Object*, 82–83) cited above.

33. Rousseau was by no means unaware of such dangers when he developed his concept of *la volonté générale* in the *Social Contract*, especially in the chapter

on "La Religion civile" (*The Social Contract,* 31–32). Rousseau, needless to say, identifies "civil society" as intrinsically antagonistic, founded in and by inequity and injustice to which his *volonté générale* is conceived simply as an antiweight. This definition was susceptible to being misconstrued once it became a received idea. See chap. 3.

34. The media dramatization of the execution of Robert Alton Harris, who is white, overtly mobilized public sentiment against capital punishment, but a major side effect of this sentiment was a suppression of awareness that such punishment is disproportionately meted out to men of color.

35. Since I first wrote this piece in 1993, the World Court at the Hague has started to prosecute for genocide, though its cases have not been in "first world" countries, but in Africa and the former Yugoslavia. When I wrote this, I was shocked to learn that the United States had consistently refused to ratify the antigenocide treaty devised by the United Nations. Apparently, if, after Rousseau, the Law is deemed less the repression of a desire than a positive form of the will— *la volonté générale,* or the formal force of the democratic polity—it seems the "popular will" in democracy must imagine itself to be good, presumed innocent, in all senses of the term. Law that would express an evil will could not afford to recognize its desire.

36. "The law as empty form in the *Critique of Practical Reason* corresponds to time as pure form in the *Critique of Pure Reason.* The law does not tell us *what* we must do, it merely tells us 'you must!', leaving us to deduce from it the good, that is, the object of this pure imperative." Gilles Deleuze, *Kant's Critical Philosophy,* trans. Hugh Tomlinson and Barbara Habberjam (Minneapolis: University of Minnesota Press, 1984), x.

37. Žižek's *They Know Not What They Do,* suggests that such exhortation denotes an absolute prohibition at work—it is the other side of "You must not!" The point is that the absolute freedom to enjoy beyond the limit of the Law brings with it countless prohibitions. "Partial" enjoyments—witness, for example the vegetarianism of Hitler, and bans on smoking, drinking, meat, loud music, free speech, noise—are sacrificed. Such bans on one's own enjoyment produce the excess hatred of perceived *jouissance* of the other, what Lacan called *Lebensneid* (*Seminar VII,* 237). See Jacques Alain Miller, "Extimité," 74–87.

38. See Arendt, *Eichmann in Jerusalem,* 136. See also P. T. Geach, "Good and Evil," in *Theories of Ethics,* ed. Philippa Foot (London: Oxford University Press, 1967), 64–73: "Since Kant's time peoples have supposed that there is another sort of relevant reply—an appeal not to inclination but to the Sense of Duty. Now indeed a man may be got by training into a state of mind in which 'You *must* not' is a sufficient answer to 'Why shouldn't I?'; in which, giving this answer to himself, or hearing it given by others, strikes him with a quite peculiar awe; in which, perhaps,

he even thinks he 'must not' ask why he 'must not.' . . . Moral philosophers of the Objectivist school, like Sir David Ross, would call this 'apprehension of one's obligations'; it does not worry them that, but for God's grace, this sort of training can make a man 'apprehend' practically anything as his 'obligations.' (Indeed they admire a man who does what he thinks he *must* do regardless of what he actually does; is he not acting from a Sense of Duty which is the highest motive?" (70–71).

39. On this point, Lacan, in *Seminar VII*, and Rousseau in *The Social Contract* might agree that the lawgiver has to present himself as either a foreigner or a divinity: no one would agree willingly to submit to a law made by one's equal and peer. See chap. 2.

40. See Lacan's lightly ironic treatment (in *Seminar VII*, 108–9) of Kant's overly rational sense of the psychology involved with sex: Kant fails to recognize, in his famous example of the gibbet awaiting the man who would sleep with his lady love and therefore naturally chooses against it, either the compulsions of the overestimated object (love) or the impulses of the sadist (the pleasure of possibly cutting up her body).

41. Although his views on marriage as the even exchange of sexual parts could give us, as it has others, pause.

42. As the documentation and testimony piled up in the trial of Eichmann, it became quite clear to Hannah Arendt, who reported on it, that he had killed not out of blood lust or any of the traditional passions. He did not participate emotionally in the *Endlosung;* he could not even bear the few glimpses he had of actual deaths and killings he routinely ordered; Eichmann was, as Arendt showed, a murderer only "by administration." He felt desire very little, if at all (at most, he wanted to rise and succeed in the government's hierarchy). He always acted in accordance with the rules, and, far from simply following orders, he reported he felt compelled to "go beyond" the written law and attributed this to his Kantian ethics. In the end, this compulsion led to his being "mastered" by a will not his own.

43. Lacan called Kant an obsessional, keeping him this side of psychosis and perversion. But he also saw how Sade would find his perverse position in a way quite parallel to Kant. Lacan also said that "the realization of full speech" began with the opposite of "obsessional intrasubjectivity"—"hysterical intersubjectivity" (Lacan, *Ecrits*, 46).

44. See Lacan, *Seminar VII*, 73, on the link between the superego and *Das Ding*. Kant ruled out "the *Gut, das Ding*" as determining reason. But at the "level of the unconscious," Lacan tells us, "*Das Ding* presents itself . . . as that which *already makes the law*. . . . It is a capricious and arbitrary law, the law of the oracle, the law of signs, . . . the law to which [the subject] has no *Sicherung*, to use another Kantian term. That is also at bottom the bad object that Kleinian theory is con-

cerned with.... *The subject makes no approach at all to the bad object, since he is already maintaining his distance in relation to the good object.* He cannot stand the extreme good that *das Ding* may bring him, which is all the more reason why he cannot locate himself in relation to the bad.... At the level of the unconscious, the subject lies [about evil]" (emphasis added).

45. In his *Seminar VII,* 307–10, Lacan interprets all of Freud's versions of the father as adumbrations of the "malevolent superego" that, in Freud's later work, replaces the Oedipus complex by the castration complex.

46. Endless opinion polls, of course, address only prepackaged, prepared goods: they rarely tap the people's desire.

47. Lacan, *Four Fundamental Concepts,* 275.

48. Lacan, *Seminar VII,* 7.

49. Recall that this *"jouissance de l'Autre,"* with respect to Freud's discussion of drive and "the two principles of mental functioning" (the pleasure and reality principles), is always a retrospective illusion.

50. Arendt follows Raoul Hilberg in utterly rejecting the long European tradition of anti-Semitism as the principal cause of the Holocaust, an opinion for which she has borne much criticism by her fellow Jews.

51. Lacan maps three sorts of *vel* in *Seminar XI* (241): the indifferent "either/or" (where the choice does not matter), the absolute "either/or" (where choice eliminates one side), and "neither/nor." In any case, each side or set of possible outcomes holds its object in common with the opposed set. If an absolute choice is made, and one set over the other is elected, the object once shared by the sets, and which is needed to complete it, is retained by only one, and the other side ceases to exist at all. Conversely, the object itself loses a portion of its own existence, its resonance in the other set.

52. Willy Apollon, "Four Seasons in Femininity," *Topoi* 12 (September 1993): 3.

53. Recent examples of "unwritten laws" and their connection to modern mass slaughter are the more or less complete lapse, since World War II, in formal declarations of war whenever hostilities are undertaken; and the burial alive of "thousands of Iraqi soldiers" by the United States Armed Forces in the Persian Gulf War, because, as Pentagon officials explained, there was no written law against it. The Pentagon stated that there was a "gap" in the law: "The Pentagon said yesterday that a 'gap' in laws governing warfare made it legally permissible during the gulf war for U.S. tanks to bury thousands of Iraqi troops in their trenches and for the U.S. warplanes to bomb the enemy retreating along the so called Highway of Death.... *Newsday* disclosed in September that many Iraqi troops were buried alive when the First Mechanized Infantry Division attacked an 8,000 man division defending Saddam Hussein's front line" (Patrick Sloyan, "US Defends Burying Alive Iraqi Troops, *San Francisco Chronicle,* April 11, 1992, A10). The Pentagon

later claimed that the "heat of the battle" obscured Iraqi efforts to surrender; but no a priori constraint on the right to such mass solutions is conceded by U.S. officials. The law of war, they state, "permits the attack of enemy combatants at any time, whether advancing, retreating or standing still."

54. Or "above the written law," as in the famous statement by Oliver North's secretary, Fawn Hall, by which she sought to justify her illegal destruction of government records in the Iran-Contra Affair: "[A] few minutes later, she retracted her statement. 'I don't feel that,' she said." Reported by AP wire service and cited in *The California Aggie,* June 10, 1987, 6.

55. Granted that the drive to "senselessness" in the discourse of fascism is utterly without the concomitant and flexible comprehension of "form" found in Kant and in post-Kantian critical esthetics.

56. Eichmann's fantasy at first is that he will "save" the Jews by his actions. He calls himself a "Zionist": "He hardly thought of anything but a 'political solution' . . . and how to 'get some firm ground under the feet of the Jews'" (41). That "expulsion" under the guise of salvation inevitably turned to extermination is, however, predicted by Eichmann's relation to *jouissance.* Since he only felt "elated" when he was swept up as a part of the "Movement of History," Eichmann's desire to pin the Jews to the "ground" "spares" them this "elevation" and "movement," which he himself terms a "death whirl." The Jews would thus go "below" and remain in "the past," reaching the endpoint of the death drive without having to suffer its *jouissance.*

57. The true sadist, as Slavoj Žižek says, is the one who works not for his own desire but on behalf of the Other's *jouissance,* as its Agent or Executioner. See "The Limits of the Semiotic Approach to Psychoanalysis," in *Psychoanalysis and . . . ,* ed. Richard Feldstein and Henry Sussman (New York and London: Routledge, 1990), 89–110, as well as *They Know Not What They Do,* 234.

58. Arendt reports that Heydrich was pleasantly surprised at how few difficulties he had enlisting the active help of all the Ministries and the whole Civil Service needed for the Final Solution. There was "more than happy agreement on the part of the participants'; the Final Solution was greeted with 'extraordinary enthusiasm' by all present" (112–13).

59. Like others from Adorno to Ronell, Lacan implicates the mass media, but in contrast to the thinkers of technology, Lacan underscores the problematic of subject and object as essential to an anatomy of fascism.

60. In *Seminar VII,* chap. XV.

61. Notably, Horkheimer and Adorno in *The Dialectic of Enlightenment.*

62. Note that Eurodisney in France was originally restricted to only one of the "Lands" that the Disney Company devised for the Anaheim Disneyland: "Fantasyland."

6. Mothers of Necessity

1. Jane Flax, *Thinking Fragments: Psychoanalysis, Feminism, and Postmodernism in the Contemporary West* (Berkeley and Los Angeles: University of California Press, 1990).

2. Nancy Chodorow, *Feminism and Psychoanalytic Theory* (London and New Haven, Conn.: Yale University Press, 1989).

3. Immanuel Kant, *Anthropology from a Pragmatic Point of View*, trans. Mary J. Gregor (The Hague: Nijhoff, 1974).

4. Madelon Sprengnether, *The Spectral Mother: Freud, Feminism, and Psychoanalysis* (Ithaca, N.Y.: Cornell University Press, 1990).

5. Chodorow, *Feminism*, 199–218.

6. For some of the domestic social and psychic, economic and political noxious effects see Dean MacCannell, "Baltimore in the Morning . . . After: On the Forms of Post-Nuclear Leadership," *Diacritics* 14, no. 2 (summer 1984): 33–46; for foreign effects see Dennis O'Rourke's film *Half-Life* (1986).

7. See Rousseau, "Sur l'économie politique," in *Oeuvres complètes*, vol. III (Paris: Gallimard, 1966 [1755]), 24–278; and Friedrich Engels, *The Origin of the Family, Private Property and the State* (Harmondsworth: Penguin Books, 1985) (originally published in 1884).

8. The fascist-narcissistic group is described *avant-la-lettre* in Freud's study of mass or crowd psychology.

9. Rosi Braidotti, "The Politics of Ontological Difference," in *Between Feminism and Psychoanalysis*, ed. Teresa Brennan (London: Routledge, 1989), 96.

10. As shown in Chodorow's account.

11. In *Between Feminism and Psychoanalysis* (142), Elizabeth Wright makes the crucial point that "psychoanalysis-for-feminism has flourished" only in literary criticism; indeed, it was first of all in literary studies that orthodoxies about femininity, feminine psychology, and women were challenged. The first and strongest post-Freudian statements about this unexpected marriage appear in Juliet Mitchell's *Women: The Longest Revolution*, (London: Virago, 1984), and her *Psychoanalysis and Feminism* (New York: Pantheon, 1974), which leaned heavily on literary examples like *What Maisie Knew*, courtly romance, and *Love in the Western World*. One finds in the wake of the British and European merging of literature, feminism, and psychoanalysis, as in Teresa Brennan's collection of essays *Between Feminism and Psychoanalysis*, women of strong intellect, committed to thinking of woman as a class and confronting her issues radically. What is socially at stake in the American case is why only certain immigrant theories, such as object-relations, are offered naturalization in American feminism and why some are problematical. The immigrants whose entry visas have been most difficult to

obtain are Melanie Klein and Jacques Lacan. The latter's linguistic obscurities explain something of the resistance to him, but Klein is another matter, since she is the presumed originator of the popular object-relations theory.

12. Renata Salecl, " 'Society Doesn't Exist,' " *American Journal of Semiotics* 7, nos. 1–2 (1990): 45–52, and "Towards a New Socialist Moral Majority," *Emergences* 2 (Spring 1990): 93–101, has several papers on the role fantasy plays in racism and antifeminism. Slavoj Žižek, *The Sublime Object of Ideology*, "How Did Marx Invent the Symptom," explicates how unconscious fantasies, rooted in the repression of *jouissance,* are found in cultural forms, not in latent wishes or thoughts.

13. As she demands that Chodorow and Dinnerstein do. Flax, *Thinking Fragments,* 164–66.

14. *Read My Desire,* 181–209. Copjec says that Drive has shifted its topological position and has now been made manifestly audible and visible in today's climate of a "duty" to enjoy. Instead of disrupting speech, it sits enthroned beside it. This contemporary staging of Drive-as-Being voids in advance the promise of the Symbolic, that of meaning. It was an empty promise, to be sure, but it could be, from time to time, fruitfully undone by the partial drive.

15. Christopher Lasch, *The Culture of Narcissism* (New York: W. W. Norton, 1979; and Julia Kristeva, *Powers of Horror,* also fear this mutated or pseudosuperego and have confirmed its identity with the "Mother," opposing her to Oedipus and its instigation of civil, social behavior. Yet society may not exist as such—not in the way they hope. In *The Regime of the Brother* I argued the possibility that Freud's *Ego and Id* attests to a new id that does not have a *parental* function at all, so that traditional controls no longer have the power over it.

16. She and Susan Contratto write that "almost primal fantasies constitute feminist politics or theory" when feminists address the issue of motherhood (Chodorow, *Feminism and Psychoanalytic Theory,* 80).

17. Teresa Brennan, "Controversial Discussions and Feminist Debate," in *Freud in Exile: Psychoanalysis and Its Vicissitudes,* ed. Edward Timms and Naomi Segal (New Haven, Conn., and London: Yale University Press, 1988), 254–74; see especially 260. Brennan shows how object-relations theory used Lacan's enemy Michael Balint to drive the *drives* out of post-Kleinian analysis.

18. Chodorow focuses on the "self" to avoid identification with ego-psychology, and to promote identification with a venerable line of sociological inquiry, from G. H. Mead to Erving Goffman, that had amply demonstrated the social construction of the "individual."

19. Carl Jung, *The Undiscovered Self,* trans. R. F. C. Hull (New York: New American Library, 1958), 74.

20. But Lacan, in cold blood, had faced the absence of sexual relation in our

cultural systems and had marked the structural and cultural reasons for this absence, doing so with characteristic wit, in formulas designed to shock: his "no sexual relation" and "only one libido marked with a male sign," "woman is the symptom of man," and so on. But he did so precisely to block the only other psychoanalytic road for woman and the mother to walk down, the Jungian one, once their roles became mired in mythified cultural symbols.

21. Jane Gallop, "The Monster in the Mirror," in *Feminism and Psychoanalysis*, ed. Richard Feldstein and Judith Roof (Ithaca, N.Y., and London: Cornell University Press, 1989), 13–24. Gallop errs in assigning Chodorow the same concept of an "ongoing infantile connection to the mother" (16) as Flax, since Chodorow says the loss of the mother is inevitable.

22. That people of the greatest good will now unquestioningly use such a statistical model of the group is a tragedy of our times and the sad after-effect of the collapse of real sociological vision, which has failed to encompass the replacement of the variety of cultures with the monologue and monotony of corporate culture. It also dovetails with that "artificial" group of Freud's *Group Psychology*, a grouping that strikes me as radically antidemocratic.

23. Readers should consult the "cryptonomic" accounts of Maria Torok and Nicolas Abraham, *Cryptonomie: Le verbier de l'homme aux loups* (Paris: Aubier Flammarion, 1976), wherein pathological relations are entertained by the ego, which internalizes (incorporates or cannibalizes) others in its "pseudo" unconscious. See also the English translation, *The Wolf Man's Magic Word: A Cryptonymy*, trans. Nicholas Rand (Minneapolis: University of Minnesota Press, 1986).

24. Cite in Flax, *Thinking Fragments*, 113.

25. See Toril Moi, "The Missing Mother: The Oedipal Rivalries of René Girard," *Diacritics* 12, no. 2 (1982): 195. In the logic of feminine narcissism as self-sufficiency, "women cannot think because they suffer no lack at all; they are complacent, cow-like, content."

26. See Lasch, *Culture of Narcissism*, 82–84, for whom the return of a repressed maternal superego is a prologue to fascism. The Frankfurt School also gave a feminine body to the fascist mass; and Kristeva, *Powers of Horror*, made the maternal body the origin of abjection and anti-Semitism. But in postmodernism narcissism (said to spring from maternal attachments) is getting better press; recent defenses come from both psychoanalysis and literary criticism of predominantly male critics like Leo Bersani, who defends end-of-the-millennium neodecadent narcissism.

27. See Joan Copjec, "The Phenomenal Nonphenomenal: Private Space in Film Noir," in her edited anthology *Shades of Noir* (London: Verso, 1993), 167–97.

28. Chodorow tries bravely to reconcile her own predilection for norms and

the emotions that cluster around them, with what is patently abnormal in our lives. She cites Hans Loewald, who recognizes a "psychotic core" in our most normal self. Chodorow wants to bring Freudian Oedipal guilt together with Kleinian atonement—that is, both the Father and the Mother, and so forth. It's a good dream.

29. Melanie Klein had her theories of an early superego that is vengeful and cannibalistic. Freud writes a note to her on this thesis in *Civilization and Its Discontents*. It is perhaps no accident that some of her theories are developed in her analysis of Robert, where father, brother, and Hitler are confused in the child's way of gridding his relations. "The Oedipus Complex in the Light of Early Anxieties," in *Love, Guilt and Reparation* (New York: Delta, 1975).

30. Klein's clear-cut confrontation of the alternate fantasies the child must choose between contrasts with Winnicott's morally equivocal vocabulary ("good enough mother"), which has had enormous appeal for feminist psychologists. Likewise, Klein's sense of the way passionate fantasies play on the real body of the mother differs greatly from Winnicott's much more abstract—and in the Lacanian sense "imaginary"—terms like *center, periphery, kernel*, and so forth. Interestingly, Freud had contrasted two factors in the control of "bad" instincts—internal and external (Freud, "Thoughts on War," 282). The infant learned to restrain its aggressivity "from within" (282) by tempering egoistic and aggressive impulses with "erotism." This had, however, to be seconded in most cases by an "external factor," "the force exercised by upbringing," that is, by the rules and regulations encountered in the social order, which are only gradually internalized. The person whose "civilization" consists mainly of the latter, of conformity to rules, has little resistance to uncivilized behavior if the rules of the game appear to change, as they do under conditions of war.

31. Lacan, *Seminar VII*, 81. Teresa Brennan, "Controversial Discussions," in her *Between Feminism and Psychoanalysis*, 258–59, points to "an Oedipal tinge" in Klein's speculation on the earliest unconscious fantasies.

32. See Lisa Jardine, "The Politics of Impenetrability," in Brennan's *Between Feminism and Psychoanalysis*, 63–72.

33. See Danielle Bergeron, Lucia Villela-Minnerly, and Lucie Cantin, dossier on *Fatal Attraction*, in *American Journal of Semiotics* 7, no. 3 (1990).

34. Barbara Johnson, "Is Female to Male as Ground Is to Figure?" (in Feldstein and Roof, *Feminism and Psychoanalysis*, 265–68). Johnson's genial account attacks both Freud's opposing clitoris (as phallic) to vagina (as feminine), and Naomi Schor and Gayatri Spivak's opposition between clitoris (sexual pleasure beyond or absent from heterosexual intercourse) and motherhood (coitus between male and female—the former sine qua non of motherhood—modeled on "fusion" with the mother's body, not woman's separate pleasure). For Johnson,

the female body is the site of sensual motivations, not libidinal drives (as for Lacan), and she discounts the unconscious both from a personal disposition, and as programmatic of her optimistic American sense of freedom of choice, somewhat like the way Butler did later. Johnson imagines that our sexual, social, and intellectual behaviors can either conform to the norm or not, at will; women are equipped with two sex organs and are therefore especially free to reproduce or not, and to engage in love relations along masculinist or feminist lines.

35. The essays in this volume result from a 1986 conference. Feldstein and Roof's "Introduction" (1–10) is a very valuable survey.

36. Freud, "Female Sexuality," *Standard Edition*, vol. XXI: 223 ff.

37. "The Dissolution of the Oedipus Complex" (1924), in *Standard Edition*, vol. XIX: 173 ff.

38. Freud, "Female Sexuality," 230.

39. Freud, " 'Civilized' Sexual Morality and Modern Nervousness," in *Standard Edition*, vol. IX: 179 ff.

7. On Woman's Speech

1. Juliet Flower MacCannell, "Signs of the Fathers: On Freud's Collection of Antiquities," in *Excavations and Their Objects: Freud/History/Art*, ed. Steven A. Barker (Albany: SUNY Press, 1996), 33–55.

2. Juliet Flower MacCannell, *Regime*, 14–15 .

3. I use *feminine subjects* here and not male and female because I include those like Stendhal. He wrote "Death of the Author" in the margins of a copy of his 1822 book *De L'Amour* when he learned of the passing, in 1825, of his greatest love, the radical rebel Mathilde Dembowski. However Stendhal intended that genitive *of (De)*, he ceded the word to Mathilde.

4. Maya Angelou, *I Know Why the Caged Bird Sings*, 98.

5. Catharine Millot, *Nobodaddy: L'Hystérie dans le siècle* (Cahors: Point Hors Ligne, 1988), 54–57.

6. Renata Salecl, "Woman as Symptom of Rights." See also her more recent "The Sirens and Feminine Jouissance," *differences* 9 (Spring 1997): 14–35.

7. Kristeva, "Motherhood According to Bellini," in *Desire in Language* (New York: Columbia University Press, 1982), 167. She seeks a breakthrough of the sentence-meaning-significance triad by "what may be called 'primary' processes those dominated by intonation and rhythm."

8. See *Topoi* 12, no. 2 (September 1993).

9. See MacCannell and MacCannell, "The Beauty System," in *The Ideology of Conduct*, ed. Nancy Armstrong and Leonard Tennenhouse (London: Methuen Books, 1987). Reprinted in *Fields of Writing: Reading across the Disciplines*, 4th ed.,

ed. Nancy R. Comley, David Hamilton, Carl H. Klaus, Robert Scholes, and Nancy Sommers (New York: St. Martin's Press, 1994), 443–63.

10. See Lisa Appignanesi and John Forrester, *Freud's Women* (New York: Basic Books, 1992).

11. See Dean MacCannell and Juliet Flower MacCannell, "Violence, Power and Pleasure: A Revisionist Reading of Foucault from the Victim Perspective," in *Up against Foucault: Explorations of Some Tensions between Foucault and Feminism,* ed. Caroline Ramazanoglu (London: Routledge, 1993), 203–38.

12. Marguerite Duras, *Hiroshima, mon amour,* trans. Richard Seaver (New York: Grove Press, 1961).

13. My son Daniel MacCannell has suggested to me that I am looking down because I am in my father's arms, and that I am impressed because he is telling my older sister why our mother is weeping and unable to speak.

14. Maya Angelou, *I Know Why the Caged Bird Sings,* 98.

8. Things to Come

1. Margaret Atwood, *The Handmaid's Tale* (New York: Fawcett Books/Ballantine, 1985).

2. Only Hélène Cixous, in her *Portrait de Dora* (Paris: Des Femmes, 1976), has emphasized the revolutionary potential of hysteria over a more compliant attitude, acquiescing to hysteria's silence.

3. Jacques Lacan, *Le Séminaire XVII: L'Envers de la psychanalyse,* ed. J.-A. Miller (Paris: Seuil, 1991), 62 (not yet in English; translations are my own).

4. Woman's "choice" and consent remained narrow for Freud—she could basically choose her father or her brother. The Quebec analysts Apollon, Bergeron, and Cantin (*Topoi* 12, no. 2 [September 1993]: 17 ff) grant femininity high status in the triple options for identity in contemporary life: the relation to the State, the aesthetic relation, and the ethical relation (to one's desire).

5. Beyond some pointers taken from Lucie Cantin's elaboration of an "ethic of the impossible" (*Topoi*), there is the work of Willy Apollon and Danielle Bergeron in the same issue.

6. See Joan Copjec, "Sex and the Euthanasia of Reason," for the formulas of sexuation and their logical universe.

7. Catharine Millot's analysis of *jouissance* gives the definite impression that she sees it as a kind of original sin, an inherent human failing. In her reading, Lacan would have pitted Spinoza's optimistic universalization of desire against Kant's universalizing of *jouissance.* See *Nobodaddy.*

8. Derrida's general reading of "woman" is as a function of the phallus, though he never makes this explicit.

9. As Millot puts it, the "presencing" of the phallus within permits her to fan-

tasize a father who is all-*jouissant.* For a critique of the phallus as misplaced by theory with "the father," see my *Regime of the Brother.*

10. Rare exceptions include Lucie Cantin among the post-Lacanians, and Jean-Joseph Goux among the poststructuralists. Goux's article "The Phallus: Masculine Identity and the 'Exchange of Women'" appears ironically enough in the special issue of *differences: the journal of feminist cultural studies* 4, no. 1 (1992) on "The Phallus," where the Freudian paradigm of woman's "bearing" the phallus as non-castrated is unerringly and unreflectively aggravated in most of the other articles.

11. Although this is the crux of the matter, as Millot has correctly seen. She is resigned to this.

12. Catharine Millot's work summarizes best the central impasse: woman is denied identification with any woman/ego-ideal as long as that ideal must include the factor of phallic power. She is stuck with a Father with whom she cannot identify, and a Mother who, if phallic, remains mythic, since no real woman could fulfill this requirement (*Nobodaddy,* 54–57). As Millot describes the logic, the woman has only an "external" superego, structurally homologous to the "maternal," so that consequently, her love object is never anything but a "real" Other from whom she continually demands the phallus. She has no internal limit.

13. In *The Regime of the Brother,* I commented this way: "The girl under patriarchy is faced with an inhuman choice: to do without an identity, or to identify with what she is not (it amounts to the same thing). She can accept that she has no symbol, no way of expressing her special needs, and thereby identify with what is 'only an absence,' as Lacan puts it (p. 198). Or, she can identify with what she is *not*: her father, a man. Under Oedipus her 'identity' is either absent or the reverse of her reality—and her 'desire' is always a misstatement: her *lack* is seen as a quite literally unsatisfiable *desire.* Now, a 'missing' body part is a terrible model for her 'identity': the woman is set-up from the start as one who cannot have one" (25).

14. See Danielle Bergeron, "Femininity," 9. See also Juliet Flower MacCannell, *"Jouissance,"* in *Critical Dictionary,* ed. E. Wright. Remarking that Freud saw the girl as striving to find man's organ as a bodily limit that would enable her to endure her lack, Bergeron counters that none of Freud's resolutions ("phallic phase," "Oedipus complex," "penisneid") is anything but imaginary. Yet the *symbolic* signifier cannot resolve this lack either, because it is too "unreliable." Instead, the "Father's word of love, manifesting his love for his girl in the absence of sexual lust," alone "situates her as subject in the order of language and manages the libidinous writing of the body" (13). This word of love is seen as "putting a limit to the Other's *jouissance* that is insisting in the girl-child's body." By inserting her mark of lack, the girl is placed "in the register of the desiring subject. . . . a failing in the father may result in psychosis or hysteria" (13). Offred has no father.

15. Bergeron, "Femininity," 9.

16. "Vérité, soeur de la jouissance," in Lacan, *Séminaire XVII*, 76 ("underside, seamy side, dirty side, backside"). The quotation on the pure imperative comes on p. 70.

17. Jacques Lacan, "Function and Field of Speech and Language," in *Ecrits*, 47.

18. Lacan, *Le Séminaire XVII*, 61.

19. Lacan, *Le Séminaire XVII*, 74.

20. Letter 59 (1897), in *Standard Edition*, vol. I: 244–45.

21. Jacques Lacan, "Function and Field of Speech and Language," in *Ecrits*, 30–113.

22. Ibid., 46.

23. Lacan puns on "verbalize it": give it a ticket, and therefore lock it up (ibid.).

24. As in Bakhtin's anatomy of *epic* as pseudopatriarchal discourse. See "Epic and Novel," in M. M. Bakhtin, *The Dialogic Imagination* (Austin: University of Texas Press, 1982).

25. Lacan, *Ecrits*, 46–47. This internal hypnotic drama functions for wide-awake consciousness like the theater in Antiquity, "in which the original myths of the City State are produced before its assembled citizens stand in relation to a history that may well be made up of materials, but in which a nation today learns to read the symbols of a destiny on the march. In Heideggerian language one could say that both types of recollection constitute the subject as *gewesend*—that is to say, as being the one who thus has been." Lacan objects, of course, to how this picture distorts, decrying the extent to which alternative outcomes have been cast aside *(écartée)* in this destinal marching: "Other encounters being assumed to have taken place since any one of these moments having been, there would have issued from it another existent that would cause him to have been quite otherwise" (47). It is this "other side" that Lacan tracks by way of *hysterical revelation*.

26. Lacan, *Ecrits*, 47.

27. Ibid.

28. See Freud, "A Child Is Being Beaten: A Contribution to the Study of the Origin of Sexual Perversions," in *Standard Edition*, vol. XVII: 177 ff. The root fantasy is where the subject, according to Lacan, is receiving his enjoyment under the form of the "jouissance de l'Autre" (*Séminaire XVII*, 74). The subject Freud was analyzing when he wrote this may have been his daughter, Anna.

29. "La tautologie de la totalité du discours, c'est cela qui fait le monde" (67).

30. Lacan plays on this: "Je dis toujours la vérité," he avers in *Television*. But he immediately qualifies this enunciation, following up his mention of "Je" and "vérité" in the same breath with "mais pas toute."

31. In "Le Champ Lacanien," in *Le Séminaire XVII*, 79.

32. Lacan used Freud's analysis of "A Child Is Being Beaten" for his first formulations here. Later, in logical formulations, Lacan depicted hysteric discourse as

$$\frac{\$}{a} \quad \frac{S_1}{// \ S_2}$$

This matheme implies that the hysteric's way of existing as a split subject consciously and conscientiously relates directly to the "first" or master subject, subject of mastery, and unconsciously represses the object a of her fantasy. And her relation to any other subject (S_2) who is less than, "under," or an underling to the master S_1 leaves the object of enjoyment out of play.

33. Sigmund Freud, *The Interpretation of Dreams*, book IV, "The Butcher's Wife," in *Standard Edition*, vol. IV: 147–51.

34. Moreover, she even puts herself in the place of her husband, who has expressed a desire to be thinner.

35. Freud asks why the butcher's wife stands "in need of an unfulfilled wish" (148). Her husband had praised a thin lady friend of hers, who had subsequently expressed the wish to grow stouter, and requested an invitation to dinner from the wife. At this point, the butcher's wife's dream of having virtually nothing in the house (only "a little smoked salmon") and thus of being forced "to abandon my wish to give a supper-party" (147) must be understood as her "identifying" with the imagined rival, with the extended implicit demand that this rival give up her desire and its subsequent *jouissance:* "It is just as though . . . you said to yourself: 'A likely thing! I'm to ask you to come and eat in my house so that you may get stout and attract my husband still more! I'd rather never give another supper party'" (148).

The demand entails a further interpretation, which Freud does not miss. At another level, the woman in the dream is the rival, not the wife, and she "had put herself in her friend's place . . . 'identified' with her" (149) at the level where, outside the dream, the wife had attempted a renunciation (of her beloved caviar). Freud located the hysteria of the dream at this second interpretative level, the level that requires us to ask "Who enjoys?" The point is that the butcher's wife does not want her husband to desire, but only to enjoy. He must not be permitted to be seen as lacking. In Lacan's terms, the husband, the full subject or S_1, must appear the most powerful in order to set the limits on the Thing, or the nonphallic *other jouissance* that drives within the wife. Her renounced *jouissance* circulates around the salmon/caviar, which functions as an object a.

36. The Fates, Clotho, Atropos, and Lacassis, all—phallically—deal with the threads of narrative or textual life: web, length, cut. The Latin word *fatum* is, moreover, the perfect passive participle of the word *to say.*

37. Yet her "cultural memory" is preset for her, in predigested (reader's digested?) renditions. Once she is within the space of preconditioned "memories" of her past, she sounds like a perfectly normal modern, educated woman, of

independent mind and critical judgment. Yet Atwood is careful to ensure that the context, the precise situation in which Offred's memory is allowed to return to her, and where an object or event over which she can exercise powers of judgment, criticism, and insight, is shown to be part of an overall phallic discourse, male "history." Then *and* now.

Offred, for example, marvels at how free women used to feel before Gilead; but she only remembers that freedom when her own Commander, breaking the rules, dangles a forbidden copy of *Vogue* before her: "Like fish bait, I wanted it" (200–201): "I wanted it with a force that made the ends of my fingers ache. At the same time, I saw this longing of mine as trivial and absurd, because I'd taken such magazines lightly enough once. I'd read them in dentists' offices, and sometimes on planes; I'd bought them to take to hotel rooms, a device to fill in empty time while I was waiting for Luke. After I'd leafed through them I would throw them away . . . and a day or two later I wouldn't be able to remember what had been in them. Though I remembered now. What was in them was promise. They dealt in transformations; they suggested an endless series of possibilities, extending life like the reflections in two mirrors set facing one another, stretching on, replica after replica, to the vanishing point.

They suggested one adventure after another, one wardrobe after another. They suggested rejuvenation, pain overcome and transcended, endless love. The real promise in them was immortality. . . . I took the magazine from him and turned it the right way round. There they were again, the images of my childhood: bold, striding, confident, their arms flung out as if to claim space, their legs apart, feet planted squarely on the earth. There was something Renaissance about the pose, but it was princes I thought of, not coiffed and ringleted maidens. Those candid eyes, shadowed with makeup, yes, but like the eyes of cats, fixed for the pounce. . . . Pirates, these women, with their ladylike briefcases for the loot and their horsy acquisitive teeth" (201–2).

38. Lacan, "The Direction of the Treatment and the Principles of Its Power," in *Ecrits*, 236.

39. Offred/Atwood taps the resources of the Book of Luke for crucial imagery. In Luke chapter 1 of (King James version), Luke declares himself an "eyewitness," writing because he has "had perfect understanding of all things from the very first" (Luke 1:3, 50). Mary submits to the Angel of the Annunciation with the words, "Behold the handmaid of the Lord; be it unto me according to thy word" (Luke 1:38, 51). Luke also deals with the "sisterhood" of birthing, as Mary's elderly, barren cousin Elisabeth "quickens" as a result of Mary's linkage to annunciation: "When Elisabeth heard the salutation of Mary, the babe leaped in her womb and Elisabeth was filled with the Holy Ghost" (Luke 1:41, 51). "Blessed is the fruit of thy womb" is first enunciated in Luke 1:42, and the parable of the barren fig tree

appears (Luke 13:7–9). The tree must be cut down if it fails to bear fruit for the third season (*Tale*, 68). It relates to Offred's memory of being told to "pretend you're a tree" in childhood dance classes, as well as to her general identification with plant life. Finally, Jesus tells us that "life is more than meat" (Luke 12:23, 67). My argument that Offred is a hysteric requires that none of these biblical references exists at a conscious level for Offred (the novel cites only Genesis 30: 1–3 and the story of Rachel and Leah as its Biblical "source"). It is also crucial that they not be unconscious either. They are preconscious. As such they surface repeatedly in fragments. The repressed unconscious wish of hysteria has to take the "path" of a preconscious memory, a "mnemic fragment," from which it draws an inference and extends it (Freud, *Interpretation of Dreams*, in *Standard Edition*, vols. 4–5: 183). The hysteric's speech and gestures are not an imitation but an "assimilation on the basis of a similar aetiological pretension" (183). See also 608. Thanks to Jonathan Cohen and Tracy McNulty for pointing the Luke connection out to me.

40. Lacan, *Ecrits*, 47.

9. Becoming and Unbecoming a Man

1. Regarding the epigraphs: "Lituraterre" was published in *Ornicar* 41 (1987): 5–13.

Colette Soler, "Literature as Symptom," in *Lacan and the Subject of Language*, ed. Ellie Ragland-Sullivan and Mark Bracher (New York: Routledge, 1991), 213–19. "In any case, Freud lapsed into applies psychoanalysis, treating the artist's know-how as equivalent to what he himself called the work of the unconscious, putting artistic and literary works on the same level as dreams, slips of the tongue, bungled actions, and symptoms, all of which are interpretable. Lacan reverses Freud's position concerning this point: it is not that the written text must be psychoanalyzed; rather, it is that the psychoanalyst must be well read."

Stendhal, *The Life of Henry Brulard: The Autobiography of Stendhal*, trans. Jean Stewart and B. C. J. G. Knight (Chicago: University of Chicago Press, 1958), 86–87.

2. The way Poe puts it in "The Purloined Letter" concerning the Minister D——, who steals the queen's letter, who "dares all things, those becoming and unbecoming a man." Lacan's translation (*Ecrits*, 33) is: "Ce qui est indigne aussi bien que ce qui est digne d'un homme." Baudelaire, says Lacan, "laisse échapper la pointe en la traduisant: ce qui est indigne d'un homme aussi bien que ce qui est digne de lui. Car dans sa forme originale, l'appréciation est beaucoup plus appropriée à ce qui intéresse une femme." *Unbecoming* means unseemly, but one might take the word literally, seeing in it a light suggestion of undoing one's masculinity—un-becoming.

3. "My mother, Mme Henriette Gagnon, was a charming woman and I was in love with my mother. I must hurriedly add that I lost her when I was seven. When

I loved her at about the age of six, in 1789, I showed exactly the same characteristics as in 1828 when I was madly in love with Alberthe de Rubempré. My way of pursuing happiness was basically unchanged; there was just this difference: I was, as regards the physical side of love, just as Caesar would be, if he came back into the world, as regards the use of cannon and small arms. I would have learned very quickly, and my tactics would have remained basically the same . . . I abhorred my father when he came to interrupt our kisses" (*Brulard*, 21–22).

4. Stendhal changes his name to avoid the "appalling quantity of I's and me's" but also, he later remarks, to avoid having his reader throw an inkpot at him—in short, staining him (*Brulard*, 219).

5. There is, for example, a bird with whom the young Beyle identifies when he himself is indoors but that he nevertheless freely hunts and shoots when outdoors. There are orange trees planted in pots; the old woman standing up, worn shoes in hand, against the regiment crying, "I'm in revort!" (*Brulard*, 42); "Je me révolte! Je me révolte!"). The peculiar, halting, fragmentary but by no means incoherent structure of Stendhal's autobiography is formed around such bits, the kind that Lacan and Freud saw as anchoring or absorbing the "mycelium growth"—which Stendhal called "crystallization"—of the unconscious and its passions. Stendhal will be found, once read correctly, to have entirely reordered the narrative of his life in the manner that Freud suggested necessary for analysis, that is, in relation to those primal scenes where one's passions are first born.

6. As between the words *ballet* and *balai* (broom; *Brulard*, 4), when he hears the Revolutionary Maréchal de Vaux is coming to Grenoble and his parents say that his coming here will be like a balai, which he hears as *ballet*.

7. "*A letter, a litter,* une lettre, une ordure. On a équivoqué dans le cénacle de Joyce, sur l'homophonie de ces deux mots en anglais" (Lacan, *Ecrits,* 25).

8. Freud, *The Wolfman,* in *Standard Edition,* vol. XVII: 20.

9. See his extraordinary list of wishes, "Les privilèges de 10 avril, 1840," in *Oeuvres intimes* (Paris: Pléïade, 1955): 1559 ff, article 3: "La *mentula* [penis], comme le doigt indicateur pour la dureté et le mouvement, cela à volonté. La forme, deux pouces de plus que l'article, même grosseur. Mais plaisir par cet organe seulement deux fois par semaine." In article 7, he states his final anti-Aristotelian wish: "Le privilégié pourra quatre fois par an, et pour un temp illimité chaque fois, occuper deux corps à la fois." This wish is the reverse of Rousseau's express wish in *The Confessions* to have two souls, masculine and feminine, in one body (his own). Stendhal's formula also exceeds Kaja Silverman's of the "female soul trapped in the male body," in her *Male Subjectivity at the Margins* (New York: Routledge, 1992).

10. *Brulard,* 16. See "Les privilèges," article 7: "Quatre fois par an, il pourra se changer en l'animal qu'il voudra; et, ensuite, se rechanger en homme."

11. Terrifying is the word Fabrice uses when he sees that Clélia Conti desires him in Stendhal's *La Chartreuse de Parme*. See *The Charterhouse of Parma*, trans. Margaret R. B. Shaw (Harmondsworth: Penguin, 1958).

Critics of *Brulard* have attributed its formal idiosyncrasies to its being a "rough draft, unfinished, unrevised"—the product of only vaguely formed introspective reveries. For all that, there is greater penetration into the "interior" regions than anyone—from Joubert to Gide—has ever quite obtained in their autobiographical writing. Stendhal blends Condillac/Destutt de Tracy's materialist analysis (called, following de Tracy, *idéologie*) with the idealism of Rousseau and Kant. It is this same mixture that conspired at the birth of psychoanalysis itself. See my preface to *Thinking Bodies* (Stanford, Calif.: Stanford University Press, 1994).

12. *Brulard*, 330–31. Much earlier in the text he had qualified this feminine identity as follows: "My self-respect, my self-interest, my very personality vanished in the loved one's presence, I became transformed into the other person. And supposing that other was a hussy like Mme Pietragrua? But I keep anticipating" (15).

13. There is evidence by several of his mistresses on this count: the letters of the Comtesse Curial and Alberthe de Rubempré give very explicit physical testimony. René Andrieu, *Stendhal ou le bal masqué* (Paris: J. C. Lattes, 1983), 174–75, calls Stendhal a man of "extrême sensibilité" who freely admitted momentary aberrations (as in the case of "le fiasco complet" due to excess love), but whose sexuality "relève davantage d'une norme très habituelle que d'une épouvantable perversion."

14. Stendhal does not lament his feminization. His attitude is distinctive in this respect. For a contrasting view of the feminization by letters, see Nancy Armstrong, *Desire and Domestic Fiction: A History of the Novel* (New York: Oxford University Press, 1987).

15. Michael Sharingham, "Visual Autobiography: Diagrams in Stendhal's *Vie de Henry Brulard*," *Paragraph* 8, no. 3 (1988): 249–73. Sharingham sees death as punishment for desire for the mother, and claims homoerotic overtones to the "death of Lambert" in the text (257). Lambert, however seems to me to be as much an allegory of the abuse of the working class as a misplaced and guilty desire for the mother.

Sharingham assumes Stendhal's drawings, "their enigmatic, visual dimension," work "therapeutically": like Michel Crouzet, Sharingham argues that in *Brulard* Stendhal "not only relives the emotional struggles of his youth, experiencing again in all their fury his antagonistic feelings for his father and his Tante Séraphie and his incestuous desires for his mother, but also comes to terms with these feelings by externalizing and comprehending them, making autobiography a process of therapy and 'acting-out' (Stendhal's word is 'mimique') and 'working through'" (251). The simple verbal-visual combination is, according to Sharingham, converted to pleasure out of what was "experienced as an excessive *jouissance*" (being burned by joy, as with Mlle. Kubly): "There is undoubtedly a powerful tendency for Stendhal to revel in images and to spurn explanations" (251).

I disagree with Sharingham's reading of the diagrams. His view remains essentially *figural* (that is, "radically anachronistic" moments of past and present are "superimposed") rather than *psychoanalytic* and the drawings do not suffer the necessary displacement of "originating" in their narrated future. Sharingham never accounts for the necessary inversion of future/past relations that psychoanalysis does.

16. What is so radical about Stendhal's technique is that the Carthage allusion is a throwaway line, meant to appear as a slip or mistake: this is not reading under erasure à la Heidegger-Derrida, an ontological but dispassionate gesture whose sophistication pales by comparison. The importance of "the other scene" is in proportion to the apparent slightness in its sign. As in Freud, the slip accesses a fully elaborated, completely different narrative/historical line, which threatens to intersect with the dominant one and dislodge its supremacy.

17. Where, as Gérard Genette points out, *La Chartreuse de Parme* begins. See Genette, *Figures, essais* (Paris: Editions du Seuil, 1966).

18. That "shameless hussy" of note 10, *Brulard*, 15.

19. *Brulard*, 177: "Son mot si simple fit sur moi tout l'effet possible. Il ajouta en riant: 'Tu ne savais que nous montrer ton gros derrière!'"

20. *Brulard*, 259–60. Jeffrey Librett has suggested the following to me: that *RP*—which I find unusual for the letters describing the line segment—might signify the "renversement du père P-R," with the *C* in the middle as the "cul." At any rate, the overcoming of the "anality" of the eighteenth century that Lacan saw Sade as putting the lie to in "Kant avec Sade" is surely what is at stake in Stendhal's giving up his passion.

21. His grandfather, who is a "Fontenellish sort of man," stands in here, obviously, for the Enlightenment. See the repeated parallel: "à la Fontenelle"; "véritable Fontenelle"; "dans le genre de celui de Fontenelle" (*Brulard*, 37, 49, 53, 57).

22. "Mon excellent grand-père qui dans le fait fut mon véritable père" (*Brulard*, 45. Earlier he had recalled how his well-spoken grandfather had cursed only once in his presence, when he had chastised a woman with the imprecation, "May the devil spit on your arse!" (138): "Mon grand-père employait son grand juron contre cette Mme Vignon: Le Diable te crache au cul!"

10. Love outside the Limits of the Law

1. The four other discourses are Master, University, Hysteric, Analytic. "Forms of the social tie" is Lacan's definition of *discourse (Séminaire XX).*

2. Jean-Jacques Rousseau, "Second Preface" to *Julie, ou la nouvelle Héloïse,* in

Oeuvres complètes, vol. II, ed. Bernard Guyon, Jacques Scherer, and Charly Guyot (Paris: Bibliothèque de la Pléïade, 1964), 15 (my translation).

3. Rousseau writes: "Had all my dreams become realities, they would not have sufficed me; I would have imagined, dreamed, desired still *[encore].* I found in myself an inexplicable void that nothing could have filled; a certain launching of the heart towards another sort of enjoyment *[jouissance]* of which I had no idea and of which I nonetheless felt the need. . . . This in itself was enjoyment *[jouissance]* because I was transpierced by it with a very vivid feeling and an attractive sadness that I would not have wanted not to have." Jean-Jacques Rousseau, *Quatre Lettres à M. de Malesherbes,* in *Oeuvres complètes,* vol. I, ed. B. Gagnebin and M. Raymond (Paris: Bibliothéque de la Pléïade, 1960), 1140–41 (my translation).

4. Jacques Lacan, "A Love Letter" ("Lettre d'amour"), in *Feminine Sexuality: Jacques Lacan and the École Freudienne,* ed. Juliet Mitchell and Jacqueline Rose (New York: Pantheon Books, 1982), 146. Reprinted from *Séminaire XX: Encore* (Paris: Seuil, 1975).

5. Jacques Lacan, *Seminar VII,* 294.

6. Ibid., 119.

7. Ibid., 110.

8. The original center of the labyrinth was "(BE)LONGING TO BE HER(E)," according to the artist.

9. "Completion," in the far upper right, does not come directly, if at all, from the "Landscape as Lies" or, rather, what "Lies as a Landscape," but only from a route taken obliquely from the "Mother" section of the map.

10. *A Thousand Plateaus: Capitalism and Schizophrenia,* trans. Brian Massumi (Minneapolis: University of Minnesota Press, 1987), 155–56. "There is, in fact, a joy that is immanent to desire, as though desire were filled by itself and its contemplations, a joy that implies no lack or impossibility and is not measured by pleasure since it is what distributes intensities of pleasure and prevents them from being suffused by anxiety, shame and guilt"; "it would be an error to interpret courtly love in terms of a law of lack or an ideal of transcendence. . . . Courtly love does not love the self, any more than it loves the whole universe in a celestial or religious way. It is a question of making a body without organs upon which intensities pass. . . . 'Joy' in courtly love, the exchange of hearts, the test or 'assay': everything is allowed as long as it is not external to desire. . . . The slightest caress may be as strong as orgasm; . . . all that counts is for pleasure to be the flow of desire itself" (156).

11. Rousseau, "Second Preface" to *Julie,* 15. The quotation continues on toward an idealization, beyond where Deleuze and Guattari put the endpoint of desire and pleasure: "When it is at its peak, it sees its object perfected; it then makes an idol of it; it places it in the Heavens; and just as the enthusiasm of [religious]

devotion borrows the language of love, the enthusiasm of love borrows also the language of devotion."

12. Rousseau, *Lettres à M. de Malesherbes*, 1142.

13. Stendhal, *Love*, 265. English citations are from the Penguin edition of the text.

14. "I don't want to end up on the issue of so-called frigidity.... Unfortunately, in Freud's discourse, as in courtly love, the whole thing is covered over with petty considerations which have caused havoc. Petty considerations about clitoral orgasm or the jouissance designated as best one can, the other one precisely, which I am trying to get you to along the path of logic, since, to date, there is no other" (Lacan, "Love Letter," 145–46) The signifier limits *jouissance*—but therefore also causes it, in the sense of its being the "final cause" (*Séminaire XX*, 27). If her jouissance stops short of the word, then, this is structural and formal, involuntary.

15. Women are first to eschew their specialness in this regard; it was Lou Salomé who saw the vagina as a misplaced rectum. But isn't this misplacement the first metaphoric deviation, the necessary one? And didn't Cixous already tell us, in *Angst* (Paris: Des Femmes, 1977), that autoeroticism is not a sufficient model for feminine *jouissance?*

16. "If, on the one hand, Lacan is careful not to hypostatize sexual difference, it is none the less true that the function of that which exceeds all discourse is characterized as 'feminine,' thus leaving open for contemporary debate what links women to 'the feminine,' and as a result the question of their position in discourse as speaking subjects." Marie-Claire Boons, "Other/Other" entry for *Critical Dictionary*, ed. Elizabeth Wright, 299.

17. See Dean MacCannell, "Faking It: On Face-Play in the Pornographic Frame," *American Journal of Semiotics* 6, no. 4 (1989): 153–74. He argues that the most characteristic facial gesture during the act of love is holding one's tongue with one's teeth. This gesture makes a double reference to language. It is made by a speaking being who states, in effect, "I can, but I will not, speak." This same tongue gesture also registers an attitude toward the regime of grammar that goes back to the very origin of language in the incest taboo.

18. Lacan termed this "the pain/pleasure of deferral *of jouissance*" (Lacan, *Seminar VII*, 152). Pain in pleasure it may be, from the masculine side; but pressed into the service of love, it is reversed so that it becomes "rather, the pleasure of experiencing unpleasure" (*Ethics*, 152), a back door to the pleasure of desire, as in Rousseau. But from the point of view of the feminine Thing, "techniques of holding back, suspension" (152) are the absolute precondition for *feminine jouissance*: "Isn't courtly love just another set of terms for foreplay, *Vorlust*, which persists in opposition to the pleasure principle?" Lacan asks. The verb *domnoyer* from which the Courtly Lady as Domnei comes, Lacan reminds us, is not just a term of

mastery, but of play, even foreplay: it means to "caress, to play around" (Lacan, *Seminar VII*, 150).

19. I am grateful to Alain Badiou for reminding me to distinguish *desire* from *love* in all matters pertaining directly to sexual difference. In my very early writing on Rousseau's *Dialogues*, I conceptualized this difference as one based on temporality ("Nature and Self-Love: A Re-Interpretation of Rousseau's 'Passion Primitive,'" *PMLA* [1977]). Badiou's book *Conditions* (Paris: Seuil, 1992) discriminates between them on several levels but focuses (as I do here) on the "two-ness" involved in love, a two not inherent in the structure of desire.

20. The feminine Thing (or the feminine object that stands in for it) is less the representative of the Ideal Woman than of the Other Sex. Marie-Claire Boons (in "Other/Other") confirms: "Even if the Other is not a real interlocutor, it can be embodied, not only in the maternal Other, but also in the Other sex which, despite the claims of tradition, is not necessarily the female sex."

21. Stendhal, *Love*, 265; Boons, "Other/Other," in *Critical Dictionary*, 298–99. Lacan's matheme refers to one part of feminine logic, the logic of "not all": the subject (S) is looking for the truth of the barred Other (Ø).

22. Martin Heidegger, *The Question Concerning Technology and Other Essays*, trans. William Lovitt (New York: Harper Torchbooks, 1977), 3–35.

23. See *Ethics*, 117, on the transformation of the object into a Thing.

24. But of cultural rather than moral activities. See Julia Lupton, "Sublimation," in *Critical Dictionary*, 416–17.

25. "Woman is the object it is impossible to detach from a primitive oral drive and yet in which she must learn to recognize her genital nature" (Lacan, "Love Letter," 90–91).

26. Lacan let us know, in his "God and the Jouissance of the Woman," that there are subjects who, "Despite, I won't say their phallus, despite what encumbers them on that score, they get the idea, they sense there must be a jouissance that goes beyond" ("Love Letter," 147).

27. Georges Bataille, *The Tears of Eros*, trans. Peter Connor (San Francisco: City Lights Books, 1989), 9.

28. Slavoj Žižek, *Metastases of Enjoyment*, 89–112.

29. Stendhal, *The Charterhouse of Parma*, 319.

30. Ford Madox Ford, *The Good Soldier: A Tale of Passion* (New York: Vintage Books, 1989), 127–28 (originally published in 1914).

31. *Ethics*, 152. This "salutation" is delivered in Stendhal's *Charterhouse of Parma*: Clélia, the jailor's daughter, arrives punctually to give water to the pigeons outside the window of her apartment in a building adjacent to, but separated from the Farnese tower where Fabrizio is not only imprisoned but doubly and triply immured, his window not only barred, but with wooden shutters nailed

across it. Because she is certain he cannot see her, she feels free to gaze with sympathy at his shuttered window, which, however, he has cleverly managed to carve a small door in: " 'Will she blush when she catches sight of me?'" Fabrizio wonders. "Why did he imagine she came punctually to feed her birds out of love for him? Love detects shades invisible to the indifferent eye and draws endless conclusions from them. . . . Now that Clélia could no longer see the prisoner, she would raise her eyes to the window," but when she discovers that indeed he has made a door, she spills the water she is giving the birds: "This was, beyond all comparison, the happiest moment of Fabrizio's life" (318).

32. See Willy Apollon, "Four Seasons in Femininity: Or Four Men in a Woman's Life," for an analysis of the way the Other *jouissance* is a challenge to science. According to Apollon, a "look" may open a girl's body to the knowledge of this Other *jouissance* that "sex can neither limit nor extinguish" (107). See also his "Nothing Works Anymore!" *differences* 9 (Spring 1997): 1–13.

33. The girl in the story—good citizen, on the debate team—transforms into a "woman" only (but rather easily) when she becomes the object of pursuit. Atwood, "The Man from Mars," in *The Dancing Girls*.

34. Lacan, "Kant avec Sade," 60.

35. Stendhal wrote *De L'Amour* to "combat the horrors of *Justine*"—surely not from any evasion of the freedom Sade pronounced. He mentions Sade near the opening of this book, which was his favorite of his writings, and credits a certain faith in men's judging "everyone after their own heart" to be the source of the "horrors of Justine" (*Love*, 44).

36. Stendhal's *crystallization* has mainly been read from the masculine subject position, however sympathetically. See the novel *What's Called Love: A Real Romance* by Jim Paul (New York: Villard Books, 1991), 136. Yet Stendhal's crusty branch marks a fundamental sexual disproportion. In the formula for crystallization, Stendhal counts five steps to the completeness of crystallization, the fifth culminating in "proof of love." That is when the beloved, loaded with all the imaginary perfections with which he can endow her, grants him sexual access, *le don de merci* in courtly terms. This moment marks, of course, precisely when a *negative* crystallization begins—for her. Having "given herself" as "proof" of love to him, she finds that his final step is her first one into the state of the cruellest doubt (did he just use me? did he just make me another notch on his belt?). Masculine and feminine positions within crystallization thus overlap only at this step and take opposing attitudes toward the same central experience.

37. Of course, with characteristic irony, Stendhal shows "crystallization" in his novels only through male personae (or an impotent character, like Octave in *Armance*). The anxiety appears in Julien, not Mathilde de la Mole, despite her thrill at claiming that she has given herself a master by sleeping with him.

38. Lacan's emphasis on the Thing as radically inaccessible, and which therefore founds a point of exception that "cracks" the universal for Kant, is interestingly paralleled and mimicked not by Thing-ness, but by no-thingness in philosophical discourse. In an unmarked reprise of Lacan's chapter on "Courtly Love as Anamorphosis" in the *Ethics*, Jean-Luc Nancy expresses this new foundation without the sexual implications but nonetheless provides a way of reading the significance of Lacan's Thing. Nancy critiques Heidegger's notion of the abyssal foundation of foundation together with Hegel's "intensification of nothingness" in favor of a renewal of *experience* and of a different version of *poeisis*, in his *The Experience of Freedom* (Stanford, Calif.: Stanford University Press, 1993): "The word "abyss" says too much or too little for this intensification: too much figure, in spite of everything (the contours of the abyss), and too little intensity. But the truth of the abyss and of intensification, as the truth of the no-thingness, can be named as experience" (85). Nancy is edging toward what is "foundation" from the other side of the paternal metaphor, that is, foundation from the viewpoint of the Feminine Thing.

39. "Religion in all its forms consists in avoiding this emptiness," Lacan, *Seminar VII*, 130.

40. Although she does so in the published version. Pretty Boy joins in and makes it a threesome. Trish Thomas, "Me and the Boys," in *The Best American Erotica*, ed. Susie Bright (New York: Collier Books, 1993), 91–104.

41. Bataille, *Tears*, 9.

Epilogue

1. Marguerite Duras, *Destroy, She Said*, trans. Barbara Bray. Jacques Rivette and Jean Narboni, "Destruction and Language: An Interview with Marguerite Duras," trans. Helen Lane Cumberford (New York: Grove Press, 1970), 91–133. The interview first appeared in *Cahiers du cinéma* (November 1969).

2. Such is the narrator's younger brother (who according to some biographers did not exist) in Duras's *The Lover* and in the later *The North China Lover* (trans. Leigh Hafrey [New York: New Press, 1992]). He is drawn as an almost pure contrast to the vicious elder brother, the one who destroys everything in the novel. (In life, Duras's brother was apparently a Fascist sympathizer and some believe he joined the dreaded *milice*, French civilians who worked for the Gestapo.)

Index

Juliet Flower MacCannell is professor emerita at the University of California at Irvine. She is the author of *The Regime of the Brother* and *Figuring Lacan.*